KW-484-888

SERVING LITURGICAL RENEWAL

SERVING LITURGICAL RENEWAL

Pastoral and Theological Questions

Essays in Honour of Patrick Jones

Edited by
Thomas R. Whelan
Liam M. Tracey

VERITAS

Published 2015 by
Veritas Publications
7–8 Lower Abbey Street
Dublin 1, Ireland
publications@veritas.ie
www.veritas.ie

Copyright © Individual Contributors, 2015

ISBN 978 1 84730 562 6

10 9 8 7 6 5 4 3 2 1

The material in this publication is protected by copyright law. Except as
may be permitted by law, no part of the material may be reproduced
(including by storage in a retrieval system) or transmitted in any form
or by any means, adapted, rented or lent without the written permission
of the copyright owners. Applications for permissions should be
addressed to the publisher.
A catalogue record for this book is available from the British Library.

Photo of Patrick Jones, p. 5, copyright Ebony and Pearl Photography,
Dublin. Used with permission.
Translation of Irish language Nuptial Blessing, from Padraig McCarthy,
A Wedding of Your Own (Veritas, 2003). Used with permission.
Article by John O'Keeffe, represents an expanded and updated version
of John O'Keeffe, 'Mass Settings in English and Irish', *The
Encyclopaedia of Music in Ireland*, Harry White and Barra Boydell, gen
eds. (Dublin: UCD Press, 2013), 633–5, on vernacular Mass settings.
It is included here with the permission of UCD Press

Designed by Colette Dower, Veritas Publications
Printed in Ireland by SPRINT-print Ltd, Dublin

*Veritas books are printed on paper made from the wood pulp of
managed forests. For every tree felled, at least one tree is planted,
thereby renewing natural resources.*

On the occasion of his seventieth birthday

Patrick Jones

caring pastor

astute scholar

wise leader

gracious host

loyal friend

CONTENTS

※ ※ ※

PRESENTATION

℈ ℈ ℈

For Paddy Jones, liturgy is important! Throughout all of his ministry, both as an ordained priest of the local Church of Dublin and as one who has taught generations of people to worship with a deeper awareness of what they were doing, Paddy Jones serves the Church he loves with generosity. He taught his students that it is in the environment of worship that believers become graced in their faith-encounter with God in Christ. It is this encounter, and nothing else, that creates 'relevance'. Of course, Paddy always knew how this faith experience needs to be sustained in the ordinary language and life of people in their parishes and communities. Culture becomes important here and he always placed great store on how an Irish context can enhance the faith-experience and growth in faith of people.

Paddy is a scholar who is rooted in tradition, as well as a pastor who knows how to translate this into a ritual language that carries people in prayer – something that has been experienced by many over long years when he preached homilies that were simple but thought-provoking and appropriate to the liturgical moment. He is first of all a man of faith who, in simplicity and in a deeply human way, serves Church in its awesome task of gathering all of creation into the gentle arms of a loving God.

We are honoured, as friends and colleagues, to present this collection of essays to Patrick Jones, as a token of our gratitude to him for his broad learning worn lightly, for his self-less service to liturgy in Ireland, for his great sense of diplomacy which kept everybody together as they worked on a project, thereby moving matters forward for a greater good, but above all for his loyal friendship which is always characterised with a welcome smile.

Daniel Murphy
Director, National Centre for Liturgy, Maynooth
Executive Secretary of the Council for Liturgy

1 February 2015
Feast of St Brigid
Secondary Patron of Ireland

FOREWORD

Those of us who know Fr Paddy Jones know something of the roots of his passionate interest in liturgical matters. The roots, as is illustrated in the final contribution of this Festschrift, written by Moira Bergin RSM, are to be found in his own family with its ecumenical background, and with his Parish Priest in Greystones, Fr John Fennelly.

Meeting Fr Fennelly was quite an experience. Father Fennelly was what we call a man ahead of his time, with all the characteristics that men ahead of their time often have. He was driven, rather than patient. He knew what he expected at a liturgical celebration, while many of his parishioners had other expectations. Going to Mass in Greystones you encountered Mass leaflets, indications of how the liturgy should be celebrated, encouragement to sing parts of the Mass and a hearty discouragement to producing your rosary beads.

Paddy learned much from Fr Fennelly, even if in character they were totally different. Paddy was, and is, a man not of clash but of bringing people together, of patience, of taking time to explain, but not giving in on principle. He is one who prepares and expects others to prepare the liturgy. He is not the sort of person who would be happy in a sacristy where liturgical roles are being distributed at the last minute and would not be happy to be asked, just as the Alleluia verse was being sung, to read the Gospel.

As a young student in Clonliffe, Paddy was one who was already well-read in liturgical matters as the Second Vatican Council began and commenced publishing its first documents. His library must be filled with everything from scholarly works, to draft liturgical texts, down to the pamphlets and magazine articles of varied value which did a booming business at the time of the early liturgical renewal in Ireland.

Already as a seminarian he was widely informed not just about liturgical theology but also on the personalities who were the leaders in the post conciliar liturgical renewal on the international scene and especially in Britain and Ireland. As students in Clonliffe College, we shared that same passion for liturgy, but in different ways. I was a Master of Ceremonies in the seminary, and was also involved in the complex ceremonies in the Pro-Cathedral presided over by Archbishop John Charles McQuaid. Such high traditional ceremony was not quite Paddy's natural liturgical home but neither was he a proponent of light-weight liturgy. He recognised good liturgy in a wide variety of forms, and he recognised poor liturgy!

The experience of that early period of liturgical renewal at the time of Vatican II has served him in all his years as he himself became a key figure in Ireland for over thirty years, his name now among the list of liturgical pioneers that he had earlier admired. His range of expertise gradually extended. He became a respected figure on the international scene, especially at ICEL. He was a respected commentator on the whole range of liturgical interest, including the language of liturgical prayer, the place of music in the liturgy and liturgical art and architecture. Wherever he travelled he took interest in the local liturgy, both in the Western and Orthodox traditions.

The National Centre for Liturgy at Maynooth grew in prestige during his years as Director, attracting students from many parts of the world due to its academic excellence and the unique atmosphere and interaction of faculty and students.

Both the recent Synod of Bishops on the Eucharist and *Evangelii Gaudium,* which gathered together the fruits of the Synod, speak about the 'art of celebration'. This is a real challenge still for the liturgy in Ireland. The art of celebration is not just about rubrics or about handy hints for being a presider. It is about an understanding of the nature and the structure of the liturgy which helps all of us to enter prayerfully into the mystery being celebrated and to avoid any sort of personal protagonism and putting ourselves at the centre of the celebration. A genuine art of celebration also involves many technical and practical questions. (There is nothing which upsets me more than to find celebrants or readers who are not trained to use a microphone and who simply cannot be understood.)

Here in Ireland we have the enormous challenge of fostering singing during worship. I spent more than thirty years outside Ireland where the concept of singing by the congregation is normal. In German-speaking churches there is a vast wealth of hymns which are remarkably well-known to congregations. In the French and Italian churches you encounter extraordinary forms of antiphonal singing. Curiously the only hymns which get a rousing response from congregations in Ireland are those which some of our contemporary liturgical music was supposed to banish. In Ireland we can get the impression that the main task of parish choirs is to ensure that people do not sing. Cantors often replace the congregation. We need a renewed repertoire in liturgical music and especially music with a strong Irish foundation and not simply imported music.

Alongside a deep understanding of the theological aspects of the liturgy, Paddy had acquired an encyclopaedic knowledge of rubrics and calendar. He was never inflexible or arrogant, but his word would go unchallenged by many a Bishop who was less sure of his terrain. Paddy was always available with an opinion and a suggestion.

He is a well-respected figure on the international scene and yet is also well rooted in concrete pastoral liturgy, whether through the daily Mass for students of Maynooth University or his Sunday Masses in Cloverhill Prison.

I am very pleased that his colleagues have decided to mark Paddy's retirement with such a prestigious Festschrift. I hope that Paddy realises that retirement is a relative term and that his contribution to liturgical research will continue, and that his new parishioners in Saint Columba's Parish appreciate that they are blessed with their new pastor.

⚜ Diarmuid Martin
Archbishop of Dublin
5 April 2015
Easter Sunday of the Resurrection of the Lord

ABBREVIATIONS

⁊ ⁊ ⁊

AAS *Acta Apostolicae Sedis.* Vatican City: Polyglot Press, 1909–

CIC *Codex Iuris Canonici*, 1983: Code of Canon Law; translations as found in the Vatican website

DOL *Documents on the Liturgy 1963–1979: Conciliar, Papal, and Curial Texts*, International Commission on English in the Liturgy, trans. Collegeville, MN: Liturgical Press, 1982

DV *Dei verbum*, Vatican II 'Dogmatic Constitution on Divine Revelation', 1965

GIRM *General Instruction of the Roman Missal*, fifth edition of 2002 (amended in 2008), as found at the beginning of the *Roman Missal* (English translation of 2011)

GS *Gaudium et spes*, Vatican II, 'Pastoral Constitution on the Church in the Modern World', 1965

ICEL International Commission on English in the Liturgy [A translation agency serving eleven full member English-speaking Episcopal Conferences and fifteen associate member Conferences; tasked with supplying Episcopal Conferences with good pastoral English language versions of the original Latin liturgical books]

LG *Lumen gentium*, Vatican II, 'Dogmatic Constitution on the Church', 1964

PG	*Patrologia Greca*. Paris: Éditions Garnier, 1857–68; Turnhout: Brepols, 1958–; 222 vols.
PL	*Patrologia Latina*. Paris: Éditions Garnier, 1884–55; Turnhout: Brepols, 1958–; 168 vols.
SC	*Sacrosanctum concilium*, Vatican II, 'Constitution on the Sacred Liturgy', 1963
UR	*Unitatis redintegratio*, Vatican II, 'Decree on Ecumenism', 1964

All citations from documents from the Second Vatican Council and from recent papal and curial texts are taken from the Vatican website, unless otherwise stated.

Roman Missal: Third edition of 2011; all citations are from the *Roman Missal*, Dublin: Veritas, 2011.

Scripture: all citations are taken from *New Revised Standard Version* (NRSV), unless otherwise stated by the author.

EXPLORING THE LITURGICAL EVENT: PRAYER, RITE AND MUSIC

HOW MANY HANDS DOES IT TAKE TO ORDAIN A MINISTER?

꙳ ꙳ ꙳

PAUL F. BRADSHAW

There seems to have been a growing tendency in recent years for more and more people to participate in the laying on of hands at an ordination. This is even observable in the case of denominations like the Anglican and Roman Catholic Churches, which have traditionally included priests along with the presiding bishop at the imposition of hands during the ordination of a priest. As well as those from the presbyterate of the particular diocese, other priests who are particular friends and relatives of the ordinand are often granted a place as well, swelling the total gathered around each ordinand to unwieldy proportions. But it seems to be especially the trend in other churches. So, for example, the United Methodist Church in the USA, where traditionally the laying on of hands had been performed by bishop and elders, made provision in 1988 for lay people to share in the gesture at the ordination of an elder, and in 1998 for deacons to do the same at the ordination of a new deacon. The latest form for the ordination of elders directs: 'Representatives from the laity, the ecumenical Church, and the order of elders who are to join in the laying on of hands stand with the bishop. When the bishop lays hands on the head of the candidate, others may lay hands on the candidate's back or shoulders'.[1]

In so doing, the United Methodist Church was merely following what has become increasingly the custom at many

Baptist and Congregationalist ordinations, where not merely representatives of the laity but often everyone present is given the opportunity to join in. Even in churches where this does not happen, the whole congregation sometimes joins in saying part of the ordination prayer together with the presiding minister. This is so, for instance, in the Presbyterian Church (USA).[2]

Historical precedent

These developments are interesting because they run contrary to what appears to have been the standard practice in early Christianity and remains the case in eastern Christian churches. Here the presiding minister alone laid his hands on a candidate for any of the ordained ministries – bishop, priest, or deacon. Even the requirement of the Council of Nicaea that no less than three bishops had to be present at the ordination of a bishop did not lead to all three joining in the laying on of hands. Instead, while the presiding bishop laid on hands and said the ordination prayer, the other two usually held the Gospel book open over the head of the ordinand. They had taken over this ceremonial action from deacons who had previously performed it (except in Rome where deacons retained responsibility for it at the ordination of the Bishop of Rome and it was not part of the rite of ordaining other bishops there), presumably because they desired to have a more active part in the ordination rite. The same desire seems to have been responsible for other bishops eventually laying their hands on the candidate's arms while the presiding bishop laid his right hand on the man's head in the Coptic rite and on the sides of his body in the East Syrian rite.[3]

From where then did the later western custom originate of other bishops joining in the imposition of hands at the ordination of a bishop and of priests doing the same at the ordination of a priest? The earliest literary evidence for this is found in the ancient and mysterious Church order known as the *Apostolic Tradition* of Hippolytus. At one time there was general agreement that this document represented the practice of the Church at Rome in the early third century, which is why a version of its eucharistic prayer came to be adopted not only in the modern Roman Catholic rite but also in the revised rites of various other churches too, and its ordination prayer for a bishop used today in both the Roman Catholic Church and the Episcopal Church in the USA. However, a growing number of scholars now seriously question that attribution, and suggest that on the contrary it is a piece of 'living literature', made up of various strata from different time periods from the second to the fourth century and from different geographical regions. As it stands therefore, it does not reflect the actual liturgy of any one Church, and in particular there is no reason to connect it specifically with Rome. We cannot even be sure that all its prescriptions were ever practised anywhere, but some of them simply might not have been the theoretical ideals of a compiler.[4]

Be that as it may, we possess no evidence that its directions about the imposition of hands at ordinations were imitated or appropriated anywhere until they were incorporated into a document known as the *Statuta ecclesiae antiqua*, perhaps written by Gennadius of Marseilles c. 490 CE. From here they found their way into the liturgical texts of ordination in France, presumably because they were thought to be truly the customs of the ancient Church even though they had previously formed no part of the indigenous traditions. When these Gallican texts were later combined with the Roman rites, these same directions migrated with them into the standard practice of the medieval west. In the case of the ordination of bishops and of priests, this made the act of imposing hands quite complex and time-consuming, especially when there was more than one candidate, and this seems to have been responsible for it eventually taking place at the point where the direction came in the written text – in silence before the ordination prayer was said, rather than during it, as it continued to be in the case of the ordination of deacons.[5]

In the modern Roman Catholic rite the silent imposition of hands separated from the ordination prayer continues to be mandated for bishops and priests, even when there is only one ordinand, and has also been extended to the ordination of deacons.[6] And in 1944 Pius XII declared in his apostolic constitution, *Episcopalis consecrationis*, that the bishops who participated in the imposition of hands at the ordination of a bishop were themselves co-consecrators and not merely assistants to the presiding bishop (although the priests who participated in the imposition of hands at the ordination of a priest were not so regarded). Pius XII directed that those bishops were also to recite the ordination prayer that followed 'and likewise for the duration of the rest of the rite to read in a low voice everything else that the consecrator reads or sings, with the exception of the prayers prescribed for blessing of the pontifical vestments, which are put on in the rite of consecration'.[7] In the modern revision of the rite, however, this verbal participation is restricted to the central portion of the ordination prayer, the part regarded as essential for the validity of the sacrament.

Full, active participation and representative ministry
What seems to be the ultimate root of the considerable increase in the numbers of those becoming involved in the laying on of hands at ordinations in most churches in the latter part of the twentieth century is the influence of the modern liturgical movement with its call for greater involvement of the laity in liturgical services, reinforced by the Roman Catholic Constitution on the Sacred Liturgy, *Sacrosanctum concilium*, in 1963:

> 14. Mother Church earnestly desires that all the faithful should be led to that fully conscious, and active participation in liturgical celebrations which is demanded by the very nature of the liturgy. Such participation by the Christian people as 'a chosen race, a royal priesthood, a holy nation, a redeemed people' (1 Peter 2:9; see 2:4-5), is their right and duty by reason of their baptism.
>
> In the restoration and promotion of the sacred liturgy, this full and active participation by all the people is the aim to be considered before all else; for it is the primary and indispensable source from which the faithful are to

derive the true Christian spirit; and therefore pastors of souls must zealously strive to achieve it, by means of the necessary instruction, in all their pastoral work.

The consequences of this laudable aim have sometimes gone beyond what was originally envisaged. Not only have lay people joined in singing or saying the parts of the liturgy that are rightfully theirs, but in some cases they have also begun to join in prayers or parts of prayers that were intended to be said by the presiding minister. And such participation is not restricted only to words. The Roman Catholic rite for the Baptism of children already officially encourages parents and godparents to join in the making of the sign of the cross on the child, and this has not only been adopted in some other churches but extended to the participation of lay people in other ritual actions too, so that, for example, congregations may sometimes be asked to stretch out their hands to share in the blessing of an individual or group within their number. Some other forms of individual participation are of much longer standing. In some places at a funeral not only has the officiating minister traditionally cast a few grains of earth on the coffin after it is lowered into the grave, but mourners have been invited to do the same, and in more recent times individual stems of flowers have sometimes been substituted.

Similarly, quite early in the liturgical movement some Roman Catholic communities began to adopt the custom of inviting each of the intending communicants to place an individual host into a ciborium as they arrived for Mass.[8] The ciborium was then carried up to the altar at the presentation of the gifts. This was intended not only to recall the early Christian practice of worshippers contributing bread and wine from their own homes for the eucharistic meal but also to give visual expression to the belief, advanced by Augustine of Hippo, that it was the worshippers themselves, symbolically present in the gifts, who were being offered to God.[9] It also had the practical side effect of providing a means whereby a count could be made of those who were going to receive communion.

The involvement of individuals in verbal or ritual acts of this kind powerfully increases their feelings of personal participation in what is happening. This is confirmed by the widespread popularity with which the introduction of such practices is generally greeted, even in congregations that have previously not been accustomed to much ceremonial in their worship. For example, the suggestion made to one low-church congregation on Easter Day that individuals might wish to go to the font and dip their fingers in the water – as a sign of the renewal of their baptismal affirmation of faith that had just taken place – had been expected by the clergy to elicit a response from only a very small number, and so a hymn with just a few verses had been announced to cover the action. So great was the actual response that the organist became fatigued in his attempts to improvise on the tune for an extended period of time!

If taken too far, however, such personal involvement in ritual action can have the unintended consequence of eroding the notion of a representative ministry. In other words, it can create the impression in people's mind that 'if I have not personally said the same words or performed the same physical gesture as the minister, then I have not really participated in the rite'. Signs of such an attitude may be seen at the exchange of the sign of peace in some congregations, where it appears vital that one greets every other person who is present there, no matter how long it takes. While it is certainly essential that every single person is greeted by someone else, it is not equally vital that I must greet everyone. Other people can represent me.

At this point we need to distinguish between those actions in which the participation of every individual is ritually important and those in which someone else may appropriately represent others. If we take as an example the custom described earlier, of intending communicants depositing a host into a ciborium as they arrive for Mass, the symbolism is lost if someone else – an usher or a server, for instance – performs the action on my behalf: how can I think of myself as symbolically present in the ciborium if I had nothing to do with it? On the other hand, it is not necessary for me subsequently to be the one who personally carries the ciborium to the altar: someone else may then act on behalf of us all.

The same practice of certain individuals intended to represent others also occurs in those congregations where there is a presentation of the eucharistic gifts without the prior ceremony of individuals placing hosts in the ciborium having taken place. But is this always *perceived* to be a representative ministry, and especially on those occasions when the persons chosen to undertake this task may be unfamiliar to most or all of the rest of the congregation? It certainly is by the clergy, who view the many individuals present in the church for the service as the assembly, the congregation, the laity, the people – collective nouns for a corporate body. But do the people see themselves in the same way or instead just as many individuals who have *come* to church, but not *as* the Church? So often the latter seems to be the case, in spite of the efforts of the liturgical movement over many years to promote the opposite understanding.

Here we may reach the heart of the problem – worshippers viewing themselves as an aggregate of individuals attending a service, but not as a community acting together. In such a situation, it is hard for people to understand how one of their number can represent them, and especially if the one was not openly appointed or elected to do so, as they do not form a single unit that can have a representative. Only I can then represent me unless I give consent in some way for someone else to do so.

If we return to the question of the exchange of the peace referred to earlier, each individual present certainly needs to receive the greeting from someone in order to be assured that they are part of the community, but each individual does not need to offer the greeting to every other person – unless they do not understand themselves to be a community but just an aggregate of individuals who therefore all need to make personal contact with everyone else there.

If we then apply this reasoning to the ordination practices outlined at the beginning of this essay, we can begin to see what may be happening there. The instructions of the *Statuta ecclesiae antiqua* with regard to the imposition of hands at the ordination of bishops and priests were probably adopted in the western Church not merely because they were thought to be very ancient but because they provided a response to the desire of individual bishops and priests to play a more active part in the rite. It was not enough simply to be there and signify their assent to the action by their presence close to the presiding bishop; they wanted to associate themselves more closely by engaging in the same physical gesture. Nevertheless, whether by their presence or by their gesture, they were still acting in a representative capacity. The bishops represented the whole college of bishops who were not able to be there, the priests the whole presbyterate of the diocese.

What has been happening in recent years, however, appears to be a decline in the appreciation of the corporate character of the ministerial order and a growth in the sense of a personal connection to the individual. 'I want to join in because I want to express my personal association with him/her; I am here as the friend of this particular candidate and not as a representative of the clergy of the diocese giving assent to all being ordained. It is not even enough that I should stretch out my hands towards him/her while the prayer is said: I need actually to touch him/her.' And what has been true of the clergy has in some other denominations also been extended to the laity. In a Church with a congregational polity, for example, it is apparently no longer sufficient that certain individuals represent the local congregation; everyone must have an opportunity to join in. Even in denominations that officially have no such polity, there is often the desire that lay people should not feel left out of what seems otherwise an exclusively clerical affair, and so the wish to be inclusive is allowed to override any notion that different groups of people may have appropriately different roles in a rite, or that there might be other parts of the service instead in which lay people ought to be taking a much more active part.

Thus, the tendencies evident in ordination practice today are but symptoms of a broader movement in the Church that in turn reflects the trend in western societies at large away from a collective understanding of a community in which certain individuals may represent the whole and towards a greater individualisation. You may act, but not in my name. Only I can do that.

ᔭᡫ ᔭᡫ ᔭᡫ

Notes

1. General Board of Discipleship, *Services for the Ordering of Ministry in the United Methodist Church: Provisional Texts* (Nashville: United Methodist Publishing House, 1998); General Board of Discipleship, *Services for the Ordering of Ministry in the United Methodist Church* (Nashville: United Methodist Publishing House, 2012).
2. Presbyterian Church (USA), *Book of Occasional Services* (Louisville: Geneva Press, 1999).
3. For further details, see Paul F. Bradshaw, *Ordination Rites of the Ancient Churches of East and West* (New York: Pueblo, 1990); idem, *Rites of Ordination: Their History and Theology* (Collegeville, MN: Liturgical Press, 2013).
4. See further, Paul F. Bradshaw, Maxwell E. Johnson and L. Edward Phillips, *The Apostolic Tradition: A Commentary*, Hermeneia Series (Minneapolis: Fortress Press, 2002), 6–11.
5. See Bradshaw, *Rites of Ordination*, Chapter 6.
6. Text in *De Ordinatione Episcopi, Presbyterorum et Diaconorum, editio typica altera* (Vatican City: Libreria Editrice Vaticana, 1990); English translation in *Rites of Ordination of a Bishop, of Priests, and of Deacons* (Washington, DC: United States Catholic Conference of Catholic Bishops, 2003).
7. Latin text in AAS 37 (1945), 131–2.
8. For evidence from the 1940s, see Alden V. Brown, *The Grail Movement and American Catholicism, 1940–1975* (Notre Dame: University of Notre Dame Press, 1989), 36. I am indebted to Dr Katharine Harmon for this reference.
9. See St Augustine, *Sermon*, 272.

THE ORGAN:
A LITURGICAL FORCE OF
CONSIDERABLE SIGNIFICANCE

Ꭷ Ꭷ Ꭷ

GERARD GILLEN

The organ has an historical uniqueness in the canon of western musical instruments, given the continuity of its history, the sheer range and diversity of its national styles of building and construction, its variety of timbres and colours, and the manner in which it is inextricably wedded to the building for which it has been designed and the liturgy it serves. Hand in hand with this development of instrument, there goes a repertoire of some six hundred years of music of the most amazing stylistic diversity (French, German, Austrian, Bohemian, Italian, Spanish, Dutch, English). No other instrument has such an historical richness and diversity of repertoire to draw on, nor such a variety of instruments on which the music may be played. This historical richness is part of the reason the instrument is a source of absorbing and endless fascination for those of us who are organists, and it is also part of the reason why its proponents can so easily become colossal bores to those who are not so absorbed with the instrument!

The organ repertoire and organ-building reached its climax in the eighteenth century with the music of J.S. Bach and the great instruments of builders such as the Alsatian Gottfried Silbermann and the north German Arp Schnitger. Thereafter it went into a cyclic decline, so to speak, from which it emerged in the late-nineteenth century with renewed musical energy, to take its place as a major force in twentieth-century music when so many leading composers from César Franck (in the late nineteenth century) through Edward Elgar, Vaughan Williams, Benjamin Britten, Michael Tippett, Olivier Messiaen, Maurice Duruflé and James MacMillan, composed music, inspired largely by the new symphonic instruments developed by that nineteenth-century French genius of organ building, Aristide Cavaille-Coll, and by William Hill and Henry Willis in England, and William Telford in Ireland. Once again the organ was projected into the mainstream of music-making, a position it had not enjoyed since the middle of the eighteenth century.

Throughout its long life the Church has been at the centre of its function and purpose (since organs were and are, for the most part, built for ecclesiastical buildings), assisting worship through its role in accompanying congregations, solo, schola, choral and instrumental voices, and through its own instrument-specific repertoire, so much of which is connected with the illumination of Church doctrine and the praise of God. It was for so long the liturgical instrument *par excellence*. Whether it remains so today is a matter of some doubt, as society in 2015 is so very different from what it was fifty years ago, not to mention 150 or two hundred or more years ago. The organ and its broad range of repertoire (service and solo music) belong to what we might loosely call the contemporary 'classical' music world. So, before considering the micro-world of the organ, organists and organ music, it is instructive to look at the macro world of which it is part.

The distinguished American music scholar at Berkeley, California, Professor Lawrence Kramer, wrote as follows:

> It is no secret that ['classical' music] is in trouble. It barely registers in our schools, it has neither the prestige nor the popularity of literature and visual art, and it squanders its capacities for self-renewal by clinging to an exceptionally static core repertoire. Its audience is shrinking, greying and overly pale-faced, and the suspicion has been voiced abroad that its claim to occupy a sphere of autonomous

artistic greatness is largely a means of veiling, and thus perpetuating, a narrow set of social interests.[1]

Kramer is a proponent of the so-called 'new musicology' which espouses the view that music must be examined and evaluated in the social and cultural context in which it was created and in which it is performed, and this view very much informs general educational philosophy and music educational attitudes in particular today. For example, the (Irish government's) Department of Education and Skills' music syllabus (especially for Junior and Leaving Certificate examinations) will attest that a pop song is treated with the same critical interest and weight as a Beethoven sonata or symphony. Function is perceived to be everything, and the notion of absolute values is, to post-modern thinking, elite and outdated. This sort of outlook reflects a prevalent view of music in the modern world where, to quote the distinguished British academic, Professor Nicholas Cook, 'deciding whether to listen to Beethoven or [David] Bowie, or Balinese music becomes the same kind of choice as deciding whether to eat Italian, Thai, or Cajun tonight'.[2]

Where do classically trained musicians stand in this matter? Do we accept the *status quo*, and accept that we are just another niche interest in a crowded market place? Do we stand firm and hope that the integrity of our art will carry us through, or that market forces may be more favourably disposed to us in the future? Do we attempt to redress the balance by promoting our art to a wider constituency? This is a complex topic admitting of no simple answers.

One of the ways in which the classical music secular world, as it were, has hit back has been through various public promotion or education 'outreach' programmes. In Ireland we have become familiar with various classical music outreach programmes: the annual national programme of 'Music in the Classroom' events sponsored by *The Irish Times*, and the National Concert Hall's own Music Education initiatives ('tiny-tots' etc.). Outreach programmes have indeed become part of the general educational process.

When we consider the organ in this context, I think we have to admit that the instrument is in particular need of wider and greater promotion. Culturally and numerically, organists are a niche within a niche. And when we consider that we operate in the context of Church worship with declining numbers of regular attenders for whatever reason, we have a real problem.[3]

While we organists love our instrument and need no evangelisation to convince us of its inherent beauty and of its power to uplift the spirit, we have to accept that we have a serious problem with the general public's perception of the instrument, one for which organists must accept some responsibility. Peter Hall, artistic director of Manchester's Bridgewater Hall (of which the £1.2 million Danish-built Marcussen organ is a feature) spoke for many people, I think, when he said in the course of an interview that 'the common perception of organists is that they are generally uncommunicative except among their own kind'. Major figures of twentieth-century music such as Sir Thomas Beecham, Igor Stravinsky and the great English critic, Ernest Newman, have been less than complimentary about organists, the latter having written that, to him 'one organist sounded much the same as another'. Added to this is the reality that the organ has declined as *the* liturgical instrument over the past half century. Despite its pre-eminent historical place in the music of Christian worship, modern liturgical democracy would appear to accord it little more than equality with its jumped-up johnny-come-lately competitors, be it guitar, flute, harp, rock group or whatever. When it comes to weddings or funerals, people are apt to request a string quartet or other instrumental combination in preference to the organ.

No doubt over the years we organists had become complacent regarding the unchallenged monarchical position the organ enjoyed in our churches, propped up, as it were, by a raft of Church legislation (in the case of the Roman Catholic pre-1962 Church), and by a strong feeling among the international Christian community that the music of the Church had to be of an other-worldly ethos, and that the organ was the only instrument sufficiently removed from the secular world to fulfil that role. (The Christian Church has always been nervous about the power of music and the emotions of which music is so capable of stirring. This fear of the corruptive power of music goes right back to Plato and later Augustine and the early Church fathers. In the Reformation time, Luther firmly saw the power of good to which music could be used, while some of the non-conformist Reformers, such as John Calvin and John Knox, were much more fearful of its effect. In fact it was not until the end of the nineteenth century that Presbyterians admitted organs into their churches.)

Given that the organ was on the whole the only instrument admitted in formal Christian worship, the Church and Church-music community became careless in the wake of such security of role: we neglected our instruments, and organists often became careless and static in the development of their skills, with the result that Church music's relationship to music became rather analogous to military intelligence's relation to 'general' intelligence. It became somehow disassociated from its *fons et origo*, its source and strength. Church worshippers suspended musical belief and judgement as they came to church: Church music was different, and different standards of composition and performance were to be applied. All of this is summed up in the frequently heard expression: 'the organ plays', as somehow human intervention is unnecessary. Do we ever hear the expression 'the piano plays, or the violin plays'? For one reason or another, the organist's art and craft is so often little appreciated (as is that of the organ-builder).

How do we fight back, or indeed should we fight back? I certainly think we should, and for several reasons. First, the longevity of the organ and its music's place in the history of western civilization is unique among musical instruments. The organ when built by skilled craftsmen is an object of beauty not only to the ear, but also to the eye. In fact there's an aphorism in the organ-building world to the effect that if an organ looks well it will sound well, or a variant of this is that an organ is seen for much longer periods than it is played. This is indeed a wondrous instrument, the craft of human hands at its best, which must be shared with and preserved for all humanity.

Second, the repertoire is wider – and still very much growing – and more varied than that of any other instrument, and that is something also to be shared with as many as are willing to lend an ear. The contemporary composer is as likely to compose today for the organ as for any other instrument.

Third, its liturgical role is unique: only the organ can accompany a large congregation with the power sufficient to sustain and stimulate fully participative singing. (It is no disrespect to other instruments, or combination of instruments, apart perhaps from a large brass ensemble or fullish orchestra, to suggest that in this function the organ is indeed supreme.)

Very often an organ's only vital contribution to liturgy can be gauged when it is missing for some reason or other. Let me cite an example: on Christmas Eve a few years ago at Dublin's Pro-Cathedral the grand organ 'sat down' just as our midnight Mass was about to commence, in the presence of the largest congregation of the year. Fortunately, the day was more than saved musically as we had an orchestra involved in the special celebratory music for the feast. Yet the organ's absence was palpable, with several members of staff and congregation commenting to me on how its contribution to liturgical continuity was missed.

Fourth, it has a choral accompanimental role that it alone can discharge in much of the service repertoire, with the music of, for instance, Stanford, Howells, Rheinberger, Widor, Duruflé, or MacMillan – choral music that is organ-specific in its accompaniment and cannot be substituted for by piano or indeed even by orchestral ensemble. The presence of the organ in the accompaniment of this sort of music is absolutely vital to the colouring of the texture, without which the presentation of the music is but a travesty of what is required. Similarly its continuo role in music from Purcell through Handel and Bach to Mozart and Haydn is vital for essential colouring that does not admit of satisfactory substitution. The same *sine qua non* role applies to the instrument's accompanimental role in so much solo voice or solo ensemble service music (such as verse anthems or solo cantata movements), where the organ has quite frankly an indispensable role.

Fifth, there is the solo repertoire, extending over a period of some six hundred years, of huge diversity of style and wide range of technical difficulty, from the very simple to the mightily demanding and complex. There is surely something for everybody here in this important function of the organ and organist in creating atmosphere and adding literally an unspeakable dimension to Church liturgy.

Sixth and finally, there is the element of improvisation which organists uniquely continue to employ as a living art form, together with jazz musicians – an art that was long a skill practised by all performing musicians, but that today only survives among practising musicians with organists and our much respected jazz colleagues.

These are all good reasons, I think, why we as organists should be proud of what we do, but the reverse side of this particular coin is that if we do our job badly, we reinforce the stereotype of the 'organ plays' rather than the organ is played, and we perform a considerable disservice to the art we practise and the liturgy we serve.

It is essential, of course, that we should have an instrument that is in good working order at our disposal. (It does not have to be a big three-manual organ, for example, but it must be one capable of discharging a modest *musical* function.)

As organists we must also fulfil our role with taste and artistry. In this connection our professional training is paramount. If we play slovenly and inaccurately, without having put due thought and preparation into whatever we play, be it hymn accompanying, psalm accompanying, anthem or motet accompaniment, or pre-service or end of service voluntary, we do a great dis-service to our art and to the act of worship we serve. We cannot then really complain if the general public regard us as second-class citizens of the musical world: it is no more than we deserve. All of us who play in church and are remunerated for our services are professional in that sense, and so it behoves us to act professionally and prepare accordingly in the discharge of our musical duty. It is our duty and responsibility to choose music that is within our capacity to perform, be it hymn, song, anthem or service accompaniment, or voluntary. There is very little merit in having a 'bash' at something that is far beyond our technical capacity, when we could play musically and satisfactorily something less demanding but perhaps less flattering to our musical 'egos'. We do the reputation of the organ and its role in the liturgy little service by such self-indulgence.

The time-honoured way in which instrumental skill is imparted is at the hands of a teacher. Those of us who are teachers have the greatest responsibility, not just to teach and pass on a skill which we have been taught by someone else, but to teach our students to use their ears and their brains in a creative and critical manner. Just because something is old does not mean that it is great art. We organists are so often accused, with some justification, that we are only interested in the past, in how things were done, in old music by dead composers. To be only interested in the music of the past for living worship is to impose on the liturgy a stamp of antiquarianism which is as inappropriate as the opposing view which holds that living worship can only have contemporary music as its fitting accompaniment. True worship belongs to the cosmos where past, present and future merge seamlessly, and it seems to me that the music we provide for the liturgical act should similarly not be bound by time, the only criteria being set by the questions, is it *good* music, and does the music we offer serve and illuminate the liturgical moment? To answer these questions appropriately and honestly implies an openness of mind in musical-liturgical matters which we should all have, but, perhaps, do not always demonstrate. As the economist J. M. Keynes famously wrote, 'The difficulty lies not in new ideas but in escaping from the old ones'.[4]

In the process of acquiring our organ skills, it is so important that the regular (organ) lesson, so vital a part of the learning strategy, does not become an end in itself, but rather that these lessons should become a means of turning the student into an effective independent learner. It is also important that we all acquire what educational psychologists call 'meta-cognitive' skills, that is, 'learning to learn' skills. The great pianist and scholar Charles Rosen has said that the best method of teaching is to practise with a student, or to demonstrate how one practises and then watch the student until the passage comes right.[5] This may very well be the best method, but it is hardly a very practical one.

It was in response to the need for such a process of learning and training that the National Centre for Liturgy, under the direction of Fr Patrick Jones, instituted its courses and examination certificates in liturgical organ training, and it was such a concern for the development of promoting liturgically appropriate organ expertise that prompted the Centre's founding father, the late Seán Swayne, with scant resources at his disposal, to purchase the Peter Collins' pipe organ, an instrument that enhanced the many and varied liturgical ceremonies celebrated in Richard Hurley's beautifully adapted chapel in the Irish Institute of Pastoral Liturgy until the demise of that Institute on the Carlow College campus and the move to an hospitable and welcoming Maynooth. Such practical and academic support for the ongoing development of the art of the organ and organist in the context of a constantly renewing liturgy stands is a beacon of light in a national liturgical music firmament that has had to endure some squally weather.

༄ ༄ ༄

Notes

1. Lawrence Kramer, *Classical Music and Postmodern Knowledge* (Berkeley: University of California Press, 1995), 3–4.
2. Nicholas Cook, *Music: A Very Short Introduction* (Oxford: Oxford University Press, 1998), 40.
3. I recently came across a twenty-year-old Dutchman, fanatical about the organ, and now living in Ireland. When I commented to him how lucky he was to come from a country with its fabulous historical legacy of wonderful instruments – Haarlem, Alkmaar, Zwolle, etc. –

and assuming this was where his passion for the organ originated, I was quite taken aback when he told me that he had never heard nor seen an organ while living in Holland, as he had never gone to church, coming as he did from a non-religious background.

4. John M. Keynes, *The General Theory of Employment, Interest and Money* (London: MacMillan, 1936; repr. 1964), viii.

5. See Charles Rosen, *The Frontiers of Meaning* (London: Hill and Wang, 1994).

THE SONG OF SONGS AS A MARIAN LITURGICAL TEXT:
THE *SIGILLUM SANCTAE MARIAE VIRGINIS* OF HONORIUS OF AUTUN

꙳ ꙳ ꙳

BRENDAN McCONVERY CSsR

The most innovative reading of the Song in the twelfth century monastic tradition was one that interpreted it in a thoroughgoing Marian key, identifying the woman in the Song as Mary, the Mother of Jesus. A number of commentaries in this vein have survived. The most significant include those of Honorius Augustodunensis (also known as Honorius of Autun), Rupert of Deutz, William of Newburgh and Alan of Lille. There is also a sermon ascribed to Hugh of St Victor. Marian interpretation of the Song may not have been a total innovation. There are signs that liturgical hymnody applied some verses of the Song to Mary at a comparatively early date. Epiphanius of Salamis in the fourth century, for example, had used a catena of verses from the Song as a basis for a hymn in which the praises of Mary, virgin mother of Christ, and the Church, virgin mother of the faithful, intermingle:

> Come from Lebanon, O spouse, you are altogether beautiful.
> There is no stain in you.
> O paradise of the great architect, city of the holy King,
> Betrothed of the immaculate Christ, virgin most pure.
> Promised in faith to the only Spouse, you shine forth
> and gleam like the dawn.
> You are beautiful as the moon, pure as the sun,
> Terrible as an army set in battle array!

Queens proclaim you blessed, women celebrate you
And young girls praise your beauty.
You come up from the desert, gleaming with an overpowering brightness,
You come in a cloud of perfumes.
You come up from the desert like a column of smoke,
Breathing forth myrrh and incense,
with all the spices of the perfumer and giving forth the sweetest of scents.
The one who announced your coming said
'Your perfumes have a pleasant odour,
therefore the young girls love you'.
You stand at the right hand of the king,
clothed in a glittering robe, woven from the purest gold.
Once you were black, but now you are beautiful and altogether fair.
When we come close to you, we forget all the sad trails of heresy
And we take rest from the tempests which toss the waves,
O Holy Mother, O Church,
And we take heart in your holy doctrine, in one faith and in the truth of God.[1]

The trigger for a more thoroughgoing Marian reading of the Song was probably the increasing use of verses drawn from it as liturgical antiphons and reading texts in the increasing number of liturgical feasts in honour of the Mother of Jesus, especially that of the Assumption, or *Transitus Mariae*. From about the year 1000, this feast appears to have been celebrated in the form of a liturgical drama with a solemn procession representing the entrance of Mary into heaven.[2] In the monastic Office, the readings at the Vigil Office of Matins were taken from the Song and from a text ascribed to Jerome (but in fact the work of the French monk, Paschasius Radbertus, 786–860).[3] As Rachel Fulton points out, the Assumption was a popular feast and Mary's dormition was described in some detail in the hagiographical legends of the apocryphal tradition, but its lack of a clear scriptural foundation posed a problem for the compilers of liturgical texts.[4] The earliest of the Marian commentaries on the Songs by Honorius Augustodunensis seems to have been intended to explain the unexpected use of this unusual book in the liturgy.

Who was Honorius of Autun (Augustodunensis)?

The author of the article on Honorius (c. 1090?–1156) in the *Dictionnaire de Théologie Catholique* remarks that 'no writer of the Middle Ages is as deeply mysterious as this man'.[5] Although he has been associated for centuries with the cathedral school of Autun, he is now more commonly referred to by the Latin name Augustodunensis ('from the hill-fort of Augustus'). This, however, may be simply a way of sidestepping the question of his origins. In the early twentieth century, his name was associated with the monastery of St James at Regensburg (Ratisbon) in Germany. This was one of several Irish monastic foundations on the European mainland and it continued to maintain its Irish links during the period Honorius was presumed to be a member of the community. Christian (or Conon), abbot of St James (1133–53) to whom Augustus dedicated several of his works, was an Irishman who ended his life as Archbishop of Cashel.[6] European scholarship has been content to refer to him in a somewhat general way as 'British', but it has been argued more recently that the influence on his thought of Anselm of Canterbury points to his English origins, and more specifically to the monastery and cathedral of Worcester.[7]

By the standards of the time, Honorius was a prolific and popular author with widely ranging interests. Some twenty-five works ascribed to him are collected in Migne's *Patrologia Latina*, including the *Elucidarius*, a summa of theological lore that was frequently translated into vernaculars (including Old Icelandic, Old French and Welsh), a treatise on the sun, six books of biblical commentary, and others on different areas of theology including an allegorical treatise on the liturgy (*Gemma Animae*), and one (*De Esu Volatilium*) on whether monks were permitted by the Rule to eat fowl.[8] While not regarded as a creative thinker, the breadth of his interests 'is a valuable witness to the learning considered respectable by his contemporaries'.[9]

Honorius composed two commentaries on the Song but the order in which they appeared is uncertain. The *Expositio in Cantica Canticorum*, the longer of the two, covers almost one hundred and fifty columns of Migne.[10] It plays on the novel idea that the Song represents allegorical marriages between Solomon and four different women. Honorius had set out to treat each section of the Song in accordance with the four medieval 'senses' of Scripture – the historical, allegorical, tropological and anagogical senses – but such an exhaustive programme seems to have proved too much even for his energies and he confines himself more regularly to the allegorical.

A Biblical-Liturgical Commentary: *Sigillum Sanctae Mariae Virginis*

Honorius' second commentary, *Sigillum Sanctae Mariae Virginis* (the Seal of St Mary the Virgin) is briefer, covering a mere twenty-two columns of text. It is probably the earliest commentary to engage in a thoroughgoing Marian reading of the Song. It takes the form of a brief treatise on the liturgical readings for the feast of the Assumption.[11] While it will not be possible to treat it all in equal detail, an exploration of how Honorius expounds the first chapter may enable readers to get the flavour of this largely unknown text. It begins by recording the request of a younger monk or pupil who apologises for burdening Honorius with yet more questions, but hoping that he might find an hour to explain briefly why certain biblical texts had been chosen for the liturgy of this feast. Honorius addresses the texts in the sequence of Gospel (Luke 10:38-42), the first reading of the Mass (Sirach 24:11-31) and finally, the Song of Songs, from the Vigil Office. There is an almost conversational tone in the way he begins to address the query of the young monk:

You say you are wondering why the Gospel that begins with the words, 'Jesus went into a certain town' (Luke 10:38-42) and the Song of Songs are read on the feast of holy Mary, since there seems to be no reference to her in either of them. As regards the Gospel, you might recognise that there is none more fitting, apt or worthy of her than this to read on her feast day. It says that Jesus 'went into a certain castle'.[12] A castle has a high tower as a defence against the enemy and an outer wall which defends the citizens within. This castle was the sanctuary of the Holy Spirit, namely Mary, the glorious mother of God which was defended by the angels and was fortified on all sides. The 'high tower' is humility, which reaches the heights of heaven, hence it is said, 'The Lord looked down on the lowliness of his handmaid' (Luke 1:48). The outer wall was her chastity which acted as a defence for the other virtues within. The Lord entered this castle when he joined human nature to himself in the womb of the virgin. 'And a certain woman called Martha received him into her house: she had a sister called Mary.' Martha is the active life, Mary the contemplative life, both of which the ever-virgin Mary is said to have cultivated in Christ to a high degree.[13]

This brief exposition of the Gospel reveals several features to which Honorius will return. In the main, it takes as its starting point a straightforward and relatively literal exposition of the meaning of the Gospel's words. Since his young questioner is puzzled by this particular choice of reading, the master moves towards the more spiritual sense, pointing out the appropriateness of this text about two women, since the Mother of Jesus united in her person the excellence of both the active and contemplative states they have traditionally represented in monastic exegesis. Although a monk, and probably expected to speak in defence of the contemplative life, Honorius realises that Mary of Nazareth is also a primary exemplar of the active life of virtue to hearers of the word and there is an earthiness in the way in which he records the details of child-care:

> For all the works of the Gospel depend on the service of her active life. For us she received Jesus as a guest in her virtuous womb when she was still a girl. She fed him from her breasts when he was hungry, consoled him in her lap when he cried. She bathed him when he was weak, she wrapped him in swaddling clothes when he was naked, she clothed him for his journeys, she kissed him sweetly when he was happy. She was always concerned about serving him, fleeing into Egypt in the face of Herod, and returning in the time of Archelaeus. She was much concerned about the places where he could hide from all who sought him.

The praise of Wisdom in the reading from Sirach is also appropriate to the feast, since the womb of Mary was the place in which God's wisdom took flesh. Yet the reading describes Wisdom as a woman in search of her true dwelling place. For the original author, this was intended as praise for the Jerusalem and the temple cult as the resting place of Wisdom, the *Shekinah* or divine presence of later Jewish tradition. Applying a typical medieval allegorical interpretation to the text, Honorius can also render this as a foreshadowing of the mystery of the day: 'Sion is to be understood as the Church of this age: Jerusalem as the heavenly homeland. That is why Mary is called the Queen of Heaven'.

It is to the longer readings of the Vigil that Honorius next turns his attention. The *Seal* is not a work of innovative learning. There is a strong popular feel to Honorius' exposition, which suggests that the author may have had a homiletic purpose in view. Stories of miracles performed at Mary's intercession on behalf of sinners were probably taken from popular collections designed as preaching *exempla*.[14] They would set the tone for a type of Mariological writing that would endure for centuries, continuing to be seen, for example, in St

Alphonsus Liguori's eighteenth century Italian classic, *The Glories of Mary*. The *exempla* reflect both the positive and negative sides of medieval piety. For all its weaknesses, the *Seal* is nonetheless a neglected key document in the history of a developing Catholic theology of Mary. It is not merely intended to be an edifying text, or perhaps to put it more accurately, medieval theology admits no chasm between popular devotion and sound theology. This might be noticed, for example, as Honorious begins his exposition of the Canticle with its opening words which express the bride's desire to kiss her beloved: 'let him kiss me with the kiss of his mouth' (1:1a).[15] In expounding these opening words, Honorius is also giving expression to some sound basic Mariological principles that might be said to presage Vatican II's teaching on Mary as believer, mother and type of the Church in *Lumen gentium*, chapter 8:

> The glorious Virgin Mary is a type of the Church, which is Virgin and Mother. She is called Mother, because, rendered fruitful by the Spirit, she brings forth children for God every day through baptism. She is called virgin, because she preserves inviolably the wholeness of the faith and is not corrupted by the contagion of heresy. Mary became a mother when she brought forth Christ, and she remained a virgin after his birth. That is why it is fitting to read everything written about the Church as though it referred to Mary. The text says, 'Let me kiss him with the kiss of his mouth.' The Virgin did not simply merit to see the one kings and prophets did not deserve to see, or even to carry him in her womb: once he was born, she kissed him and received many kisses from his mouth in return.

Honorius has also awarded himself a certain amount of hermeneutical liberty by stating as a principle that 'it is fitting to read everything written about the Church as though it referred to Mary'. This gives him imaginative access to a wide range of Old Testament texts, including the Song.

The second half of this verse, 'for thy breasts are better than wine' is an instance where Honorius' Vulgate differs from the majority of modern versions.[16]

> 'For your breasts are better than wine'. The one who feeds the angels in the bosom of the Father was suckled at the breasts of the Virgin Mother. 'The fragrance of the finest perfume', that is, it is full of the gifts of the Holy Spirit. It would not be a frivolous interpretation to assume that the virgin often anointed her dear son with the finest perfumed oils. 'Your name is like oil poured out'. When oil is mixed with other liquids, it floats to the top: oil also heals the sick. The virgin's name is Mary, which means star of the sea. She will help those who call on her in any tribulation to rise above adversity as oil rises. She protected a young Jewish boy whose father cast him into the furnace because he had received the body of Christ with his Christian playmates. Even those who are weak from their sins, but continue to trust in her, will speedily find Christ, the oil of salvation. They may be like Theophilus, who denied Christ and handed himself over to the devil: with Mary's help, he got back a pact he had signed with the devil and so won pardon. In the same way, many people who are trammelled in sin not only find pardon through Mary, but even have miracles done for them on her account.

Several features of this short exposition might be noted. There is, as has already been noted in our comments on the Gospel text, a homely and well-observed interest in the child-care arrangements of the Mother of the Lord – breast-feeding him and anointing him with the finest perfumed oils, perhaps the medieval equivalent of Johnson's baby lotion! Second, the liturgist in Honorius cannot fail to equate any reference to oil with its sacramental equivalents, first as the baptismal symbol of the fragrant gifts of the Holy Spirit and then as the healing oil of the anointing of the sick. In giving the meaning of Mary's name as 'Star of the Sea', Honorius is reflecting a traditional interpretation that may go back as far as Jerome. Third, it contains two preaching *exempla*. The story of the Jewish boy saved from the furnace by Mary is a form of a common anti-Semitic legend. It is found in both Gregory of Tours (538–94)[17] and in Paschasius Radabertus (785–865).[18] The legend of Theophilus, a cleric who entered into a pact with the devil signed in his own blood in a desperate search for preferment within his diocese and from which he could only be freed from it through the direct intervention of Mary, was an early form of the Faust legend. It appears to have been popular in the Middle Ages, as an early form of it may be traced back to Paul the Deacon (c. 720–90). It appeared frequently in the decoration of medieval churches and several scenes dramatically illustrating it appear on one of the transept doors of Notre Dame Cathedral in Paris.[19] Jacobus a Voragine (1230–89) gave it classical status in his *Golden Legend*.[20]

The emphasis on devotion to Virgin as a motif of hope continues in the immediately following section, combining the imagery of Mary, star of the sea by whom the mariner pilots his boat, with yet another an *exemplum* that will constantly reappear in popular preaching of devotion to Mary. It appears in several forms in Alphonsus Liguori's *Glories of Mary*, usually with the argument that even a vestigial devotion to Mary is a sign that faith and hope are not totally dead.

> Those who sail on the ocean of this life, imitating her humility and chastity as though they were plotting a course by the stars, will enter the safe harbour of eternal life with her help. There is a story told of someone who knelt and prayed one Hail Mary every day as he passed before the Virgin's altar. When he was on his deathbed and the demons had already arrived to carry him off to hell, the Virgin herself suddenly appeared and, with her mantle, snatched the man who was by now on the edge of despair from the evil one and brought him safely to the heights.

As a preacher with a pastoral end in view, Honorius can also use the love poetry of the Song as an invitation to a life of virtue. The next verse of the Song reads 'draw me: we will run after thee to the odour of thy ointments' (Song 1:3).

> 'Therefore the young girls love you', that is to say, 'they imitate you.' 'Draw me after you' she says to her Son, meaning 'draw me in the exercise of the virtues'. Mary never commanded her Son to create the universe, but she anchored herself in humility and meekness, for he says, 'Learn from me, for I am meek and humble of heart' (Matthew 19:29). Hence she is drawn into heaven after Christ. 'We will run in the odour of perfumes', that is, the faithful will hasten in joy to imitate the example of her life. 'The king has brought me into his wine-cellar', or the King of Glory has taken her up into eternal life. 'We will be glad and rejoice in you:' the faithful will rejoice in her intercession. 'Remembering your breasts:' the breasts of Mary are chastity and humility in which the company of the just takes delight. 'More than wine', that is, more than human glory; 'do they love you' that is, the angels honour you.

Mary is to be imitated because she was, in the first instance, a disciple who learned virtue by imitating her son. Honorius returns again discreetly to the mystery of the day, the Assumption of Mary into heaven. This was the goal of the attraction of virtue, the royal wine-cellar of eternal life.

> 'I am black', or born of poor people. 'Like the tents of Kedar:' that means with something of the sinner. 'Beautiful as the covers of Solomon:' that is as if to say 'I am the veil of true peace that covered the ark who is Christ'. 'Do not consider me that I am black, that the sun has altered my colour', for although I have come from poor people, the Sun of Justice chose me, lowly as I am, to be his mother. 'My mother's sons fought against me:' that is to say, the prophets, who were the sons of the

synagogue, spoke about me or else the apostles, sons of the mother of grace, preached about me or on my behalf against the heretics who claim Jesus was not God but merely a phantom or else they deny that he was conceived in a human manner. 'They set me as a guardian of the vineyard', or as an example of virginity for all the churches. 'I did not keep my vineyard' that is, my virginity, but it was the Holy Spirit who protected it. 'Tell me whom my soul loves'. Mary's soul loves Christ, therefore all the Father's secrets are made known to her. 'Where do you pasture your flock, where do you make them lie down at noon?' The most chaste Virgin Mary was like the noonday, shining with the Holy Spirit, through whom Christ caused the heat of passions to subside. Humility rested in her. Chastity dwelt in her.

The famous 'black but beautiful' verse offers Honorius a way to speak of Mary's solidarity with sinful humanity. She has 'come of poor people' but has been transformed by grace. Honorius does not yet know the tradition which will flower in the doctrine of the Immaculate Conception. While the bride in the Song can lament that she did not keep her vineyard, Honorius suggests that Mary as the Bride recognised that is was the Spirit, not herself, who was the keeper of her virginity.[21]

Conclusion

There is much more one could say about the liturgical use of the Song of Songs. The medieval Roman Rite, as it survived down to the reform of Vatican II, primarily used it as a quarry for Marian texts, especially for antiphons for the Feasts of Mary. Its repertoire of reading texts was limited to two, the first for the Feast of the Visitation (Song 2:8b–14) and the second for the feast of St Mary Magdalene, a compound text of Song 3:1-5 and 8:6-7. If truth is to be told, however, the revisers of the Roman Lectionary did not treat it much better. It does not appear at any Sunday or major feast day liturgy. There is just a single reading for a weekday celebration (Song 2:8-14 for 21

December within the liturgically privileged time of late Advent). It still survives for Visitation and St Mary Magdalene, but alternatives are provided and one short text (Song 8:6-7) is an alternative reading for the Common of Virgins. It has been ignored in the two-year lectionary for the weekdays in Ordinary Time but it does figure in the Ritual Masses for marriage and religious profession. One senses that it is a text with which compilers of lectionaries feel uncomfortable!

There has long been a certain reserve about the public reading of the Song of Songs. When I entered the Redemptorist novitiate in 1964, hanging near the reader's pulpit in the community refectory was a table of biblical passages that were not to be read as part of the meal-time reading: it included the Song of Songs in its entirety. Such reserve might be traced back to Judaism at the turn of the Christian era. Origen, who was familiar with this tradition, tells the readers of his commentary on the Song of Songs that

> It is said that, among the Jews, no one is allowed even to hold this book in their hands until they have arrived at a mature and perfect age. It is from them that we have received this practice, for their learned men and scholars teach all the scriptures to children, but they reserve until last four books that they call *deuteroseis*, namely the beginning of Genesis describing the creation of the world, the beginning of the prophet Ezekiel describing the cherubim and the last part of the same book that describes the rebuilding of the temple and this book of the Song of Songs.[22]

Jewish hesitation, unlike that of religious communities, it should be noted, was based not on the poem's sexually explicit language, but on complications its mystical interpretation opened up. On the other hand, the *Glossa Ordinaria* on the Song, which combined the text with a *florilegium* of patristic exegesis, was one of the most copied and studied texts in the Middle Ages.[23]

In his *Gemma Animae*, Honorius says that it is the office of the presbyter 'to celebrate Mass, to offer sacrifice for the people, dispense the Body of the Lord, preach, baptise, absolve penitents, anoint the sick, bury the dead, call the people to Mass, bless marriages, arms, walking-sticks, water, candles, palms, ashes and indeed anything pertaining to food'.[24] He might have been describing the programme of the National Centre for Liturgy under the leadership of Patrick Jones, aided and abetted by Sister Moira Bergin. The Roman playwright Terence perhaps put it more directly when he said, '*Homo sum, humani nihil a me alienum puto*', or 'I am a human being, I consider nothing that is human alien to me'. The Liturgy Centre has tried to show us the human depths of worship both in the study of its history and in its attempts to show how the right celebration of the liturgy can respond to the deepest human needs. In so doing, it helps us glimpse the face of God.

In the little commentary whose surface we have skimmed in this paper, Honorius tries to open the liturgy with the key of Scripture. He is, I think, also doing something much more difficult, namely, finding how these two can converse with that other language of 'popular devotion' or piety. Scholars have found him a frustratingly obscure man, yet what emerges from this commentary is the living voice of someone who was willing to take time to open the scriptures to a young, puzzled beginner, who may have had more traditional piety than theology. I have taught a course on the Lectionary for several years at the Centre. I know how deeply Paddy respects the Word as nourishment for God's people assembled. I also have learned to respect him as a homilist at the daily celebration in St Mary's Oratory, whether it is an 'of the day' in the middle of winter, a feast day, a celebration of some student occasion or one of those more difficult moments when the college community comes to mourn the unexpected death of a young person. Perhaps we can all learn with Honorius the importance to trying, when we preach liturgically, to respond to the question – 'what does this reading really mean, and why are we reading it today?'

Notes

1. My translation of the French version given in *Le Cantique des Cantiques du Roi Salomon à Umberto Eco*, Anne Mars ed. (Paris: Cerf, 2003), 106–7.
2. For detailed accounts of the Roman procession and its counterpart in the Monastery of Cluny, see Rachel Fulton, *From Judgement to Passion: Devotion to Christ and the Virgin 800–1200* (New York: Columbia University Press, 2002), 268–74.
3. The Latin text, *Cogitis a me, O Paula* is in PL 30, 122c–142c.
4. Fulton, *From Judgement*, 248.
5. Émile Amann, 'Honorius Augustodunensis', in *Dictionnaire de Théologie Catholique*, Alfred Vacant, Eugene Mangenot, and Émile Amman, eds. (Paris: Letouzey et Ané, 2005), 7: 140.
6. Aubrey Gwynn, 'The Continuity of the Irish Tradition at Wurzburg', in *Herbipolis Jubilans: 1200 Jahre Bistum Würzburg. Festschrift zur Säkularfeier der erhebung der Kiliansreliquien* (Würzburg: Bischofliches Ordinariat, 1952), 66–8. It has been suggested that 'Augustodunensis' might represent 'Cashel of the Kings' which would make Honorius a Tipperary man!
7. See the series of articles by Valerie I.J. Flint: 'The Career of Honorius Augustodunensis', *Révue Bénédictine* 82 (1972), 215–42; 'The Commentaries of Honorius Augustodunensis on the Song of Songs', *Révue Bénédictine* 84 (1974), 196–211; 'The *Elucidarius* of Honorius Augustodunensis and Reform in Late Eleventh-Century England', *Révue Bénédictine* (1975), 178–89; and 'Henricus of Augsburg and Honorius Augustodunensis: Are they the same person?', *Révue Bénédictine* 92 (1982), 148–58. Fulton, *From Judgement*, 251–4 supports the Worcester connection.
8. See PL 172, 499ff.
9. 'Honorius of Autun', *New Catholic Encyclopaedia*, 2nd ed. (Washington, DC: Catholic University of America, 2003), Vol. 7, 88–9.
10. See PL 172, 347–496.
11. On the contribution of the liturgy to the medieval interpretative tradition, see Anne E. Matter, *The Voice of My Beloved: The Song of Songs in Western Medieval Christianity* (Philadelphia: University of Pennsylvania Press, 1990). See also Fulton, *From Judgement to Passion*.
12. Honorius uses the Vulgate word *castellum*. It originally meant something like a farmstead, but by the Middle Ages was applied to the fortified house, hence 'castle' in English. The architectural form of the castle will be put to good use here to advance Honorius' homiletic intentions.

13. Translation is my own, based on the Latin text in PL 172, 499ff.
14. Flint, 'The Commentaries of Honorius Augustodunensis', 201, notes their popularity in popular English preaching manuals of the period.
15. Since Honorius is citing from the Latin Vulgate, I am using the Douai-Rheims translation as it is closer to his text, unless otherwise noted.
16. While it is unnecessary to go into too many details of translation here, the Vulgate 'ubera' follows faithfully the Septuagint *mastoi* (breasts). Most modern translations are closer to the underlying Hebrew *dodeka*, 'your lovers', itself a difficult reading.
17. *Liber de Gloria Martyrum* X [PL 71, 714].
18. *Liber de Corpore et Sanguine Domini.*
19. Emile Mâle, *L'Art Religieux du 13e siècle en France* (Paris: Colin, 1923), 262–7, has noted the importance of these two miracles in the religious art of thirteenth-century France.
20. It occurs among the miracles at the end of the account of the Nativity of the Blessed Virgin Mary, 8 September, *Legenda Aurea* 131.
21. Many critics, e.g. Ariel and Chana Bloch in *The Song of Songs: A New Translation with an Introduction and Commentary* (Berkeley: University of California Press, 1998), suggest that her admission that she has not 'kept her own vineyard' is a metaphor or euphemism for loss of virginity. The biblical evidence for equating vineyard and sexuality is, however, comparatively slight. The Valiant Woman of Proverbs invests the fruit of her labour in purchasing and planting a vineyard, which remains her own property and does not accrue to her husband's estate (Proverbs 31:16). Her failure to keep it represents a lack of wisdom that might be expected in an inexperienced young woman.
22. *Commentary on the Song of Songs* 1:7; my translation of the Latin text in *Origène: Commentaire sur le Cantique des Cantiques*, Sources Chrétiennes, Luc Bresard and Henri Crouzel, eds., with the collaboration of Marcel Borret (Paris: Cerf, 1991), 375–6.
23. There is a very fine illuminated copy in the Russell Library in Maynooth.
24. *Gemma Animae* I. 181 [PL 172, 599].

WORDS OF SALVATION: THE VERNACULAR IN CONTEMPORARY CATHOLIC LITURGY

ɜ ɜ ɜ

NEIL XAVIER O'DONOGHUE

The change from celebrating the liturgy in Latin to celebrating in the vernacular is arguably the most significant development in Catholic liturgy over the last hundred years.[1] As the vernacular was not widely used in western Catholic worship for many centuries, this article will attempt to trace the history of the vernacular in Catholic worship and show how its introduction was an overwhelmingly positive event in the Church's recent history.[2]

Looking at the New Testament, it would seem that there is a preference for the use of the vernacular and there is no reference to a sacred language to be used in prayer and worship. One of the most relevant texts is Chapter 14 of the First Letter to the Corinthians (vv. 6-19). Here St Paul deals with the problem of language at prayer and with the phenomenon of praying in tongues during the liturgical celebration. Admittedly he is probably not directly referring to the language that is used for the central prayers of the Eucharist, but nonetheless it is clear that he values the use of the vernacular when the assembly is gathered together.

The book of Revelation often refers to the universality of God's election and message as the Church is made up of people from 'every tribe, and tongue, and people, and nation' (see Revelation 5:9; 7:9; 14:6). Indeed we are not even sure which language Jesus used in the Last Supper: was it the biblical language of Hebrew or the common tongue of Aramaic, or was it some combination of the two?[3] In any case the New Testament reports of the Last Supper are written in Koine Greek, the common form of Greek that was used in vast sections of the Roman Empire.[4]

It seems that initially all Christians attended eucharistic liturgies celebrated in a language that they actually understood, although in some assemblies this language might have been a common language, as the members of the worshipping community might have spoken a number of different local languages. Echoing St Paul, but now explicitly referring to the Eucharist, St Justin emphasises the importance of the assembly giving their assent to the thanksgiving expressed by the president of the assembly in the eucharistic prayer by saying Amen to what they have heard.[5] As late as the year 600, St John Moschos tells a story in his *Spiritual Meadow* of some children who perform a play Mass where God has to intervene and send fire from heaven to consume the eucharistic elements as the children had managed to celebrate a 'valid' Mass because they knew the eucharistic prayer by heart, 'for in those days it was the custom for children to stand before the holy sanctuary during divine worship and to be the first after the clergy to partake of the holy mysteries. As it was the custom in some places for the priests to say the prayer out loud, children were found to learn it by heart from continually hearing it audibly recited.'[6]

While in the East a multiplicity of different languages were used depending on the region, in the provinces of the western Roman empire the liturgy was initially celebrated in Greek. Greek was an official language and a language that many people understood, and everyone was accustomed to public events being held in Greek. However, Latin was a more common language. In the third century, as the use of Greek in the West was in decline, the Church in North Africa introduced Latin into the liturgy.[7] In the fourth century the liturgical use of Latin was adopted by the Churches of Gaul and Rome itself and thus Latin became almost universally the liturgical language in the West. In 390 St Ambrose of Milan is able to quote the oldest known reference to the Roman Canon, already treating it as a venerable prayer text.[8]

But soon after Latin was introduced into the liturgy of Rome, the Latin language itself began to suffer decline as the western Roman empire began to disintegrate and give way to the nations of western Christendom. While the faithful in Italy and Iberia continued to understand some Latin for a longer time, as their languages were closer to Latin, already by the sixth century Latin was unintelligible in France.

While in the East the principal of translating the liturgy into the language of newly evangelised people was to remain (at least in theory) to this day, in the evangelisation of the non-Roman peoples of western Europe Latin was used as the language of the scriptures and the liturgy. The Irish were the first non-Roman people whose evangelisation was to be accompanied by the introduction of Latin, now a fully foreign language, as the language of the liturgy and the scriptures. The experience of the evangelisation of the Irish, along with the many missionaries to the barbarian tribes of Europe who came from the young Irish Church, was to be of great importance in the spread of a Latin liturgy throughout the West.[9]

However, while the use of Latin as the language of the liturgy in Northern Europe did facilitate the adoption of Latin as the language of the educated throughout the West, it also had some unforeseen consequences. The renewed interest in Latin, particularly among the scholars coming from the newly evangelised peoples and who didn't speak a Latin dialect as their native language, gradually transformed Church Latin into a purer form, particularly with regard to pronunciation and grammar. But as the standard of Latin used in the liturgy improved from a technical point of view, it became harder to understand for those southern Europeans whose dialects had developed from the Latin of the Empire. Thus the adoption of Latin as the language of liturgy in northern Europe had the converse effect of transforming the Latin of the liturgy from a vernacular into a language used exclusively by the clerical and educated classes in areas of southern Europe.[10] This is in contrast to earlier generations who had been able to understand a less refined Latin that had been close to their vernacular. Thus in the West the liturgy came to be celebrated in a language that was incomprehensible to the vast majority of the faithful. The fact that people could not understand the words of the liturgy was to have a profound effect on their spirituality and on their understanding of the Mass. To compound this problem, between the seventh and the ninth centuries in the West the Canon, or eucharistic prayer, of the Mass began to be prayed inaudibly or 'secretly'. This meant that even the few who understood Latin were still excluded from understanding the words of the Mass.[11]

One of the principal effects of this change was to facilitate the transformation of the people's liturgical spirituality from one of understanding the Mass through the prayers of the liturgy to one of an allegorical interpretation.[12] In this allegorical interpretation the rites of the Mass are no longer 'Mysteries' in and of themselves, but they rather now point to other more distant divine 'mysteries'.[13] Also on an interpretive level the Paschal Mystery of Christ's death and Resurrection was no longer the key to understanding the Mass, but the Mass was now interpreted solely on the basis of Christ's Passion and death. Using the allegorical method of understanding the liturgy as popularised in the west particularly by Amalarius of Metz, the Mass was understood to be a presentation of the life of Christ, and indeed the whole history of salvation, culminating in Christ's death on the Cross. No action in the Mass could be understood at face value – even the most simple of actions were understood to be shadows of some deeper reality. For example, the priest washing his hands at the lavabo was understood to be a reference to Pontius Pilate washing his hands during the Passion. It is true that earlier patristic authors had seen some allegory in the Mass, but 'whereas the Fathers see the Old Testament fulfilled in New Testament worship, [Amalarius] finds in Christian worship, not a fulfilment of Old Testament worship, but allusions to it'.[14] The Church never lost track of the fact that the eucharistic celebration was important and attendance at the Sunday Eucharist was mandatory for all Catholics. However, one could question what people actually understood about the Mass during the Middle Ages.[15]

The divisions resulting from the Reformation are one of the greatest tragedies in the history of Christianity. Today's Christians are still living with the wounds to the Body of Christ caused by this, and the Church's mission of bearing witness to the Gospel is impaired by this disunion. John O'Malley has recently examined the Council of Trent and came to the conclusion that the state of the Catholic Church in the period before the Reformation was, echoing the words of Dickens, 'neither the best nor the worst of times'.[16] Nonetheless, in the sixteenth century the Catholic Church needed renewal. In fact Vatican II teaches us that Christ calls the Catholic Church to 'permanent reform, which it perpetually needs insofar as it is a human and worldly institution' (UR 6).

For the purposes of this paper our concern is with Trent's treatment of the vernacular in the liturgy, as in that council we find a more theological treatment than we do in Vatican II. The Protestant reformers introduced the vernacular into their liturgical celebrations. This was part of the enlightenment emphasis on the modern European languages and a desire to go back to the sources of early Christianity, as well as the obvious emphasis on the Word of God. Unfortunately, while there were many good aspects to early Protestant liturgy, these formed part of a whole reformulation of liturgy that cannot be seen simply as a renewal, revival or revitalisation of the traditional liturgy of the Great Church, but which instead constitute a total rejection of the traditional Catholic worldview and gave way to a totally different conception of reality:

> Behind the repudiation of ceremonial by the reformers lay a radically different conceptual world, a world in which text was everything, sign nothing. The sacramental universe of late medieval Catholicism was, from such a perspective totally opaque, a bewildering and meaningless

world of dumb objects and vapid gestures, hindering communication.[17]

When the Fathers of the Council of Trent considered the vernacular they did so as a matter of discipline and not of dogma and their conclusion did not mandate the exclusive use of Latin in the liturgy. In fact, in answer to some of the reformers who totally rejected the use of Latin, the Council only decreed that Latin was a legitimate liturgical language: 'If anyone says ... that the Mass should be celebrated only in the vernacular ... let him be anathema'.[18] Earlier in the same session the Council gave some more context:

> Although the Mass contains much instruction for the faithful, the Fathers did not think that it should be celebrated in the vernacular indiscriminately. Therefore, the ancient rite of each Church, approved by the holy Roman Church, the mother and teacher of all the Churches, being everywhere maintained, the holy council, in order that the sheep of Christ may not be unfed, lest the children beg for food but no one gives to them, orders that pastors and all who have the care of souls must frequently either by themselves, or through others, explain during the celebration of Masses some of the readings of the Mass and among other things give some instruction about the mystery of this most holy sacrifice, especially on Sundays and feast days.[19]

In the wake of the Council of Trent Latin was to retain its dominance as the virtually universal language of Catholic liturgy in the West. While there were a few attempts to translate parts of the Mass into the vernacular, these attempts failed to gain any widespread support. The sermon was in the vernacular, although it was often unconnected to the liturgy of the Mass, very rarely being based on the Scripture texts of the celebration. The Scripture texts were read or chanted in Latin and occasionally they were re-read in a vernacular translation prior to the sermon. Other than that, some Masses had vernacular hymns that were sung by the assembly. But it would not have been uncommon, particularly at a weekday Mass, to find an exclusively Latin celebration. However the idea that people should actually understand the words of the liturgy and the possibility of Mass in the vernacular was appreciated particularly in mission lands. For example, Archbishop John Carroll of Baltimore (d. 1815), the first bishop of the United States, was a proponent of vernacular liturgy. He came to this view principally through his pastoral and missionary work in the American colonies.[20]

While Trent emphasised that the people should understand what was happening at Mass, in its wake this understanding centred on appreciating the Mass from the point of view of the Catechism and not understanding the Mass texts *per se*. Indeed Sunday duty was basically understood as a precept to be physically present in the church building while Mass was being celebrated.[21] In 1602 when St Francis de Sales was ordained bishop of Geneva, he made the pious resolution to pray the rosary when his episcopal duties required him to attend public Mass, so that he wouldn't waste valuable prayer time![22] The great French bishop and master of spirituality Jacques-Bénigne Bossuet (d. 1704) counselled that one can 'obey the precept of hearing Mass while spending the whole time on other readings and prayers'.[23]

It wasn't until the birth of the liturgical movement in the nineteenth century that attention was finally paid to Trent's desire that the faithful understand what is happening at Mass. This was done mainly through the hand missal. These missals contained the texts of the prayers of the various Masses of the Church's year, in both Latin and vernacular, along with some catechetical and devotional material. This allowed people to follow along with the priest. The hand missal was to become very popular towards the end of the nineteenth century. By this time literacy was much more common and the industrial revolution of the mid-1800s meant that paper and book production had become much more affordable.

Naturally the hand missal, whereby people could read in their own language what the priest was saying in Latin, changed people's devotional attitude at Mass. This development dovetailed nicely with the promotion of an active participation in the liturgy by the laity, another aspect of the liturgical movement. The concept of active participation was introduced by Pope St Pius X in his motu propio *Tra le sollecitudini* of 1903. The nascent liturgical movement took up this idea. While Pius X meant it principally to mean that the assembly take part in singing at Mass, Dom Lambert Beauduin, one of the pioneers of the liturgical movement, opened it up to more than singing to actually understanding the liturgical texts in a 1909 conference in Mechlin, Belgium.[24]

At Vatican II the introduction of the vernacular in the celebration of the Sacraments was one of the most debated topics of the Council.[25] Eventually the Council reached a compromise whereby 'in Masses which are celebrated with the people, a suitable place may be allotted to their mother tongue. This is to apply in the first place to the readings and "the common prayer", but also, as local conditions may warrant, to those parts which pertain to the people'.[26]

However the majority of the Fathers had been in favour of the introduction of the vernacular and the initially limited introduction of the vernacular was almost universally acclaimed.[27] Almost immediately after the Council, bilingual altar missals containing the (Tridentine) Order of Mass began to appear. The central eucharistic prayer remained in Latin, but the readings and many other prayers of the Mass were in the vernacular. Hearing the Word of God in their native language was another remarkable benefit for the spiritual life of Catholics as the Bible had been an almost forbidden book since the Reformation.

The faithful were very pleased to hear parts of the Eucharist celebrated in their mother tongue and finally being able to understand the Mass without having to read along in a hand missal, but 'the resultant Mass, partly in Latin, partly in the vernacular, was a hybrid, lacking in continuity'.[28] There was a popular groundswell for an extension of the use of the vernacular and this, combined with the fact that the great majority of bishops had favoured the use of the vernacular in the Council, led eighty-seven separate conferences of bishops to petition the Holy See for permission to celebrate the whole Mass in the vernacular. And so, on 13 January 1967, Pope Paul VI granted permission to celebrate the whole Eucharist in the vernacular.[29]

Thus in little more than three years after the Council, the Eucharist was being celebrated wholly in the vernacular. Some have criticised the use of the vernacular, claiming that it is a 'distortion' of the Council's decrees. Archbishop Annibale Bugnini, the secretary of the *Consilium* for the Implementation of the Constitution on the Liturgy, counters:

> It cannot be denied that the principle, approved by the Council, of using the vernaculars was given a broad interpretation. But this interpretation did not spring from a desire to take risks or from an itch for novelty; it was adopted after deliberation, with the approval of competent authority; and in line with the spirit of the conciliar decrees.
>
> It is the prerogative of the Holy See and, within the limits set by law, of the episcopal conferences and individual bishops to regulate the sacred liturgy. These various authorities saw it as a pastoral necessity that the faithful should understand the Canon of the Mass; they simply extended the principle of intelligibility that had already been admitted for the other parts of the Mass. They examined the problem in their plenary meetings, made their decisions, and presented these to the Holy See for approval. The Pope, as we have seen, engaged in lengthy consultation with the competent Roman agencies, studied the concrete situation and needs and the spirit of the Council, and finally approved the requests of the episcopal conferences.[30]

As with any great change, not everybody was in favour and indeed some people were scandalised by the Mass in the vernacular. This scandal was particularly felt by converts. In England a petition was circulated in which a number of prominent non-Catholic intellectuals and cultural figures petitioned for permission to continue celebrating the Tridentine Mass in Latin after the introduction of the new edition of the Missal. Pope Paul VI gave an indult to Cardinal Heenan of Westminster in 1971, which earned the nickname the 'Agatha Christie indult' due to the famous (nominally Anglican but non-practising) mystery author's name on the petition. Evelyn Waugh, the author of *Brideshead Revisited* and a convert to Catholicism, was one of those scandalised by the Mass in the vernacular and was very unhappy with the liturgical changes of Vatican II.[31] Waugh considered the status quo before Vatican II whereby most Catholics come to worship 'often dumbly and effectively' as a positive spiritual quality that the Church should maintain.[32] However, the relatively few mainly intellectual lovers of Latin must be balanced with the thousands of English speakers, Catholic and Protestant alike, who wrote to Archbishop Bugnini petitioning for the use of the vernacular in the liturgy.[33]

In an address to translators of liturgical texts given on 10 November 1965, Pope Paul VI presents the basic principles of liturgical translations. The pope emphasised that vernacular translations of liturgical texts 'have become part of the rites themselves' and explained why the adoption of the vernacular instead of Latin was necessary:

> The introduction of the vernacular will certainly be a great sacrifice for those who know the beauty, the power and the expressive sacrality of Latin. We are parting with the speech of the Christian centuries; we are becoming like profane intruders in the literary preserve of sacred utterance. We will lose a great part of that stupendous and incomparable artistic and spiritual thing, the Gregorian chant. We have reason indeed for regret, reason almost for

bewilderment. What can we put in the place of that language of the angels? We are giving up something of priceless worth. But why? What is more precious than these loftiest of our Church's values? The answer will seem banal, prosaic. Yet it is a good answer, because it is human, because it is apostolic. Understanding of prayer is worth more than the silken garments in which it is royally dressed. Participation by the people is worth more – particularly participation by modern people, so fond of plain language which is easily understood and converted into everyday speech.[34]

Undoubtedly today the use of the vernacular in the liturgy has opened the treasures of the Bible and the liturgical prayers of the Church to countless millions. However we cannot enter into complacency thinking that the introduction of the vernacular has solved all liturgical problems or guarantees full active participation of the whole liturgical assembly.[35] Today, perhaps the greatest challenge for all Christians is to make the words of the liturgy a part of their innermost life so that, echoing the desire of St Benedict, our minds may always be in harmony with the words our voices utter when we attend the liturgy.[36]

Notes

1. Latin remains as the official language of the Roman Rite, but the overwhelming majority of Catholics attend Mass celebrated in the vernacular. The choice of the vernacular as being the most significant liturgical development of the last hundred years is now a much clearer choice as the reintroduction of frequent Communion by Pope St Pius X took place over one hundred years ago.
2. The vernacular is somewhat of a technical term in liturgical theology, but it simply refers to 'the language or dialect spoken by the ordinary people in a particular country or region' (from the *Oxford English Dictionary*).
3. Robert F. O'Toole, 'Last Supper', *The Anchor Yale Bible Dictionary*, David Noel Freedman, ed. (New York: Doubleday, 1992), 235.

4.   Gerard Mussies, 'Languages: Greek', *The Anchor Yale Bible Dictionary*, 202.
5.   See Justin *Apology* I, 65; ET, *Worship in the Early Church: An Anthology of Historical Sources*, Lawrence J. Johnson (Collegeville, MN: Liturgical Press, A Pueblo Book, 2009), Vol. 1, no. 246, 68. This section of St Justin is quoted in the *Catechism of the Catholic Church*, 1345, as a description of 'the Mass of all ages'.
6.   *The Spiritual Meadow: (*Pratum Spirituale*) by John Moschos (also known as John Eviratus)*, John Wortley, trans. and ed., Cistercian Studies Series 139 (Kalamazoo, MI: Cistercian Publications, 1992), no. 196, 172–4.
7.   Orthodox polemicists sometimes propose that, in the ninth century, certain German Catholic theologians persecuted SS. Cyril and Methodius for translating the liturgy into the vernacular, and that this was a western heresy called trilingualism that taught that the liturgy could only be celebrated in Hebrew, Greek and Latin, the three languages of the inscription of the Lord's Cross. However, a recent study has proven that this accusation is a mere invention by earlier generations of Orthodox polemicists. See F. J. Thomson, 'SS. Cyril and Methodius and a Mythical Western Heresy: Trilingualism. A Contribution to the Study of Patristic and Mediaeval Theories of Sacred Languages', *Analecta Bollandiana* 110 (1992), 67–122.
8.   For more details on the shift of languages, see Uwe Michael Lang, 'Rhetoric of Salvation: The Origins of Latin as the Language of the Roman Liturgy', *The Genius of the Roman Rite: Historical, Theological, and Pastoral Perspectives on Catholic Liturgy*, Uwe Michael Lang, ed., A Hillenbrand Book (Chicago: Liturgical Training Publications, 2010), 22–45.
9.   See Neil Xavier O'Donoghue, *Eucharist in Pre-Norman Ireland* (Notre Dame, IN: University of Notre Dame Press, 2011), 7, 50–4.
10. Uwe Michael Lang, *The Voice of the Church at Prayer: Reflections on Liturgy and Language* (San Francisco: Ignatius Press, 2012), 121.
11. For a summary of the ample evidence that the eucharistic prayer was prayed in an audible way in the early Church, see Robert F. Taft, 'Was the Eucharistic Anaphora Recited Secretly or Aloud? The Ancient Tradition and What Became of It', *Worship Traditions in Armenia and the Neighboring Christian East: An International Symposium in Honor of the Fortieth Anniversary of St Nersess Armenian Seminary*, Roberta R. Ervine, ed. (Crestwood, NY: St Vladimir's Seminary Press, 2006), 15–57.
12. The East also witnessed similar allegorical interpretations, although a stronger liturgical spirituality was to survive in many parts of the East where the language of the liturgy remained closer to the vernacular.

13. For a contemporary explanation of the Christian understanding of mystery in the liturgy, see the *Catechism of the Catholic Church*, 1066–1068.

14. See Edward J. Kilmartin, *The Eucharist in the West: History and Theology*, Robert J. Daly, ed. (Collegeville, MN: Liturgical Press, 1998), 93.

15. During the Middle Ages at Sunday Mass the laity were not even able to see the high altar. However, there were often other celebrations on the more accessible side altars of the parish church. These were used for votive Masses and for other weekday eucharistic celebrations and Eamon Duffy has shown how by the end of the Middle Ages, at least in England, these celebrations had a much more popular dimension, oftentimes with the laity crowded around the altar for the celebration. Even if they did not understand many of the actual words of the liturgy, it would be wrong to say that they understood nothing. Indeed, a rich sacramental life was often based on the attendance at such celebrations. Eamon Duffy, *The Stripping of the Altars: Traditional Religion in England 1400–1580*, 2nd ed. (New Haven, CT: Yale University Press, 2005), 111–16.

16. John W. O'Malley, *Trent: What Happened at the Council* (Cambridge, MA: Belknap Press of Harvard University, 2013), 48; see 38–48 for a fuller analysis of the problems facing the Church in the period before Trent.

17. Duffy, *The Stripping of the Altars*, 532.

18. Council of Trent, Session 22 (17 September 1562), can. 9. In Heinrich Denzinger and Peter Hunermann, eds., *Enchiridion Symbolorum: A Compendium of Creeds, Definitions, and Declarations of the Catholic Church*, 43rd ed., ET, Robert Fastiggi and Anne Englund Nash (San Francisco: Ignatius Press, 2012), no. 1755, p. 421. For more on the Council see O'Malley, *Trent: What Happened at the Council*, 190–1.

19. Council of Trent, Session 22 (17 September 1562), chap. 8; see *Enchiridion Symbolorum*, no. 1749, pp. 419–20.

20. See Keith F. Pecklers, *Dynamic Equivalence: The Living Language of Christian Worship* (Collegeville, MN: Liturgical Press, 2003), 25–6. There was also some liturgical inculturation in the Algonquian and Iroquoian Missions in North America (in present-day US and Canada) with the congregation singing some of the parts of the Mass in the local Native American vernaculars. See Claudio R. Salvucci, *The Roman Rite in the Algonquian and Iroquoian Missions*, Massinahigan Series (Merchantville, NJ: Evolution Publishing, 2008). However, note that Salvucci's presentation tends to be overly enthusiastic about the past and he seems to fall into the trap of

promoting a return to the time-period he is studying rather than simply presenting the historical picture or even trying to see what lessons this history can teach us today.

21. For example, see the treatment of 'attendance at Holy Mass' in Heribert Jone, *Moral Theology*, translated and updated to the Customs of the United States by Urban Adelman (Westminster, MD: The Newman Press, 1961), 123–6.

22. See Louis Bouyer, *Liturgical Piety* (Notre Dame, IN: University of Notre Dame Press, 1955), 2.

23. Quoted by Denis Crouan, *The History and the Future of the Roman Liturgy* (San Francisco: Ignatius Press, 2005), 81.

24. See Martin Stuflesser, '*Actuosa Participatio*: Between Hectic Actionism and New Interiority. Reflections on "Active Participation" in the Worship of the Church as Both Right and Obligation of the Faithful', *Studia Liturgica* 41 (2011), 92–126, at 97.

25. For more on the debate, see John W. O'Malley, *What Happened at Vatican II* (Cambridge, MA: Belknap Press of Harvard University, 2008), 135–40.

26. SC 53, also see 36.

27. For an example of a first-hand account of what the Council Fathers thought, see Joseph Ratzinger, *Theological Highlights of Vatican II*, new ed. (Mahwah, NJ: Paulist Press, 2009), 20–1 and 36–7.

28. Annibale Bugnini, *The Reform of the Liturgy 1948–1975*, Matthew J. O'Connell, trans., (Collegeville, MN: Liturgical Press, 1990), 104.

29. See Bugnini, *The Reform of the Liturgy*, 107.

30. Bugnini, *The Reform of the Liturgy*, 110.

31. His correspondence and occasional writings on the Mass in English can be found in *A Bitter Trial: Evelyn Waugh and John Cardinal Heenan on the Liturgical Changes*, Alcuin Reid, ed. (San Francisco: Ignatius Press, 2011).

32. Cited in *A Bitter Trial*, 39.

33. See Pecklers, *Dynamic Equivalence*, 158.

34. Paul VI, Address to translators of liturgical text, 8–11 (10 November 1965), in AAS 57 (1965), 967–970; English translation from taken from: *L'Osservatore Romano* Weekly Edition in English (4 December 1969).

35. Lack of space prevents us from treating here the issues involved with the new 2011 English translation of the *Roman Missal*. While the earlier 1973 translation was clearly in need of revision, and in many details the current edition of the Missal is more accurate, this newer edition is often quite difficult to understand, thus threatening Vatican II's guiding liturgical principle of promoting an active

participation of the faithful in the liturgy. For background on the Congregation for Divine Worship's 2001 Instruction on the use of the vernacular in Catholic liturgy see Peter Jeffrey, *Translating Tradition: A Chant Historian Reads* Liturgiam Authenticam (Collegeville, MN: Liturgical Press, 2005). For an analysis of the new translation of the Missal itself, see Edward Foley, ed., *A Commentary on the Order of Mass of The Roman Missal: A New English Translation* (Collegeville, MN: Liturgical Press, 2011) and Anscar J. Chupungco, *The Prayers of the New Missal: A Homiletic and Catechetical Companion* (Collegeville, MN: Liturgical Press, 2013). Also scant attention is paid to the 1998 second edition of the *Sacramentary* that was approved by the vast majority of English-speaking bishops, only for the complete project to be definitively rejected by the Congregation for Divine Worship and to be replaced by the current translation of the *Roman Missal*. For more on this see J. Peter Nixon, 'A Crisis in Reception: The Constitution on the Sacred Liturgy and the Debate over the English Translation of the *Roman Missal*', M. A. Thesis Graduate Theological Union, Berkeley, California. This thesis is available at www.praytellblog.com/index.php/2010/07/15/a-crisis-of-reception/ (accessed 23 October 2013).

36. See *Rule of Benedict* 19, 7.

SINGING THE MASS:
MASS COMPOSITION IN IRELAND
SINCE VATICAN II

꒰ ꒰ ꒰

JOHN O'KEEFFE

The spring issue of *New Liturgy*, 1996 contained an interesting
article on the subject of Mass settings.[1] Compiled by the editor,
Patrick Jones, in conjunction with members of the then
Advisory Committee on Church Music, the article simply listed
various Mass settings composed in Ireland during the previous
thirty years. Though not claimed as definitive or exhaustive, the
list testified to an extremely rich national outpouring of musical
creativity over the first three decades of liturgical renewal, and
signaled early on in Jones' tenure as director of the National
Centre for Liturgy a genuine interest in the music employed in
liturgical worship. Almost two decades later, as we approach a
half-century of vernacular liturgical composition in this country,
this brief article tries to place in some sort of context the
information recorded on that list, combining it with
developments which have taken place in the meantime.

Mass Composition in Irish and English Post-Vatican II
The liturgical reforms of the Second Vatican Council in the
1960s heralded a new era of liturgical celebration in the
vernacular, and with it new opportunities for Irish Church
musicians and composers, as the musical emphasis shifted from
choirs towards congregations. The principal focus was to be on
the musical requirements of the Mass Ordinary, and for
musicians the historical template of the Latin rite (*Kyrie,*

Gloria, Credo, Sanctus, Agnus Dei) provided an obvious starting point. Composers once more faced the challenge of setting metrically irregular given liturgical texts, this time however in the distinctive vernacular structures of Irish and English.

English Language Settings (1966–2001)

Early vernacular settings such as *The Ordinary of the Mass* (1966) from Glenstal Abbey and *Congregational Mass* (1967) by Staff Gebruers of Cobh Cathedral adhere strictly to the traditional format, their through-composed musical approach drawing overtly on the language of plainchant and on the basic premise of a musically unified Mass setting (the Creed being presented as an independent musical entity). Very soon however, a new template, more closely based on the ritual requirements of the revised rites, would emerge, with attention shifting away from the Creed to other congregational texts such as the Gospel and Memorial Acclamations, the 'Great' Amen and Our Father.

New official translations of key musical texts appearing from 1969 onwards and culminating in the publication of the *Roman Missal* in 1973 (complete with its own sung Mass establishing fixed ritual formulae for the greetings, dialogues and prayers of the priest) mapped a clearer way forward for Church music. This new Missal provided the context for a series of congregational Mass settings commissioned from four leading Irish composers by the Music Panel of the Irish Commission for Liturgy: *Mass of Peace* (1976) by Seóirse Bodley; *Mass of the Immaculate Conception* (1977) by Fintan O'Carroll; *Mass of Peace* (1976) by Thomas C. Kelly; and *Mass of the Resurrection* (1977) by Gerard Victory. Kelly's attempt to integrate the distinctive roles of congregation and choir, and Victory's deliberate move away from traditional to bolder and more modern musical expression, address some of the issues of the time. A setting which takes particular account of the sung ritual formulae of the new Missal is that of Fintan O'Carroll. This composition successfully integrates the musical roles of presider, choir, congregation and the emerging role of cantor within a distinctively melodic, though recognisably European musical style. The Mass, in its use of refrains and congregation-oriented text repetitions, also reflects growing international trends away from the principle of through-composition and the concept of fixed liturgical/textual forms. Of the four commissioned composers, Bodley arguably proved most successful in the task, providing a through-composed indigenous setting, integrated within the broader musical context of the *Roman Missal*, which engaged and would continue to sustain Irish congregational singing for decades.

Whilst the organ provided the standard backdrop for these and other mainstream settings, other accompanimental solutions were also being explored, and compositions such as the *Folk Mass in Honour of St Teresa* (1982) by Natuca Cordon and Hilda Geraghty signal the growing influence of the guitar and the emergence of a more consciously popular, youth-oriented musical style.

During the 1980s, heightened international interest in the musical possibilities of the eucharistic prayer is reflected in Tom Egan's stand-alone *Eucharistic Prayer II* (1985), in Margaret Daly-[Denton]'s *Kainos Mass* (1986) and Ite O'Donovan's *Mass of St Attracta: A Festive Liturgy for Children* (1985). These Mass settings also attest to an increasing integration of supplementary hymns and psalm settings, signaled early on in the decade by the inclusion of an 'Entrance Psalm' in Fintan O'Carroll's *Mass of the Annunciation* (1982). Scored for cantor, congregation, choir, organ and brass ensemble, this Mass represents a musically substantial and highly successful synthesis of varied musical and liturgical possibilities.

Ronan McDonagh's 1991 *Mass of St John of the Cross*, with its 'properised' hymns, responsorial psalm and traditional instrumental meditation, signals a fuller and more thematically unified concept. Of note here are the newly composed ritual formulae for the priest, a chanted version of the Lord's Prayer, and an example (unusual for the time) of a through-composed English language 'Holy Holy'. Thematic concepts and supplementary material tend to predominate over Mass parts in the hugely popular liturgical collections of Liam Lawton, whose *Sacred Story* (1996), a work based on the life and legacy of Edmund Rice, is scored for cantor, choir, congregation and guitar. His *Mass of the Celtic Saints* (1997), sustained by strong melodies and propelled by the regularised patterns of song forms, typifies the compositional approach. Amongst these and other settings which followed, Lawton's first Mass setting from *Light the Fire* (1996) remains the most interesting, with its set of seasonal through-composed Alleluia verses, Intercessory Refrain (incorporating double choir) and memorable troped 'Kyrie' structure.

Mass composition in the vernacular was given fresh musical impetus and renewed liturgical focus by two national competitions run by RTÉ Radio 1 in 1997 and 2001. *Mass of the Holy Spirit* by 1997 winner John McCann features a set of musically unified 'eucharistic acclamations' for the congregation, a freshly contemporary unison setting of the Pentecost sequence, and a festive *Gloria*, notable for its independent instrumental and harmonically adventurous choral writing. The thematic, tonal and textural variety evident in Sue Furlong's prizewinning *Mass of Thanksgiving* (2001) for choir, congregation and cantor suggests a series of compositional responses to a wide range of individual liturgical texts. Notable elements include the 'Lamb of God' setting for cantor and choir only, and a festive 'Dismissal' (a once-traditional liturgical element re-introduced by the competition organisers). The broader context of *Roman Missal* sung ritual is once more recalled and integrated in John O'Keeffe's *Jubilee Mass* (2000), a setting involving congregation, choir and organ, which combines Latin and English textual elements.

Irish Language Settings (1966–2003)

From 1963 onwards, Seán Ó Riada and the members of the emerging Cór Chúil Aodha were experimenting with native liturgical settings in the Irish language. The first fruits of their work were brought together in Ó Riada's *Ceol an Aifrinn* (1971), a seminal collection containing a congregational Mass setting supplemented by native devotional texts (both prose and metrical). Though *An Leabhar Aifrinn* (the Irish version of the *Roman Missal*) would not be published until 1973, the official translations of *Ord an Aifrinn* (The Order of Mass) were available to Ó Riada. The musical language chosen by the composer was drawn directly from the *Múscraí sean nós* tradition and applied to the Mass texts as they stood. The Creed is omitted from the standard Mass Ordinary template, to which Ó Riada adds settings of the Our Father and the Preface Dialogue (with a suggested Preface reciting-tone). Ó Riada's other Irish Mass (composed in 1970 and published posthumously in incomplete form as *Aifreann 2* [1979]), also through-composed, includes liturgical additions such as the Alleluia and presider-led chants for the Gospel, Memorial Acclamation and Doxology/Amen. These last additions are significant in light of the fact that *An Leabhar Aifrinn* would include no standard sung ritual formulae for priest and people.

Tomás Ó Canainn's *Aifreann Cholmcille* (1978) mirrors Ó Riada's template (a combination of Mass Ordinary and Proper) and unison compositional approach (the Mass is through-composed, apart from the refrain-based Gloria), adding to the structure a responsorial psalm and congregational communion-rite acclamations. *Aifreann in onóir Muire, Máthair Dé* (1973; published in 1975), by Fintan O'Carroll, engages with the Mass Ordinary texts from a different standpoint, integrating Irish melodic shapes within a more substantial and recognisably European musical structure, characterised by independent choral and instrumental writing. Eastern European (specifically Hungarian) influences are evident in Pat Ahern's adoption of a strictly pentatonic four-part texture in *Aifreann Phádraig Naofa* (1984), which includes a choral Introit, Responsorial Psalm, Gospel Acclamation and Recessional Hymn in honour of the saint. Proper elements predominate over Mass parts in Peadar Ó Riada's substantial *Aifreann Eoin Na Croise* (1991), which features an extended Entrance Chant, a setting of the Prayers of the Faithful and a sung Communion Rite. Liam Lawton's *Aifreann Laiserian Naofa* (1992) treats the Mass texts in a rather free manner and adopts the song-style approach which would characterise his later English settings. *Aifreann Réalt na Mara* (2000) by Máire Ní Dhuibhir features an interesting non-responsorial strophic psalm setting, a Marian Litany and a *Kyrie* based around a native penitential text. On a larger scale is Patrick Davey's *Aifreann na Feirste* (2003), a more orchestrally conceived setting for tenor soloist, choir and congregation. In this substantial offering which integrates traditional and classical instrumental contributions, baroque-influenced harmonies and occasional polyphonic elements underpin a convincingly traditional melodic treatment of a wide range of Irish texts (including a responsorial *Gloria* and a native strophic version of the Creed). By contrast, Ronan McDonagh's 2000 *Aifreann* distils the art of Mass composition to its purest essentials in a concentrated work which stands closest in compositional intent to that of Seán Ó Riada's *Ceol an Aifrinn*.

The *Roman Missal* – Third Edition

A decrease in compositional activity from around 2003 onwards coincided with plans for a new translation of the *Roman Missal* (published in 2011), for which key musical texts were eventually ratified in 2009. In the same year, as part of the preparation for this new liturgical reality, the Irish Bishops' Advisory Committee on Church Music[2] issued a call to Irish liturgical composers to submit settings of these newly translated Mass texts with a view to establishing a new core repertoire of specifically congregational material. Guidelines issued to composers by the ACCM, reflecting Irish and broader Church thinking on Mass composition in the intervening decades since Vatican II, re-focused musicians' attention on the setting of the *given* liturgical text as the most effective means of engaging and sustaining congregational (as opposed to merely choral) singing. The following excerpt from the opening section of the guidelines sets the challenge:

> One of the hallmarks of the music of the Roman Rite is the variety of textual forms used. Each 'part' of the Mass

has a specific function to carry out within the overall context of the rite.[3] This function is related to the nature and form of its text. Thus the Gloria, for example, is described as a *hymn* and the Sanctus as an *acclamation*. Finding music answerable to these texts is the main challenge of the liturgical composer. Over the past number of decades, many composers have treated such given liturgical texts in a more or less free manner, introducing refrains, repetitions and additions which go beyond what is given in the original text. Recent liturgical documents have been encouraging composers to re-engage with the principle of through-composition (i.e. setting the given liturgical text just as it stands, without alteration or repetitions) as a potentially more fruitful approach.[4]

As a frame of reference for the broader context of sung liturgy, musicians were directed to the recently ratified English chant setting for the forthcoming Missal, together with specific examples from the Gregorian tradition. In proposing through-composed vernacular congregational models for younger composers to emulate, the guidelines significantly returned to the 1970s, to the work of O'Carroll and, more specifically, Bodley, singling out the latter's *Gloria* and *Sanctus* settings for particular attention.

Irish composers strove to meet the specific challenges of the project, and following an enthusiastic response three new settings, by Ephrem Feeley (*Mass of St Paul*), Columba (John) McCann (*Mass of St Columba*) and Bernard Sexton (*Mass of Renewal*), were selected by the ACCM for inclusion in the collection *Sing the Mass*, published jointly by Veritas and the National Centre for Liturgy.[5] As a parallel track to the soliciting of newly composed settings and with the aim of maintaining a continuity of repertoire, the ACCM also commissioned for inclusion in the collection re-workings of Seóirse Bodley's *Mass of Peace*, Fintan O'Carroll's *Mass of the Immaculate Conception* and the *Lourdes Mass*. An appendix to the main project included revisions of settings by T.C. Kelly and Tom

Egan, a selection of Gospel acclamations and a congregational setting of the Apostles' Creed. Published in July 2011, six months ahead of the launch of the revised *Roman Missal*, *Sing the Mass* continues to establish itself as a foundational national resource. Meanwhile, the revised English language Mass texts continue to provide inspiration and challenge to the skills of younger composers, experimenting in a range of musical styles.

Revision of *An Leabhar Aifrinn*

The principles of literal translation employed in the 1969 Irish language Order of Mass, *Ord an Aifrinn*, meant that the changes required as part of worldwide Missal re-translations would be of a far lesser nature than was the case with the English version. Revised versions of popular existing settings will, however, still be required. In 2011, *Sapienti* (the Rome-appointed working group to oversee the re-translation of the Irish-language missal, *An Leabhar Aifrinn*) commissioned two musical settings (as yet unpublished) of *Ord an Aifrinn*, following the melodic formulae of the 2002/2008 *Missale Romanum*, thus bringing it into line with the approach adopted by English and other vernacular revisions. A more melodically indigenous setting of the Mass in Irish was commissioned independently by Comhchoiste Liotúirge na Gaeilge from an tAth Pat Ahern,[6] and a project currently under way by the ACCM envisages that this, together with other new Mass settings and revisions of existing ones, will form the basis of a worthy compendium of music for Mass celebrated in the Irish language into the future.[7]

Selected Bibliography (in chronological order)

Staff Gebruers, *Congregational Mass* (Birmingham: Goodliffe Neale, 1967).

Seán Ó Riada, *Ceol an aifrinn* (Baile Átha Cliath: An Clócomhar Teo, 1971).

Fintan O'Carroll, *Aifreann in onóir Muire, Mathair Dé* (Dublin: Cumann Ceol Eaglasta na hEireann, 1975).

Thomas C. Kelly, *Mass of Peace* (Dublin: Irish Commission for Liturgy, 1976).

Fintan O'Carroll, *Mass of the Immaculate Conception* (Dublin: Irish Commission for Liturgy, 1977).

Gerard Victory, *Mass of the Resurrection* (Dublin: Irish Commission for Liturgy, 1977).

Fintan O'Carroll, *Mass of the Annunciation* (Dublin: Irish Church Music Association, 1982).

Pat Ahern, *Aifreann Phádraig Naofa* (Dublin: Veritas, 1984).

Margaret Daly, *Kainos Mass* (Carlow: Irish Institute of Pastoral Liturgy, 1986).

Ronan McDonagh, *Mass of St John of the Cross* (Dublin: Carmelite Publications, 1991).

Liam Lawton, *Light the Fire* (Dublin: Veritas, 1996).

John McCann, 'Eucharistic Acclamations', in *Seinn Alleluia 2000*, Patrick O'Donoghue, ed. (Dublin: The Columba Press, 1999).

Ronan McDonagh, 'Aifreann', *Music to Honour God's Name* (Dublin: Veritas, 2000).

Seóirse Bodley, *Three Congregational Masses*, Lorraine Byrne, ed. (Dublin: Carysfort Press, 2005).

Sue Furlong, 'Mass of Thanksgiving', *I Sing for Joy* (Dublin: Columba Press, 2006).

Ephrem Feeley, 'Mass of St Paul', *Sing the Mass* (Dublin: Veritas, 2011).

Liam Lawton, 'The Glendalough Mass', *Sing the Mass* (Dublin: Veritas, 2011).

Columba (John) McCann, 'Mass of St Columba', *Sing the Mass* (Dublin: Veritas, 2011).

Bernard Sexton, 'Mass of Renewal', *Sing the Mass* (Dublin: Veritas, 2011).

Notes

1. 'Mass Settings', *New Liturgy* 89 (1996), 23–6.
2. This is the successor to the 'Music Panel' of the 1970s, referred to above.
3. Chapter II of the 2002/2008 *General Instruction of the Roman Missal* (GIRM) provides a useful commentary on the various sung elements of the Mass.
4. John Paul II, *Chirograph for the Centenary of the* Motu Proprio *'Tra le sollecitudini' on Sacred Music* [2003], art. 5; see also the Fifth Instruction 'For the Right Implementation of the Constitution on the sacred Liturgy of the Second Vatican Council' (SC 36) *Liturgiam authenticam*, on the use of Vernacular Language in the Publication of the Books of the Roman Liturgy [2001], art. 60.

5. An independently conceived fourth setting, Liam Lawton's *The Glendalough Mass* (Chicago: GIA Publications), was also included in the collection.

6. Key elements of this setting have been integrated into the composer's forthcoming *Aifreann na ndaoine*.

7. This article represents an expanded and updated version of John O'Keeffe, 'Mass Settings in English and Irish', *The Encyclopaedia of Music in Ireland*, Harry White and Barra Boydell, gen. eds. (Dublin: UCD Press, 2013), 633–5, on vernacular Mass settings. It is included here with the permission of UCD Press.

'A MISSIONARY IN HIS WAY AND PLACE'
THE FIVE-MINUTE SERMONS OF FR ALGERNON BROWN CSP (1848–78)

꙰ ꙰ ꙰

SALVADOR RYAN

It is perhaps fitting that this chapter recalls an individual for whom the preached word became a priority.[1] This was Fr Algernon Brown (1848–78), a young Paulist priest who spent most of his short priestly ministry (a mere four years) at St Paul the Apostle Church on West 59th Street in New York City. He was one of the early pioneers of the Paulist 'five-minute sermons' which began to be preached at Low Masses in 1876 at the Paulist mother Church where he was based. The unidentified author of the Preface to a volume of these sermons, published in 1879, explains the rationale behind the five-minute sermons:

> ... that the great number of persons who generally attend only a Low Mass on Sundays might enjoy the advantage of hearing the word of God preached without being delayed too long for their convenience. For this reason they were limited in time to five minutes, while the effort was made to condense within this brief compass a sufficient amount of matter at once instructive and hortatory, in plain and simple language, to answer the practical purpose of a popular discourse.[2]

The Society of St Paul had been founded as recently as 1858 by a former Redemptorist, Fr Isaac Thomas Hecker (1819–88), and its earliest members were all former members of the congregation, many of them converts and adherents of the Oxford Movement.[3] They were welcomed to the New York diocese by Archbishop John Hughes in the same year.

For those interested in reading something of Fr Algernon Brown's life and his short period of ministry, sources are difficult to come by. A simple internet search (as of December 2013) under the term 'Fr Algernon Brown CSP' simply turns up a website entitled findagrave.com. It sketches a short biography of Brown along with two photographs of him dressed as a Paulist priest, in which he seems much younger and more boyish in appearance than the age he must have been when these were taken – just a year or two beyond his mid-twenties. This biography is supplemented by the details found in the preface to the *Five-Minute Sermons* publication. We are told that he was born in Cobham in Surrey, England, the son of a prominent British physician in 1848. He converted from Anglicanism to Catholicism at the Brompton Oratory at the age of eighteen and went on to study at St Edmund's College and Prior Park where he took minor orders. He and his younger brother, Louis (who would also become a Paulist priest), immigrated to the United States in 1871 and settled in Cincinnati. Algernon would be ordained a priest by Archbishop Francis Purcell on 25 May 1872. The following year a mission in the diocese, delivered by one of the Paulist Society's priests, Walter Elliott (1842–1928), who later wrote the first biography of Hecker, impressed both brothers so deeply that they resolved to enter the society. Archbishop Purcell released Algernon to the society, but wondered whether his weak health might fail him while undertaking a hectic schedule of mission activity. In the event, it did, and he was soon assigned to the society's New York City parish of St Paul the Apostle, where he seems to have assumed the duties of sacristan. Here, according to the anonymous author of the preface to the volume of sermons, he displayed an 'accurate knowledge of the rubrics, ceremonial, and sacred chant', coupled with 'zeal for the order and decorum of the divine service and ... untiring assiduity in the work assigned him'.[4] By 1877 his health was in steep decline, and having made one last visit home to England, he collapsed as he commenced the Introit on the Feast of the Immaculate Conception, 8 December. He lingered for some months before passing away on the Monday of Holy Week, 8 April 1878. He was just twenty-nine years old. Incredibly, his younger brother, Louis, would die at the very same age two years later.

The volume of *Five-Minute Sermons* which was published in 1879 contained sermons that had already been preached by members of the Paulist society. The preface to the volume explains that these were designed to contain 'a sufficient amount of matter at once instructive and hortatory, in plain and simple language, to answer the practical purposes of a popular discourse'.[5] In addition, they were intended to be 'so solid and pungent that they would furnish a real nutriment and stimulus to the hearts and minds of the audience'.[6] Yet these sermons had not only already been preached; they had also appeared on a weekly basis in *The Catholic Review*, a newspaper founded by Mr Patrick Valentine Hickey, formerly of the New York *World*, and published in Brooklyn and New York from 1872–98. This was later described by the Catholic literary critic, novelist and diplomat, Maurice Francis Egan, as 'a paper intended for Catholic gentlemen written by Catholic gentlemen'.[7] The aim of the volume was to present these sermons in a 'more convenient and permanent form'.[8]

The Paulist publication, *Catholic World* (founded in 1865) carried a review of the volume in its issue of December 1879.[9] This review provides further information on how the volume came about. It explains that these sermons had been delivered by the Paulists over the previous three years and were almost simultaneously printed in *The Catholic Review*; but not quite. The printed copy was received in advance from the newspaper and was pasted on a tablet, which was left on the desk for the priest who was about to celebrate the Low Mass. He would then read the text to the people after the Gospel. The reviewer explains that 'there is only one way of preaching very short sermons which are really useful and interesting, and this is to write them out carefully and deliver them exactly as they are written'. He also points to the danger of ad-libbing a shorter sermon, which is 'likely to be a mere random declamation without pith or marrow, and the preacher will often be tempted to overrun his time'. However, even Algernon Brown's confrère, the Paulist, Rev. Alfred Young (1831–1900), writing on the topic of street-preaching in the *Catholic World*, was far from convinced that the five-minute sermon was the perfect panacea for a preacher's predicament: 'five-minute sermons are better than no sermon at all, but such a short time, snatched between the announcement of a lot of parish notices and proclamations of all sorts of regulations ... is not sufficient to present with any force the proofs for doctrine which any indiscriminate audience are capable of appreciating'. He continues:

> I believe it to be a very great mistake to suppose that one must adapt the presentation of the great truths of faith and of private or social duty to an imaginary intellectual weakness or infirmity of mind among the common people. More than once I have heard unfavourably from some such attempt, made by an ill-prepared preacher, to palm off a lot of platitudes upon those whom he thought were worthy of nothing better.[10]

The provision of a volume of carefully prepared short sermons by the Paulists can be conceived then as an effort to address some of the poorer examples of preaching that they no doubt heard much of.

The volume of sermons proved to be largely successful. Some years later, *The Sacred Heart Review*, in an issue dated 16 September 1893, referred to the sermons as follows:

> All Catholics in this country and many abroad know the five-minute sermons, those brief little addresses delivered by the Paulist Fathers to their early morning congregations in New York. They have been printed in our papers all over the land and have had innumerable readers.[11]

By 1893, the Catholic Book Exchange advertised the volume in the *Catholic World* with the claim that there was 'no better manual for altar use' and promised that 'on receipt of One Dollar we will mail you a copy'.[12]

With some exceptions, the 1879 volume contains three five-minute sermons for each Sunday of the year. In each case, at least one of these was marked with a 'B'; this indicated that the sermon could be attributed with certainty to Brown. The authorship of those lacking this marker was deemed to be less certain. Having said that, the review of the volume that appeared in the Paulist *Catholic World* in the same year as its publication claimed (most likely with some authority) that 'Brown wrote nearly all the sermons until his fatal illness put a stop to his priestly labours'.[13] For the purposes of this introduction to the Paulist five-minute sermons, this distinction will not be strictly adhered to. Rather, the aim here is to provide a flavour of the material which was preached by Brown and his confrères in the mid-to late 1870s.[14]

Inspired by the thought of its founder, Isaac Hecker, one of the priorities of the Paulist mission was to address the issue of how lay Catholics might accommodate themselves to the prevailing American culture and yet, at the same time, transform that culture from within. This would lead to charges of 'Americanism' in the late 1890s after a French translation of Walter Elliott's biography of Hecker appeared in 1897.[15] In 1866 Hecker had addressed the Second Plenary Council in Baltimore and had urged the bishops to take seriously the task of converting America.[16] For him, the soil was already rich and perfect for the sowing of the seed of faith. He remarked, 'Nowhere is there a promise of a brighter future for the Church than in our own country ... here Christianity is promised a reception from an intelligent and free people that will bring forth a development of unprecedented glory'.[17] Not everyone would remain as convinced of this as Hecker, however. Nevertheless, the Paulist emphasis would remain fixed on the idea that the lives of ordinary Catholics, if lived in an exemplary manner, could act as the leaven that would 'raise' the wider culture.[18] Well-lived Catholicism would be its own attraction and a major tool of evangelisation. This approach is clearly in evidence in the texts of the Paulist five-minute sermons. The themes of the sermons themselves, and the language employed in their delivery, afford the reader a fascinating window into what were considered by the Paulist preachers to be some of the most pressing issues for the spiritual lives of ordinary Catholics living in the city of New York in the late nineteenth century.

The Paulist sermons might be identified as, first and foremost, rallying cries to the lay Catholic faithful to engage with the modern world while, at the same time, avoiding becoming enslaved by it. They called their hearers to be witnesses of faith to their families and friends. In the simplest of acts could the piecemeal work of converting America begin. In a sermon for the Second Sunday of Advent, based on the line from Matthew 9:10 ('Behold, I send my angel before thy face'), Fr Algernon Brown, explaining that the word 'angel' meant messenger, stated that 'all of us ought to be messengers of God to our neighbour and to the world'.[19] More specifically, he claimed that 'we Catholics ought to be the *angels of God on earth* to those who are not Catholics … By our lives we ought to show the world that the Catholic religion makes us better citizens, better and more honest men of business, and truer lovers of our neighbours and mankind'.[20] This had a particular resonance in late-nineteenth-century America when to be Catholic routinely involved being part of a little trusted minority.[21] But what did this mean in practical terms? Brown was addressing a congregation in which many of his hearers were employed in the service of non-Catholic families (the language is very much of its time, speaking of non-Christians as 'infidel families'). Here was an opportunity, Brown continued, to:

> show by your fidelity to work, by your strict honesty, by your modest behaviour, that you belong to a religion that comes from God. By a seasonable word, by the loan of a book, by showing your horror of cursing and swearing

and of bad talk, you would be doing God's work, and showing to those outside the Church that there is *something* in your belief which makes you good.[22]

Not only should such action show Catholics to be good, according to Brown, but even that they are better than others and that it is their religion that makes them so.[23] Even the very youngest of Catholics could be evangelisers in their own home. Brown offers the example of the young child who abstained from meat on a Friday after hearing a sermon to this end, even though his less Gospel-greedy parents beat him as a result. Ultimately, his perseverance was to bring about his parents' conversion. This example becomes the *pièce de résistance* of Brown's sermon, appearing just before its close.

The exhortation to congregations to be missionaries in their daily lives was common in the Paulist five-minute sermons. An alternative sermon for the Second Sunday of Advent, based on the verse from Matthew 12:30 ('He who is not with me is against me'), also took up the question of how to conduct oneself when associating with persons 'whose mouths are full of impious and impure talk'; these were identified as 'either infidels, Protestants or bad Catholics'.[24] In this instance, in a concession to practicality (and perhaps also as a health and safety measure!) the sermon states that one is not bound on each and every occasion to reprove these particular sins; nevertheless, the author continues, 'I do say that you are sometimes'.[25] The crucial point of this sermon is perhaps best captured in the line, 'Do not, then, keep your faith and piety shut up in your prayer-books, only to be brought out when you are on your knees before God'.[26] The Paulists were quick to hold to account those who exhibited a devotion that was devoid of an evangelising mentality; in the third sermon offered for the same Sunday in Advent, the preacher was to remind his congregation that 'there is a great deal of piety nowadays, but it seems often to be of a very superficial kind'.[27] If the Paulists never construed themselves as so-called 'sacristy priests', neither did they wish for their congregations to keep their faith for the church pews. Rather, as a sermon for the Sixth Sunday after the Epiphany (based on Matthew 13:33, 'The kingdom of heaven is like to leaven') puts it:

> there are many Catholics who do not seem to understand the world has got to be converted, and that they themselves have got to do their share towards it; that they are part of that leaven with which our Lord meant that the world should be leavened ... every Catholic ought to be a missionary in his way and place ...[28]

Of course a poorly lived Catholicism could render one what might be termed an 'anti-missionary' to one's non-Catholic associates, thus causing them to stumble, or at the very least to dismiss from their minds any thoughts of enquiring further about the Catholic faith. The same sermon identifies the practice of swearing as one instance in which this might come about, sternly warning its hearers that 'if you are the cause, by this abominable habit of yours, of his [the interested Protestant, in this case] turning away in despair from the Church, most assuredly you will have to give an account for it when your soul shall come to be judged'.[29]

The perennial challenge for any preacher is to draw some connection between the world of the liturgy and the world of daily living. At many points, the Paulist sermons clearly identify a yawning disconnect between the two. For instance, in a sermon for the First Sunday of Lent (based on Matthew 4:4, 'Man liveth not by bread alone'), Brown addresses in particular all working men who spend their time earning a living while neglecting their souls. He warns them, 'Don't leave piety to priests, religious women and children, but let the men also be seen in the church and at the altar-rail'.[30] The reluctance of some men to receive Holy Communion is also highlighted in a sermon for the Second Sunday after Pentecost (based on Luke 14:18, 'And they began all at once to make excuse'), which treats of the objection 'Piety is very good for priests and religious; but I am living in the world and can't be good enough to go to Communion' with a dismissive 'Humbug! ... are you more in the world than St Henry, Emperor of Germany; St Louis, King of France; the two Saints Elizabeth, of Hungary and Portugal? ... Don't make any more foolish excuses, then'.[31] The idea of the lay apostolate, which emerged in the later nineteenth century, was strongly supported by the Paulists. In a sermon for Septuagesima Sunday (the ninth Sunday before Easter), reflecting upon the verse 'Why stand ye here all day idle?' (Matthew 20:6), the following categories of persons are addressed:

> ... such among you as have means, or who are able to help your pastor by active service in the charge of the sick and the poor, who can teach the uninstructed, help along in sewing-schools and in forming sodalities and pious organizations of various kinds – to you also the cry comes 'why stand ye all the day idle?' Why, when called upon to bear a little part of the priest's burden, are so many people like an old gun that hangs fire? Why is it often so difficult for the priest to get the active co-operation of the lay people? ... How often they say 'I have no time'; 'What are the priests for anyhow?'; 'Let *them* look after these things ...'[32]

Here we have a call for active participation of the laity in the apostolate; yet, in the late nineteenth century (and, indeed, for much of the twentieth century) it would remain a sharing in the mission of the hierarchy.[33]

There were other ways to ensure that one's Catholicism was reflected in the manner in which one lived – and, in the main, these involved avoiding certain practices, situations and entertainments. Among the areas highlighted in a sermon for Gaudete Sunday (which Brown terms 'a little *let-up* ... on the solemn season of Advent') is that of fashion: 'when you deck yourselves out in clothing, in fashions which are beyond your means, unsuited to your calling as a Christian'; he calls such individuals 'nothing but jackdaws in peacock's feathers'.[34] This problem also extended to what was worn in church and Brown comments in a sermon for the Ninth Sunday after Pentecost (on Luke 19:46, 'My house is the house of prayer'), that 'the church is not the place to see what kind of clothes people have on, or to show off one's good clothes ... it is the place to dress neatly but not showily'.[35] A sermon for the Fourteenth Sunday after Pentecost (based on Galatians 5:19, 'The works of the flesh are manifest') raised the issue of the 'dances which have become fashionable in the last few years', concluding that even the most scrupulous of Catholics seem to see no harm in them; and yet,

> the harm is in the improper positions assumed in what are called round dances and which have lately been brought into almost all others. These mutual positions of the parties, these embraces – for that they simply are – are in themselves evidently contrary to modesty and decency ... every person pretending to be respectable would blush to be detected in such positions on any other occasion, unless united to the other party by very near relationship or marriage. And let no one say that fashion justifies them.[36]

This question of what was considered 'fashionable' exercised many of the early Paulists in their preaching. A sermon for the Seventeenth Sunday after Pentecost declares that 'we hear a great deal nowadays, my dear brethren, about toleration. It is a thing which the nineteenth century takes a special pride in ... but if we examine this pretended toleration and charity we shall have to confess that it is simply a sham, having nothing whatever in it to make it deserve the name it takes.'[37]

Indeed, elsewhere, in a sermon by Brown for the Seventh Sunday after Pentecost, which warned of the dangers of false prophets, he critiques a number of 'false' principles which he finds to be particularly prevalent in his own time: that religion is a matter of choice; that it doesn't matter what a man believes as long as he is good; that education is the business of the state; that religion has nothing to do with science; that a man cannot help his nature; that a young man is expected to sow his wild oats; that 'we are in the world and must go with it'. For Brown,

SERVING LITURGICAL RENEWAL

these were the principles of the 'false newspaper prophet' who offers for sale 'his filthy, licentious, and lying sheet'.[38] In a sermon for the Fourth Sunday after Pentecost, Brown complained of Catholics who never thought of reading 'a good religious book or a Catholic newspaper', but instead turned to 'the trashy, beastly stuff that is served up daily and weekly to pander to depraved appetites'.[39]

The five-minute sermons also comprise an important commentary on aspects of the social condition of American Catholics at the time. One of the great concerns of the Paulists was the problem of alcoholism within families. In a sermon on the verse 'No man can serve two masters' (Matthew 6:24) for the Fourteenth Sunday after Pentecost, Brown calls alcohol the 'master of the poor', a 'devil' which takes a poor man's wages on a Saturday night

> and from the bar-room he sends him home to be a scandal to his little children, and maybe to beat his wretched wife. Others this master sends from that liquor-store to steal, and so to prison and hopeless ruin; others he sends to brothels; many a one he afflicts with frightful diseases and sudden accidents, and so brings them to hell.[40]

The effects of such behaviour on families comprises the subject matter of a sermon for the Third Sunday of Lent on the verse, 'Every kingdom divided against itself will be brought to desolation' (Luke 11:17). Here, Brown depicts the drunken husband arriving home 'in a dull, heavy stupor, or else in a perfect fury of rage; he worries his wife, scares his children, disgraces himself; all his family shrink from him' and, in a passionate plea, urges his hearers 'For God's sake, *stop this evil war*. Stop these things which make the family miserable'.[41] However, alcoholism was just one aspect of a wider social problem which the Paulists identified in their sermons: the phenomenon of parental neglect of their children. This is clearly expressed in a sermon by Brown for the Sunday within the Octave of Christmas:

There are some who let their children eat just as they please, who pamper their appetites, who give them all kinds of unwholesome food. Such children will never be healthy. There are others who spend all their money on drink – who leave their poor little ones at home, moaning and starving with hunger … no wonder that our city children are unhealthy; no wonder death sweeps them away as it does.[42]

Addressing parents directly, he states, 'you make your home uncomfortable by your crossness, by your curses, by your slovenly, untidy habits. Your children, from their earliest infancy, take to the streets'.[43] There they learn impurity, blasphemy and cursing and smoke, chew tobacco and flirt 'like little men and women'.[44] And, in a story which anticipates Dorothy Law Nolte's 1954 poem, 'Children Learn What They Live', Brown continues, 'You know the story of the old crab who said to her little ones "Why do you walk sideways?". "Suppose, mother", they said, "*you* show us how to walk straight"'.[45]

But there were others, too, within the family household, to whom a duty of care was owed. Brown makes this clear in a sermon for the Third Sunday after the Epiphany, which took its cue from the account of the good centurion in Matthew 8:8 ('Only say the word and my servant shall be healed'). Here he takes the opportunity to ask how Catholics treat their hired help, especially in cases where they fall ill: 'You grumble at the inconvenience to which you are put, but what do you do to help them? … Often a servant is made to work when bed would be a more fitting place to be than in the kitchen'.[46] However, the duty of care was expected to stretch beyond the temporal to the spiritual needs of their employees, seeing that they get to Mass, that they are afforded time to confess their sins, and that they receive Holy Communion when ill. The message was clear: 'God will require all these souls at your hands'; the corollary, of course, was that 'No Catholic man or woman ought to keep in their houses a servant who is negligent of his or her religious duties'.[47]

The language and rhetoric of the Paulist five-minute sermons was designed to hold the attention of the congregation, and their home-spun style must have been very effective. A sermon for Septuagesima Sunday, based on 1 Corinthians 9:24 ('So run that you may obtain the prize') refers to the contemporary 'great rage ... for walking, running, or footing it in any way', alluding to its health benefits and the fact that it is also good for the pocket (in a time of recession, such that it was).[48] This segues into a discussion of the journey that one must make on foot to heaven and the preparation or training needed for this. In a line which might be regarded by some as somewhat Pelagian in tone, it continues, 'If we are to get there [heaven], it must be by our own exertions'.[49] One also finds references to contemporary events, which were undoubtedly fresh in the minds of the congregation. In this way, the Paulists were perhaps Barthian before Barth in their approach to the combined use of newspapers and the scriptures. One such example is in a sermon for Christmas Eve which refers to a fire which occurred at the Brooklyn Theatre just weeks before, on 5 December 1876, claiming the lives of at least two hundred and seventy-eight people:

> But a little while ago we read in the papers of an awful calamity – the burning of the Brooklyn Theatre ... brethren, some of those poor creatures who perished in the Brooklyn fire were so charred, so burnt that they could not be recognised. Take care that you do not become so disfigured by sin that at the last day God will say to you 'I know ye not'.[50]

The sermon went on to draw a comparison between returning to a life of sin and re-entering the theatre building and exposing oneself once more to the conflagration.[51] Sobering words for a Christmas Eve. In a further example, a sermon for Passion Sunday warned against the escalation of the passions in verbal quarrels that quickly get out of control. The potential ramifications of a careless word uttered in the white heat of anger were captured in the line, 'A cow kicked a lantern in a stable, and Chicago was on fire for days', referring to the Great Fire of Chicago on 10 October 1871, some five years earlier, the cause of which has traditionally been attributed to 'Mrs O'Leary's cow'.[52]

However, there were many lighter moments for a congregation listening to a five-minute sermon. In a sermon for Quinquagesima Sunday (the Sunday before Ash Wednesday), which set out to explain what is meant by a fast-day (namely, the consumption of only one full meal), the preacher raises the objections of his audience, 'I will get very hungry and lose a good many pounds on such a scant diet as that', to which he replies, 'It wouldn't do some of you any harm to lose a few pounds; you will recover from it, I am sure'.[53] A sermon for the previous Sunday, which focused on the passage, 'A sower went out to sow his seed' (Luke 8:5), covered the topic of how to profitably hear sermons. It contended that 'you do not get any fruit from the word of God, though you often think your neighbours ought to. You say "I hope Mr. and Mrs. Smith, Brown, or Jones heard that"'.[54] In the Candlemas Day sermon it was observed that there are some Catholics who are not adequately equipped to welcome a priest arriving on a sick-call, having to borrow a candle from some pious neighbour and then having no candleholder to place it in, resorting to the use of a bottle instead. At this the preacher quipped, 'It would look much better, in some houses which we have to visit, if there were fewer bottles and more blessed candles'.[55] Meanwhile, a sermon on the calming of the storm episode in Matthew 8:26 opens with the lines, 'Some people are always worrying. It would seem that they must enjoy it, for they always find something to worry about ... they are so fond of their amusement that if they cannot get their favourite matter to worry about, they will take something else rather than not have any at all'.[56] In another effective image used in a sermon for the Feast of Pentecost, Brown explains that it does not automatically follow that the person who likes to pray really loves God very much (at least in the short term when he feels that he is rewarded for it): 'He may like it in the same way that a child would like the company of anyone who would give him candy. If the supply of candy stops his affection is gone'.[57]

The five-minute sermons of Algernon Brown and his Paulist confrères, short as they may have been by nineteenth-century preaching standards, nevertheless punched well above their weight. Although communicated in an accessible style and pitched at a broad audience, the challenges that they set before their hearers were not always so easy. For the Paulists, Catholicism solely lived between the covers of a prayer-book was not Catholicism at all. Indeed, one of its Christmas sermons castigates those who 'seem to imagine that it is enough to be a Catholic to be quite sure of one's salvation', associating it with the Reformation idea 'that a man may be justified by faith without good works'.[58] For the Paulists, the proof of true conversion entailed a real change of heart and a demonstrable change of one's habits. And they were sufficient realists to conclude that this was not always the case. In fact, in a sermon by Algernon Brown for Low Sunday, based on the 'Doubting Thomas' passage in John 20:25 and adapted from Matthias Faber SJ (1586–1653), the preacher likewise takes a sceptical approach to the individual sinner's repentance. It seems a fitting passage in which to conclude our discussion of the evangelising five-minute sermons of the Paulists and their emphasis on the necessity of a fully-lived Catholicism in late-nineteenth-century America:

> I will not believe that you have come out of the grave of mortal sin unless I see in you the signs of a former crucifixion. First I want to see the print of the nails. I want to see in your hands and feet – that is, in your inclinations and passions – the print of the nails that the priest drove in, in the confessional. I want to see that these hands strike no more, handle no more bad books, pass no more bad money, write no more evil letters, sign no more fraudulent documents, are stretched forth no more unto evil things,

raised no more to curse ... I want to see these hands smoothing the pillows of the sick, giving drink to the thirsty, food to the hungry, and raiment to the naked ... These feet, too – I must see them bearing you to the confessional regularly, taking you to Mass, carrying you to Benediction, bent under you in prayer. In a word, I must see in you the signs of a true conversion, or I will not believe that you have really risen from the death of sin ... Lastly, I want to put my hand into your side to see if your heart is wounded. I want to see if there is true contrition there ...[59]

So much more could be said of these sermons; the short account above hardly does them justice. Neither does the fact that they have been little worked on so far. It is to be hoped that this situation will soon be remedied.

Notes

1. Some of the most abiding memories I have of Fr Paddy Jones' time in Maynooth College revolve around the 12.15 p.m. liturgies of the Eucharist which he celebrated most weekdays in St Mary's Oratory, and especially the homilies he delivered. These were firmly rooted in the readings of the day and, although always suitably brief, were invariably thought-provoking. Although he did not speak from a text, Paddy always carried a small slip of paper with some short guiding notes. In concluding his few words, he would fold this tiny *aide-mémoire* over a couple of times and make his way back to the presider's chair. What was important for Paddy was clearly not the length of his preaching; the critical point was that it should be undertaken daily and should flow from the Word just proclaimed.
2. *Five-Minute Sermons for Low Masses on All Sundays of the Year* by the Priests of the Congregation of St Paul (New York: The Catholic Publication Society, 1879), iii.
3. For the early history of the society, see David J. O'Brien, *Isaac Hecker: An American Catholic* (New York/Mahwah, NJ: Paulist Press, 1992).
4. *Five-Minute Sermons*, vi.
5. Ibid., iii.
6. Ibid.

7. Maurice Francis Egan, *Recollections of a Happy Life* (New York: George H. Doran Company, 1924), 118.
8. *Five-Minute Sermons*, iv.
9. *Catholic World*, Vol. 30, Issue 177 (December 1879), 426–7. See the database 'Making of America', quod.lib.umich.edu/m/moajrnl/bac8387.0030.177/430:14?g=moagrp;rgn=full+text;view=image;xc=1;q1=Five-Minute+Sermons (accessed 11 December 2013).
10. Rev. Alfred Young, 'Street Preaching', *Catholic World*, Vol. 46, issue 274 (January 1888), 502.
11. Newspapers. Boston College: newspapers.bc.edu/cgi-bin/bostonsh?a=d&d=BOSTONSH18931216-01.2.21# (accessed 11 December 2013).
12. *Catholic World*, Vol. 58, issue 348 (March, 1894), A26.
13. Ibid., Vol. 30, Issue 177 (December 1879), 426.
14. It should be noted that in 2010 the print-on-demand publishing company, Kessinger Publishing, re-printed this volume of sermons as part of its Legacy Reprint Series.
15. In fact, it was the preface to this French translation, written not by Elliott but by Abbé Félix Klein of the Institut Catholique, which proved to be most controversial, suggesting that Hecker was a model priest of the future and idealising the new American way of Catholicism as the way forward. After Pope Leo XIII's Apostolic Letter, *Testem benevolentiae*, which appeared on 22 January 1899 and which condemned 'Americanism' and specifically mentioned the French translation of Hecker's biography as one of its roots, Klein submitted to papal authority and withdrew the volume from circulation. See Thomas T. McAvoy, 'Abbé Klein and Americanism', *The Review of Politics* 11: 3 (July 1949), 379–81.
16. It should be noted that already, according to one estimate, between 1831 and 1860 the number of converts to Catholicism, stood at some 57,400. See Jon Gjerde, *Catholicism and the Shaping of Nineteenth-Century America* (New York: Cambridge University Press, 2012), 109.
17. Timothy E. Byreley, *The Great Commission: Models of Evangelization in American Catholicism* (Mahwah, NJ: Paulist Press, 2008), 74–5.
18. This language is actually used in a five-minute sermon for the Sixth Sunday after the Epiphany. See the discussion of this below.
19. *Five Minute Sermons*, 27.
20. Ibid., 28.
21. For a useful discussion of anti-Catholic sentiment during this period, see especially Susan M. Griffin, *Anti-Catholicism and Nineteenth-Century Fiction* (Cambridge: Cambridge University Press, 2004).

22. *Five Minute Sermons*, 28.
23. Ibid., 29.
24. Ibid., 30–1.
25. Ibid., 31.
26. Ibid.
27. Ibid., 33.
28. Ibid., 119.
29. Ibid., 119–20.
30. Ibid., 156.
31. Ibid., 293–4.
32. Ibid., 123–4.
33. For the history of the development of this concept, see especially Joseph Sasaki, *The Lay Apostolate and the Hierarchy* (Ottawa: St Paul's University/University of Ottawa Press, 1967), 73–102.
34. *Five Minute Sermons*, 38.
35. Ibid., 351.
36. Ibid., 398.
37. Ibid., 422–3.
38. Ibid., 331–2.
39. Ibid., 309.
40. Ibid., 395–6.
41. Ibid., 171–2.
42. Ibid., 56–7. For a useful study of this area, see Samuel H. Preston and Michael R. Haines, *Fatal Years: Child Mortality in Late Nineteenth-Century America* (Princeton, NJ: Princeton University Press, 1991). It argues, however, that the relatively high rates of childhood mortality of the period should not be attributed solely to parental neglect or socio-economic factors, but to the widespread communicable disease in an age when germ theory had not been widely accepted.
43. Ibid., 57.
44. Ibid., 58.
45. Ibid.
46. Ibid., 92.
47. Ibid., 92–3.
48. Ibid., 128.
49. Ibid.
50. Ibid., 47–8. Vivid descriptions of the awful scenes as the fire raged were gathered from eyewitnesses and were carried in local newspapers such as the *Brooklyn Eagle*. Few people within the congregation would not have been familiar with the details of the tragedy.
51. Ibid.

52. Ibid., 190.
53. Ibid., 149.
54. Ibid., 137.
55. Ibid., 105.
56. Ibid., 98.
57. Ibid., 272.
58. Ibid., 50.
59. Ibid., 215–16.

WHEN THE REFORM BECOMES PRAYER: THE STRANGE CASE OF 1 JANUARY

LIAM M. TRACEY OSM

In a volume honouring the contribution of Fr Patrick Jones to the celebration and study of liturgy in Ireland, mention must be made of his editing of the annual *Liturgical Calendar for Ireland*,[1] a task on which he collaborated with Fr Brian Magee, CM, and for which he took responsibility after the untimely death of the latter in 2003. This contribution is a study of the first day of the civil year which appears in the liturgical calendar, now entitled 'Mary, the Holy Mother of God' with the rank of solemnity, and is also named 'World Day of Peace' and 'Octave Day of the Nativity of the Lord'.

Liturgical Cult to the Virgin Mary

Alongside the cult and veneration of those early Christian heroes and witnesses, the martyrs, devotion to and veneration of Mary the mother of Jesus appears to have developed quite early in the history of the Christian Church. However, precisely when this devotion and veneration took a distinctive liturgical shape remains a matter of debate and conjecture.[2]

As the Second Vatican Council document on the Church, *Lumen gentium*, notes in article 66, a remarkable growth in piety toward Mary followed the declaration of the divine maternity of Mary at the Council of Ephesus in 431.[3] Recent Church teaching has also reflected on this foundation of Marian piety. In the first document of the Council we find the following article in the section dealing with the Liturgical year.

Sacrosanctum concilium 103 (with emphasis added):

In hoc annuo mysteriorum Christi circulo celebrando, Sancta Ecclesia Beatam Mariam Dei Genetricem cum peculiari amore veneratur, quae indissolubili nexu cum Filii sui opere salutari coniungitur; in qua praecellentem Redemptionis fructum miratur et exaltat, ac veluti in purissima imagine, id quod ipsa tota esse cupit et sperat cum gaudio contemplatur.	In celebrating this annual cycle of Christ's mysteries, holy Church honours with *especial love* the Blessed Mary, *Mother of God*, who is joined by an *inseparable bond* to the saving work of her Son. In her the Church holds up and admires the most excellent fruit of the redemption, and joyfully contemplates, as in a faultless image, that which she herself desires and hopes wholly to be.

Ignazio Calabuig notes that SC 103 is key to considering the place of Mary in liturgical piety:

> The Constitution on the Sacred Liturgy of Vatican II, *Sacrosanctum Concilium*, synthesises, in an authoritative way, what the Church teaches about the place of the holy Theotokos in the liturgy.

He goes on to note that:

> Liturgical devotion to holy Mary encompasses a vast area. It is necessary, however, to interpret it correctly both in order to dispel doubts about the legitimacy of such devotion in a liturgical setting and also to make evident how valuable it is in the liturgy, which has as its ultimate

aim nothing other than the perfect glorification of God and the sanctification of humanity.[4]

This brief text is both dense in its construction and significant in its meaning. It clearly establishes that the liturgical year is one festal cycle which celebrates the saving mystery of Christ, its past, present and future dimensions; and that there is not a parallel liturgical cycle of feasts of Our Lady (as had been suggested by many preconciliar authors on the liturgical calendar). Devotion to Mary is rooted in the mystery of Christ to whose saving work she is indissolubly and profoundly linked. Interesting is that the authors of SC text select the title of Mother of God as the motive for the Church's veneration of Mary.

Similar affirmations are to be found in the Constitution on the Church, *Lumen gentium* 53 (with emphasis added):

Virgo enim Maria, quae Angelo nuntiante Verbum Dei corde et corpore suscepit et Vitam mundo protulit, ut vera Mater Dei ac Redemptoris agnoscitur et honoratur. Intuitu meritorum Filii sui sublimiore modo redempta Eique arcto et *indissolubili vinculo* unita, hoc *summo munere* ac dignitate ditatur ut sit *Genitrix Dei Filii,* ideoque praedilecta filia Patris necnon sacrarium Spiritus Sancti quo eximiae gratiae dono omnibus aliis creaturis, coelestibus et terrestribus, *longe antecellit.* Simul autem cum omnibus hominibus salvandis in stirpe Adam invenitur coniuncta, immo

The Virgin Mary, who at the message of the angel received the Word of God in her heart and in her body and gave Life to the world, is acknowledged and honoured as being truly the Mother of God and Mother of the Redeemer. Redeemed by reason of the merits of her Son and united to Him by a close and *indissoluble tie,* she is endowed with the *high office* and dignity of being the *Mother of the Son of God,* by which account she is also the beloved daughter of the Father and the temple of the Holy Spirit. Because of this gift of sublime grace she far *surpasses all creatures,* both in 'plane mater membrorum (Christi), ... quia cooperata est caritate ut fideles in Ecclesia nascerentur, quae illius Capitis membra sunt.' Quapropter etiam ut supereminens prorsusque singulare membrum Ecclesiae necnon eius in fide et caritate typus et exemplar spectatissimum salutatur eamque Catholica Ecclesia, a Spiritu Sancto edocta, filialis pietatis affectu tamquam matrem amantissimam prosequitur.

heaven and on earth. At the same time, however, because she belongs to the offspring of Adam she is one with all those who are to be saved. She is 'the mother of the members of Christ ... having cooperated by charity that faithful might be born in the Church, who are members of that Head.'[5] Wherefore she is hailed as a pre-eminent and singular member of the Church, and as its type and excellent exemplar in faith and charity. The Catholic Church, taught by the Holy Spirit, honours her with filial affection and piety as a most beloved mother.

LG 55 speaks of the office and the dignity of Mary which is rooted in her divine maternity and of her relationships with three divine persons. This is seen as exalting her above all other creatures, in heaven and on earth and yet, by quoting Augustine, the article recalls her oneness with those who are to be saved.

The consequences of these affirmations for Marian piety are not dealt with until article 66 of the same document:

Maria,
per gratiam Dei
post Filium
prae omnibus angelis et
hominibus exaltata,
utpote *sanctissima Dei Mater*,
quae mysteriis Christi interfuit,
speciali cultu
ab Ecclesia merito honoratur.

Placed by the grace of God,
as *God's Mother*,
next to her Son,
and exalted above all angels
and men, Mary intervened in
the mysteries of Christ
and is justly honoured by a
special cult in the Church.

This article offers a rapid synthesis of the history of the Church's devotion to Mary, and in two places makes explicit reference to the title Mother of God in its allusion to the antiphon *Sub tuum praesidium* and its direct reference to the Council of Ephesus. In both of these conciliar texts from LG, the divine maternity of Mary is seen as the motive for the devotion of the people of God towards Mary.

The Apostolic Exhortations *Signum Magnum* and *Marialis Cultus*

These two Council documents (SC and LG) were followed by two apostolic exhortations of Paul VI, *Signum magnum*[6] and *Marialis cultus*,[7] both of which directly treat the topic of Marian devotion. The first of these texts (SM) is little known in the English-speaking world, or indeed elsewhere, and in this particular exhortation Paul VI clearly notes that the liturgical reform flowing from the Second Vatican Council is not detrimental to Marian piety (a charge often levelled by traditionalists of various hues). He is also clear that veneration is due to Mary because of her prerogatives, and first among these is her divine maternity.

Nec verendum est, ne reformatio liturgica – modo ad eam formulam efficiatur, quae hisce exprimitur verbis: *lex credendi legem statuat supplicandi* – detrimentum cultui *singulari omnino* (see, LG 66) iniungat, qui Mariae Virgini sanctissimae, ob praecipua eius privilegia, *debetur,* in quibus *Matris Dei dignitas eminet.*	Nor is it to be feared that liturgical reform, if put into practice according to the formula 'the law of faith must establish the law of prayer' may be detrimental to the 'wholly singular' (see LG 66) veneration due to the Virgin Mary for her prerogatives, first among these being the dignity of the Mother of God.

A similar affirmation is made by Paul VI in the later document, MC 56, when, towards the end of the text, he recalls the root of Marian devotion:

Hic autem marialis cultus altas veluti agit radices in Verbo Dei revelato ac firmiter innititur in doctrinae catholicae veritatibus, quae sunti *singularis dignitas Mariae*, quae est *Genetrix Dei Filii, ideo que praedilecta filia Patris necnon sacrarium Spiritus Sancti* (LG 53).	Such devotion to the Blessed Virgin is firmly rooted in the revealed word and has solid dogmatic foundations. It is based on the *singular dignity of Mary, 'Mother of the Son of God, and therefore beloved daughter of the Father and Temple of the Holy Spirit'* (LG 53)

Already in MC 22, Paul VI lists the various cultic attitudes that the Church has in regard to the person of Mary and notes that her singular dignity results from her being the Mother of God:

È importante, d'altra parte, osservare come la Chiesa traduca i molteplici rapporti che la uniscono a Maria in vari ed efficaci atteggiamenti cultuali: in venerazione profonda, quando riflette sulla *singolare dignità della Vergine*, divenuta, per opera dello Spirito, *madre del Verbo incarnato*;[8]	It is also important to note how the Church expresses in various effective attitudes of devotion the many relationships that bind her to Mary: in profound veneration, when she reflects on the *singular dignity of the Virgin* who, through the action of the Holy Spirit has become *Mother of the Incarnate Word*;

While Paul VI is merely repeating traditional Catholic doctrine, he is also indicating how the divine maternity of Mary is the foundation of the piety of the Church towards her. It was also during the pontificate of Paul VI, that another 'magisterial act' regarding the divine maternity of Mary occurred, that is, the institution on 14 February 1969 of the celebration of the Solemnity of Mary, Mother of God. The solemnity was not instituted with a particular decree but rather forms part of the *motu proprio Mysterii paschali* of Paul VI, which promulgated the new *Calendarium Romanum Generale.*[9]

Deus, qui salutis aeternae, beatae Mariae virginitate, fecunda, humano generi praemia praestitisti, tribue, quaesumus, ut, ipsam pro nobis interceder sentiamus per quam meruimus Filium tuum auctorem vitae suscipere. Qui tecum vivit.	O God, who through the fruitful virginity of Blessed Mary bestowed on the human race the grace of eternal salvation, grant, we pray, that we may experience the intercession of her, through whom we were found worthy to receive the author of life, our Lord Jesus Christ, your Son. Who lives and reigns ...
Die 1 ianuarii. Sollemnitas sanctae Dei Genetricis Mariae; Collecta[10]	1 January. Solemnity of Mary, The Holy Mother of God; Collect (*Roman Missal*, 43)

That the celebration is ranked as a *sollemnitas,* that in many parts of the world it is still a holy day of obligation, and that the date to which it was assigned is the first day of the new civil year, all underline the importance with which this celebration was considered by the Church.[11] The feast of Mary Mother of God first came into the Roman Calendar in 1932, following the encyclical *Lux veritatis* of Pius XI which commemorated the fifteenth centenary of the Council of Ephesus. This encyclical established the feast and gave a mandate to the Sacred Congregation of Rites to compose the texts for the Mass and the Divine Office. The Congregation assigned the feast to 11 October with its decree *Ingenti populi* of 6 January 1932.

Paul VI writes in MC 5 that:

> [i]n the revised ordering of the Christmas period it seems
> to us that the attention of all should be directed towards
> the restored Solemnity of Mary the holy Mother of God.
> This celebration, placed on 1 January in conformity with
> the ancient indication of the liturgy of the City of Rome,
> is meant to commemorate the part played by Mary in this
> mystery of salvation. It is meant also to exalt the singular
> dignity which this mystery brings to the 'holy Mother ...
> through whom we were found worthy to receive the
> Author of life'.

Of note here is that his thoughts reflect the views of Dom
Bernard Botte, later to be taken up by Antoine Chavasse and
others, and, perhaps more interestingly in this case, those of
Calabuig (the principal author of *Marialis cultus*).[12]

The Reforms of Vatican II and 1 January
Bernard Botte put forward his views on the Marian character of
1 January in a celebrated article in 1933.[13] For Botte, 1 January
celebrated Mary, Mother of God, and this celebration preceded
the introduction of the four great Marian feasts (Assumption,
Nativity, Purification and Annunciation) in Rome which began
in the first half of the seventh century, and only later did 1
January celebrate the Octave of Christmas.[14] Following on from
the work of Botte, other liturgical scholars suggested that there
was a Roman memorial of *Natale sanctae Mariae* established in
the mid-sixth century and celebrated on 1 January. A formulary
was composed sometime between 560 and 590, and use was
made of the scriptural readings from the Common of Virgins,
but the euchological texts, according to Chavasse, are original.[15]

Botte based his hypothesis on what he believed to be three of
the most ancient antiphonaries (those of Monza, Mont-Blandin
and Corbie) which give for 1 January the indication, *In natale
sanctae Mariae*, and under this title provide a set of chants. He
found similar indications in two ancient evanglaries (Gospel

books). For Botte, a Marian collect found in a Georgian Sacramentary confirmed his view, as did margin notes in another supplement to the Sacramentary of Hadrian. Two years later in the pages of the same journal, Joseph Beran, the future Cardinal Archbishop of Prague, responded to Botte's article, which in rather typical fashion Botte summarily dismissed.[16] The crucial and still relevant questions raised by Beran were not answered by Botte: what are the differences between a collect, a full euchological formulary, the indication of a stational church, and a feast day indication in the calendar? These differences are still unclear as is a sense of exactly what they tell us regarding an actual celebration.

In a 1936 article, again in the same journal, Bernardo Opfermann, writing about a ninth-century liturgical fragment from Fulda, notes that the feast of Saint Martina is given for 1 January,[17] and he goes on to comment on the hypothesis of Botte who claimed that this is a copyist's error, an argument which he finds unconvincing, ignoring as it does other calendars and martyrologies which place Martina on 1 January (a point made some forty years later by Pierre Jounel).[18]

As already noted, Antoine Chavasse adopted the view of Botte in his 1958 study of the Gelasian Sacramentary.[19] Dom Georges Frénaud, in his much admired 1961 study of the origins and development of the Roman cult of Our Lady, accepts the conclusions of Chavasse but notes the weaknesses of the thesis of Botte, especially his dismissal of the cult of St Martina and her feast on 1 January.[20] He argued that the celebration of Mary already took place in some of the Roman *tituli* between 560 and 590; he is less certain about its presence in possible papal celebrations.

In his study of the liturgical year, the Italian liturgist Mario Righetti notes that 1 January has had to balance several different liturgical celebrations over the course of the centuries.[21] Righetti sees the office *ad prohibendum ab idolis* as the most ancient liturgical memorial for this date. Dating back to Tertullian, Christians were urged by their bishops to avoid the pagan celebrations of the *Kalends* of January. Local Church councils invited the faithful to fasting and public prayer over these days of the New Year. To this Mass formulary of 1 January against all surviving forms of idolatry, the Roman Church added the celebration of the Mother of God as part of its resistance to these celebrations. Righetti speculates that the celebration may be associated with the Church of *Santa Maria Antiqua,* the earliest Christian monument in the Roman Forum, and dedicated to the Mother of God, which was built on the site of the temple of Mother Vesta where tradition held a dragon devoured one of the Vestal Virgins every year on 1 January. The Church was in the care of Greek monks who may well be responsible for what Righetti sees as the 'Byzantine feel' to the antiphons of Lauds and Vespers.

Adolf Adam treats this movement in a more nuanced way, seeing the growing popularity in Rome of the two Byzantine feasts of Annunciation and Assumption as overshadowing the 1 January celebration. He notes that the Circumcision of the Lord does not in fact come to be celebrated in Rome until the thirteenth–fourteenth centuries, and then with a decidedly Marian emphasis. Lastly, Adam regrets that no mention is made of 1 January being the start of the civil year.[22] Annibale Bugnini notes the debate over 1 January in his account of the reform of the calendar:

> The liturgy of January 1 was always a composite liturgy, that is, various rites had been combined on that day: the Motherhood of Mary, the octave of Christmas, the Circumcision, the Name of Jesus, New Year's Day, day of peace. The liturgical expression of all these commemorations could not be but composite and unparalleled in the liturgical year. All the themes of the day found benevolent supporters in the Consilium. It was agreed that the Gallican theme of the Circumcision should be completely eliminated. The Name of Jesus is recalled in the gospel for the octave of Christmas; it was thought that the prayer of the faithful should be used for recalling New Year's Day, although some of the Fathers would have like

to see it mentioned in the texts of the Mass. The view prevailed that January 1 should be once again the feast of the Motherhood of Mary, which goes back to the origins of the Roman liturgy and links Rome with the East, where on December 26 'Our Lady is congratulated' (Mansourati, A Syrian Archbishop living in Rome). In the texts of the Mass, too, the Marian feast is given primacy, although other themes are mentioned.[23]

In a little commented upon 1994 article, the chant scholar Jacques-Marie Guilmard challenges the existence of an ancient Marian feast on 1 January in Rome.[24] Guilmard argues that the hypothesis of Botte needs serious revision in the light of developments in the historical study of liturgical books, and especially in the growing understanding of the relationship between Old Roman and Gregorian chant.

For Guilmard, Gregorian chant is Gallican (indeed for him the Marian feast of 1 January is a Gallican misreading of an earlier Roman source) and it cannot be used as a means of establishing the shape of the Roman liturgical calendar. He also questions Botte's quick dismissal of the confusion in some of the manuscripts between Mary and Martina, an early patroness of Rome celebrated on 1 January. Her feast day was later moved to the end of January. Guilmard usefully points out that in speaking of a liturgical feast, one must distinguish between a Mass and a Mass with an Office. When coming to study a Roman Mass formulary one must clearly distinguish between what is a local Mass, a stational Mass (which presumably gathered people from beyond the immediate locality), and a Mass that was celebrated across the city of Rome. A similar pattern exists for an Office. Following an attentive examination of the claims of Botte and Chavasse, Guilmard concludes that there was no religious feast, no city wide Mass, Marian celebration, nor even preparatory period for a Marian feast to be found on 1 January.

Looking at the chant evidence, he notes that there is no Old Roman chant for a Mass on 1 January and that it is in Gaul that the Mass chants are Marian. For Guilmard, this new feast of Mary on 1 January is the result of a liturgical mistake, the inspiration of which is to be found in eighth-century Gaul. It is surprising to find a euchological formulary without something similar for chant, but this may be more to do with how we expect liturgical books to be complete ensembles without inner contradictions, something which does not always exist even in our current liturgical books. One finds a Gregorian Mass, he speculates, because the Frankish composers of the liturgy found a prayer and a station in their Roman source material, the Gregorian Sacramentary. This led them to create a repertory of Marian chant. Guilmard holds that the earliest feast of the Virgin Mary in Rome is the Assumption.

In the light of this study I would argue that the action of Paul VI may well be a case of the reform (or rather than reform, it may have been more a new intuition about an ancient truth, or even a scholarly hypothesis advanced by an influential liturgical consultor) becoming prayer. If the divine maternity is understood as the foundation of the cult of the Church in regard to the Virgin Mary, the question emerges as to how it is understood in terms of teaching and, for our purposes, praying. The characteristics of the divine maternity as traced in recent magisterial teaching have found their way into the euchology of the liturgy with words like:

> *predestined,* found in the bull of Pius IX, *Ineffabilis Deus* (1854) and taken up in LG 56 and 61. It is found liturgically in a hymn for the 22 August, celebrating the Queenship of Mary;

> *saving:* this characteristic of the divine maternity of Mary is read often in conjunction with Genesis 3:14-15. John Paul II took up the title *Mater Redemptoris* from LG 53, 55, and 61, and used it right throughout his pontificate. The title is used throughout the Roman liturgy both in texts for the Liturgy of the Hours and for the celebration of the Eucharist;

virginal: this particular characteristic has links with the typologies of Adam – Christ; Eve – Mary and the Church as Virgin and Mother – a theme of LG 63 and 64.

Other characteristics of the divine maternity of Mary are its humanness or even fleshiness (that is a free and responsible action of Mary); and its spousal dimension, one that is found especially from the third century onwards in patristic commentaries on Psalm 18 (19) especially on v. 6. There are also Trinitarian, eschatological and singular (it is a unique event)[25] dimensions to the divine maternity.

Conclusion

This brief survey of some Conciliar and post-Conciliar texts views the divine maternity of Mary as the fundamental principle and foundation of the liturgical cult to the Virgin Mary, and it may well be the source of piety towards her. However, the divine maternity of Mary is not the only reason for honouring her in the liturgy. As SC 103 points out, there is also her role in the work of salvation. This has been characterised by the biblical title of *Mater Domini,* the patristic use of *Nova Eva,* or in recent magisterial writings, *Socia Redemptoris.* In the desire to establish a liturgical celebration at the start of the year to honour that intuition, the reading of the past may well have been forced or over emphasised.

Notes

1. Produced annually by Veritas Publications, Dublin.
2. A recent discussion can be found in Paul F. Bradshaw and Maxwell E. Johnson, *The Origins of Feasts, Fasts and Seasons in Early Christianity* (London: SPCK, 2011), 196–214.
3. See Ignazio M. Calabuig, 'The Liturgical Cult of Mary in the East and West', *Handbook for Liturgical Studies,* Vol. V, *Liturgical Space and Time,* Anscar Chupungco, ed. (Collegeville, MN: Liturgical Press, 2000), 244: 'The canons of Ephesus were directly Christological both in scope and in intent. Nevertheless, scholars recognize that the declarations of Ephesus are extremely important in Mariology and see in them one of the most important factors in the development of Marian piety'. Interestingly though, Calabuig

argues that the establishment of the feast of Christmas a hundred years previously had a greater liturgical influence. Bradshaw and Johnson have also argued that approaches to Ephesus need to be much more nuanced than they have been in the past: see Bradshaw and Johnson, *The Origins of Feasts, Fasts and Seasons*, 212: 'Devotion to and liturgical celebration of Mary *Theotokos* did not spring out of thin air or somehow fall out of heaven in a tin box in the context or aftermath of the Council of Ephesus. Nor did it begin to spread only after that council. Rather, such devotion is rooted in developing piety and devotion from at least the third century'. Helpful on the wider social context of the Council is the study of Miri Rubin, *Mother of God. A History of the Virgin Mary* (London: Penguin, 2010), esp. 43–9.

4. Calabuig, 'The Liturgical Cult of Mary in the East and West', 220.
5. St Augustine, *De S. Virginitate*, 6 (PL 40: 399).
6. Paul VI, Apostolic Exhortation, *Signum magnum*, on the necessity of Veneration and Imitation of the Blessed Virgin Mary, Mother of the Church and Exemplar of all Virtues, 13 May 1967. Hereafter SM.
7. Paul VI, Apostolic Exhortation, *Marialis cultus*, for the Right Ordering and Development of Devotion to the Blessed Virgin Mary, 2 February 1974. Hereafter MC.
8. This article is one of the many in MC that shows that this document was written in Italian and that in various places the Latin version is inexact. Here the Italian reads 'divenuta, per opera dello Spirito, madre del Verbo incarnato' and is translated into Latin as 'Spiritus Sancti virtute matris effectae', omitting mention of the Incarnate Word.
9. See AAS 61 (1969), 222–6.
10. The collect is from the current Eucharistic liturgy of the day and is found in the eight century Greogrian Sacramentary under the title, 'Mense ianuario in octabas domini ad sanctam mariam ad martyres'. The revised formulary adds in the words 'Filium tuum', not found in the last line in the Gregorian version, which simply reads, 'per quam meruimus auctorem vitae suscipere'. This prayer is found as no. 82 in the critical edition of the Hadrian (Gregorian) Sacramentary by Jean Deshusses, *Le Sacramentaire Grégorien* (Fribourg: Éditions Universitaires, 1982).
11. As will be seen further on, this level of importance reflects the view of Bernard Botte and others who have claimed that this feast day is an ancient celebration of the city of Rome, a claim which influenced the adoption by Paul VI and by the revised Roman Calendar. There are significant objections to this historical reconstruction that deserve further study.

12. See Calabuig, 'The Liturgical Cult of Mary in the East and West', 243–4.
13. See Bernard Botte, 'La première fête mariale de la liturgie romaine', *Ephemerides Liturgicae* 47 (1933), 425–30. Patrick Regan has summarised the argument of Botte as follows: 'January 1 was originally set aside at Rome to honour the Mother of God and in fact for a long time was the only feast of Mary. In the course of the seventh century the Roman Church adopted other Marian feasts that had originated elsewhere – Assumption, Nativity, Annunciation, and Purification. These had greater popular appeal and quickly gained ascendancy over the older generic festival of the Virgin Mother, allowing it to be eclipsed by the octave of Christmas except for the mention of Mary in the collect and post-Communion, but not in the secret'. See Patrick Regan, *Advent to Pentecost. Comparing the Seasons in the Ordinary and Extraordinary Forms of the Roman Rite* (Collegeville, MN: The Liturgical Press, 2012), 59. The feast was quickly moved aside in favour of the Gallican feast of *In circumcisione Domini*. For an account of the feast of the Circumcision of the Lord and its development and disappearance, see Arnaud Join-Lambert, 'La Disparition de la fête liturgique de la Circoncision du Seigneur: une question historico-théologique complexe', *Ephemerides Liturgicae* 127 (2013), 307–27.

   Rina Avner in recent article, which also includes the material evidence found on the archaeological site, has noted that the Theotokos was celebrated on August 15 in Jerusalem: 'However, in accordance with the Armenian lectionary, the Kathisma was the only strictly Marian *locus sanctus* devoted solely to the figure of Mary, as the Theotokos, and it was not a *locus sanctus* shared with the figure of Christ. Furthermore, the Armenian lectionary indicates that the feast of the Theotokos was initially celebrated in the Kathisma on 15 August, a date which was later moved to 13 August (a fact recorded in the Gregorian lectionary). Moreover, the central theme of the celebration was the glorification of the Theotokos, focusing on Mary's virginal motherhood, as most scholars have observed'. See Rina Avner, 'The Initial Tradition of the Theotokos at the Kathisma: Earliest Celebrations and the Calendar', *The Cult of the Mother of God in Byzantium: Texts and Images*, Leslie Brubaker and Mary Cunningham, eds (Farnham: Ashgate, 2011), 9–29, at 19.
14. Patrick Regan, drawing on the work of Placid Bruylants, notes that: 'In all the early sacramentaries January 1 bears the title *Octava Domini*, "Octave of the Lord". The first printed edition of the *Roman Missal* in 1474 supplies reference to the nativity, expanding the title to "Octave of the Nativity of the Lord." Only in 1570 does

the first typical edition of the Missal of Pius V, or Tridentine Missal, place *In die Circumcisione* in front of the existing title. The 1962 Missal, however, removes this phrase leaving only "Octave of the Nativity of the Lord"'. See Regan, *Advent to Pentecost*, 58.

15. For a useful summary on the shift from the Common of Virgins to the celebration of the Virgin Mary, see Killian McDonnell, 'The Marian Liturgical Tradition', *Between Memory and Hope. Readings on the Liturgical Year*, Maxwell Johnson, ed. (Collegeville, MN: Liturgical Press, 2000), 385.

16. Joseph Beran and Bernard Botte, 'A propositio della prima festa mariale della liturgia romana', *Ephemerides Liturgicae* 49 (1935): 261–4.

17. See Bernardo Opfermann, 'Un frammento liturgico di Fulda del IX secolo', *Ephemerides Liturgicae* 50 (1936): 207–23. On p. 209 he notes regarding the article of Botte: '... pensa che questa sia la più antica festa della B. Vergine nella liturgia romana e che solo un copista l'abbia trasformatata in Martina. Sembra tuttavia che il caso sia più complicato in quanto in molti calendari, martirologi e altri manoscritti romani dall'ottavo secolo in poi troviamo sempre santa Martina al primo gennaio. Questa circostanza rende necessaria una speciale indagine perché l'ipotesi di B. Botte non coincide coi fatti. É strano che la designazione "Octava Domini" si trovi nel nostro frammento in mezzo al succedersi delle domeniche del tempo dopo l'Epifania'. Opfermann goes onto note that the chant texts indicated in this Fulda manuscript are different to the other antiphonaries and their so called marian texts.

18. In his study of Roman calendars Pierre Jounel notes that a local Roman cult of St. Martina existed and was introduced into Rome by Pope Donus (676–678), who dedicated a church in her honour in the Roman Forum, located in or near the Senate house. As the Senate house was placed under the patronage of St Hadrian fifty years later, and given the nearness of the two basilicas, Martina became the wife of Hadrian! Some authors place the small church dedicated to her on the site of the temple dedicated to Mars Ultor or in the ruins of the *secretarium senatus*. See Pierre Jounel, *Les calendriers des Saints dans les Basiliques du Latran et du Vatican au douzième siècle* (Rome: École Française de Rome, 1977), 211. A perusal of several of the various calendars contained in this study of Jounel confirms Opfermann's affirmation that Martina appears in several of these calendars.

　　Mary Schaefer notes that it was Donus or one of his predecessors, Honorius I (625–638), who was responsible for converting the Senate House into a church on the discovery of her supposed body, see Mary M. Schaefer, *Women in Pastoral Office: The Story of St. Prassede* (New York: Oxford University Press, 2013), 317, n. 9; also Andrew J. Ekonomou, *Byzantine Rome and the Greek Pope* (Lanham, MD: Lexington Books, 2007), 254; and Jörg Martin Merz, 'Saint Martina Refuses to Adore the Idols: Pietro da Cortona's Painting at Princeton in Context', *Record of the Art Museum, Princeton University* 62 (2003): 84–104. The Church of St Hadrian became the starting point for the public processions held on the four Marian feast days and established in Rome by the seventh century; see Bradshaw and Johnson, *The Origins of Feasts, Fasts and Seasons*, 212.

19. See Antoine Chavasse, *Le sacramentaire gélasien (Vaticanus Reginensis 316): Sacramentaire presbytéral en usage dans les titres romains au VIIe siècle* (Tournai: Desclée 1958), 318. The Gelasian sacramentary is a liturgical book for use by presbyters in the *tituli* of the Church of Rome, unlike the Georgian sacramentary which reflects the city's episcopal usages.

20. See Georges Frénaud, 'Le culte de Notre Dame dans l'ancienne liturgie latine', *Maria: Études sur la sainte Vierge*, Vol. VI, Hubert du Manoir de Juaye, ed. (Paris: Beauchesne, 1961), 157–211.

21. See Mario Righetti, *Manuale di storia liturgica*, Vol. II, *L'anno liturgico* (Milano: Editrice Ancora, 1969), 93.

22. See Adolf Adam, *The Liturgical Year: Its History and Its Meaning after the Reform of the Liturgy* (Collegeville, MN: Liturgical Press, 1990), 139–41. Similar sentiments have been expressed by others: 'As revised after the Second Vatican Council, the formulary for the eucharistic celebration on January 1 is unassailable from a historical and theological viewpoint and is an advance over its predecessor, which repeated much of the Christmas Masses. Its shortcoming is that apart from the invocation just citied [the solemn blessing] and a few allusions and hints elsewhere, it fails to express openly and directly that this is New Year's.' Regan, *Advent to Pentecost*, 62.

23. Annibale Bugnini, *The Reform of the Liturgy 1948–1975* (Collegeville, MN: Liturgical Press, 1990), 306–7, n. 5. An account of the discussions can also be found in Lauren Pristas, *The Collects of the Roman Missals* (London: Bloomsbury, 2013), 63–5.

Since the appearance of the 2002 edition of the *Roman Missal*, the commemoration of the Most Holy Name of Jesus had been moved to January 3, which is when it is celebrated today as an optional memorial. The celebration of the Most Holy Name of Jesus on the Sunday between 2–5 January (and 2 January when there is not Sunday falling between these dates) can be traced to the *motu proprio* of Pius X, *Abhinc duos annos* (1913). Its celebration had been extended to the whole Church by Innocent XIII in 1721 and celebrated on the Second Sunday after the Epiphany. A useful study on the origins and development of this liturgical memorial can be found in Richard W. Pfaff, *New Liturgical Feasts in Later Medieval England* (Oxford: Clarendon Press, 1970) 62–83.

There seems to have been some kind of a Marian feast day on 26 December in fifth-century Constantinople and, as noted by Bugnini, the Syrian Churches celebrate the same day as a congratulations to the Mother of God: see Bradshaw and Johnson, *The Origins of Feasts, Fasts and Seasons*, 210.

24. Jacques-Marie Guilmard, 'Une antique fête au 1er Janvier dans la ville de Rome?', *Ecclesia Orans* 11 (1994): 25–67. One of the few references to his article can be found in Margot Fassler, 'The First Marian Feast in Jerusalem and Constantinople: Chant Texts, Readings, and Homiletic Literature', in *The Study of Medieval Chant. Paths and Bridges, East and West*, Peter Jeffrey, ed. (Woodbridge: Boydell and Brewer, 2001), 25–87, at 27. While outside the scope of this article, Guilmard's critique of the work of Chavasse is enlightening and requires attention from liturgical historians. Scholarship on Roman and the later mixed Franco-Germanic-Roman liturgical books in the Carolingian world requires serious collaboration with chant scholars and musicologists working on similar material. These liturgical books may well use Roman material but that they are being copied and used in a Frankish Church is sometimes forgotten by liturgical scholars. Helpful in this regard is the important contribution of James McKinnon, 'Antoine Chavasse and the dating of early chant', *Plainsong and Medieval Music* 1 (1992): 123–47. Yitzhak Hen has also noted that Chavasse's findings are not universally accepted; see Yitzhak Hen, 'The Liturgy of the Bobbio Missal', in *The Bobbio Missal. Liturgy and Religious Culture in Merovingian Gaul*, Yitzhak Hen and Rob Meens, eds. (Cambridge: Cambridge University Press, 2009), 145, n. 36.

25. The third antiphon for Lauds on 1 January notes that 'Genuit puerpera Regem, cui nomen aeternum, et gaudia matris habens cum virinitatis honore (or pudore); nec primam similem visa est nec habere sequentem'. 'One in childbirth has borne a King, whose name is eternal, having the joy of a mother with the chastity of virginity; she seemed to have neither a first similar nor one following'. As Hesbert has pointed out, this antiphon, based on a poem of Sedulius, was once used for Lauds on Christmas Day.

IMPLICATIONS
FOR BELIEF

DOES THE REFORM OF THE REFORM HAVE A FUTURE?

꙳ ꙳ ꙳

JOHN F. BALDOVIN SJ

Resistance to the post-Vatican II reform of the Roman Catholic liturgy began within months of the promulgation of *Sacrosanctum concilium*, the Council's Constitution on the Sacred Liturgy. The Constitution itself had received final approval on 4 December 1963, but like any document of the sort it contained only general directives and policies. Particular reforms had to be carried on by an ecclesiastical organ suited to the task. Instead of giving this task to the Congregation of Rites, Pope Paul VI decided to create a new commission, the *Consilium* for the Implementation of the Constitution, headed by a non-curial Cardinal, Giacomo Lercaro of Bologna, with the assistance of a long-time official and expert in liturgical matters, Fr (later Archbishop) Annibale Bugnini CM. The first Instruction on Carrying out the Liturgical Constitution (*Inter oecumenici*) was issued on 26 September 1964, less than a year after the Constitution itself.[1]

It is the aim of this essay to trace the development of resistance to the reform of the liturgy, and especially as it was characterised by a loosely organised group calling itself the 'Reform of the Reform', to discuss the pros and cons of its proposals and finally to assess its future.

Beginnings of Opposition to the Post-Vatican II Liturgical Reform
The Constitution on the Sacred Liturgy was approved by a vote

of two thousand one hundred and forty-seven to four. The tiny opposition to the Constitution was later led by Archbishop Marcel Lefebvre CSSp, one of the Council Fathers. It became a movement under the aegis of his Society of St Pius X.[2] Lefebvre and his followers were opposed to the Constitution itself and so will not be the focus of this essay. The opposition we are dealing with here reacted to the subsequent reform. Many of the vigorous opponents of that reform initially greeted the Constitution with approval and even enthusiasm. Among them were two German theologians who subsequently became vigorous opponents, Mgr Klaus Gamber and Joseph (later Cardinal and then Pope Benedict XVI) Ratzinger.[3] Both of these scholars understood that the pre-Vatican II liturgy was in need of even more reform than had been carried out in the 1950s under Pope Pius XII. They knew that liturgy is not a fossil but a living organism. But they were horrified at the chaos unleashed by the reform in the late 1960s. I think it fair to say that the rash experimentation that followed the Constitution was (if somewhat understandable after centuries of rigidity) unfortunate.

At the same time both Gamber and Ratzinger judged that the *Consilium* had gone well beyond its brief in applying the principles of *Sacrosanctum concilium*. One of the first and most significant changes that was mandated in the Instruction *Inter oecumenici* of 1964 was the establishment of free standing altars in churches which made for the possibility of the celebration of the Eucharist facing the people (*versus populum*). In a book on the Reform of the Roman Liturgy published in 1979 and translated into Italian, French and English, Gamber laid out his objections to this decision.[4] One should note that Cardinal Joseph Ratzinger wrote a preface to the French edition and his own writings on the subject of the position of the celebrant at the altar owe a great deal to Gamber.

Gamber points out the novelty of thinking that there was ever a time that priests regularly faced the people as a matter of principle. The priest faced eastward, toward the rising sun and the Coming Lord, and that position depended on the orientation of the church building. For example, at St Mary Major and St Peter's in Rome the priest celebrant faced the doors of the church, which were located in the east. In his important work, *The Spirit of the Liturgy*, Ratzinger further comments that a cross or other representation of the Lord was placed on the east wall of churches as a symbol of the eschatological Lord. Eventually he acknowledged that it was unlikely that free-standing altars would be removed and he recommended that a large cross and six candles be placed on altars to ensure that Christ would be the focus of the celebration rather than the priest.[5] For Ratzinger the position of the priest *versus populum* became emblematic of the problem of post-Vatican II liturgical reform since it created a kind of self-enclosed circle by which the assembly celebrates itself rather than worshipping God.

To some extent Ratzinger is correct in pointing out the difficulty of a self-celebratory act of worship. The position of the priest *versus populum* can and does lead to the temptation to make the assembly turn in on itself and (worse) to make the priest into a kind of performer. This is an ongoing problem of the reform and it needs to be faced. On the other hand, the value of the assembly gathered around the Table of the Lord is so important that a great deal would be lost if the Church reverted to the eastward position. A balance needs to be sought, not in the creation of a kind of altar screen by means of cross and candles, but by training priests to be self-effacing in their presiding as well as by a church architecture that coveys both transcendence and communal celebration. In this area, in my opinion, the Reform of the Reform movement opts for much too simple a solution.

The Reform of the Reform

Let us turn now to the heart of the post-Vatican II critique. A major factor that characterises the 'Reform of the Reform' is the claim that the post-Vatican II reform of the liturgy broke so radically with the past that it made it seem like the liturgy was a human construct rather than a divine gift. Ratzinger put it this way:

The liturgical reform, in its concrete realisation, has distanced itself even more from its origin. The result has not been a reanimation, but devastation. In place of the liturgy, fruit of a continual development, they have placed a fabricated liturgy. They have deserted a vital process of growth and becoming in order to substitute a fabrication. They did not want to continue the development, the organic maturing of something living through the centuries, and they replaced it, in the manner of technical production, by a fabrication, a banal product of the moment.[6]

This criticism of the reform liturgy as product rather than gift is underlined by Sven Conrad who submits: 'The reform after the Second Vatican Council for the first time in history subordinated the assessment of the established rites to a theological premise'.[7] For him the result was losing 'the fundament of the Roman tradition – at least in the realm of gestures and rites, as well as the hierarchical understanding'.[8] We shall return to the notion of the gift below.

Ratzinger's very serious criticism of the reform represents many who oppose the new liturgical books and their implementation. Similar to his criticism that Mass *versus populum* creates a closed circle whereby the community celebrates itself rather than the Lord, this critique regards the liturgy as a human product. To some extent this criticism is warranted for the impression given in the aftermath of the Council was that liturgy was up for grabs, the more creative the better.[9] By the time there was a definitive edition of the *Roman Missal* (1970) it must have seemed that the 'official' Roman liturgy was an option among many possibilities. Some of the critics, like James Hitchcock, never seem to have recovered from that period of liturgical anarchy.[10] But others, like Ratzinger and Laszlo Dobszay,[11] regard the 1970 *Roman Missal* itself as much too radical a departure from the pre-Vatican II liturgy. They claim that the *Consilium* rejected the directive of par. 23 of the Liturgy Constitution:

That sound tradition may be retained, and yet the way remain open to legitimate progress careful investigation is always to be made into each part of the liturgy which is to be revised. This investigation should be theological, historical, and pastoral. Also the general laws governing the structure and meaning of the liturgy must be studied in conjunction with the experience derived from recent liturgical reforms and from the indults conceded to various places. Finally, there must be no innovations unless the good of the Church genuinely and certainly requires them; and care must be taken that any new forms adopted should in some way grow organically from forms already existing.

What they neglect to mention, however, is that this statement about continuity must be balanced by the earlier call for significant revision of the liturgy in SC 21:

In order that the Christian people may more certainly derive an abundance of graces from the sacred liturgy, holy Mother Church desires to undertake with great care a general restoration of the liturgy itself. For the liturgy is made up of immutable elements divinely instituted, and of elements subject to change. These not only may but ought to be changed with the passage of time if they have suffered from the intrusion of anything out of harmony with the inner nature of the liturgy or have become unsuited to it. In this restoration, both texts and rites should be drawn up so that they express more clearly the holy things which they signify; the Christian people, so far as possible, should be enabled to understand them with ease and to take part in them fully, actively, and as befits a community.

It seems to me that Ratzinger et al. have rejected the painstaking historical research that led to many of the post-Vatican II reforms as well as the pastoral wisdom that understood that the liturgy must be more accessible to the Christian faithful. For this reason Ratzinger called for a new liturgical movement that would work to reverse the unorganic developments of the post-Vatican II reform.[12] That call was taken up by many including Ratzinger's former student Fr Joseph Fessio SJ and in particular by a blog calling itself 'The New Liturgical Movement', headed by Jeffrey Tucker.[13] This blog devotes itself to promoting traditional sacred music, art and architecture as well as celebration *ad orientem* and what its contributors consider faithful celebrations of the Mass of Paul VI. Often as not, however, contributions focus not on a new liturgical movement at all but on the restoration of the pre-Vatican II Missal of Pius V.

Although proponents of a new liturgical movement differ among themselves as to what authentic Catholic worship faithful to *Sacrosanctum concilium* would look like they tend to support the proclamation of the Word in the vernacular, the addition of new prefaces to the eucharistic prayer,[14] and the introduction of the General Intercessions. On the other hand, a number of these authors see no good reason for the elimination of the prayers at the foot of the altar, the traditional introits, graduals, offertories, etc. (only in their original form), and the offertory prayers of the Missal of Pius V. They also argue for a single eucharistic prayer, the Roman Canon, in Latin.[15]

The Fate of ICEL

There is a real sense in which the reform of the reform gained an upper hand in the fate of the International Commission on English in the Liturgy. The Commission, consisting ultimately of eleven national episcopal conferences together with fifteen associate conferences, was initiated even before the end of Vatican II since it was clear that few conferences had the resources on their own to undertake the massive project of liturgical translation. As noted by John Wilkins in his fine 2005 *Commonweal* article, ICEL's initial work was completed by 1978.[16] ICEL's translations followed the principles that were laid down in a 1969 document from the Consilium entitled

Comme le prévoit. The translation strategy recommended in that document has often been referred to as 'dynamic equivalence', a strategy which attempts above all to render the sense of an original in a colloquial way. A clear example of this approach can be found in the *Good News Bible*.

Understandably ICEL's translations were done rather quickly and were criticised even by those sympathetic to the reform. Starting with a revision of the *Order of Christian Funerals* in the 1980s the commission produced revised translations, often with a number of original texts; i.e. texts that were not to be found in the Latin typical edition. It had been ICEL's brief to produce such texts in its 1964 charter. The 1973 (1975) edition of the *Sacramentary (Roman Missal)* produced by ICEL had also contained alternative collects for Sundays and major feasts.

As Wilkins ably recounts, the story the 1978 election of Pope John Paul II signalled a shift in the Roman Curia's attitude toward ICEL, overseen by a series of cardinal-prefects of the (renamed) Congregation for Divine Worship and the Discipline of the Sacraments, beginning with Cardinal Paul Augustin Mayer OSB and ending with Cardinal Jorge Medina Estévez. One of the major complaints against ICEL was that it took far too much liberty in translating texts so that they might be gender inclusive. In fact, the 1995 ICEL translation of the Psalter (and Biblical Canticles) went so far as to eliminate many of the gender references to God. By the late 1990s, under Cardinal Medina, it was evident that ICEL's fortunes had shifted. In 1997 ICEL's proposed translation of the 1992 second edition of the Rite of Ordination, which had been approved overwhelmingly by all of the eleven ICEL episcopal conferences, was rejected with a harsh letter from Cardinal Medina enumerating some one hundred and fourteen errors in the translation. This was the beginning of the end, for the following year the new American episcopal representative, Cardinal Francis George, made it quite clear to ICEL's bishops that the Vatican was demanding a change in ICEL's approach to translation.

Finally, the Congregation issued the Fifth Instruction on the Implementation of the Liturgical Reform, a document on translation entitled *Liturgiam authenticam*, on 28 March 2001. Among the provisions of this instruction were ideas that corresponded well to the desires of those who espoused the reform of the reform. For example, translations had to adhere as closely as possible to the words and even the word order of the original (nos 20, 55); translations should adhere to a 'sacred style' which can be valuable precisely because of its difference from ordinary language (nos 27, 47); with regard to the Bible 'a version of the Sacred Scriptures [should] be prepared in accordance with the principles of sound exegesis and of high literary quality, but also with a view to the particular exigencies of liturgical use as regards style, the selection of words, and the selection from among different possible interpretations' (34); 'great caution is to be taken to avoid a wording or style that the Catholic faithful would confuse with the manner of speech of non-Catholic ecclesial communities or of other religions, so that such a factor will not cause them confusion or discomfort' (40); contrary to SC 22 and 36, the Congregation reserves to itself the right to be involved in the translation process (nos 76, 104).[17] A Vatican agency to oversee English language translation (*Vox Clara*) was established to vet the work of ICEL for its 2010 translation of the *Roman Missal*. That translation was widely seen as a triumph for the reform of the reform.[18] The new translation of the Missal represents a low point for many who were involved in promoting the post-Vatican II liturgical reform.[19]

The Future?

To ask a question about the future of the Reform of the Reform is to ask a question about the future of the post-Vatican II reform itself. In my opinion there are some positive aspects to the Reform of the Reform. They have to do not with specific proposals for changing the current liturgy rites but with the spirituality and theology that undergird them.

A number of years ago M. Francis Mannion proposed a helpful taxonomy of approaches to Catholic liturgical reform.[20]

He outlines five agendas. The 'Official Agenda' is the reform of the liturgical books issued by the Vatican and implemented by the International Commission on English in the Liturgy and its counterparts. The 'Restorationist Agenda' favours a reform to the pre-Vatican II liturgy *tout court*. The 'Reform of the Reform Agenda' is dissatisfied with the state of the reform but does not advocate a wholesale return to the pre-Vatican II liturgy, but something more like the state of the liturgy in 1965 (without the priest facing the people). 'Inculturating the Reform' refers to a group who consider the official reform just the beginning of the liturgical reform, which must be thoroughly adapted to various cultures. He associates this agenda with groups like the North American Academy of Liturgy, an interfaith organisation. The final agenda he names 'Recatholicizing the Reform'. This approach is satisfied with the official books. What is lacking, however, is the spiritual and theological assimilation of the revised liturgies. It seems to me that Mannion has a valid point. The reformed rites have been put in place but their spirit has not been inculcated – at least among a very large number of Catholics.

I believe that Joseph Ratzinger/Pope Benedict XVI was correct in insisting on a rediscovery of the vertical dimension of the liturgy.[21] What a number of people today would call a loss of the sense of the sacred I would prefer to call a need for greater reverence. Where I part company with Ratzinger/Benedict and the group that identifies as the 'Reform of the Reform' is in the means to achieve the goal of greater sensitivity to transcendence in the liturgy. We need not return to practices like the *ad orientem* posture of the celebrant or even to insist on kneeling during the eucharistic prayer as to enable a new 'choreography' of the liturgy which emphasises reverence and communal engagement at the same time. We need to practise what (in dealing with textual hermeneutics) Paul Ricoeur called a 'second naïveté' with regard to our worship.[22] Intellectually responsible people simply cannot dispense with the historical-critical method as the traditionalists would have us do. At the same time, the deconstructive element in the historical-critical method is not sufficient to support belief and faithful engagement. Therefore, we must learn to accept our worship ultimately as God's gift even as we understand its symbolic, ritual, historical and theological makeup.

The value of a movement like the Reform of the Reform is that it has helped us to appreciate the need for greater reverence in the liturgy. The disadvantage of this movement is that it has searched for answers in outworn liturgical forms. I do not believe that the Reform of the Reform has much of a future as such. But ongoing liturgical reform is certainly a necessity and will provide a great deal of work and reflection for faithful Catholics for decades to come.

꒐ ꒐ ꒐

Notes

1. A full chronicle of the reform up to 1975 is given in Annibale Bugnini, *The Reform of the Liturgy 1948–1975*, ET by Matthew J. O'Connell (Collegeville, MN: Liturgical Press, 1990). Bugnini discusses the first three Instructions on 825–47. See also Piero Marini, *A Challenging Reform: Realizing the Vision of Liturgical Renewal 1963–1975* (Collegeville, MN: Liturgical Press, 2007) as well as John Baldovin, *Reforming the Liturgy: A Response to the Critics* (Collegeville, MN: Liturgical Press, 2008).

2. A number of groups dedicated to the preservation of the pre-Vatican II liturgy followed, e.g. the Benedictine Monastery of Barroux (France) and the Institute of Christ the Sovereign King.

3. On Gamber's initial enthusiasm, see Manfred Hauke, 'Klaus Gamber: Father of the New Liturgical Movement', in *Benedict XVI and the Sacred Liturgy: Proceedings of the First Fota International Liturgy Conference, 2008*, Neil Roy and Janet Rutherford, eds. (Dublin: Four Courts Press, 2010), 24–69; on Ratzinger's initial response, see Helen Hull Hitchcock, 'Benedict XVI and the "Reform of the Reform"', in Roy and Rutherford, *Benedict XVI and the Sacred Liturgy*, 70–87, esp. 71–2. Here she cites his *Theological Highlights of Vatican II* (New York/Mahwah: Paulist Press, 1966, repr. 2009), 216–63.

4. See Klaus Gamber, *The Reform of the Roman Liturgy: Its Problems and Background* (San Juan Capistrano, CA: Una Voce Press, 1993). Hauke's review of Gamber's work (see note 3, above) provides an

excellent summary. See as well Klaus Gamber, *Liturgie und Kirchenbau: Studien der Geschichte des Messfeier und des Gotteshauses in der Früzeit*, Studia Patristica et Liturgica 6 (Regensburg: Pustet, 1976).

5. See Joseph Ratzinger, *The Spirit of the Liturgy* (San Francisco: Ignatius Press, 2000), 70–3. On this same subject, see Uwe Michael Lang, *Turning Toward the Lord: Orientation in Liturgical Prayer*, ET (San Francisco: Ignatius Press, 2004). This book also has a Foreword by Ratzinger. One might also consult the argument of Stefan Heid, *Kreuz, Jerusalem, Kosmos: Aspekte früchristliche Staurologie* (Münster: Aschendorff, 2001). Heid argues that during prayer Christians all looked, not to the altar, but to an apse mosaic of Christ.

6. Joseph Ratzinger in *Theologisches Revue* 20 (Feb 1990), 103–4.

7. Sven Conrad, 'Renewal of the Liturgy in the Spirit of Tradition: Perspectives with a View towards the Liturgical Developments of the West', *Antiphon* 14 (2010): 122.

8. Conrad, 'Renewal of the Liturgy in the Spirit of Tradition', 123.

9. A good example is Robert Hoey, ed., *The Experimental Liturgy Book* (New York: Herder and Herder, 1969).

10. See James Hitchcock, 'Continuity and Disruption in the Liturgy: A Cultural Approach', *Benedict XVI and the Sacred Liturgy*, Roy and Rutherford, 88–97; also his earlier, *The Recovery of the Sacred* (San Francisco: Ignatius Press, 1974, repr. 1995).

11. See Laszlo Dobszay, *The Bugnini-Liturgy and the Reform of the Reform* (Front Royal, VA: Catholic Church Music Associates, 2003).

12. See Joseph Ratzinger, *Milestones: Memoirs 1927–1977* (San Francisco: Ignatius Press, 1998), 148–9; see also Joseph Murphy, 'Joseph Ratzinger and the Liturgy: A Liturgical Approach', in Roy and Rutherford, *Benedict XVI and the Sacred Liturgy*, 132–55, here at 135.

13. See http://www.newliturgicalmovement.org/ (accessed 28 October 2013).

14 Particularly Benedict XVI (Ratzinger), Post Synodal Apostolic Exhortation, *Sacramentum caritatis* (2007), 48; Joseph Ratzinger, *Feast of Faith: Approaches to a Theology of the Liturgy* (San Francisco: Ignatius Press, 1986), 87; idem., 'Assessment and Future Prospects', in *Looking Again at the Question of the Liturgy with Cardinal Ratzinger. Proceedings of the July 2001 Fontgombault Liturgical Conference*, Alcuin Reid, ed. (Farnborough [UK]: St Michael's Abbey Press, 2003), 145–53, at 153. See also the interesting effort by William Johnston to argue that Ratzinger/Benedict XVI basically favoured the post-Vatican II

reform, 'Pope Benedict XVI on the Postconciliar Reform: An Essay in Interpretation', *Antiphon* 17 (2013), 118–38.

15. The bibliography here is immense. See, for example, Thomas Kocik, *The Reform of the Reform? A Liturgical Debate: Reform or Return* (San Francisco: Ignatius Press, 2003); idem., 'The Reform of the Reform in Broad Context: Re-engaging the Living Tradition', *Antiphon*, 21 (2008): 26–44; Editorial, *Usus Antiquior* 1 (2010), 1–4; Nicola Bux, *Benedict XVI's Reform: Between Innovation and Tradition*, ET (San Francisco: Ignatius Press, 2012); and Alcuin Reid, 'The Reformed Liturgy: A "Cadaver Decomposed"? Louis Bouyer and Liturgical *Ressourcement*', *Antiphon* 16 (2012), 37–51.

16. John Wilkins, 'Lost in Translation: The Bishops, Vatican II and the English Liturgy', *Commonweal* 132 (2005), 12, 14–16, 18–20. The narrative that follows relies heavily on Wilkins' report as well as on the memoirs of ICEL's episcopal chairman during its period of crisis, Maurice Taylor, *Being a Bishop in Scotland* (Dublin: Columba Press, 2006), esp. 131–8.

17. An articulate apologia for *Liturgiam authenticam* can be found in Dennis McManus, 'Translation Theory in *Liturgiam Authenticam*,' in Roy & Rutherford, *Benedict XVI and the Sacred Liturgy*, 116–31.

18. See, for example, www.newliturgicalmovement.org/2009/09/new-english-roman-missal-translation.html#.Um7BliSzBAI; and, www.newliturgicalmovement.org/2011/12/one-month-out-reactions-to-revised.html#.Um7B-ySzBAI (accessed 28 October 2013).

19. In my experience many priest-celebrants are exercising a certain freedom with regard to some of the more awkwardly worded texts.

20. M. Francis Mannion, 'The Catholicity of the Liturgy: Shaping a New Agenda', *Beyond the Prosaic: Renewing the Liturgical Movement*, S. Caldecott, ed. (Edinburgh: T&T Clark, 1998), 11–48.

21. See the fine summary of his thought on this issue in Murphy, 'Joseph Ratzinger and the Liturgy: A Liturgical Approach', *Benedict XVI and the Sacred Liturgy*, Roy and Rutherford, 153–4.

22. See, for example, Paul Ricoeur, *The Rule of Metaphor* (Toronto: University of Toronto Press, 1977).

LITURGY AND THE BOOK OF REVELATION

꙳ ꙳ ꙳

WILFRID J. HARRINGTON OP

Bewilderment, in all likelihood, is the reaction of one who comes, for the first time, to the Book of Revelation.[1] Those scrolls and plagues, those elders and living creatures, the dragon and the beasts – what can it be about? Is there any sense to be made of it? Revelation is not readily understood. Indeed, without some appreciation of its apocalyptic genre, it is wholly puzzling.[2]

In truth, it *is* a thoroughly Christian writing which, despite first impression, carries a message of startling hope.

Revelation opens with a prologue (1:1-3), which is in fact an elaborate title. The author names himself: John – an otherwise unknown Christian prophet, for this apocalyptic *letter* (1:4; 22:21) is firmly characterised as 'prophecy' (1:3; 22:7, 10, 18). He does not, unlike all other apocalyptists, need to resort to pseudonymity in respect of what is a 'revelation of Jesus Christ' with God as the ultimate source (1:1), a revelation which, at the close, will be attested by Christ himself (22:6).

Two figures dominate Revelation: the Almighty One on the heavenly throne, and the Lamb. The One on the throne displays his power in and through the Lamb who was slain. In his manner, John makes the same point as Paul: 'We proclaim Christ crucified ... Christ the power of God and the wisdom of God' (1 Corinthians 1:23-24).[3] So fully is the Lamb the manifestation and the very presence of God that, at the end of all, in the New Jerusalem, in place of a temple is a single throne, 'the throne of God and of the Lamb' (Revelation 22:1).

Revelation is explicitly designated for public reading in a liturgy – most likely, a eucharistic liturgy: 'Blessed is the one who reads aloud, and blessed are those who hear the words of this prophecy and heed what is written there' (1:3).[4] It is designed to be *heard*. Somewhat as with radio drama, the listener assimilates its words imaginatively. Spangled with heavenly liturgies, it maintains a liturgical dimension throughout. John's heavenly liturgies are, surely, echoes of community celebrations of his churches. These songs of heaven are songs of Christians. Not surprisingly then, there is an aura of eucharistic celebration.

Not alone by its liturgical setting, but also through a constant and insistent liturgical interest, Revelation makes its statement on the centrality of worship in Christian life. So central, indeed, is worship that the inimical 'inhabitants of the earth' are also intent on worship: they are worshippers of the 'Beast' (Rome, as instrument of Satan). John is making a thoroughly biblical point: humans, as creatures, are subject to some lordship. One must serve God or Mammon, whatever shape Mammon may assume. The choice is of fundamental importance. John is sure that idolatry corrupts the created order. Worship of God and of the Lamb prepares for and hastens the coming of the new heaven and new earth where righteousness dwells.

Yet, Revelation does *not* figure largely in the liturgical prayer of the contemporary Church. In the Lectionary it provides the second readings for Sundays Week Two to Seven of Easter in Year C.[5] In the Divine Office it supplies canticles for Evening Prayer.[6] In view of the four-week breviary cycle, these passages are familiar. But there are several other canticles in Revelation. Here we look at some of the relevant texts. One would suggest that reform of liturgy might well prompt us to reconsider our neglect of the liturgical riches of Revelation.

Canticles
4:8-11

John, introduced to heaven (4:1), had a vision of a throne and One seated on it: the Lord God Almighty. The 'twenty-four elders' around the throne (v. 4) are kings, seated on thrones and wearing crowns. Throughout Revelation they have a cultic role (4:9-10; 5:8-11; 11:16-18; 19:4). They fittingly represent the people of God, that 'royal house of priests' (1:6). They are heavenly counterparts of the earthly Church. The 'four living creatures' (4:6) symbolise the created cosmos. The canticle of v. 8, based on Isaiah, is the unceasing song of nature in praise of its Creator:

> Holy, holy, holy is the Lord God Almighty,
> who was, and is, and is to come!

Human minds and tongues give shape and voice to that praise of animate and inanimate creation as the twenty-four elder sing:

> Worthy are you, our Lord and God
> to receive glory and honour and power;
> for you created all things;
> by your will they were created and came into being! (v. 11)

5:8-14

Chapter 5 of Revelation depicts a transfer of power. God hands over to the Lamb (the crucified and risen Christ) a sealed scroll – since the Lamb alone has been found worthy to open it and reveal God's saving purpose for humankind. The living creatures and the twenty-four elders whom we had heard worship God (4:8-10) here worship the Lamb. In keeping with their cultic function, the elders hold harps and censers. They exercise the priestly office of mediation, offering the prayers of the faithful to God. Their 'new song' celebrates the redemption wrought by Christ:

You are worthy to take the scroll and break its seals.
for you were slain
and by your blood you bought for God
those of every tribe, tongue, people and nation;
you have made them a royal house of priests for our God,
and they shall reign on earth. (vv. 9-10)

This doxology addressed to the Lamb is more fulsome than that earlier addressed to the Creator (4:11). Finally, the whole of creation, without exception, joins in the great canticle:

Blessing and honour, glory and might,
to the One seated on the throne and to the Lamb
for ever and ever! (v. 13)

John *heard* the sound of the great acclamation. To it the four living creatures, heavenly representatives of the created universe, give their 'Amen' (v. 14) – and the elders worship as in 4:9-10.

7:9-12

Before the last of the first series of seven plagues (8:1),[7] the servants of God were signed with the seal of the living God, one hundred and forty-four thousand of them (7:1-8). That plague of 8:1 will unleash the plagues of Trumpets (8:6–11:19), which are modelled on the plagues of Egypt. The sealing of the elect recalls the immunity of the Israelites to the plagues that struck the Egyptians. John's unexpected twist here is that God's servants will be sealed for protection *through* the great tribulation (not preserved from it). They achieve their victory, yes, but in the only Christian manner: 'love of life did not bring them to shrink from death' (12:11). The vast throng – 'I looked, and there was a vast throng, which no one could count, from all nations and tribes and peoples and tongues, standing before the throne and the Lamb, robed in white and with palm branches in their hands' (v. 9) – is not a group distinct from the one hundred and forty-four thousand of 7:4-8. It is the same group, now viewed beyond the great tribulation: the Church triumphant in heaven. They stand before God and Lamb celebrating a heavenly feast of Tabernacles – the most joyous of Jewish feasts. They chant:

> Victory to our God who sits on the throne.
> and to the Lamb! (v. 10)

The vision is proleptic: it anticipates the future destiny of those now faithfully enduring tribulation. The angels, the countless host of 5:11, join in the heavenly liturgy, first by adding their Amen to the prayer of the faithful, and then with their own doxology:

> Amen! Praise, glory and wisdom
> thanksgiving and honour, power and might,
> to our God for ever and ever! Amen. (v. 12)

8:3-4

In 8:3-4 an angel officiates as priest in the heavenly temple and offers incense at the altar:

> An angel came and stood at the altar, holding a golden censer. He was given much incense to offer with the prayers of all God's people on the golden altar before the throne, and the smoke of the incense went up before God with the people's prayers from the angel's hand.

The prayers of the saints are the prayers of the martyrs of 6:9-10 who 'had been slaughtered for the word of God and for the testimony they bore'. While Revelation never directly refers to the worship of the earthly Church, Christians would recognise their prayers in the incense rising before the heavenly throne.

15:2-4

The victors appear again in the vision of 15:1-14. They have been 'victorious against the beast' (Rome). They have won the victory in the same manner as 'the Lamb who was slain' (5:6). Though termed 'song of Moses' (v. 3) their song, unlike the song of Exodus 15:1-18, is not one of triumph over enemies; it is solely praise of God:

> Great and marvellous are your works,
> Lord God Almighty!
> Just and true are your ways,
> O king of the nations!
> Who shall not fear you, Lord,
> and do homage to your name?
> for you alone are holy.
> All nations will come
> and worship before you,
> for your righteous deeds have been revealed. (vv. 3-4)

This song holds out hope that the nations, in view of the righteous deeds of the Lord, will fear him – that is, acknowledge him – and render him homage and worship. In other words, God is King of the nations, and the nations will come to acknowledge him as their King.[8]

19:6-8

In 19:1-10 a heavenly liturgy anticipates the vindication of God's people. A voice from the throne (19:5) summons the servants of God to praise the Lord. The throng of victors takes up the hymn:

> Hallelujah!
> For the Lord God the Almighty has entered on his reign.
> Let us rejoice and be glad and give glory to him,
> for the marriage of the Lamb has come.
> His bride has made herself ready,
> And it is granted her to attire herself in fine linen
> Shining and clean –
> for the fine linen is the righteous deeds of God's people.
> (vv. 6-8)

The victors rejoice that their often repeated prayer – 'Your kingdom come' – has been answered: the Lord reigns! They are invited guests at the marriage feast of the Lamb. His bride has made herself ready – but her wedding gown is his gift. And yet it is woven of the righteous deeds of God's people. Thus, it appears that while the bride is the Church, the wedding guests are the members of the Church, and their deeds are her bridal dress. The seeming jumble of John's imagery here holds a salutary reminder. He reminds us that the Church has no existence apart from the living community (a living community, too, beyond death) of Christian men and women. It is we, all of us together, who form the bride of Christ; it is our righteous deeds that clothe her. The Church is not some entity 'out there' or 'up there'! It is not represented by a hierarchy. Leaders in the Church have a servant role, not a representative role (see Mark 9:35; 10:42-35). It is, simply, the people of God – 'all who fear him, small and great' (19:5).

The New Jerusalem
21:9–22:5

The book closes with a magnificent vision of the New Jerusalem, the heavenly city, the veritable kingdom of God. John surpasses himself in his surrealistic painting of this New Jerusalem. The twelve gates of the city are inscribed with the names of the twelve tribes of Israel; its twelve foundation-stones bear the names of the twelve apostles of the Lamb (21:12, 14). John maintains the continuity of the Christian Church with Israel. In vv. 24–26 it is declared that the gates remain always open, inviting the entry of the nations. All traffic is *into* the city (vv. 24–27).

We might expect the glowing description of the city to be followed by a particularly striking description of the temple (the temple was the glory of the earthly Jerusalem). Instead, a brilliant touch, we learn that there is no temple, nor any need of one: God himself dwells there with the Lamb. Now indeed, 'God's dwelling is with humankind' (21:3) and the glory of his presence pervades the whole city (vv. 11, 18). God and Lamb reign indeed, but not in the formality of a cultic setting. They dwell in the midst of their people. Consistently, the waters which in Ezekiel 47 (the model text) flow from the temple, here flow from 'the throne of God and of the Lamb' (22:1). It is the river of the first paradise, and the tree of life is found again (Genesis 2:9-10). There the elect will look upon the face of God and will reign for ever and ever.

Most evocative is John's picture of the nations streaming into the New Jerusalem (vv. 24–26). They bring into it splendour and wealth – all that is lovely and worthy in human achievement. Though city of God, it is their city, the true home of humankind. God's saving purpose prevails. John's glowing description is not only encouragement: it is challenge. We are to look, beyond evil, to what is good in our world. We are to turn with confidence to the God who, though the One seated on the throne, is the gracious God who wipes away every tear.

Epilogue

An epilogue (21:6-20) gives the closing words of the angel, the seer and the Lord. Inspired by the Spirit, the Church ('the bride') prays its *marana tha*, 'Our Lord, Come!'. The Church (the earthly Church) responds with eager joy to the Lord's announcement of his coming. The prayer is to be caught up by every hearer of the book (see 1:3); the Lord looks for the response of the individual Christian (see 3:20-21). For the Church is no vague personification: it *is* a living organism, of living men and women. Attention turns to the community: 'the one who is thirsty' is invited to come to Christ. In 3:20 there is a eucharistic flavour to the promise of a meal shared by Christ and Christian, and also a look to the 'marriage feast of the Lamb' (19:9): 'Here I stand knocking at the door; if anyone hears my voice and opens the door, I will come in and dine with such a one and that one with me'. It would seem that the eucharistic interest is present here too in this offer of the water of life. The invitation of Spirit and bride blends into an invitation to eucharistic fellowship.

'Behold, I am coming soon!' (vv. 12, 20). It is an assurance that John's hearers/readers longed to hear. Life was not easy for them in the present. John's prospect of imminent tribulation augured much tougher times ahead. His promise to victors was all very well; the reality was that 'conquering' meant dying! It was comforting to look eagerly to the One who was coming soon 'bringing his reward with him'. He was the one who had conquered by laying down his life. They, if they were faithful, would share his victory and his triumph. They look to his coming.

In the meantime, as they celebrate their Eucharist, they have his presence with them. They have the reminder of his victory and the assurance of his promise: 'As often as you eat this bread and drink the cup, you proclaim the Lord's death until he comes' (1 Corinthians 11:26). They do not have to wait, bereft, for his final coming. Yet, they long. 'My desire is to depart and be with Christ, for that is far better' (Philippians 1:23). It is in their going to him that the Lord will come to them. *Marana tha!*

Perhaps it is in our eucharistic celebration that Revelation might challenge us. It was on the night on which he was delivered up that the Lord took, gave thanks, and broke bread: 'This is my body which is for you'. He is the Lamb who was slain. His death is victory for all. The Victim is the Victor. That is the 'remembrance' of the Eucharist. That is the message of Revelation. Behind the surreal visions of the plagues is the Lamb. And, with the Lamb is the One on the throne – the Father of our Lord Jesus Christ. 'The grace of the Lord Jesus be with all' (22:21). This 'revelation of Jesus Christ' (1:1) is a word of grace. 'Blessed is the one who hears' (1:3), for these words are trustworthy and true (22:6).

Notes

1. The contribution of Fr Patrick Jones to renewal of liturgy in Ireland has been tireless and very significant. My association with him has been in his role of Director of the National Centre for Liturgy. I have lectured at the Centre over many years, first in Carlow, then in Maynooth. I have enjoyed working with Paddy and I value his friendship. An invitation to contribute to this *festschrift* is a privilege.
2. 'Apocalypse', from the Greek *apocalypsis* ('revelation') designates a type of Jewish literature which flourished from about 200 BCE to 100 CE. As a literary form it is presented as a revelation, or series of revelations, of heavenly secrets made to a seer and conveyed in highly symbolic imagery. It is a crisis literature. The biblical

apocalypses are the book of Daniel (more precisely, Daniel 7–12) and the Revelation of John. Apocalypticism is the worldview of an apocalyptic movement. In this view it is taken for granted that a supernatural world stands above our earthly world. That heavenly world is the 'real' world. There is a twofold dualism: vertical, the world above and our world, and horizontal, our age and the Age to come. There is always a definitive eschatological judgement: the final clash between good and evil, issuing in the total victory of God and the end of evil. Apocalyptic ideas pervade the New Testament.

Revelation addresses a group of seven Christian communities in the late first-century CE Roman province of Asia (the western part of modern Turkey). The author, John, knows these churches thoroughly, and in his estimation, all is not well (chapters 2–3). He perceived a radical incompatibility between the Roman world of his day and the Gospel message. In his dualistic view, the perennial conflict between good and evil was being played out between Rome and the Church. There were those Christians who did not share his assessment, who sought accommodation. However, in his radical view, there was no room for compromise.

John had come to regard Rome as evil through and through. The Empire was instrument of the Dragon – Satan – implacable foe of the Lamb (Christ) and his followers. He was upset that some Christians did not see as clearly as he. He set out, then, to focus their attention on the true situation as he viewed it. He did so by demonizing Rome, by painting it in luridly negative colours. He sought to motivate his readers (hearers) to reject Rome wholly. Their rejection will not be marked by violence; but it will be total. He had no illusion about the outcome. Rome will respond; there will be tribulation. John's was a minority position. First-century Christians, by and large, had learned to live with, and within the Roman system. John stands as a challenge: a reminder, then and now, that the demands of Caesar may be in conflict with the claims of God.

For further reading, see, M. Eugene Boring, *Revelation: Interpretation* (Louisville: John Knox, 1989); G.B. Caird, *The Revelation of St John the Divine* (London: A & C Black, 1966); Adela Y. Collins, *The Apocalypse* (Wilmington, DE: M. Glazier, 1979); Adela Y. Collins, *Crisis and Catharsis: The Power of the Apocalypse* (Philadelphia: Westminster, 1984); Wilfrid J. Harrington, *Revelation. Sacra Pagina* (Collegeville, MN: Liturgical Press, 1993); Wilfrid J. Harrington, *Revelation. Proclaiming a Vision of Hope* (San Jose: Resource Publications, 1994); Gerhard A. Krodel, *Revelation* (Minneapolis: Augsburg, 1989).

3. All Scripture citations are the translation of the author.

4. It has been plausibly suggested that 1:4-8 might be read as a liturgical dialogue:

   Lector: Grace to you and peace, from him who is, who was and who is to come ... and from Jesus Christ, the faithful witness, the first born of the dead, and ruler of the kings of earth.

   Assembly: To him who loves us and has loosed us from our sins with his blood, and has made us a royal house of priests to his God and Father – to him be glory and dominion for ever and ever. Amen.

   Lector: Behold, he will come with the clouds, and every eye will see him, even those who pierced him. And all the tribes of the earth will wail because of him.

   Assembly: So be it. Amen.

   Lector: 'I am the Alpha and the Omega,' says the Lord God, who is, who was, and who is to come, the Almighty. See Ugo Vanni, 'Un esempio di dialogo liturgico', *Biblica* 57 (1976), 460–1.

5. Thus: Sunday 2 of Easter: 1:9-13, 17-19; Sunday 3 of Easter: 5:11-14; Sunday 4 of Easter: 7:9, 14-17; Sunday 5 of Easter: 21:1-5; Sunday 6 of Easter: 21:10-14, 22-23; Sunday 7 of Easter: 22:12-14.16-17, 20.

6. Revelation 4:11, 5:9-10, 12; 11:17-18; 12:10b-12a; 15:3-4; 19:1-3, 5-7.

7. A notable feature of Revelation is the three series of seven 'plagues': Seals (6:1–8:5), Trumpets (8:6–11:19), Bowls (chapters 15–16). The series flow one into the other, becoming increasingly more destructive. Seals follows the pattern of events in the Synoptic 'apocalypse' (Matthew 24; Mark 13; Luke 21). Trumpets and Bowls are modelled on the plagues of Egypt (Exodus 7–11). Especially in light of these plagues, Revelation can easily give an impression of implacable divine wrath – even a strong flavour of vindictiveness. A first step toward a proper grasp of this aspect of the book might be a consideration of the Genesis flood story (Genesis 6:1–9:17). There too, at first sight, Yahweh/God is stirred to violent action against sin and sinners. The Flood story is myth, a story of fundamental symbols which are vehicles of ultimate meaning. Myth speaks timeless truth, truth vital for human existence; it brings out the *super*natural dimension of events. In the flood story we see the holy God's radical incompatibility with evil – God's grief over human sin. The flood is not an historical event; it is a mythical event. Myth expresses truth. The flood story assures us that God will have the last word: 'never again shall there be a flood to destroy the earth' (Genesis 9:13). God will bear with sinful humankind. Revelation, too, is myth. The plagues exist in vision only. The great battle of Armageddon (Revelation 19:11-21; see 16:16) is not an historical but a mythical

141

battle. None of the violence of the plagues is literal violence against our world; it is violence in visionary scenes of the future, couched in metaphorical language. Again, just as there was no 'real' flood, there were no 'real' plagues of Egypt, and there were not, nor will be, 'real' plagues of Revelation. John is convinced of universal human sinfulness (Christians also are sinners – 1:5). The eschatological terrors are an expression of his sense of justice. That is why God and Lamb are the source of violence; Christians can only be victims, not perpetrators, of violence (13:9-10). After all, it is the Lamb, by breaking the first seal, who unleashes the plagues – for all three cycles are interconnected – the Lamb 'who was slain from the foundation of the world'. There is *no* human violence against evil.

8. If John were only an apocalyptist, he might have settled for the conventional scenario. In that case, the faithful followers of the Lamb, and they alone, would have a place in the New Jerusalem. As a prophet, he knows his God better than that. Throughout he is careful to distinguish between the 'destroyers of the earth' and the 'inhabitants of the earth'. The former, the Dragon and the two beasts, are symbols of pervasive evil. The others are deluded humans, swayed by evil. The plagues are not only an expression of God's incompatibility with sin and evil, they are aimed at the repentance of the victims of evil. John's Christian faith in the mercy and saving power of God inspired him to sustain a chain of startling 'inconsistencies'. He never forgot that his foolish God will have the last word.

One may discern in Revelation a doctrine of universal salvation. At first blush, suggestion of such a presence must seem absurd. Revelation displays such a spirit of vindictiveness and revels so in destruction of earth and its inhabitants that it can scarcely be taken for a Christian book. Closer study, based on an understanding of the genre and of the purpose of the writing as well as of the strong prophetic element, does lead one to a very different assessment. Note, for instance, the following:

> Great and marvellous are your works, Lord God Almighty;
> Just and true are your ways, O King of the nations.
> Who shall not fear you, Lord, and do homage to your name?
> For you alone are holy.
> All nations will come and worship before you,
> for your righteous deeds have been revealed (15:3b-4).

See also 1:7; 5:13; 14:6-7; 20:11-15; 21:3; 21:24-27. See Harrington, *Revelation*, 229–235.

THE GIFT OF THE EUCHARIST: A REFLECTION

꒰ ꒰ ꒰

PATRICK McGOLDRICK

What is the gift of the Eucharist? The short, and familiar, answer is: his body and blood given to us by Christ at the Last Supper. But the Eucharist itself has a fuller answer to offer.

The best teacher of the Eucharist is the eucharistic celebration itself. The Church has a long and ancient tradition of mystagogy, allowing and enabling the action of the liturgy to lead us into the mystery it celebrates. In the case of the Eucharist, it helps us to connect with the riches and the vitality that underlie what we say and do in the Eucharist in all its breadth and depth and dynamic.

We ask: what should we be doing to make our celebration of the Eucharist better? How are we to infuse life into the celebration? These are important questions, but perhaps not the best starting point. We should examine the understanding of God that may lie behind them. Is it of a God who is impassive, waiting on us to move and then reacting, primarily the recipient of our praise and petition?

Gift of God

The Eucharist starts from God and not from us. It is a gift of God, a dynamic gift made in and through God's action, to draw us into the divine mystery. God is pro-active rather than reactive, and this gives a quality of divine dynamism to the Eucharist. God is always there before us, in each celebration,

SERVING LITURGICAL RENEWAL

with greater energy and urgency than we bring. The Eucharist does not start with us, it is not our initiative. Rather, it comes to us, already living and life-giving. It belongs to God before it is ours: that's what gives it its depth of being, its density, its power.

If we start from the Eucharist as gift, we must acknowledge that it is not we who give meaning or purpose to what we do in celebrating it. We receive the Eucharist and respond to it; we find meaning and purpose there and we must engage with them. In the Eucharist God's plan is actively revealed and put into effect, and so draws us into it as we participate, into the mystery of God.

The Scope of the Eucharistic Gift

One of the most striking additions to the *Roman Missal*, made after the Second Vatican Council, was Eucharistic Prayer IV, with its magnificent sweep from the mystery of God in God-self, to creation, through the history of salvation to fulfilment in God's kingdom. Though this was a new composition, it was very strongly influenced by the eastern tradition. Why do we use such a prayer during the Eucharist? Is it just a general enrichment of the prayer of the Mass? Or is there a deeper and closer connection between them? Is it a eucharistic prayer in the sense of a prayer of thanksgiving said during the Eucharist or is it a eucharistic prayer in the sense that it is expressing the full scope of the mystery and the gift of the Eucharist?

Surely what we celebrate in the Eucharist is the mystery in all its fullness as presented by Eucharistic Prayer IV? We impoverish our understanding of the Eucharist if we reduce the Mass to anything less. Eucharistic Prayer IV evokes the fullness of what the Eucharist is in God's intention. All that comes from God is a gift, and the Eucharist can be understood as the sacrament of God's action from creation to fulfilment.

What has been said up to this lays emphasis on the Eucharist as God's action: it reveals God's plan and it embodies God's action in fulfilment of that plan. The Eucharist 'sacramentalizes' the divine plan and the divine action. The mystery of the

Eucharist is in the first place the mystery of God in God-self revealed in the saving plan for all creation and being worked out, realised, in the evolution of the world and in the movement of human history. There are many accounts of this evolution and this movement, but it is God who writes the narrative. The Eucharist recounts this narrative and plays a central part in its development.

The Gift of Creation

Creation is often seen by us as just a pre-Christian reality, not well integrated into our full Christian theology. But scriptural teaching on creation cannot be confined to Genesis 1–2. Parts of the New Testament link creation and Christ very closely: 'He is ... the firstborn of all creation, for in him all things in heaven and on earth were created ... all things have been created through him and for him ... in him all things hold together' (Colossians 1:15-17).

Creation is not just a given, a datum to be examined and explored, but a gift, to be received and responded to. Creation is God's continued gift, a gift always newly given, and it is given to us in Christ. It enters into the Eucharist; in ourselves, of course (we are the products of creation, and so we are God's gift); but also in the bread and wine that we present, as the prayers of preparation make clear: what they are, where they come from, what gives them their present form, what they are to become. They are signs of that creation in and for Christ, sacraments of that creation transformed and fulfilled in Christ. And they are intended for us, to eat and to drink, for the transformation and fulfilment of that creation in us.

So God's gift of creation is present in the Eucharist and is part of the eucharistic mystery. We can say that the Eucharist is a sacrament of God's gift of creation in Christ.

The History of Salvation

Eucharistic Prayer IV moves from creation to the history of salvation as it continues its narrative of God's great plan. Again, the Eucharist is part of that plan and has its role in its being worked out. It inserts us into a movement that is driven forward by God's purpose towards the goal, the consummation, that God wills. This history, with its dynamic, is God's gift. We do not start from cold or from scratch; we enter a history and a dynamic and we are caught up in them. We don't have to find directions for ourselves, nor are we on our own, because we join a people, one already on the march. All of that is God's gift, given freely and renewed in each celebration of the Eucharist.

What this means is seen in a familiar passage from Eucharistic Prayer III: '... and you never cease to gather a people to yourself, so that from the rising of the sun to its setting a pure sacrifice may be offered to the glory of your name'. And so God is gathering this people, here, today, in ongoing fulfilment of his purpose. This eucharistic assembly is God's doing, the result of God's own action, to insert it into a wider salvific work all through time and all over the world, and to contribute its part to that work. Our assembly is God's gift. As already mentioned, we can understand the Eucharist as the sacrament of that divine plan and that divine action in all their fullness.

The Gift of Christ

At the centre of it all is Christ. Just as all was created through him and in him and for him and all will find its perfection in him, so the lines of God's action converge on him and the dynamic of God's history leads to him. To put it the other way round: Jesus sums up all that God has achieved over previous time, he fulfils all that God has been working towards. In a real sense, all that is past is now present in him. And that is why and how it is all present to us in the Eucharist.

If then all is gift from God, Christ is the supreme gift: his very person, his incarnate life, his death and Resurrection. He comes to us in the fullness of time, as the scriptural phrase, with its sense of culmination and completion, has it. When we come shortly to consider the Eucharist as Christ's gift of his body and blood, and therefore of himself, we should remember that before that mystery and in that mystery. Christ is himself the historic gift of the Father and the Holy Spirit to the world.

The Eucharist is the gift of Christ in two different senses of that phrase: the gift that Christ gives us, the gift that is Christ. Christ gives himself in the gift he makes. But Christ is also the gift of the Father, or, better, of the Trinity. And in giving us Christ, surely the Father gives us as a gift all that went into his preparation and his formation? And the promise of the perfection of all things in him? That is the breadth of the Eucharist as the sacrament of God's gift, of God's action in its totality.

In approaching Christ in this way, we come to the heart of the Eucharist – and indeed to the heart of the mystery of God.

The Paschal Mystery

In the Eucharist God draws us into Christ's paschal mystery. The paschal mystery is the living core of the Eucharist and its focal point. The paschal mystery, of course, is Christ's death and Resurrection, his passage from this life of human weakness and sin through his Passion of suffering and death to his glorification, to the utter transformation of his humanity by the Holy Spirit and the new life of the Resurrection with the Father.

On the night he was betrayed (or handed over), at the Last Supper, Jesus took bread, gave thanks over it and gave it to his disciples with the words: 'Take, eat: this is my body, which will be given up for you'. And similarly with the cup, he gave thanks and gave it to them with the words: 'Take, drink: this is my blood of the covenant, which will be poured out for you'.

Two things in particular are noteworthy. What he gave them was not just his body but his body 'given up for you'; not just his blood but his blood 'poured out for you'. Jesus is looking forward to his death, he is interpreting that death, and in this ritual he is celebrating his death in anticipation. There are elements and tones of sacrificial language in his words, and he is offering his disciples a share in that sacrifice in anticipation.

There is a second point to note. What we have here is an act involving not just Jesus and his companions at table. The context is of prayer to the Father, and here in this ritual Jesus is offering himself in his forthcoming death to the Father. Jesus' words and actions at the Last Supper look to his imminent Passion and begin the great offering that gives it its deepest meaning and its true power. The Last Supper is, as it were, the Passion, the sacrifice, in anticipation, as the Eucharist will be the Passion, the sacrifice, in memorial.

Jesus went on to say: 'Do this as my memorial/in memory of me/as a memorial of me'. So the Eucharist is Christ's gift of the sacrament of his paschal mystery in all its fullness and all its salvific power. It is the gift of the sacrament of his sacrifice. Again, the Eucharist, to the very depth of its reality, and primarily, is a gift.

But we must go further still: whose gift? Christ's undoubtedly, but the Father's too. The Eucharist is the Father's action giving to the Church the sacrament of Christ's great saving deed. This is no more than Eucharistic Prayer IV itself says: 'Lord [= Father], look upon the sacrifice which you yourself have provided for your Church.' And there is a similar expression in the second Eucharistic Prayer for Reconciliation: ' ... we offer you what you have bestowed on us, the Sacrifice of perfect reconciliation'. But there is a deeper level of mystery here. When the New Testament account (see 1 Corinthians 11:23), closely reflected in Eucharistic Prayer III, places the Last Supper on the night Jesus was 'handed over', in the final sense isn't it the Father who does this, who, like Abraham, hands over his Son to death for us?

A Gift Made Anew in Each Mass

It is not adequate to the mystery of the Eucharist to see it just as a gift bequeathed once by Christ at the Last Supper or given by the Father in his raising of Christ from the dead. It is a gift made anew in each Mass.

The Church 'remembers' Christ and his paschal mystery by its obedient 'doing' of what he did at the Last Supper. But this requires the ministry of a priest configured to Christ by God in his ordination, who will thus be empowered to act *in persona*

Christi. This is not to say that he acts in the name of an absent Christ but rather that Christ is present in his action, that Christ acts *in persona ministri* at the heart of the Eucharist.

Or consider the Church's fulfilment of Christ's command in trinitarian terms, as the Eucharistic Prayer does in the epiclesis. It is only the power of God that can bring the Church's memorial to life so that it becomes effective in the present, so that past and present are brought into living contact through it. It is the Holy Spirit, the gift of the Father, who achieves this: the Holy Spirit who has been active in the working-out of God's great design all through history, from his hovering over the primeval waters at the beginning, through his role in the incarnation when he overshadowed Mary, and his coming upon Jesus at his Baptism in the Jordan and his work in Christ's death and Resurrection right through to his descent upon the Church at Pentecost. The Spirit's role in the Eucharist – in each Eucharist – mirrors that activity and continues it. What the Spirit did in history, the Holy Spirit continues to do now in the Eucharist in fulfilment of the same divine plan of salvation.

In Eucharistic Prayer IV the Holy Spirit is presented as the first fruit sent from the Father by the risen Christ for those who believe, sent in order to bring to perfection Christ's work on earth and so to sanctify creation to the full. In the epiclesis that follows immediately, we ask the Father that 'this same' Holy Spirit sanctify the bread and wine with the effect that they become the body and blood of Christ for the celebration of the great mystery that he left us.

So, by the working of the Holy Spirit, the Father gives to the Church the living sacrament of Christ's paschal mystery. To celebrate the Eucharist, then, is to be drawn by the Spirit into Christ's paschal mystery and through this into the totality of Christ and into the dynamic of history that reached its culmination in Christ – to be drawn into the fullness of the mystery of God, in other words. This, of course, is primarily God's act, and therefore God's gift to us in every Eucharist.

A Gift of the Future and for the Future

It has been said that the liturgical mystery is the future celebrated in the present on the foundations of the past. The Eucharist joins not just past and present; it joins also present and future, future and present. That future is already achieved in the humanity of Christ in glory. And the Eucharist is the sacrament of the fulfilment of all things in God and his kingdom at the end of time. 'Sacrament' is to be understood here not in any weak sense of a mere sign or promise but as a sign and promise already filled with that reality, a true anticipation of what is to be, which is already reaching out to us into our present. It is already present in its sacramental pledge but not yet in all the fullness of its true reality.

This is true of elements of the created world – bread and wine – which are transformed even now into the body and blood of Christ transfigured in glory. It is true of the movement of history to which God has joined us – already completed in Christ, even if we are still on the way and perhaps far from that goal, and completed also in those who are united with Christ in heaven. It is true of us too, already living by divine grace and receiving even now the body and blood of the risen Lord and in this way sharing in the fullness of his eternal life.

The tension between 'already' and 'not yet' runs through the New Testament and through the whole life of the Church, but God's gift of the Eucharist emphasises strongly the reality of the 'already', while never underestimating the dimension of 'not yet'. 'Already', because the future is even now reaching into the present and exercising its influence there; 'already', because the Church on earth is even now united with the Church in heaven and even now united with it in communion of life and in the worship of God.

In the Eucharist the Christian people sits down together to share the heavenly food and drink in the communion of saints. It is a sign filled with the reality, because the food and drink are even now the body and blood of Christ.

Eucharistic Prayer IV began by linking closely God's original work of creation and the creation of the human race. It ends with its vision in hope of a heavenly inheritance of God's children in the kingdom, where, with the whole of creation freed from the corruption of sin and death, we may glorify the Father through Christ, through whom the Father bestows on the world all that is good. It is a soaring conclusion, a consistent and inclusive culmination to the sweep and the dynamic of the divine plan as Eucharistic Prayer IV presents it.

Conclusion

The Eucharist is a mystery of immense breadth and depth and dynamism. It joins past, present and future, the beginning and the end. It brings together all God's creation and the whole human race. It celebrates the great divine plan that embraces all of us, the mystery of God's design and will for all that he has made. It draws us into that mystery, and in doing so it draws us into the heart of the very mystery and the very life of God. All of it is God's gift to us in and through Christ: a gift to be received and celebrated in the Eucharist itself, a gift to be received and lived in the everyday life of Christian, Church and world.

THEOLOGY OF MARRIAGE IN THE NUPTIAL BLESSINGS APPROVED FOR USE IN IRELAND (1970, 1980)[1]

꙳ ꙳ ꙳

DANIEL MURPHY

In Vatican Two's *Gaudium et spes*, the Council Fathers have given us a rich and life-giving treasure of theology of marriage that is biblical and modern, traditional yet prophetic. Prominent phrases proclaim marriage as a relationship-in-growth through partnership, equality, and life-long love. In Part Two of its text, *Gaudium et spes* discloses a new theological framework for marriage.[2]

a) The millennia-old patriarchal order is set aside in favour of one that expresses equality and an 'intimate partnership of life and [the] love (....)' between the spouses (GS 48).[3]

b) This term 'intimacy', by itself, highlights the Council's Fathers' departure from the earlier view that saw procreation as the 'primary purpose' of married life. As well as saying 'marriage and married love are by nature ordered to the procreation and education of children', they also stress the quality of friendship between husband and wife, recognising it as underscoring the kind of parents spouses would be (see GS 50).

c) Furthermore, the life-long sacramentality of Christian marriage is affirmed. It is in the realm of covenant-relationship in union with Christ, and it is more than a passing liturgical event (see GS 48).

According to Kenneth Stevenson, this 'careful and perceptive theology', which was influenced by current advances in scriptural studies and social science, complemented the initial document of Vatican Two, *Sacrosanctum concilium* (77-78), and, in time, shaped the *Ordo celebrandi matrimonium* first published in 1969.[4]

This paper seeks to focus on one section of the euchology in this Order, namely, the Nuptial Blessings [NB]. I propose to examine the extent to which this 'framework for human love' actually pervades Nuptial Blessing texts promulgated for use by the Church in Ireland, and will seek to examine the implications of this new theology for these rites.[5] As we will see, what quickly emerges is that no one prayer completely integrates this new marriage theology of GS. When a blessing succeeds in being fully explicit in one particular aspect, it will be less so in the others. However, Nuptial Blessing IV, an original prayer in the English language approved for use in Ireland, seems to be an exception. Of the two that appear to come next in terms of reflecting the theology of GS, one is also an original prayer, NB V (composed for use in Irish-speaking parishes). These original prayers have captured the attention of liturgists from France, Canada, England and the United States.[6] These scholars will, in the first place, highlight the success the Irish Bishops have had in incorporating the theology of *Gaudium et spes* into the prayer life of the Church and, secondly, they will point out where improvements have yet to be made.

Equality
The biblical witness to the equality between the sexes lies in the creation myths which open the Judeo-Christian Scriptures (Genesis 1:27; and 2:18-24). A Canadian pastoral commentary noted that:

> [t]he biblical images in our present nuptial blessings are primarily those of Genesis chapters 1 and 2, and Ephesians 5. These of course are very important.

However, other images could be incorporated as well, including the famous married couples of the Old Testament.[7]

Commenting on Genesis 2, Chauvet highlights the complementarity between man and woman, and notes that the Yahwist writer does not deny the role of fertility in marriage here, which, however, remains subordinate to the 'fulfilling delight of loving union'.[8]

Immediately after recounting the creation of man and women, the Genesis text says that the first man and the first woman, as a partnership, were commissioned to participate in the divine creating power: 'God blessed them, and God said to them, "Be fruitful and multiply, and fill the earth and subdue it" (Genesis 1:18)'. Nuptial Blessing I consists of verses 27 and 28 succinctly, and NB II reaches into Genesis 2:18-23 to speak of woman being given as a companion to man. Michael G. Lawler says this creation account also emphasizes the equality of man and woman for both are of the same biological matter.[9] However, it is NB V, the original prayer in the Irish language, which most fully utilises this biblical basis for spousal equality:

God our Father, you created the universe. You made a human person from the soil of the earth and into the nostrils you blew the breath of life thus making a living being. And you said: It is not good that this person be alone; I will make a worthy helpmate to match. And, causing a deep sleep to fall on him, You took a rib and covered it in flesh. This you made into woman, and brought her to the man, who said: This at last is bone of my bone and flesh of my flesh! She shall be called woman because she was called into being from man. For this reason, a man leaves father and mother and holds fast to his wife and they come to be one flesh. You blessed them and said, Be fruitful and multiply and fill the earth and subdue it.

Nuptial Blessing IV, the original prayer in the English language, also makes substantial use of this Scriptural motif:

> Father from you every family in heaven and on earth takes its name. You made us. You made all that exists. You made man and woman like yourself in their power to know and love. You call them to share life with each other, saying, 'It is not good for man to be alone'. You bless them with children to give new life to your people, telling them: 'Increase and multiply, and fill the earth'.

God, in the fullness of time, dignified 'adam and their descendants[10] in a definitive way in Christ.[11] Nuptial Blessing III connects the Old Testament creation story with this new covenant in Christ. However, the New Testament reference has an ambivalent application of the equality motif, which is repeated at the conclusion of the prayer.

> Father, you created man and woman in your own image and united them in body and heart so that they might fulfil your plan for the world. To reveal your loving design you made the union of man and *wife* a sign of the covenant between you and your people; through the sacrament of marriage you perfect this union and make it now a sign of Christ's love for his bride the Church.[12]

Partnership and Intimacy

In the patriarchal approach to marriage, a woman was handed over to her new owner. Faithfulness to one's husband was obliged, but there was leniency regarding his infidelities. It was the norm to gender-stereotype the tasks generated by family life.[13] In a marriage understood as an intimate partnership of life and love, women are not men's property. Familial duties and responsibilities will be approached according to, among other considerations, preference, competence, availability and rationale. Regarding fidelity, it is a mutual responsibility. This theology, however, is not uniformly applied in the euchology under examination.[14] For instance, in NB II, there are undertones of patriarchal possessiveness:

> Look with love upon N., as *she* asks your blessing. May *she* live in peace with you and follow the example of those women whose lives are praised in the scriptures. May N. place his trust *in her* and see *her* as his companion. May he always honour *her* and love *her* as Christ loves the Church. [Emphasis added]

This prayer does, however, admit mutual fidelity: 'May they be faithful to each other'. While it recalls biblical examples of fidelity, examples relating to women only are given and appear simply in generic form. It avoids mentioning division of labour.

The original prayer in Irish (NB V) also carries undertones of patriarchal possessiveness. The line, 'May she be blessed in her looks and in her speech', unfortunately echoes the media driven characterisation of women as sex objects, as status-bearing trophies to decorate male pride. While this prayer can be lauded for imploring God's blessing and protection on *both* his servants, for its most extensive use of male/female scriptural models, and for avoiding the pitfall of labor stereotyping, it is unfortunate that it has elements of bride-fixation. It is *she* who must earn trust, *she only* who has been singled out to, hopefully, follow the example of people praised in Scripture:

> Therefore, Lord God, grant your generous blessing to your servants here, N. and N. Bless them as you blessed Abraham and Sarah, Isaac and Rebecca, Zachary and Elizabeth, Joachim and Anne. Protect them, Lord, as you protected Noah from the flood, the three in the fiery furnace, Isaac from the sword, and the people of Moses from slavery in Egypt.

> Look kindly on N. May she live in peace with you and follow the example of those women who are praised in the Scriptures. May she have the cheerfulness of Rachel and

the wisdom of Rebecca and a long life of faithfulness like Sarah. May she be blessed in her looks and in her speech. May she be blessed in her health and in her beauty. May she be blessed in love and in grace.

May N. put his trust in her, and may she be a companion to him. May he always esteem her and love her as Christ does the Church.

Nuptial Blessing III contains explicit role stereotyping and is, therefore, patriarchal. It fails to show the sense of equality between the sexes characteristic of modern social science. It reads:

May N. be a good wife (and mother), caring for her home, faithful to her husband, generous and kind. May N. be a good husband (and a devoted father), gentle and strong, faithful to his wife, and a careful provider for his household.

One wonders why should the invocation not be as follows?

May N. be a good husband (and father), caring for his home, faithful to his wife, generous and kind. May N. be a good wife (and a devoted mother), gentle and strong, faithful to her husband, and a careful provider for her household.

Joncas offers a considered opinion: 'While one might argue that the emphasis placed on the wife's role exalts her status in a culture that degrades women, I think the text as heard in the liturgical assembly suggests that the husband has fewer responsibilities for maintaining the household than does the wife.'[15] In its favour, this prayer contains petitions, other than that quoted above, articulated on behalf of the couple rather than separately as 'bride' or 'groom'. That there are no scriptural models of fidelity included is a weakness.

Nuptial Blessing IV (the original English language text for use in Ireland) is most evocative of Vatican II's 'intimate partnership of life and love'. On mutual fidelity, its Celtic poetry is most compliant.[16] It prays, 'Let their love be strong as death, a fire that floods cannot drown, a jewel beyond all price'. It avoids entirely the tensions inevitable in labeling the spouses with stereotyped duties and responsibilities. Of the mindset that has a woman becoming the property of her man through marriage, this prayer never broaches that dark world. Instead, the prayer is introduced by words that refer to the couple as 'children' of God our Father and it maintains its focus on the couple in all its petitions.[17] However, 'it can be criticised for an anamnesis that only presents First Testament patriarchal types for Christian marriage, but lauded for the balancing of male and female scriptural models'.[18]

Of the five Nuptial Blessings being studied, NB I is the shortest in length and the most concise in content. It is entirely 'couple' oriented and promotes equality in its generic mention of work, and states that mutual happiness can be the fruit of mutual love. Popular because it is so short and also because it is rhythmical, it nonetheless lacks the male and female scriptural models of NB V and the otherwise rich exposition of Vatican II's marriage theology in NB IV.

> The 1917 Code of Canon Law spoke of marriage as the exchange of the permanent and exclusive rights of one's body for acts of sexual intercourse that were suitable for procreation. The spirituality required to fulfill that definition was quite minimal: remain married, do not commit adultery, and respond to each other's 'request' for sexual intercourse (or, as the pre-Vatican Two moral theology books put it, 'render the debt'). Once one accepts marriage as a call to a unique kind of intimacy with one's spouse, the horizons of one's marital spirituality are dramatically expanded. While the demands of the Code's definition can easily be delimited, the challenge to grow in intimacy has no bounds.[19]

Intimacy (the knowing of oneself and another in a deep and personal way) in marriage is an adventure within the parameters of love. Michael G. Lawler, after C.S. Lewis, says that married love is *'agape,* the love of the spouse for the spouse's sake; it is *philia,* the love of the spouse as friend, and it is also *eros,* the love of the spouse for one's own sake'.[20] While this adventure of love must, according to Vatican II, be open to the generation of new life, the quality of that adventure is now also emphasised. Self-revelation and generous communication of this revelation to one's spouse is an important factor in determining that quality. Growing in love after having fallen in love, being a source of joyful enrichment to one another, and accepting sexual intercourse from God as a profound vocabulary for that love and means for their healing, each of these is essentially important too.[21] All these characteristics of marital intimacy must nurture the fruits of this love, of which its greatest manifestation is new human life (see GS 48). How obvious are these characteristics though in the Nuptial Blessings under review? NB III successfully includes them:

> Lord, bless this husband and wife and protect them. Grant that as they live this sacrament they may learn *to share with each other the gifts of your love.* May they become *one in heart and mind* as witnesses to your presence in their marriage. (*Bless them with children who will be formed by the gospel* and have a place in your family in heaven). [Emphasis added]

Nuptial Blessing IV, however, while giving partial illustration of the nature of 'married love', only obliquely evokes the parental role of nurturing children (see GS 50). It reads, 'Father, you take delight in the love of husband and wife, that love which *hopes and shares, heals and forgives.* May their children bring them your blessing, and give glory to your name' [emphasis added]. Nuptial Blessing V is less forthcoming on marital intimacy, though it does pray, 'Father, (...) may they be faithful to each other, examples of Christian living, and witnesses to Christ'.

While it reads, 'May they see their children's children', this Scriptural motif does not explicitly account for their role as nurturers and educators.[22] NB II makes mention of some characteristics of the economy of married love, but these references do not reflect the mutuality and reciprocity that these imply of necessity.[23] For example, this prayer reads, 'May N. place his *trust* in her and see her as his *companion*. May he always *honor* her and *love her as Christ loves the Church*' [emphasis added]. Nuptial Blessing I, restricted by its brief form, says, 'May they find happiness in their love for each other, (be blessed in their children) and enrich the life of the Church'. Again, this reference to children fails by not explicitly alluding to the nurturing and educating role of parents. Certainly, while *they* will be blessed in their children, *Gaudium et spes* insists, I believe, that they should also be a blessing for their children.

The Sacrament of Marriage Lived
The third pillar of the theology of marriage in *Gaudium et spes* is that Christian marriage has been broadened to include not just the liturgical event as sacrament but the entire married life of the couple as sacrament. Goh explains:

> ... Marital sacramentality cannot be restricted to the wedding rituals. We press this latter issue as an authentic presentation of a *performative* faith that refuses to reduce the presence of Christ in the Church to a magical formula. God's saving action consists essentially in the divine self-giving. In the fidelity and loving relationship of a married couple, God's presence unfolds. It takes the freely-given, wholly gratuitous and unearned grace of God and the response of the human couple, in a love that perseveres, to perfect the sacrament. The essence of a Christian marriage is revealed in a sacramental process and is not a once-for-all attainment. And because the love of Christ for the Church is steadfast, a man and a woman in a marital vow pledge to care of each other in big matters of life as well as in small, for better, for worse, in sickness and in health,

till death them do part. Christian marriage is a unique commitment between two baptised persons in community before their Lord. We have argued that it is a *Realsymbol* to the extent that, through steadfast love, in words that are attested in actions, it serves as the visible and efficacious symbol of the presence of Christ.[24]

More than juridical contract, it is a covenant relationship between the spouses and a confirmed Christian vocation by the power of the Holy Spirit.[25] 'Christian marital covenant demands not only the creation of a life of equal partnership but also the sustaining of that life'.[26] 'Marriage is always in process or continually becoming'.[27] We now return to the texts of the Nuptial Blessings to see how these reflect this dimension of marriage, defined for the Catholic Church by *Gaudium et spes*.

The first Nuptial Blessing certainly projects the liturgical event of marriage into the future and its broader meanings is implied.

> May they praise you *in their days of happiness and turn to you in times of sorrow*. May they know the joy of your help *in their work* and the strength of your presence *in their need*. May they *worship you with the Church* and *be your witnesses in the world*. May old age come to them *in the company of their friends*, and may they *reach at last the Kingdom of heaven*. [Emphasis added]

However, this text is not as clear as it might be in exposing the new theology of marriage as sacrament, that is, that Christian marriage is as much a framework for everyday life into the future as it is a liturgy in church.

Nuptial Blessing II also looks to the future, and hopes, as well, that the vocation of marriage will be lived so as to gain the rewards of heaven.

> Father, keep this husband and wife strong in faith and true to your commandments. May they be faithful to each

other, examples of Christian living, and witnesses of Christ. And after a long and happy life together, may they enjoy the company of your saints in heaven.

Nuptial Blessing III has explicit and commendable lines which expand the meaning of the sacrament:

> Grant as they *live this sacrament* they may *learn* to share with each other the gifts of your love. May they *become one* in heart and mind *as witnesses to your presence in their marriage.* [Emphasis added]

The fourth Nuptial Blessing asks God to bless the couple as they set out on their new life together. It is essentially a rephrasing of what is found in NB I. It then calls for a new outpouring of a number of gifts of the Holy Spirit, deemed necessary for a covenantal marriage.

> We ask you to bless N. and N. as they set out on their new life. Fill their hearts with your Holy Spirit, the *Spirit of understanding, joy, fortitude and peace.* Strengthen them *to do your will* and in the trials of life to bear the cross with Christ. May they praise you during the bright days, and call on you in times of trouble ... *May their life together give witness to their faith in Christ.* May they see *long* and happy days, and be united forever in the *kingdom of your glory.* [Emphasis added]

This is the most explicit invocation of the Holy Spirit in any of the five Nuptial Blessings. In fact, the absence of a direct *epiclesis* of the Holy Spirit is, here and in each of the blessings, a serious flaw. German Martinez comments: 'Unfortunately, the *epiclesis* component is missing in the 1969 rite of marriage. Contrary to what happens in the eastern liturgies, the specific function of the priest would appear better defined with the more explicit pneumatic dimension'.[28]

Nuptial Blessing V also seeks to embrace a God-filled future for the couple but, again, like the majority of these prayers (NB III being the exception), it does not explicitly express that future by using the word 'sacrament'. It says:

> Father, keep this couple strong in faith and true to your commands. May they be faithful to each other, examples of Christian living, and witnesses to Christ. May they see their children's children. And after a long and happy life together, may they find joy in the company of your saints in heaven.

Evaluation

Having examined the five Nuptial Blessings in use by the Church in Ireland, three conclusions come to the fore.

Firstly, no single prayer completely expresses the theology of marriage expressed in GS. One can now rate, in descending order, the success with which each of these Blessings actually testifies to the theology of marriage according to GS.[29]

Nuptial Blessing IV appears to reflect the theology of GS most successfully. It is explicit in stating that marriage is an intimate partnership of life and love.[30] It strongly implies spousal equality from biblical sources and, also, how the quality of a marriage relationship is as important as that marriage being open to producing new life. It strongly implies that marriage is a sacrament for life, that it is more than simply a liturgical event.

Nuptial Blessings I and V seem to be somewhat equal in how they reflect the theology of GS. Of all the prayers, NB V excels in setting forth the biblical basis for gender equality. However, while implying that marriage is an intimate partnership between a couple, it then undermines this insight by praying, 'May she be blessed in her looks and in her speech'. Nuptial Blessing I, perhaps because it is so brief, never expresses any of the three pillars explicitly but does imply them to varying degrees. Coming in behind these is NB III. It expresses well the idea that the Sacrament of Marriage is a lifelong vocation rather than a once-off church event.[31] It fails drastically, however, by setting out stereotyped labour divisions, something that fails to elucidate the meaning of GS 52. Least successful of all in expressing these three pillars of the theology of marriage is, I believe, NB II. Its weakest sections are on marriage as an intimate partnership of life and love and on the point that the quality of relationship between the couple is as important as being open to the possibility generating new life.

A second conclusion, based on what we have stated in our first conclusion (that is, that NB IV, I and V best reflect the theology of marriage found in GS), is that, therefore, the three Blessings given in the *editio typica*, 1969 (with a partial exception of NB I) are more seriously flawed theologically than are the extra and original prayers for use in Ireland (NB IV and V). These texts from the Latin *editio typica* are less in harmony with the theology of marriage according of GS than are NB IV and V.

While the theological weaknesses of these foundational prayers may be excused due the speed with which Study-Group (*Coetus*) 23 had to produce new texts for the 1969 first edition,[32] certainly the later *editio typica altera* should have had such paradoxes ironed out. While Joncas is generally positive in his comments on the *editio typica altera*, he expresses two concerns:

> While I applaud the modifications made in Nuptial Blessing A by OCM 1991, at least two concerns remain. First, if the prayer is attempting to recognise the egalitarian nature of matrimonial partnership, I think the groom's name should be pronounced in the blessing as well as the bride's. Second, to mirror the shifts in focus in the prayer, it might be helpful to have the ordained officiant extend his hands over the couple at the central position and epiclesis, lay hands on the bride's head during the recitation of the petition for her, lay hands on the groom's head during the recitation of the petition for him, and resume extended hands over the couple for the

concluding petitions for them both. ... While I am heartened by the addition of an explicit *epiclesis* in the OCM 1991's Nuptial Blessing B, I believe the 'division of labor' applied to the spouses remains problematic.[33]

It is clear that those working in 2014 on the new translations for *The Celebration of Marriage – Gnás na Phósta* cannot presume the Latin texts promulgated in 1991 are free of theological incongruity.

Thirdly, we have noted above how Joncas praises the 1980 Irish ritual for its greater variety of Nuptial Blessings.[34] The variety of Nuptial Blessing texts in *The Celebration of Marriage – Gnás na Phósta* 1970/1980 is, indeed, a positive characteristic. However, the variant quality of theological content has compromised this praiseworthy characteristic in pastoral use. While one cannot downplay the advantage of having a greater variety of texts to choose from, the theological and pastoral quality of these prayers must be the primary concern. A variety of Nuptial Blessings without improved quality would be no gain at all.

Conclusion

It remains to be said, that while flaws exist, *The Celebration of Marriage – Gnás an Phósta* (1970/1980) is, nonetheless, an imaginative adaptation of the *Order for the Celebration of Marriage* published in 1969. Should we not be hopeful then that the Irish Episcopal Conference will maintain this laudable approach and produce a new Order of Marriage that is more deservingly praiseworthy and renowned?[35] We should expect that all of its prayer texts, including nuptial blessings (whether these might be re-workings of blessings in the *editio typica altera* or originals) fully comply with and richly express the life-giving theology of marriage enshrined by Vatican II.[36]

In the history of liturgy there are instances when the *lex credendi* influenced the *lex orandi*. An occasion for this may be supplied by the creation of new marriage prayers which would reflect something of the magisterium of the Irish bishops.[37] The theology of equality between the spouses is found in the Pastoral Letter of the Irish Bishops, *Prosperity with a Purpose*. That prayer texts approved for use in Ireland would suggest otherwise is a serious pastoral issue, which should be urgently addressed. A summary of this pastoral letter was published on Tuesday, 2 November 1999 in *The Irish Times*. The relevant section reads:

> Well before the economic boom, the family in Ireland was under pressure. The boom has brought new tensions arising from difficulties in reconciling work and family life. By 1997, 49 per cent of mothers with dependent children were working. The need to respond more effectively to parents' difficulties in balancing the demands of jobs with parenting roles is a key issue facing Ireland. In place of discriminatory arguments that 'the mother's place is in the home', the fairer argument is that 'each parent has a place in the home'. A great deal more is now known about the importance of active parenting by the father, for the good of children, for the mother who is freed to carry out roles outside the home at less cost to herself, for the father himself whose own life experience is enriched, and for the health and stability of the family.[38]

Another point that could be considered is the fact that people in the Church in Ireland easily identify anointing as a sacramental sign. In its liturgical use, most people know this is done, in faith, to signify a special meeting between God and the human being. If the practice of anointing married couples during the Nuptial Blessing were also established, the life-long sacramentality of a couple's marriage would be more clearly understood. It would be likened to the anointing of a priest's hands on ordination day. As well, the extra ceremonial would serve to enrich a liturgy much starved of meaningful ritual expression. Therefore, this anointing would be a more suitable ritual embellishment than the ambiguous 'unity candle', and would be more culturally acceptable in Ireland than ceremonies of crowning or binding.

There should be some emphasis in the Nuptial Blessings on the fact that the Church, in the local context (especially among family and friends), has a vital role to play in the success of the marriage process by virtue of their support, example, and experience. One might consider if, by saying the concluding words of the current Nuptial Blessings in an inclusive way could contribute to this, even in a limited way: '*We*, their family and friends, ask these graces for them through Christ, Our Lord', thus invoking a more meaningful and consequential, 'Amen'.

Finally, a consideration might be given to constructing original Nuptial Blessings in the form of the Jewish *berakah*. Henderson:

> [Nuptial Blessings] might profit being more closely modeled after the eucharistic prayer, using the form of prayer called *berakah*. This begins by blessing God, that is giving praise and thanks to God, and telling of God's mighty acts of love and deliverance through history. Such a prayer would also invoke the transforming and sanctifying presence of the Holy Spirit. Furthermore, the nuptial blessing might well incorporate periodic congregational acclamations. Finally, the couple might join hands again during the blessing.[39]

This Order and ritual will be the fruit of the work and the consultation, and indeed the witness for some of living the Sacrament of Marriage, of the Council for Liturgy of the Irish Bishop's Conference.

Appendix One

Nuptial Blessing Formulary I [= OCM C]

God our Father, creator of the universe, you made man and woman in your own likeness, and blessed their union. We humbly pray to you for this bridegroom and bride, today united in the sacrament of marriage. May your blessing come upon them. May they find happiness in their love for each other, (be blessed in their children) and enrich the life of the Church.

May they praise you in their days of happiness and turn to you in times of sorrow. May they know the joy of your help in their work and the strength of your presence in their need. May they worship you with the Church and be your witnesses in the world. May old age come to them in the company of their friends, and may they reach at last the kingdom of heaven.

We ask this through Christ our Lord. **R/.** Amen.

Nuptial Blessing Formulary II [= OCM A]

Father, you created the universe and made man and woman in your own likeness. You gave woman as companion to man so that they should no longer be two, but one flesh, teaching us that those you have so united may never be separated.

Father, you have sanctified marriage in a mystery so holy that it is a sign of the union of Christ and his Church. Look with love upon N., as she asks your blessing. May she live in peace with you and follow the example of those women whose lives are praised in the scriptures. May N. place his trust in her and see her as his companion. May he always honor her and love her as Christ loves the Church.

Father, keep this husband and wife strong in faith and true to your commandments. May they be faithful to each other, examples of Christian living, and witnesses of Christ.

(Bless them with children and help them to be good parents.) And, after a long and happy life together, may they enjoy the company of your saints in heaven.

We ask this through Christ our Lord. **R/.** Amen.

Nuptial Blessing Formulary III [= OCM B]

Father, you created man and woman in your own image and united them in body and heart so that they might fulfil your plan for the world.

To reveal your loving design you made the union of man and wife a sign of the covenant between you and your people; through the sacrament of marriage you perfect this union and make it now a sign of Christ's love for his bride the Church.

Lord, bless this husband and wife and protect them. Grant that as they live this sacrament they may learn to share with each other the gifts of your love. May they become one in heart and mind as witnesses to your presence in their marriage. (Bless them with children who will be formed by the gospel and have a place in your family in heaven.)

May N. be a good wife (and mother), caring for her home, faithful to her husband, generous and kind. May N. be a good husband (and a devoted father), gentle and strong, faithful to his wife, and a careful provider for his household.

Father, grant that as they now come as man and wife to your altar, they may one day share your feast in heaven.

We ask this through Christ our Lord. **R/.** Amen.

Nuptial Blessing Formulary IV (English Language Original)

Father, from you every family in heaven and on earth takes its name. You made us. You made all that exists. You made man and woman like yourself in their power to know and love. You call them to share life with each other, saying 'It is not good for man to be alone'. (You bless them with children to give new life to your people, telling them: 'Increase and multiply, and fill the earth.')

We call to mind the fruitful companionship of Abraham, our father in faith, and his wife Sarah. We remember how your guiding hand brought Rebecca and Isaac together, and how through the lives of Jacob and Rachel you prepared the way for your kingdom.

Father, you take delight in the love of husband and wife, that love which hopes and shares, heals and forgives.

We ask you to bless N. and N. as they set out on their new life. Fill their hearts with your holy spirit, the Spirit of understanding, joy, fortitude and peace. Strengthen them to do your will, and in the trials of life to bear the cross with Christ. May they praise you during the bright days, and call on you in times of trouble. (May their children bring them your blessing, and give glory to your name.) Let their love be strong as death, a fire that floods cannot drown, a jewel beyond all price. May their life together give witness to their faith in Christ. May they see long and happy days, and be united forever in the kingdom of your glory.

We ask this through Christ our Lord. **R/.** Amen.

Nuptial Blessing Formulary V (English Translation of Irish Language Original – Beannú an Phósta)[40]

God our Father, you created the universe. You made a human person from the soil of the earth and into the nostrils you blew the breath of life thus making a living being. And you said: It is not good that this person be alone; I will make a worthy helpmate to match. And, causing a deep sleep to fall on him, You took a rib and covered it in flesh. This you made into woman, and brought her to the man, who said: This at last is bone of my bone and flesh of my flesh! She shall be called woman because she was called into being from man. For this reason, a man leaves father and mother and holds fast to his wife and they come to be one flesh. You blessed them and said: Be fruitful and multiply and fill the earth and subdue it.

Therefore, Lord God, grant your generous blessing to your servants here, N. and N. Bless them as you blessed Abraham and Sarah, Isaac and Rebecca, Zachary and Elizabeth, Joachim and Anne. Protect them, Lord, as you protected Noah from the flood, the three in the fiery furnace, Isaac from the sword, and the people of Moses from slavery in Egypt.

Look kindly on N. May she live in peace with you and follow the example of those women who are praised in the Scriptures. May she have the cheerfulness of Rachel and the wisdom of Rebecca and a long life of faithfulness like Sarah. May she be blessed in her looks and in her speech. May she be blessed in her health and in her beauty. May she be blessed in love and in grace.

May N. put his trust in her, and may she be a companion to him. May he always esteem her and love her as Christ does the Church.

Father, keep this couple strong in faith and true to your commands. May they be faithful to each other, examples of Christian living, and witnesses to Christ. May they see their children's children. And after a long and happy life together, may they find joy in the company of your saints in heaven.

We ask this through Christ, our Lord. **R/.** Amen.

Appendix Two

A Theological Analysis of Five Nuptial Blessings Approved for Use in Ireland (1970; 1980)

	Blessing				
	I	II	III	IV	V
Theology of Marriage according to *Gaudium et spes* (GS)					
On the Biblical Sources of Equality between the Spouses	2	2	1	3	4
On Marriage as an intimate Partnership of Life and Love	3	1	0	4	1
On Intimacy as a Quality Relationship also open to New Life	2	1	3	3	2
On Marriage as a Sacrament for life; as being more than a Liturgical Event	3	3	4	3	3
Total	10/16	7/16	8/16	13/16	10/16

0 = Contradictory to *Gaudium et spes*
1 = *Gaudium et spes* is implied, but with contradictions also
2 = *Gaudium et spes* is partially implied
3 = *Gaudium et spes* is more fully implied
4 = Most explicit reference to *Gaudium et spes*

Notes

1. Just as this Festschrift is being compiled, the Catholic Church in Ireland is preparing a new English and Irish language edition of *Order of Marriage / Gnás an Phósta*, based on the translations of the *editio typica altera* of 1991 proposed by the International Commission on English in the Liturgy (ICEL) in 2013, and, for the Irish language, prepared by the *Coiste Comhairleach um an Liotúirge i nGaeilge*.

   This paper considers the Nuptial Blessings of the Order of Marriage as prayed by the Church in Ireland since 1970, and not according to the translations of the first three Blessings with which they are replaced in the new English translation of the *Roman Missal* (2011). The texts in use up to 2011 were those of the *editio typica* of 1969 prepared, not by ICEL, but by the 'Liturgical Commission of the Irish Hierarchy', and subsequently approved by the Irish Episcopal Conference and the Sacred Congregation for Divine Worship for use in Ireland.

2. See R. Kevin Seasoltz, *A Virtuous Church. Catholic Theology, Ethics, and Liturgy for the 21st Century* (Maryknoll, NY: Orbis Books, 2012), 186–8.

3. 'The treatment men have accorded women in the history of western civilization must wait for the forgiveness of God. Today women have their hands full struggling for equality, never mind being put on pedestals or deified. Even such a sturdy feminist as F.D. Maurice objected to the exaltation of one sex over the other, as in the courtly love tradition, because it betrayed his ideal of interdependence and organic unity. "The relation of man and woman, which is expressed in marriage," he advised his Cambridge audience, "the dependence of each upon the other, is lost in the attempt to exalt either at the expense of the other"'. Paul Elmen, 'On Worshipping the Bride', *Anglican Theological Review* 68 (1986), 241–9, at 248.

4. The nature of the study and research to be undertaken in the revision of the various liturgical books and rites is set out in SC 23.

5. This paper examines five Nuptial Blessings. Nuptial Blessing formularies I, II and III are translations of the Latin prayers found in the *editio typica* of 1969. However these NBs are found in an order different to that of the typical editions of the *Ordo celebrandi matrimonium* (1969 / 1991): the (Irish) NB I = *Ordo celebrandi matrimonium* [= OCM] C; NB II = OCM A; and NB III = OCM B. The Irish ritual book also carries two original prayers approved for use in Ireland: this paper refers to the English language original prayer as NB IV; and to the Irish language original prayer as NB V (but in English translation made by Pádraig McCarthy, *A Wedding*

173

of Your Own, 4th ed. [Dublin: Veritas, 2003]). Appendix One gives the texts of the Nuptial Blessings as found in *The Celebration of Marriage – Gnás an Phósta* (Dublin: Veritas, 1980).

Balthasar Fischer speaks of the right of each Episcopal Conference, based on SC 63, to prepare a ritual for marriage suited to local needs and culture. However, this ritual must be in harmony with the *editio typica* 1969 and be ratified by the Apostolic See before local promulgation: see, 'Le Droit Liturgique du Mariage', *La Maison-Dieu* 99 (1969), 154–9, at 155.

6. For example, see Jan Michael Joncas, 'Solemnizing the Mystery of Wedded Love: Nuptial Blessings in the *Ordo Celebrandi Matrimonium* 1991', *Worship* 70 (1996), 210–237; Pierre-Marie Gy, 'La réforme liturgique et les sacrements aujourd'hui', *Les Quatre Fleuves*, 21–22 (1985), 121–2; Frank J. Henderson, ed., 'Celebrating Marriage', *National Bulletin on Liturgy* 21 (December, 1988), 193–256, at 252; and, Christopher Walsh and Geoffrey Steel, 'La révision du Rite Catholique de Mariage pour l'Angleterre et le Pays de Galles', *La Maison-Dieu* 179 (1989), 99–110, at 107.

7. Henderson, ed., 'Celebrating Marriage', 252. Reference here is to NB I, II and III.

8. In Genesis 2, Chauvet notes that the woman 'was given to counter the loneliness [of the man] ... Together they become one flesh'. He lays stress on the mysterious and powerful loving attraction between a man and a woman which, he says, cements one to the other into a 'single, physical, moral and spiritual person'. Louis-Marie Chauvet, 'Le Mariage un Sacrement pas comme les autres'", *La Maison-Dieu* 127 (1976), 64–79, at 65–6.

9. See Michael G. Lawler, *Marriage and Sacrament* (Collegeville, MN: Liturgical Press, 1993), 21. Examining how the issue of equality between the spouses based on Genesis 1: 27 is addressed by Pope John Paul II in his 1980 Apostolic Exhortation, *Familiaris consortio*, Boulanger states that, despite the undoubted broad-mindedness behind reflections therein on the dignity and equality of women, he does not believe that these reflections will foster general support. Certain feminists will suggest that the pope's insistence on specific feminine merits may be allowed to give rise to the repetition of cultural stereotypes that they have fought against so much. See, Viateur Boulanger, 'Quand le couple inquiète l'église', *Prêtre et Pasteur* 92 (1989), 587–98, at 595.

10. '"We", in Hebrew *'adam*, in English "humankind", came from God. Male and female as we are, we are from God, and together we make up humankind. This fact alone, that God names woman and man

together *'adam*, establishes the equality of men and women as human beings.' See, Lawler, *Marriage and Sacrament*, 21.

11. Jesus challenged the standards of his day in which women were treated with inequality regarding, for example, adultery and divorce. Contrary to his contemporary Jewish tradition, Jesus numbered among his disciples many women who became partners in the proclamation of his Resurrection. See William P. Roberts, 'Towards a Post-Vatican II Spirituality of Marriage', *Christian Marriage and Family*, Michael G. Lawler and William P. Roberts, eds. (Collegeville, MN: Liturgical Press, 1996), 126.

12. Emphasis added. Instead of 'man and *woman*', it reads 'man and *wife*'.

13. This norm persists in the culture of Igboland, Nigeria. Patrick C. Chibuko calls for the approval of the New Igbo Rite of Marriage in which it is incorporated. '"Look upon your handmade N. Endow her with a soft tongue (the type with which the snail glides through thorny paths); and crown her with the dignity of womanhood." The dignity of womanhood according to the culture includes, motherhood, deep love of the husband, the skill to run a home efficiently. "Look upon your servant N.: shower your abundant blessings on him. May he remain the source of her encouragement as he undertakes the heavy task of fending for his family." According to cultural demands, a man must show beyond all reasonable doubts that he is first and foremost capable of being a husband and father. He needs to be strong, industrious and skillful. He must be able to feed, protect and provide the necessary means of livelihood for the family"': 'The Challenges of Liturgical Inculturation', *Questions Liturgiques* 80 (1999), 24–47, at 40–41.

14. Mouret says that none of the proposed nuptial blessing formularies are therefore prayers of blessing solely for the spouse. However, NB II (which is an adaptation of an old Roman prayer which was directed solely to the wife and prayed for her welfare and fidelity), and NB III, while affirming equal obligation and duties, still directs much of their attention to the wife. See, René Mouret, 'Le Rituel Français du Mariage', *La Maison-Dieu* 99 (1969), 177–201, at 197.

15. Joncas, 'Solemnizing the Mystery of Wedded Love', 223.

16. 'The theology and spirituality of the sacrament have to be accessible to the local churches according to the thought patterns, language and symbols of the people. This is a task that requires the expertise of local liturgists and the professional assistance of cultural anthropologists, religious sociologists, linguistic scientists and missiologists.' Anscar J. Chupungco, 'The Cultural Adaptation of the Rite of Marriage', *La celebrazione cristiana del matrimonio –*

Simboli e testi, Studia Anselmiana 93, Analecta liturgica 11, Giustino Farnedi, ed. (Rome: Edizioni Abbazia S. Paolo, 1986), 145–62, at 161.

17. For example, 'We ask you to bless N. and N. Fill their ...' (NB IV).

18. Joncas, 'Solemnizing the Mystery of Wedded Love', 233.

19. Roberts, 'Towards a Post-Vatican II Spirituality of Marriage', 129–130.

20. Lawler, *Marriage and Sacrament*, 99.

21. These categories are identified by Roberts in 'Towards a Post-Vatican II Spirituality of Marriage', 130–4.

22. See, CIC canon 226 § 2, *The Canon Law: Letter and Spirit* (Collegeville, MN: Liturgical Press, 1995), 128.

23. 'Peace,' 'trust' and 'honour' are some of the spiritual characteristics necessary to foster an intimate relationship. Both partners in marriage require these characteristics and more besides. This prayer fails, however, to express this fact when it speaks of 'peace' in terms of the woman only and 'trust' and 'honour' in terms of the man only.

24. J.C.K. Goh, 'Christian Marriage as a Realsymbol: Towards a Performative Understanding of the Sacrament', *Questions Liturgiques* 76 (1995), 254–64, at 263–4.

25. 'Another feature of the Tagalog Rite of Marriage (approved for use in the Philippians in 1983) is its elaboration of theological themes such as the role of the Holy Spirit in married life, the connection between marriage and the sacraments of initiation, and the Eucharistic dimension of marriage.' Anscar J. Chupungco, *Liturgies of the Future, The Process and Methods of Inculturation* (New York: Paulist Press, 1989), 148.

26. Lawler, *Marriage and Sacrament*, 22.

27. David M. Thomas, 'Marriage', *The New Dictionary of Theology*, Joseph A. Komonchak, Dermot A. Lane, Mary Collins, eds. (Collegeville, MN: Liturgical Press, 1990), 627.

28. German Martinez, *Worship: Wedding to Marriage* (Washington, DC: Pastoral Press, 1993), 68.

    Frank Henderson also noted that, 'At present, our nuptial blessings are primarily prayers of petition, and completely neglect the Holy Spirit. Though the role of the Spirit has been recovered in most of our post-conciliar liturgies, this is not the case with respect to marriage. This is a serious weakness'. See, *National Bulletin on Liturgy*, 251. This flaw was rectified in the *editio typica altera* of 1991.

29. See Appendix Two for summary analysis of this order.

30. The marriage ceremony belongs equally to the couple and to the Church at large. It is not 'the bride's day'. The Nuptial Blessing

should not therefore evoke this popular belief by praying for the bride and groom separately. Again, Henderson: 'Though Vatican Council II called for wedding texts to indicate equality and mutuality, two of our three nuptial blessings are still basically prayers for the bride. References to the husband have been added, but they seem awkward and inconsistent with the general thrust of the prayer. This lack needs to be attended to.' *National Bulletin on Liturgy*, 252.

31. Marriage is always a process. The liturgical ceremony is but one stage in that process, that becoming, that growing into love. This process begins in the first glance of preference. It reaches a high point in the liturgical celebration. Then in the availing of God's special graces, called down upon the couple in that liturgy, the process can and should climb to a higher plane, come what may, in the course of the couple's lives. This essential characteristic of marriage, that it is a process, needs to be better highlighted in the Nuptial Blessing and throughout the marriage liturgy.

    'Because marriage as a human relationship is necessarily developmental, Christian marriage exists first as intention, and moves toward accomplishment. The actualization of the marriage is dependent upon interpersonal revelation and the events of life which constitute the life of the married'. Thomas, 'Marriage', 627.

32. See Annibale Bugnini, *The Reform of the Liturgy 1948–1975* (Collegeville, MN: Liturgical Press, 1990), 696–706.

33. Joncas, 'Solemnizing the Mystery of Wedded Love', 220; and 223–4.

34. See note 6, above. Others support him in this view:
    On the principle of 'variety' itself, Pierre-Marie Gy, writing in 1985 in *Les Quatre Fleuves*, praises how the Order for Marriage of 1969 and the reformed rites in general, offer a great variety of texts to choose from. He says all priests who have prepared engaged couples for marriage are able to testify to the depth of interest with which couples, if they so choose, to make these choices. He goes on to say it is wrong to describe these liturgical celebrations as 'à la carte' liturgy because this is liturgy coming out of mature faith and from the discovering together of the faith response necessary for the couple's lives. *Les Quatre Fleuves*, 21–22 , pp. 121–2.

    In the 1988 December issue of the Canadian Journal *National Bulletin on Liturgy*, subtitled *Celebrating Marriage*, there is a call for the provision of an even greater variety of nuptial blessings. It cites the two original prayers in the Irish Rite as 'an improvement in several [of these] respects'. *National Bulletin on Liturgy*, 252.

The following year, in *La Maison Dieu*, Christopher Walsh and Geoffrey Steel, writing about the ongoing evaluation of the 1969 Roman Rite of Marriage being undertaken by the Church in England and Wales, also call for the inclusion of a greater number of nuptial blessings. They said it is to be hoped there will be more than the original three blessings of the Roman Ritual – texts which will address the multiplicity of pastoral situations encountered in the Church today. See *La Maison Dieu* 179 (1989), 107.

35. See, Irish Commission for Liturgy, 'Order of Christian Marriage', *New Liturgy* 99 (1998), 3.

36. An English (and Irish) translation of the second Latin edition of the Order of Marriage has been long overdue, given that the Order of Celebrating Marriage for the Roman Rite was promulgated by the Congregation for Divine Worship and the Discipline of the Sacraments on 19 March 1991 by the decree *Ritus celebrandi Matrimonium*. See Joncas, 'Solemnizing the Mystery of Wedded Love', 211.

37. On inculturation, see Kenneth J Martin, *The Forgotten Instruction The Roman Liturgy, Inculturation, and Legitimate Adaptations* (Chicago, IL: Liturgy Training Publications, 2007), 48–60.

38. See The Irish Episcopal Conference, 'Prosperity with a Purpose', *The Irish Times*, (www.ireland.com/newspaper/special/1999/bishops/: 2 November 1999) [accessed 10 October 2013].

39. See *National Bulletin on Liturgy*, 251. See the comment of Gilbert Ostdiek: 'Rituals help individuals and groups negotiate moments of transition', in 'Human Situations in need of Ritualization', *New Theology Review* 3 (1990), 41.

40. Translation taken from, Pádraig McCarthy, *A Wedding of Your Own*, 4th ed. (Dublin: Veritas, 2003).

SACRAMENTALITY AND DEVOTION: A WORD FROM AQUINAS

꒛ ꒛ ꒛

LIAM G. WALSH OP

It was hardly as a liturgist that Thomas Aquinas made his fame and fortune. Efforts that have been made to win him a place in liturgical debate[1] may not have entirely banished the sense that he belongs more readily to the domain of theory than of practice. Yet there are significant things in his writings that can have a bearing on liturgical practice. His appreciation of liturgy is evident in the attention he gives to what he calls the *ritus* of sacraments in the *Summa*. He devotes articles to the rite of Baptism (*IIIa* q. 66, a. 10) and Confirmation (*IIIa* q. 72, a. 12), and a full question to the rite of the Eucharist (*IIIa*, q. 83). In the introduction to his treatment of the sacrament of Penance (*IIIa* q. 84) he announces a question *de solemni ritu huius sacramenti*. Thomas's thinking about the practice of these rites has the advantage of being undergirded by the theological vision that he has been developing all through the *Summa*.

It will be suggested here that the thinking of Thomas on the rites of sacraments, understood in light of the teaching about ceremonial law, grace, virtues and sacraments, may not be entirely irrelevant to current liturgical debates. There is discussion today about the relative value of different liturgical rites – the *Ordo Missae* of Paul VI and the *Missale Romanum* of Pius V, for example – and about styles of celebrating the *Ordo Missae*, which vary from the introduction of contemporary innovations that delight some and shock others, to attempts to reform the reform by restoring to the *Ordo Missae* attitudes and practices that vaunt their Catholicism from the place they have had in Tridentine rituality. And there is, of course, the mixed feeling generated by the granting of liberal permission for the celebration of the Extraordinary Rite. While these debates are fuelled by historical, aesthetic, canonical and even political options, they raise at the deeper level theological issues. What will be suggested here is that the issue Thomas Aquinas would want raised in any discussion about liturgy is the relationship between sacramentality and devotion, because this is the issue that underlies his own examination of liturgical practice in the question he devotes to the rite of the Eucharist in his *Summa Theologiae*.

THOMAS'S THEOLOGY OF SACRAMENTALITY

Rituality and Grace
The build-up toward Thomas's treatment of the Eucharist and its rite in the *Summa* can be described only summarily here. His appreciation of rituality can be traced back to his discussion on the ceremonial precepts of the Old Law in the *Ia IIae* qq. 101-103. His understanding of the way the rituality of the New Testament differs from and surpasses that of the Old is presented in qq. 106-108. The basic difference is that because the New Testament is the reality of the grace of the Holy Spirit the institutions prescribed in it – and they are very few compared to the multitude of the Old – can actually have justifying grace within them. The theology of that justifying grace that he works out in qq. 109-114 makes it clear it is in no way the fruit of human works; and that if faith and other dispositions are at work in its reception it is only because they are caused by grace itself.

Grace, Virtues and God-wardness
The virtues and states of life that Thomas goes on to examine in *IIa IIae* are infused gifts of grace, accompanying grace, expressing it and bringing it to its fulfilment in glory. The life of grace comes from God and goes to God. What primarily ensures

the God-centeredness of the human laying-hold of grace is faith and its accompanying theological virtues. Among the moral virtues the one that is specifically occupied with the God-wardness that grace puts into human life is religion. Thomas says it is preeminent among the moral virtues (*IIa IIae* q. 81, a. 7).

The Virtue of Religion

As a good Aristotelian, Thomas thinks that, infused virtue though it is, religion should assume within itself the rational dictates of the corresponding acquired virtue. That allows him to give full value to the human effort in the sphere of religion that corresponds to grace, to its good actions that are the fruit of grace, but also to its human failures that spoil grace. Thomas will be expecting to find these moral values, positive and negative, in all he has to say subsequently about worship.

It is worth noting some details of what he says about this virtue that is the human heart of worship. It is a virtue: 1° that, although to be understood as a form of justice, does not measure up the equality that is the hallmark of full justice; no human acts of worship can match the infinite worship due to God (q. 80, a. 1); 2° that is realised essentially in the interior acts of devotion and prayer; where these acts of the virtue are not operative no external actions, however persuasively religious they may seem, are acts of religion; external action of devotion and vocal prayers are signs of interior acts, and have religious value only when they genuinely signify true interior devotion and prayer (q. 81, a. 7); 3° that finds its first external action in adoration, which Thomas understands to be the use of the human body to express worship; religion is exercised in and through the expressiveness of one's own body before it employs anything else (q. 84); 4° that does, however, use other things besides the human body; it uses things that have a place in the ordinary course of human life by offering them to God; sacrifice is the first of these uses of external things (q. 85); 5° that has another way of using external things in the worship of God, when those things already belong to God; such things are sacraments and the divine name itself (qq. 89-91).

The Misuse of Religion

The vices that Thomas finds opposed to the virtue of religion (*IIa IIae* qq. 92-100) are not, paradoxically, those of irreligious people, but rather of people who would consider themselves to be religious, might be considered so by others. The reasoned moderation that Thomas expects of religion as a virtue may seem to some to be an ungenerous restriction of the élan towards the divine. Perhaps the availability of the word 'religiosity' can express the ambiguity that lets religion open to excesses. Religiosity can be religion at its best or at its worst. The sciences of psychology and sociology have helped to bring clarity to the understanding of it. There are people who are religious in their psychological make-up. This can support their cultivation of the virtue of religion, but it can also leave them open to deviant forms of religion. Sociologically there are societies that by tradition or political choice are religious. The people who form them are not necessarily God-fearing and the society they form can wage wars in the name of its god that have very little of the divine about them. More religion is not necessarily better religion. And letting forms of religious practice become associated with political agendas – either to promote them or oppose them – is not necessarily in the best interest of true religion.

The vices that Thomas identifies in the domain of religion are of two types: on the one hand, excesses of religiosity (superstition, idolatry ...) and, on the other, abuses of the power that can be given by religiosity (by using holy things, but irreverently, as in sacrilege or simony). Thomas's listing of the vices of people given to religion could warm the hearts of militant atheists and agnostics, because it shows how ridiculously irrational religion can become. But it could also provide a useful examination of conscience for people who like to consider themselves religious.

Sacraments: Signs of Grace and of Worship

For Thomas sacraments are the ritual embodiment of the grace of the New Testament.[2] They are God's action through Christ and the Spirit in the form of humanly made signs (*IIIa* 60, 1). A sacrament is a *res sacra* in which grace is given and received. In his discussion on the virtue of religion Thomas introduced sacraments as the taking hold of holy things and as such as external acts of religion (*IIa IIae, Prol* q. 89). He brings this cultic reality of sacraments to light early in his questions about sacraments. In q. 60, a. 5 he says:

> In the use of the sacraments two things may be considered, namely, the worship (*cultus*) of God, and the sanctification of man: the former of which pertains to man as referred to God, and the latter pertains to God in reference to man.

For all the primacy that Thomas gives to the sanctifying action of God in sacraments, he requires one to be aware that human acts of worship are always present in their celebration (*usus*, which includes reception). To their downward movement from God to humans correspond the upward movement from humans to God.

Sacramental Characters and the Worship of Christ

But before the human act of worship in sacraments is an act of virtue it has to be sacramentalised. The upward movement of worship has to be something divinely given even on the level of sign. The expression of it has to be seen to be an act of Christ. This is the sense of Thomas's teaching about sacramental characters (*IIIa* q. 63). He sees these as designations for Christian worship given by God in Baptism, Confirmation and Ordination. They enable people to make sacraments, culminating in the Eucharist, be acts of Christian worship, of the very worship of Christ himself, the Eternal Priest. It is in being acts of Christ's worship that sacraments are grace-giving.

Devotion in Sacraments

Thomas will say with the Tradition that, being signs of Christ in virtue of the character of those who celebrate them, sacraments are real, grace-giving acts of Christ's worship even when those taking part in them do not have the appropriate dispositions to receive that grace. But what he is primarily interested in are fruitful sacraments, true acts of worship in which grace is actually given. While he would see the theological virtues as the prime requisites for the God-wardness of the upward movement of sacraments, he would expect them to have the moral worth that comes with the virtue of religion. He is sparing in his use of the word religion in his discussion on sacraments. Most often it is the word *devotio* that he uses to express the moral stance that has to be present in the grace giving of sacraments. *Devotio* is the primary act of religion for Thomas (*IIa IIae* q. 82).[3] It is a 'safer' word than *religio* in the context of sacraments. It is the inner side of *religio* and so more independent of the external forms that religion is inclined to take. It does not carry to the same extent the risk of attributing to external action some kind of power over grace that seeing them as acts of religion may do.

LITURGICAL RITES FOR THE CELEBRATION OF SACRAMENTS

The build-up of Thomas's theological position about the grace of Christian worship that has been outlined up to now must be the horizon of interpretation for what he has to say about the rites of the sacraments at the end of the *IIIa Pars*.

Which Rite

One needs to take account of what rite of the Mass Thomas is talking about. He lived in the period when the classical liturgical forms of the *Ordines Romani* had been received in the medieval world and filled out under the influence of the somewhat more exuberant devotionalism of the Germanic people. While maintaining its basic fidelity to the classical Roman rite the liturgy developed in many and varied forms across western Europe. In the thirteenth century there was no standard, centralised form of the Roman Rite of Mass. As a Dominican Thomas would have known and celebrated what came to be called the Dominican Rite.[4] There is no reference to this rite nor to any particular version of the Roman Rite that Thomas might have experienced in his question on the rite of the Mass. What he envisages are the general common features of the thirteenth century Latin Mass.

Thomas's Liturgical Authorities

That Thomas accepted there was no need to canonise any single, centrally authorised rite of the Mass is theologically and liturgically significant. It does not mean, of course, that authorisation by the Church had no place in his thinking about the rite of the Mass. In the *sed contra* of all but the first article of his question on the rite of the Eucharist he invokes the Church as the authority that justifies the ritual elements that he is about to explain. And he notes there that 'the Church's ordinances are Christ's own' (a. 3) and that the Church is the exercise of this authority is guided by the Holy Spirit and so protected from error (a. 5). The primary weight of Church authority in sacraments is exercised by its Scriptures. It is the Bible that reveals in the Church what is divinely instituted in the sacraments, and how they are therefore instruments of divine grace. This biblical regulation bears on the core sign of a sacrament, what the Scholastics call its matter and form. But it bears on much more. In presenting the sacramental sign in which the Eucharist is realised (*IIIa, q. 73*) Thomas wants account to be taken, not just of the 'words of institution' but of the entire Last Supper and also of the biblical types of the Eucharist – the bread and wine of Melchisedech, the manna and pre-eminently the lamb sacrificed in the Passover. He makes no appeal to the ceremonial precepts of the Old Testament. Jesus, in choosing to have himself remembered in simple, domestic rituals of table, bathing, anointing and blessings, parted company with the fulsome religiosity of his Jewish forebears. It is only when the Old Testament throws prophetic light on these core rituals given by Jesus that Thomas will have it appealed to.

Thomas has maintained that, viewed in terms of law, what the New Testament prescribes for sacraments is minimal (*Ia*

IIae q.107, a.4). However, he qualifies this in two ways. First he says that not everything said or done by Christ and his Apostles was written in the Scriptures (*IIIa*, q. 24, a. 3 ad 4; q. 83, a. 4 ad 2). And then he allows that, subsequent to the teaching of Christ and the Apostles, 'some things were added afterwards on the authority of the Fathers' (*Ia IIae* 107, 4). While much can be written about what Thomas means by 'Fathers' here one can at least say he is alluding to the great bishops and teachers, recognised as such by the universal Church, belonging to the age when the churches were giving the first classical shape to the tradition of faith in the cultures and institutions in which the faith first embedded itself. Whatever could trace itself back to this era, in teaching or in liturgical rites, was thought to be uniquely faithful to the Apostolic Tradition and so carried unique weight in the life of the Church.

The Mass: Sacrament of Christ's Sacrifice (q. 83, a. 1)

Thomas begins his study of the rite of the Eucharist with a question that he formulates: 'Is Christ immolated in the celebration of this mystery?'. The article is not about whether or not the Eucharist is a sacrifice. That it is has been affirmed by Thomas, as an obvious given of faith, all through his treatment of the sacrament of the Eucharist. He is concerned here with *a rite*. What he wants to establish now is that the rite of Mass, which being the rite of a sacrament realises what it signifies, realises the immolation of Christ. To speak about rite in a sacrament is to draw attention to it being an act of worship. The question here is how this particular rite is worship. Thomas has already established that the only worship acceptable to God in the New Covenant is the immolation that Christ suffered willingly on the Cross. The question about the rite of the Mass is, then, does it fulfil its function as worship by realising the unique sacrifice of Christ. Saying that it does, and explaining how, is the most fundamental and distinctive thing that Thomas has to say about the rite of the Eucharist, and the saying of it commands everything else that he will say. If any worship value is to be claimed for the rite it must come, not just from the religiosity of those who celebrate but from the cross of Christ.

Thomas's explanation is that the rite is 'a kind of image representing Christ's Passion, which is his true immolation', representing it as actually giving grace here and now. It is what later theology will call a sacramental sacrifice. In earlier questions about the Eucharist Thomas had explained how its sacrificial sacramentality is found in the consecration of the bread and wine, in the words spoken about them and in the way they present the blood of Christ separated from his body (*IIIa* q. 74, a. 1; q. 76, a. 2 ad 1; q. 80, a. 12 ad 3). He is now saying this is true of the entire rite. The complex act of worship that is the Mass must represent and realise the sacrificial act of Christ. What makes what Christians do in Mass be a sacrifice is not that it is their own act of the virtue of religion but that it is the one sacrifice of Christ (q. 83, a. 1 ad 1). The devotion that the rite of Mass calls forth is fruit of the grace that it itself embodies, not the addition of human enhancements that will make the Mass more pleasing to God in their own right.

It is noteworthy, in the light of later developments and of various temptations towards a clericalisation of the Eucharist, that Thomas does not make the sacrificial character of the Mass depend on the priesthood of the celebrant. Thomas had devoted a full question (q. 82) to the role of the priest. It is the sacramental one of representing the Christ who offers himself in the offering of his people. The priest also represents the people in their worshipful taking hold of the sacrifice of Christ, by which they are opened to the grace of the sacrament. Thomas has more to say about the people than about the priest in q. 83. The world *populus* occurs many times there, and when Thomas says 'we offer' one is entitled to think that the 'we' means the ecclesial community and not the collectivity of the ordained. It is in the theological perspective set down in a. 1 that Thomas examines the details of the rite of Mass in the remaining articles of q. 83. The rite must be, and be clearly seen to be, the sacrament of the immolation of Christ as it gives saving grace here and now. This *sacramentality* is the first and most pervasive criterion to be used in evaluating any form of liturgical celebration of the Mass. The human expressions of worship, however devout, and venerable and aesthetically rich they are claimed to be, should only find a place in Mass when they clearly enhance and promote devotion to its essential sacramentality.

Time of Celebration (q. 83, a. 2)

The authority of Scripture is the predominant court of appeal in what Thomas has to say in article 2 by way of justifying the discipline of his day about the time for celebrating Mass. He reasons that, in order to be the representation of the Passion of Christ and participation in its fruits, the Mass must have its times and places of celebration given sacramental significance by the Scriptural records of that saving event. It has to be noted that the weight given to Scripture here is nothing like what it has in determining the core rite of the Eucharist. There the texts are employed according to their strictly literal sense and as such they are absolutely determinative. But for decisions about the time and place of the celebration Thomas is able to employ all four types of exegesis that he recognises to be legitimate in the domain of faith. The texts so interpreted are not being asked to provide strict prescription for the essentials of sacramentality but to provide settings in which that sacramentality can be filled out in the Church. To the Christian imagination texts so interpreted give representative value to certain times and places, which thus make them appropriate for celebrating the Eucharist. While there is always a literal ground to Thomas's exegesis, much of what he uses here is of the prophetic and allegorical type. This lends itself to sacramentality without imposing definitive liturgical requirement.[5] Thomas, indeed, recognises that there is considerable flexibility in the discipline of his day. The important thing for him is not that one practice is right and the other wrong but that they should be redolent of the Scriptures, and in ways that make them appropriate for the sacramentalizing of the sacrifice of Christ.

Place and Furnishing of Celebrations (q. 83, a. 3)

The appeal to the authority of the Scriptures continues in the examination of where and with what furnishing and receptacles Mass is celebrated. Scripture is invoked in the body of the article, in a text from Hebrews, primarily to establish the essential sacramentality of the Eucharist. It is from this that he argues that the objects used in its celebration (church building, altar, paten and chalice etc.) should be set aside for liturgical use by being consecrated. Consecration is an act of the virtue of religion, an act of reverence for the sacrament and the holiness that is its effect. Thomas does reinforce his appeal to the rationality of religion by turning to the Scriptures in replying to difficulties raised against the need for such consecrated object. It is not to Old Testament texts prescribing the consecration of places or objects for divine worship that he turns (he has already established that the sacramentality of the New Testament is quite the antithesis of that of the Old) but to texts that make their point by being read allegorically. And the New Testament texts he uses are evocative but certainly not prescriptive.

The prescriptive material in his discussion comes from the Canons of the Church. Some of these can be given special weight when they are thought to be from the Fathers, but their formal value is as decisions of the Church. They have to be distinguished sharply from what give the Mass its essential sacramentality. Thomas formulates the distinction in his reply to objection 8, where he says:

> The dispensing of the sacraments belongs to the Church's ministers; but their consecration is from God Himself. Consequently, the Church's ministers can make no ordinances regarding the form of the consecration, and the manner of celebrating.

Thomas has been working on this principle all through his replies to the objections, in which he was justifying the current practice of the Church about consecrating churches, altars and sacred vessels. The rules and regulations about consecrations of liturgical object are, indeed, made in the Church under the guidance of the Holy Spirit. But they are still choices of human prudence, radically different to the divine determination that gives the sacraments their core truth. He has no difficulty in allowing that when the law of the Church in these matters cannot be fulfilled Mass can be celebrated outside sacred places and without sacred vessels (*ibid*).

Words (q. 83, a. 4)

Thomas introduces his examination of the words spoken throughout the Mass by using a text from the *Decretum* of Gratian in his *sed contra*. The text claims that James the brother of the Lord and Basil the bishop of Cesarea edited the rite for the celebration of Mass. It is not to the Scriptures, then, that he is going to appeal to justify the spoken features of the rite of the Mass, but to what might justly be called the Apostolic Tradition. What he justifies in this article are not an actual set of words that he finds in a particular liturgical book but the broad structure in which words are arranged in the Mass and the kind of words that are used to fill out the structure. One has also to remember that what he is considering is the form the Apostolic Tradition had taken within the Roman Rite of the Mass. Thomas was well aware there were Greek liturgies that were different to the Roman. The structure that he describes is not entirely foreign to the structures of Oriental liturgies, but his primary reference is to the liturgies of the Latin churches.

Thomas finds that in the rite of the Mass there are successively words of preparation, of instruction, of offering, of consecration, of receiving, of thanksgiving; and within each of these sets there are different groups of words. His description obviously fits the medieval forms of Mass he would have known. One might hypothetically claim it could fit the Tridentine Mass. One could with more justice claim it fits earlier forms of the Mass that are attested by the *Ordines Romani*. One could even claim that it fits the rite of Mass described in the *Apostolic Tradition* attributed to St Hippolytus.

And it obviously fits the *Ordo Missae* of Paul VI. Thomas is saying that the liturgical justification of the words used in Mass is found not in a material consideration of individual words but in the way those words serve the different parts of a structure of celebration that Thomas seems to think has been received from the Apostolic Tradition. It matches what he said in *Ia IIae* q. 107, a. 4 about what is prescribed in the New Law being from the Scriptures with *quaedam additae ex institutione Patrum*.

Actions (q. 83, a. 5)

The sacramentality of the eucharistic rite is given in a combination of words and actions. For the actions, as he had done for the words, Thomas lays down the principle for understanding them in the body of the article, and then deals with them particularly in replying to the objections. The principle is that the actions being considered here represent the Passion of Christ; they also represent, and Thomas makes it explicit here, the devotion of the people and their reception of the sacrament. Representation and devotion are the two poles of sacramental celebration. The issues raised by the objections require Thomas to bring both sides of the principle into play and to see how they interact. He brings to light the representative value of most of the actions he has to discuss – signs of the cross, hand gestures, turning towards the people, the breaking of the host, the co-mingling. He presents the devotional value in terms of reverence and says 'this sacrament calls for deeper devotion than do the other sacraments' (ad 5).

The actions that Thomas considers in the objections are ones done by the priest – washing of hands, thurification, joining of thumb and index finger after the consecration … Because the priest is acting as the minister of a sacrament of the Church his actions are at the service of his people. They express their reverence and devotion as well as his own. In article 4 he has noted that some of the chants of the Mass were *laus, exultatio populi* and envisaged the Lord's Prayer as *oratio communis totius populi*; and in his reply in ad 6 he describes the exchange of words between celebrant and people. In a. 5 he does not have much to add about actions of the people. In the liturgy of his day there was not much for them to do. Obviously it is an action of the people to just be there at the Mass. They count, and indeed should be counted. Thomas says in ad 11 that the number of hosts consecrated at a Mass should be enough to be consumed by priest, ministers and people; he does not seem to envisage reservation of hosts except for giving communion to the sick. In a. 5, ad 12, where he has to justify the use of plural form of words in *missa privata*, he says the people are always somehow there. Legally the Church requires a congregation to be there for the solemn celebration of Mass; and even when only one server is present at a Mass he *gerit personam totius populi catholici* and it is in the name of this entire Catholic people that he responds to the celebrant. It is considerations like this that help one to understand why in formulating the principle of representation at the body of this article Thomas recalls that the Eucharist represents not only the Passion of Christ but also Christ's Mystical Body.

Thomas does not consider situations in which the claims of representation and devotion might be in conflict. But his teaching about sacramentality and the place of practices of the virtue of religion in it can invite one to do so. Some speculation about how he might deal with such an eventuality could be interesting and might contribute to some contemporary debates about the value of re-introducing certain practices that were put aside in the wake of Vatican Two. The way Thomas deals in ad 3 with the signs of the cross made in the Mass, and particularly with the triple or double making of it at various points of the Eucharistic Prayer, might serve to raise the issue.[6] For Thomas the basic justification of this ritual action is clear: making the sign of the cross is appropriate because it represents the Passion of Christ, of which the Eucharist itself is a sign. But then he has to do some real exegetical gymnastics to explain why there are so many signs of the cross and why they are grouped in twos and threes. Having done so, he ends his reply with a remark into which one might read a hint of mild exasperation:

> In short, we may say that the consecration of this
> sacrament, and the acceptance of this sacrifice, and its
> fruits, proceed from the virtue of the cross of Christ, and
> therefore wherever mention is made of these, the priest
> makes use of the sign of the cross.

The combining of devotion with representation of the Passion
of Christ in the principle worked out in the body of article 5
requires one to consider the multiple signs of the cross also from
the point of view of the devotion of those who partake of the
sacrament. Whether Thomas knew it or not these multiple signs
of the cross are products of medieval devotionalism.[7] They were
developed, in accordance with what Jungmann calls 'the Gothic
principle of cumulation', as a way of exciting and expressing
devotion to the Passion in the Mass as it is present in the
Eucharist. They refer to the Passion of Christ, not in their own
right but by the reference they have to the core sacramentality
of the Eucharist, in which the bread and wine and the words
that consecrate them to be the body and blood of Christ make
the Passion of Christ present.

Obviously it is a pastorally laudable thing to help people and
priests grow in devotion as they celebrate the Eucharist.
Devotion, as an act of a moral virtue, has to be measured. While
it can never have too much intensity, its forms of expression can
be found wanting not only by deficit but also by excess. More
is not necessarily better. A recognised feature of religiosity is the
pressure to do more and more, and to claim special value for
certain numerical combinations; and this can be a compulsion
that is not necessarily healthy. Thomas treats superstition as an
excess of religiosity. Religiosity can also introduce an element of
'holy emulation' into the practice of religion. Cain put himself
in competition with Abel and it landed him in trouble. Those
who do more religious things or do them in certain numerical
patterns can seem to be better than others. One hears the
judgement, 'He/she is very religious; they make that novena
several times a year'. That can put pressure on those who do less
to match up, and even introduce superstitious fears that if they

do not, God will be less than pleased with them and with their more measured forms of religion. And this kind of dynamic can even be at work in the decisions made by Church authorities. It can influence them when they add various degrees of canonical authority to what are first called 'pious practices'.

The most serious risk in multiplying devotional expressions in the rite of the Mass is that they would somehow displace or obscure the core sacramentality of the Eucharist, which realises the Passion of Christ in the divinely given consecration of the bread and wine. Liturgical history can suggest that there were already peculiarities in medieval Latin liturgies that weakened the impact of that core sacramentality.[8] If something like multiple signs of the cross, or crucifixes placed ostentatiously on the altar between the celebrant and the congregation, were to become the focus of devotion to the Passion in a way that would further displace the devotion of the celebrant and the faithful from the core sacramentality of the consecrated bread and wine, they would be doing no great service to the liturgy. They might even encourage the feeling that the grace of Mass is somehow managed by human effort. This could explain why a restoration of attention to the core sacramentality of the Eucharist – such, for example as Vatican Two intended – could sensibly decide to scale down those personal acts of devotion.

Sacramentality and Common Sense (q. 83, a. 6)

Thomas's appreciation of the objective sacramentality of the Eucharist makes him very down to earth about the rite of the Mass. The canonists of his day were already launching an area of discussion on that would be called *defectus Missae*. To quote the first such problem Thomas records in the objections of article 6:

> it sometimes happens that before or after the consecration the priest dies or goes mad, or is hindered by some other infirmity from receiving the sacrament and completing the mass. Consequently it seems impossible to observe the

Church's statute, whereby the priest consecrating must communicate of his own sacrifice!

Thomas approves the standard canonical solutions to such liturgical contretemps. He does so by affirming again and again the principle of sacramentality: the reality of the Mass comes ultimately from its divinely instituted components, not from the practical, reverential and devotional clothing this has been given in the course of time and authorised variously by churches. The defects can only occur in this latter area. What is prescribed there must be taken seriously, but with a common-sense that leaves no place for superstitiously-fuelled scruples. As he puts it laconically but very theologically in his *sed contra*:

> Just as God does not command impossibility, so neither does the Church.

Neither does the Church think it impossible to combine the two poles of liturgical activity, sacramentality and devotion, which have been brought to light in Thomas's theology. He has seen how necessary it is that they should interact, and how undue concentration on one, or abuses in its application, can threaten and handicap the other. If more attention has been given here to the priority of sacramentality and to the need to let it discipline devotion, and the vagaries of devotionalism and religiosity, it is in the hope that this could bring to light aspects of the thought of Thomas Aquinas that are perhaps not always appreciated and that could make a useful contribution to current debates about liturgy.

Notes

1. Liam G. Walsh, 'Liturgy in the Theology of St Thomas', *The Thomist* 38 (1974), 557–83; David Berger, *Thomas Aquinas and the Liturgy* (Naples, FL: Sapientia Press, 2005); Aidan Nichols, 'St Thomas and the Sacramental Liturgy', *The Thomist* 72 (2008), 569–93; Antolin Gonzales Fuente, 'La teologia nella liturgia e la liturgia nella teologia

in san Tommaso d'Aquino', *Angelicum* 74 (1997), 359–417, 551–601; Matthew Levering, Michael Dauphinais and Kevin Thornton, *Rediscovering Aquinas and the Sacraments: Studies in Sacramental Theology* (Chicago: Liturgy Training Publication, 2009).

2.   For Thomas's teaching on sacraments see Liam G. Walsh, 'Sacraments', *The Theology of Thomas Aquinas*, Rik Van Nieuwhenhove and Joseph Wawrykow, eds. (Notre Dame, IN: University of Notre Dame Press, 2005), 326–64.

3.   On the centrality of *devotio* in Thomas's teaching about *religio* see Appendix 2, by C. Veleck in *Summa Theologiae*, Kevin D. O'Rourke OP, ed., Vol. 39, *Religion and Worship* (Oxford: Blackfriars, 1964), 256–8.

4.   This rite, worked on in the course of several General Chapters, seems to have been given its definitive form through the efforts of the Master of the Order, Humbert of Romans, and approved at the General Chapter of Paris in 1256, so within the lifetime of Thomas.

5.   Critics of Thomas's use of allegorical exegesis in his study of the rite of the Mass have not always appreciated this. See Berger, *Thomas Aquinas and the Liturgy*, 39. The passage from Jungmann referred to by Berger has a well documented and quite nuanced assessment of the use of allegorical interpretation in the thirteenth century: Albert the Great comes well out of it, Thomas also but a little less so. See Joseph A. Jungmann, *The Mass of the Roman Rite: Its Origins and Development (Missarum Solemnia)*, Vol. 1 (New York: Benzinger 1950), 113–18.

6.   Berger explains well the relationship of these signs of the cross to the sacramentality of the Eucharist: *Thomas Aquinas and the Liturgy*, 33–7; his attempts to make Thomas a champion of these multiple signs of the cross is less convincing.

7.   See Jungmann, *The Mass of the Roman Rite*, 107.

8.   Everything that distanced the faithful from what the celebrant was doing at the altar must have done so.

ON LITURGICAL TRADITION

༂ ༂ ༂

THOMAS R. WHELAN

This essay emerges in part from current discussion on 'best practice' concerning pastoral situations wherein, due to an increasing lack of ordained priests, a serious reconfiguration of the worship patterns of the weekday assembly must take place. Historical studies have been made of the frequency of Mass and Communion by Callam[1] and Bradshaw,[2] among others, and some of these early practices were brought to bear on contemporary issues by scholars like Taft[3] and Baldovin.[4] Despite increasing official reticence to promote the distribution of holy Communion from the Tabernacle when Mass is not available on weekdays, some places (not least in Ireland) have endorsed this practice – mostly by default. This practice, among others, is occasionally defended on the grounds that similar ritual customs were found in earlier centuries, and that consequently these form part of our 'tradition'.[5] The concerns raised here are primarily pastoral rather than academic. On the one hand, one wonders if the distribution of holy Communion outside of Mass as a replacement for weekday Mass best responds to a contemporary pastoral situation in Ireland. It could be suggested that this and related matters are better served – while fully honouring tradition – by recommending ways of addressing the needs of the weekday assembly that promote faith-development as well as an 'ownership' of assembly and Church at local levels that, albeit stretching narrow pastoral mind-sets, have potential for far-reaching pastoral benefit. Among these one could name the breaking down of unhealthy elements of clericalism in liturgy and worship practices.[6] On the other hand, questions arise when precedent is used to justify the importation of older forms of worship: by what criteria can later generations of christians appeal to earlier practices and attribute to these the weight of 'tradition'? In this context does 'liturgical tradition' refer to 'custom' or to liturgical history? Or is it something different? Can 'liturgical tradition' (used in this sense) have a claim to authority, and if so, what authority?[7]

This essay seeks to do no more than explore the parameters of the question.[8]

1. DESCRIBING LITURGICAL TRADITION

Appeal has always been made to 'liturgical tradition,' especially in relation to possible reform of prayer or rites. There is a vague sense in these discussions that a difference exists between liturgical tradition and liturgical history, but it is not always clear as to what it is or how one might discern it.

In liturgical studies *traditio* ('handing on') can be used in reference to anything from liturgical rites/prayer texts which are biblical in origin, to practices that are shared in the different churches, or to the complexity of customs and practices that developed within a local church, be it ancient or post-reformation. The term is also employed to refer to cultural mores which have coloured practices in worship.

Tradition[9] can be described as a living and dynamic reality that seeks to place the present in a continuum with the past with a view to influencing how the present might be shaped into a future. Therefore, it is more than simply memory of past events or concepts: we must speak of tradition as being future orientated.[10] It has been appealed to in Scripture in order to justify the establishment or continuity of a particular Christian teaching or practice.[11] For its part, liturgical studies has always involved, as an important component, an engagement with the history of liturgical form and text, and in this sense the task of 'recovering tradition' informed much of the scholarship of the liturgical movement throughout the entire twentieth century. Even the work of Dom Prosper Guéranger (1805–1875), although generally acknowledged to have been reactionary, historically misinformed in some regards and motivated by anti-Gallicanism, was carried out by what he understood to be a 'return to the sources' which would result in the recovery of 'tradition'. The recent move to 'reform the reform' similarly aspires to correct perceived erroneous interpretations of historical data and return post-Conciliar liturgy to its 'traditional' form.[12]

Understandably, if unhelpfully, the aftermath of the reform ushered in by the Council saw attention directed to the ritual and ceremonial changes that were made to liturgy. Insufficient attention has been given in popular writings, even today, to the more fundamental *theological* and *ecclesial* reform that underpins the Liturgy Constitution of 1963. A criterion proposed by *Sacrosanctum concilium* for the work of reforming liturgy was, in fact, tradition,[13] and it will be suggested later that this criterion is best understood in its theological and ecclesial dimensions and not simply that of source texts. Other criteria (including the overarching one of 'full, active and conscious participation' – SC 14) were broad and pastoral but always had to 'respect sound tradition' (SC 23).[14] For prayer texts this 'return to the tradition' was often interpreted to mean that, by means of textual and redaction criticism, the earliest and best representative of every prayer should be established and then employed. Partly driving this was a sense that a golden age of Roman liturgy once existed and that, aside from the modification to expressions of doctrine which some early prayers might now require (along with adaptations recommended by contemporary pastoral engagement), the recovery of the best of tradition, pre-eminently represented by prayers coming from earlier times, should be aspired to in the reform process.[15]

'Liturgical Tradition' and '(Sacred) Tradition'

(Sacred) Tradition [capital 'T'] refers to the apostolic teaching 'expressed in a special way' in the scriptures (DV 8) and which continues on in the Church as a living organism, enabling those who respond to God's invitation to faith to embody the values of the Kingdom as proclaimed by Jesus of Nazareth.[16] In this sense, and at this level, Tradition pertains to salvation. This Tradition is progressive in that there is a 'growth in insight into the realities and words that are being passed on' (DV 8). Included here are post-apostolic practices and precisions of the tenets of belief, such as those agreed in the early ecumenical Councils of the Church. Thus, for example, we can affirm that the ritual events referred to as Baptism and Eucharist pertain to Tradition, but not in the details of their rites or prayers.[17] For christians, both Scripture and Tradition act as a mirror of God's saving event as they journey on their pilgrim way (see DV 7). So, we must ask, when we speak of *liturgical* Tradition, do we do so by analogy with (sacred) Tradition or can the concept be applied, in its own right, to liturgy?[18]

Article 7 of the Liturgy Constitution identifies liturgy as an action of Christ in the exercise of his priestly office, Head and Members, in and through the Church. The efficacy of the liturgy is mediated by signs which become bearers of the salvific work of Christ. In a way similar but not identical to Christ's becoming the enfleshed and living revelation of God, sacramental signs embody the full weight of the saving reality of Christ which thereby brings the assembly into a deeper relationship with God in Christ,[19] in turn resulting in 'the sanctification of the human person' (SC 7).

The movement here is from the 'Mystery of God' (revealed to us through the Easter event – see SC 5 and 6 – and exercised through the priestly office of Christ), which is 'celebrated' as public worship by the living Body through rituals and prayers (SC 48), and which engages the assembly as it negotiates daily with 'life', thus persuading a transformation in human relationships. In describing the relationship of 'Mystery – celebration – life', Triacca highlights 'celebration' as the privileged place wherein 'life' and 'Mystery' meet and transact with salvific wholesomeness.[20] Such is the claim that liturgy has with regard to its saving role that 'no other action of the Church can equal its efficacy by the same title and to the same degree' (SC 7).

This means that we cannot speak of 'liturgical Tradition' by analogy with (sacred) Tradition: rather liturgy forms, in itself, a privileged expression of (sacred) Tradition. *Dei verbum* does not understand Tradition to be static content but rather as something that is embodied in and by the living *ecclesia* and transmitted faithfully through the generations in and through various cultural forms. The revealed faith of the Church, understood as Tradition, is lived and enacted daily through preaching, liturgy, and the outreach of believers to those on the margins making of them the centre (see DV 8). It can only be grasped in reference to the Paschal Mystery of Christ. If liturgy is understood to be the primordial place for a sacramental encounter and enfolding of God's saving outreach, then liturgical Tradition must be recognised as being in continuity with (sacred) Tradition as well as being a true and authentic manifestation and experience of it.[21] For Salvatore Marsili – under whom Patrick Jones studied – liturgy becomes an 'event of salvation' precisely because it is founded on the 'sacramentality of Revelation', the content of which is summarised in the Paschal Mystery of Christ (itself the culmination of God's saving work across the biblical Testaments). The liturgical event thus becomes the 'final moment in salvation history' in all its efficacy.[22] Liturgy is the privileged (but not the only) place where the word of God is preserved in a living way. If in 'a living way', then it means that revealed faith will find expression in the grammar of history (which is personal, social, political and cultural). If Pope Francis is able to speak of the Spirit as being an 'Apostle of Babel', creating difference from which a rich and diversified unity is manifested, then we might expect of liturgical tradition [small 't'] a similar diversity that does not upset the basic and fundamental unity of the faith tradition that it represents.

Paul speaks of how we are shaped by Christ in his death and Resurrection when we are baptised (see Romans 6:3-5) and of how we become sharers and co-participants in the salvific work of God in Christ. This is what is actualised in liturgy and, potentially, in the daily life of the assembly. The eternal *hodie* (= actuality; 'today-ness') of the Mystery of Christ in its salvific reality transacts with the personal *hodie* of the assembly, thereby creating the conditions for liberation and transformation. Memory, in itself, can be dangerous if it is not balanced with a radical sense of the present: therefore *anamnesis*, as the efficacious memory of the salvific workings of God for us through Christ, continues on through the Spirit and becomes less a review of what God in Christ did for us two thousand years ago and everything to do with the continual salvific invitation of God in our *hodie* (which is historically and culturally conditioned) to embrace new life through Word.

We must be able to affirm that the liturgical event becomes at once a living *locus* for the faith which is 'traditioned' (*fides quae creditur*) as well as for the personal deepening and expression of this faith on the part of the assembly in the liturgical event (*fides qua creditur*). It is the difference between faith considered 'in itself' and faith 'experienced', between the systematic conceptualisation of faith on the one hand, and graced Christian life lived in and through the Church community on the other. In this sense liturgy is the privileged, but not sole, form of traditioning Tradition.[23]

Levels of Expression of Liturgical Tradition
The theological employment of the term 'tradition' begs clarifications relating to the normativity of what is deemed to constitute its content (the phrase from the Faith and Order study of 1963, *parádosis* of the *kerygma*, is very broad). A similar concern is faced when discussing liturgical tradition. It is possible, I suggest, to see 'liturgical tradition' as operating at three levels. At the first level the liturgical event itself is understood to be a living embodiment of (sacred) Tradition ('liturgy traditioning Tradition'). The second level ('liturgical-

ritual reception of Tradition') reveals how the first level is manifested through the deep structures of liturgical ritual, including their biblical roots and forms of expression in the churches throughout history, while the third level ('liturgical tradition(s)') identifies ritual and euchological elements that frequently relate to particular local ecclesial expressions, often culturally framed. These, although characteristic of a particular church and probably important to its liturgical self-identity, are arbitrary in the sense that they do not always pertain to the central and salvific biblical revelation that is at the heart of (sacred) Tradition. It is to this third level that reform relates. The validity of each level of tradition depends on the extent to which it facilitates the assembly to actualise the Paschal Mystery of Christ in its midst. We will now explore briefly each of these levels of expression of liturgical Tradition.

(1) Liturgy Traditioning Tradition

In the liturgical event, an assembly is engaged with the Paschal Mystery, not just in a 'spiritual' manner but as a co-participant through Baptism in the salvific work of God in Christ. Thus it experiences (sacred) Tradition whose 'content' can be described as the living revelation of all that God has done for us and for our salvation in Christ (see DV 7). 'Full, conscious and active participation' (SC 14) has participation in the life of the Trinity as its purpose, however imperfectly in our present existence, and this happens through the modality of rites and prayers (*per ritus et preces*: SC 48) celebrated communally. The nature of *traditio* encountered here as a saving event is not empirically measurable but must be acknowledged as a faith reality.

If we simply speak of liturgy as being an 'authority' or witness to the act of transmission of faith, there is a danger that it could be considered to be such only to the extent that it echoes that which Tradition (systematically considered) deems to be of essence. However, the liturgical event is not extrinsic to or simply demonstrative of Tradition, pointing to it as it were from a distance: the liturgical event itself constitutes a privileged act of traditioning Tradition with the fullest salvific efficacy that is implied by the term. Thus, without excluding other manifestations of tradition, liturgy *becomes* Tradition in so far as it is the living and efficacious transmission of the salvific heart of God's self-revelation through the 'process' of human history and liturgical ritual, these latter constituting liturgical tradition [small 't'] which is expressed variously in time and place.

(2) *Liturgical-Ritual Reception of Tradition*

Liturgical ritual enables the assembly in its efficacious transaction with Paschal Mystery.[24] By engagement through space, time, movement, word, rite and other modes of social intercourse, believers embrace the Mystery of Christ (by means of Baptism, Eucharist, the praise of the Hours, to name a few) in a way that aligns ritual expression with the salvific purpose of Christ.[25] The validation of Tradition is to be found in the *receptio* that is expressed in tradition [small 't'] and in traditions. In this way, and through rite and prayer, assemblies in every place and in every generation are aligned with new life in Christ. Local churches, as well as every local assembly, are 'preeminent manifestations of the Church' (see SC 41-42) and therefore existentially embody the dynamics of the living Mystery of God. The local assembly is thus implicated ethically in this Mystery, and thereby becomes a personification of the Mystery (and not merely a witness to it).[26]

Tradition is ritually transmitted through liturgy in a privileged manner by means of the proclamation of the scriptures. This biblical proclamation, in turn, relates as 'sacrament' within the entire liturgical event (of which the celebrating assembly is subject). The breaking open of biblical word in the homily is at the heart of this and directly concerns the proclamation of the kerygma itself (presented as 'tradition' by Paul in 1 Corinthians 15:1-7). To this we must add the creedal formularies which have been used from earliest centuries as the central part of the baptismal liturgy[27] and which later found a place at Eucharist in some traditions.

Wainwright employs medieval theological language to propose how all those baptised and ordained, by virtue of these sacraments themselves, are rightly characterised as *deputati ad cultum* – 'destined for worship'.[28] As a result of baptism the believer is a participant in the Paschal Mystery of Christ,[29] no longer 'a receiver of the Gospel' but someone who 'actively embodies the faith'.[30] Those ordained, serving as part of a wider local ministry, are sacramentally charged to enable the local church to transact with salvation in its own social and political reality, thereby further transmitting and incarnating the Tradition into which they have been immersed in Baptism. Baptismal faith, which is supported through Orders and other forms of ecclesial ministry, is grounded in the Mystery of a Triune God whose salvific outreach to creation was revealed most completely and definitively in Jesus, and is extended through apostolic preaching and through the embodied witness of believers.

(3) Liturgical tradition(s)

The expression of Tradition in ritual form throughout history, as proposed in the previous section, holds a degree of consistency and ubiquity not found at a third level, that of liturgical tradition(s). At this level we are dealing with something that is somewhat more arbitrary and that reflects how liturgical expressions of Tradition are variously articulated in different epochs as well as by diverse churches.[31] Liturgical tradition(s) are no more than bearers of liturgical Tradition (second level) which, at this third level, are expressed and shaped by culture, history, customs, politics of empire (in both West and East) – all of which acted (or purported to act) as hermeneutics of Tradition (first level). Here 'tradition' [small 't'] might refer to those practices which ritually reflect Tradition and are shared by churches both East and West, but which in themselves may be described, at best, as normative *practices* which can, in theory at least, be modified in an ecclesial process.[32] From an anthropological perspective we must observe that both custom and practice, albeit culturally conditioned, collude over time to establish order and meaning in any form of ritual expression.

Using the language of DV 8, liturgical tradition(s) can be a 'witness to the life-giving presence' of the Tradition. Variations in ritual expressions to this witness have often developed along confessional lines or in traditions related to local churches. The normativity of certain practices, the non adherence to which do not necessarily represent a denial of doctrinal tenets, nonetheless do illustrate important truths of faith through ritual. One such example is the use of biblical readings as part of every sacramental celebration, mandated by the Council (see especially SC 24, 33, 35§4, 51, 78), even if the ritual history of liturgies show that this was not always the practice in the Western Church. Can, we might ask, some 'idea' feasts such as Corpus Christi, Sacred Heart (or one beloved in some post-Reformation traditions, Trinity Sunday) be considered as 'normative' in liturgical tradition in the same way that the liturgical seasons of Easter and Christmas clearly are?[33] One criterion often proposed for establishing the relative importance of certain festival days has been their antiquity and, to a lesser extent, their universality.[34]

2. DISCERNING LITURGICAL TRADITION

The identification of how liturgical Tradition [capital 'T'] is expressed in the worshipping assembly, while not a 'given', is a less complex task than sorting through the historical data that help identify and describe its ritual expression through tradition [small 't'] and traditions.[35] This raises some obvious questions. Are there liturgical traditions which are normative for the churches for today? How do we distinguish these from customs and practices which survive locally or which were found only in one or other period in history? To facilitate this, an exploration will be made of some criteria which are often presumed to function in the identification of liturgical Tradition/tradition.

Scripture

To subscribe to the proposition that 'liturgy is an authority (even a principal authority) in the transmission of Tradition, or a *locus theologicus* and source for identifying it', is, for

Geoffrey Wainwright, to suggest that worship developed from Tradition and points back to it. This would subscribe to the notion that Tradition is an 'unchanging content' to be carefully handed on. Wainwright is forthright in proposing that 'Liturgy *constitutes* the Tradition. Or even more boldly: Liturgy *is* the Tradition, and (more boldly yet) the Tradition *is* liturgy'.[36] Note needs to be taken of how the scriptures crystallise certain pre-existing liturgical practices, including some of the NT Christological hymns[37] and ritual elements, deemed by later theology to be constitutive of specific sacramental actions (e.g., imposition of hands, anointing, water) on the basis that they are to be found in Scripture. Classic among possible examples is the Institution Narrative of the Eucharist which represents a liturgical practice recorded in the NT according to *two* traditions, that of Paul/Luke and that of Mark/Matthew.

The underlying ritual patterns in the NT scriptures are themselves records of a living tradition and are historically prior to that which is deemed to be the originating biblical tradition. These ritual patterns do not simply communicate tradition by extrinsic association with the Mystery, but are incarnate modes (because they are 'ritual') making present as salvific reality that which Tradition itself transmits.[38] Thus in NT texts, the efficacy of Baptism is experienced by means of a water rite in a response to a 'coming to faith', thereby making of the newly baptised a participant in the death and Resurrection of Christ; and Eucharist, through its ritual sharing in bread and wine blessed and broken, becomes an experience (and more than just a memory) of the Resurrection. So, while respecting the permanent normativity of Scripture in Christian Tradition/tradition, we must state that the inchoate liturgical tradition embedded in the NT is normative only to the extent that it places the assembly in a human encounter with a saving God. This statement needs to be balanced by a consideration of the authority that scriptural tradition [small 't'] gives to central rites whose biblical origins help define their performance and faith-meaning.[39]

The assertion that 'the Bible was born from the liturgy' is true both as a statement of history as well as of theology.[40]

Scripture finds its natural home in liturgy, and it is in the liturgy that it becomes a living encounter for the assembly. The privileged arena for the interpretation of Scripture is worship,[41] which means that the ultimate hermeneutic of the biblical text is to be found in the faith community as it breaks open the Word as part of its sacramental enactment of the Paschal Mystery.[42] This Mystery of Christ is *really* present in Scriptures proclaimed as well as in the eucharistic species (see SC 7).[43] The context of the living faith of believers allows Scripture to take on a new meaning each time it is proclaimed in liturgy.[44] In the words of Taft, 'the liturgy is the ongoing *Sitz im Leben* of Christ's saving pattern in every age, and what we do in the liturgy is exactly what the New Testament itself did with Christ: it applied him and what he was and is to the present'.[45] Such is the relationship between Word and sacrament that the claims made for the alignment of Eucharist with the transmission of the faith must also be made of the proclamation of the biblical word, each being a different mode of participation in the same living Mystery of God of which Tradition is a bearer, and which is facilitated by liturgical tradition.[46] Scripture therefore has the qualities of sacrament and, as such, is a bearer of liturgical Tradition [capital 'T'].

Lex orandi

The principle that the worship practice of the Church is important for establishing the belief of the Church was sometimes appealed to in patristic debate, but Prosper of Aquitaine (d. c. 455) is the person who is attributed with casting the axiom in the memorable form we have today: '… so that the norm of interceding may establish the norm of believing.'[47] The binomial 'lex orandi, lex credendi' ('norm of praying, norm of believing') is a modern and abbreviated form of this fifth century axiom, and it is problematic on a number of counts.

[a] As it is usually employed, the binomial has no verb, and when given one, it is normally 'est'. This allows two misrepresentations of what Prosper initially intended: (i) both terms are now on equal footing with the result that the healthy

tension between them, present in the original axiom, has been removed; and (ii) the two elements can be reversed to imply the opposite of what was originally stated: the 'norm of believing' is/leads to the 'norm of praying'.

[b] The arbitrary presence and behaviour of a copulative verb ('est') in the binomial means that it is made to signify whatever an author wishes and to reflect a theological agenda imposed by the author.[48]

[c] From this follows the challenge that arises when the binomial is employed variously by different churches, reflecting their own particular historical and doctrinal positions. Thus, for the Orthodox and Eastern churches which understand their rich liturgy to be the place where the doctrinal teaching of the Church is most clearly expressed, the verb 'est' is important ('lex orandi EST lex credendi').[49] In contrast to this, the post-Reformation articulation, reacting to the abuses it saw in the Roman Catholic liturgical practice, set out to ensure that correct doctrine would inform how worship is shaped and worded. In these churches there is strong adherence to the principle that it is the 'lex credendi' that shapes ['est'] the 'lex orandi'.[50] Although we only find explicit reference to the principle in modern times since the sixteenth century, the binomial appears for the first time in nineteenth century Catholic circles and reflects the ancient sense that worship gives articulation to belief.[51]

[d] Just as the arbitrary role and choice of verb is problematic, so also is the employment of the term 'lex orandi' in a narrow and literal sense. This has manifested itself in two opposite directions. (i) There are those who would wish to recommend that doctrine be expressed according to how it is conceptualised in liturgical prayer. Such an extreme position, for example, was proposed by the Irish (sometime Jesuit) George Tyrrell (1861-1909) and his modernist followers (and later taken up by a group of active lay Catholics in Germany in the earlier part of the twentieth century) who stated that the 'lex orandi' produces the 'lex credendi'. For them, 'belief' must articulate the religious and faith experience of believers as expressed in liturgical prayer. (ii) In an opposite and equally extreme expression, the 1947

encyclical of Pius XII, *Mediator dei* – the first Roman document to employ the binomial 'lex orandi lex credendi' rather than the more complete text attributed to Prosper – tried to counteract this modernist position by reversing the ancient sense of the phrase and made it say that 'the norm of believing establishes the norm of praying'. Since 1947, the Roman Catholic Church has increasingly employed the protestant reversal of the original meaning of the binomial in order to assert its authority in all matters relating to liturgy. Thus the *General Instruction on the Roman Missal* (2002/2008) affirms and insists that the 'lex orandi' of the Missal corresponds with the 'lex credendi' of the Church.[52] John Paul II retained the same reversal of the traditional expression of this binomial when he stated, 'Fidelity to the rites and to the authentic texts of the Liturgy is a requirement of the *lex orandi*, which must always be in conformity with the *lex credendi*'.[53] This same stricture is to be found in the 2001 document that regulates the vernacular translation of liturgical books: '... the *lex orandi* must always be in harmony with the *lex credendi* ...' (*Liturgiam authenticam*, 80).[54]

However, if official Roman Catholic writings change the meaning and intent of the axiom of Prosper, misrepresenting in a rather simplistic fashion its original sense as well as the dynamics and complexity of a relationship that exists between the two elements, then this is not so among Catholic exponents of liturgical theology.[55] Here the discussion establishes the foundational character of how we pray liturgically (and therefore recognising liturgy to be a formal ecclesial act rather than a mere ceremonial happening) and how this relates creatively with the norm of belief: each element (praying/believing) has its own sphere of operation and both interact together in a creative fusion that sometimes has one element taking priority over another while retaining the general dynamic that moves from liturgical prayer to belief.[56]

Given the importance of the influence of the adage attributed to Prosper of Aquitaine in this discussion, it would be helpful to briefly remind ourselves of what exactly it says, and how this might best be understood. The original text states, '... so that the norm of supplicating may establish the norm of believing'. The historical and theological context of the document in which this saying is found endeavours to demonstrate the veracity of a doctrinal issue relating to grace: we do not initiate the movement towards conversion and faith but rather these constitute our response to God's prior action of grace. Many arguments are put forward by Prosper, mostly referring to papal teaching. His final argument relates to worship and the apostolic mandate to intercede for all (see 1 Timothy 2:1-4), a mandate that is carried out in liturgy when prayer is offered for all so that grace may be given to all (= 'lex supplicandi'), thereby demonstrating that grace is necessary for all (= 'lex credendi'). This practice, according to Prosper's line of reasoning, has apostolic origins (hence his reference to 1 Timothy) and to which biblical text he refers elsewhere as the 'rule of apostolic teaching (*apostolicae doctrinae regula*)'.

A few important insights can be gleaned from this very brief overview: [1] the 'rule of praying/supplicating (*lex orandi/ supplicandi*)' does not refer to the actual texts of the prayers themselves[57] but to the *fact* that intercession is made for those in need of conversion (this is, after all, one of the points at the heart of the debate he is having with the semi-Pelagians); [2] the authority of these prayers is not grounded in what is said or done, but on apostolic authority (1 Timothy). Therefore, we must conclude, liturgical prayer does not have a primacy independent of its reference back to apostolic teaching (*regula fidei*) or to Tradition as found in Scripture and the continual practice of the Church. [3] Elsewhere in the same document Prosper appeals to the universality of the rituals as well as prayers in the exorcisms employed in Baptism. This indicates that, in Prosper's argument, the 'lex supplicandi' (rule of supplicating, which we must understand to include liturgical ritual as well as text) sets the standard but, again, only to the extent that it relates to apostolic doctrine.

Therefore we need to be clear that there is no assertion that the entirety of the *credens* ('norm of believing') is to be found in the *orans* ('norm of praying'); nor that the 'norm of praying' is confined just to what is found in prayer texts. Prosper is clear that there is a dialectic relationship between both 'norms', and that these must be in conformity with apostolic teaching. These nuances cannot be easily communicated by the truncated, compact form of the binomial, 'lex orandi, lex credendi'. The axiom, in its original form, ought always to be used, thereby allowing the verb 'establish' (*statuat*) give expression to what in reality is the case. There were always times in which the liturgical rite was appealed to by theology (including patristic writers) and by Church authority when articulating some of its more formal teaching: the *lex orandi* points towards the *lex credendi*. On the other hand, there have been many instances where either heretical teaching or new doctrinal insights have required the modification of prayer texts: the *lex credendi* causing an adjustment to the *lex orandi*. This dialectic correlation is allowed for in the original axiom of Prosper but not so easily in the rather arbitrary relationship between the two terms in the binomial.[58]

The principle that 'the norm of supplicating establishes the norm of believing', despite the necessary tensions that can exist between these two elements, sets forth what is taken to be a methodological norm for liturgical theology today: how we pray (verbally and ritually) is the normative starting point for a theological investigation of liturgy and sacrament.[59] The axiom does not state that the liturgical event says all that there is to say about Christian belief, nor that prayer must be framed as doctrinal statements. (Of their nature, prayers are vehicles for praise, thanksgiving and intercession and do not have as their purpose the bearing of formal dogmatic teaching.) History, particularly in the first millennium, shows us that a healthy tension always existed between the two elements, but in such a way that the privileged priority of *orans* always creatively serves the *credens* which in turn often exerts pressure back onto the *orans*.

We must therefore consider that the axiom helps us to discern what may be of greater importance to a sense of liturgical *tradition* than simply a compilation of historical facts relating to liturgical practices. Given the inherently conservative nature of liturgy, the 'lex supplicandi [orandi]' will normally refer to the rites and prayers found within the liturgical tradition(s) of a particular christian denomination. In this way, the Prosperian axiom (in preference to its modern reductive binomial) can serve as part of a process of discernment of the extent to which a liturgical practice or element pertains to liturgical tradition, as well as what weight it might carry within that tradition. In this case the axiom needs to be employed with care and respect for the nuance that it carries in the original Prosperian context. The 'lex orandi' must never be considered a mere *auctoritas* or *probatio/protestatio* of the faith but rather as pertaining to an *actus liturgicus* which reveals the prayer and ritual context in which the believer transacts with the salvific event of Christ in her or his *hodie*.

Where systematic theology is accustomed to taking Scripture as the logical theological starting point in a discussion, a consideration of the 'lex orandi' shows how an assertion that liturgy constitutes *theologia prima* does not diminish Scripture and its privileged place in Christian life nor its normative position for establishing the limits of revelation. Rather it provides a broader basis within which the living tradition of the scriptures is intuitively understood as both revelation in action and a privileged *locus* for the transmission of the apostolic faith.

History and Tradition

Much of the work of the twentieth century ecumenical Liturgical Movement would not have been possible except for the historical study that had emerged alongside a renewed interest in the worship practices of the patristic era and the publication of early medieval liturgical sources. Students of liturgical history increasingly came to the view that, especially from the medieval period onwards, liturgies began to develop ritual and euchological excesses that were thought to be no longer pastorally appropriate today. Many of the liturgy reforms of the past sixty years or so across the churches were influenced heavily by historical research as can be witnessed, for instance, in the reforms of initiation, eucharistic practice, and Orders.[60]

Certain liturgical rites are imbedded in the biblical accounts of the ministry of Christ and the early Church and are, for that reason, irreducible. Churches have consistently transmitted the Tradition to which these referred, by means of a 'translation' through ritual and language that is coloured by history and the modalities of culture, so that this Tradition will continue to be alive and salvific for those who engage with it ritually. The core rites of initiation, eating and drinking of the eucharistic Christ, anointing, of embracing in reconciliation, of daily prayer in the name of Christ, and of formal appointment to ministry, have been shaped and reshaped in and by history. Liturgical Tradition [capital 'T'] does not exist except in the forms and words given to it by culture and language, as well as their pastoral and historical contexts. History and its study can point out to us how God in Christ engaged efficaciously with peoples in different eras and in certain cultural forms which we can refer to as 'liturgical tradition(s)'. The challenge of each generation has been to discern how, in their earlier historical expression, current liturgical practices placed assemblies in touch with the *parádosis* of the *kerygma* as this was expressed in sacrament and praise. These practices changed and developed over time, often imperceptibly, so that later generations can find in history a repertoire of rites and prayers relating to worship. A temptation, especially in times of liturgical reform, is to appeal to these and incorporate them into contemporary worship in the belief that, by so doing, a guarantee is given that there is a return to a more 'traditional' form of worship. Here the appeal to history is equated with the desire to 'recover tradition': the more ancient the sources, the more venerable and precious the tradition is perceived to be. A related danger is seen in how, at times, a more radical reform is promoted on the grounds that *everything* that history identifies as having taken place is considered to pertain equally to tradition and therefore offer viable options for their re-employment on those grounds alone.[61]

Historians today, however, observe that the research on which some reforms were based was incomplete or one-sided, or that a contemporary recovery of some ancient practices did not consider the liturgical purpose, theological meaning or cultural resonances that shaped rites or texts when initially employed. Paul Bradshaw speaks of how important it is for contemporary churches to base their reform agenda on a theologically informed pastoral strategy capable of understanding the historical and cultural context of the precedents to which it wishes to appeal.[62]

Ritual and prayer elements from a past era cannot be easily translated into a different context without changing completely the meaning and functioning of this element. Robert Cabié speaks of the artificiality and inauthenticity of importing from liturgical history 'solutions' for our times. While it can offer insights and paradigms, history is never normative as it speaks only in the 'indicative' and never with the 'imperative'.[63] Even in the academy, historians recognise that its scholarly enquiry investigates and reveals how christians of former times engaged salvifically with Paschal Mystery, and how history must now serve new generations in their search for a living expression of Tradition that is authentic and rooted.

Sacrosanctum concilium 23 requires that, in the work of reform, care be taken that new forms 'should in some way grow organically from forms already existing', a concept that owes its origins to Anton Baumstark (1872–1948) and the comparative studies of culture that has roots in the early nineteenth century. Cabié sees here the possibility of a continuity between the child and its elderly self, and how, despite all of the changes and wisdom the years brought, it is still the same person. However, neither ritual studies nor a history of how liturgical form developed over the centuries can support a sense of organic development that is unfettered by the human context within which it thrives. 'Organic' growth (be it in nature or liturgy) is never neat or predictable and is only discerned retrospectively. While the origins of a practice can be uncovered, the 'organic' development of liturgical form shows that it invariably embraces 'non-essential' matter which compromises its 'purity', modifies its shape and rarely conforms to type. Organic development in liturgy is conditioned by context and culture and must be deemed to reflect an authentic experience of faith for those who ritually engaged with it. History cannot but help us map its genesis and growth. Nevertheless Cabié's conclusion is correct: we cannot confuse Tradition with history, identifying, as history does, helpful and unhelpful experiences or suggesting directions to explore. However, history cannot dictate to Tradition [capital 'T'] what a contemporary re-reading of faith ought to be or how liturgical traditions ought to behave.[64] In different ways, both liturgical Tradition and tradition refer to a process that is never ending, always in need of discernment, and one that is guided by the Spirit as a living expression in and through the churches.

Liturgical tradition is not an atemporal or disembodied entity but a living engagement with and transmission of Tradition which needs to be translated through history and culture to a contemporary experience of faith.[65] The discernment of how liturgical history and liturgical Tradition [capital 'T'] relate with one another in a way that serves the faith of the praying assembly cannot be guided by a 'normativity' imposed on it from outside of Tradition itself, nor by a normative *magisterium* or teaching office which can decide on what constitutes liturgical Tradition.[66] One of the criteria must be that of the dynamic relationship established between the 'lex orandi' and the 'lex credendi' as described above, with the healthy tensions that the relationship implies. When ecclesial authority interferes with this natural dynamic and forces a relationship, the process of the liturgical traditioning of Tradition is compromised in its capacity to facilitate an assembly with its engagement with the Mystery of Christ. In these cases the liturgical act becomes part of ecclesiastical politics and Church authority is no longer a ministry exercised 'for the life of the world' (John 6:51).

Another valuable criterion is supplied by the ancient sense of 'unanimity, antiquity and universality',[67] the best known expression of which was famously given to us by Vincent of Lérins in the fifth century: that which is believed everywhere, always, and by everybody.[68] The extent to which one or other of these three elements of the criterion is diminished or missing, the lesser a claim will a liturgical practice have to being at the core of the liturgical traditioning of Tradition.[69] Together the elements of this Vincentian criterion refer to 'reception,' a decisive factor in determining authenticity in the transmission of doctrine (as a *consensus fidelium*): the extent and modality of 'reception' should help ascertain the universal legitimacy of certain liturgical forms found in liturgical history.

3. 'REFORM' AS A CRITERION FOR TRADITIONING LITURGICAL TRADITION

Little notice is taken of the opening article of *Sacrosanctum concilium* which states that the reform of the liturgy is in view of what amounts to being nothing less than a thorough *reform of the Church*. SC 1 states that this reform hopes to bring increasing vigour to the lives of christians and to modify what can be changed so that the unchanging gospel will speak more clearly to people today. The desired reform was also outward-looking: the promotion of union among all who believe in Christ, and the making known of God's Reign in Christ. At times of crisis and reform, Church must always rethink its identity in the light of the Gospels (and Tradition[70]): how christians of previous generations lived the Paschal Mystery needs to be interrogated once again to ensure that the contemporary Church remains faithful to the salvific message of Christ, and such a re-interrogation will be in the light of pastoral requirements today. In SC, the reform of liturgy is clearly at the service of the reform of the Church.[71]

Reform, such as the one experienced by Roman Catholics after the Second Vatican Council, brings about renewed insights into Christian belief (thereby representing a modified *lex credendi*[72]) and these in turn become a guiding principle in the subsequent reform of liturgy, steered by a keen sense of the textual and ritual repertoire of liturgical practices found in tradition. As has happened in all liturgical reform throughout history, older practices or prayers can be restored – sometimes in a modified and revised form – or new rites and prayers can be developed.[73] Decisions to revise or not will be made in view of the fact that a Church reform can require, on so many fronts, that the modified *lex credendi* bears heavily on the *lex orandi*.[74] De Clerck suggests that what is true of the reform process, which gives priority to doctrinal concerns over the *lex orandi*, also holds true for 'the transition to the vernacular,'[75] and this explains something of Rome's current pre-occupation with a more literal rendition of Latin euchology. What we witness in *Liturgiam authenticam* (2001) is a concern that liturgical prayers be in conformity with belief, this latter understood as 'Church teaching'. Thus the current Roman expectation, reflecting the narrow approach it took in the earlier part of the liturgical movement, is that liturgical texts could be used as 'proof texts' and thereby be respected as authoritative affirmations of doctrine.[76] The authoritativeness of the vernacular translation, according to *Liturgiam authenticam*, is now to be judged against its fidelity to the Latin in every detail of grammar and style.

Klöckener's study demonstrates that every reform of liturgy throughout history has been guided, not so much by a desire to reform the liturgy in itself, but in order to have the liturgy reflect more clearly contemporary (theological) insights of how the *life of the Church* might be best re-visioned, thereby to more fully 'tradition Tradition'. But behind this is also a profound sense that liturgy, because this is where the privileged sacramental encounter with the Paschal Mystery takes place, is the *fons* from which reform can mostly authentically emerge (see SC 10). If Church reform does not find its *fons* (as embodiment of Paschal Mystery) in liturgy then the reform will be superficial and irrelevant, and will not serve the *missio Dei*.

Reform and *ressourcement* are somewhat different. Liturgical reform is in view of contemporary needs and ought not to return to the 'sources' for their own sake. For its part, *ressourcement* is not a return to the past as such, nor is it an exercise in archaeology. Rather, it deepens a *contemporary* sense of Christian living, embedding it in previous experience – almost opening the present to a contemplative and 'rooted sense' of itself. These 'sources' from our two-thousand year old tradition refer to an underlying *fons* (singular rather than the plural, *fontes*) that places Christians in touch with the Mystery of God as a lived reality. (We will return to this point.) For its part, reform does not imply a break with the past but rather an understanding of the continuing presence of the saving Mystery in the circumstances of the life of the Church. However, if Church reform both requires and justifies liturgical reform, then it means that all religious practices and pieties must be open to critical investigation in the light of current pastoral needs. Such reform of liturgical practices must be carried out in deference to liturgical tradition (which is not unchangeable in all its dimensions) but only to the extent that new or renewed forms do not harm a sense of continuity with liturgical Tradition [capital 'T'] and a nourishment of faith (see SC 12-13). This raises the question of how the parameters of a liturgical tradition can be established. SC 38 asks that the 'substantial unity of the Roman rite be preserved' in any work of inculturating liturgy, but fails to reveal what this 'substantial unity' might be.[77] Contemporary developments in the Roman Dicastery responsible for Worship continue to promote a narrow ahistorical sense of this neologism,[78] but a better set of parameters would, I suggest, be supplied by a study of how liturgy traditioned Tradition throughout history, and how these found expression among the various liturgical traditions that are found in the Church of Christ (East and West), of which the Roman Catholic is one part. If the Roman liturgy was capable of accepting influences from outside of the City (however reluctantly at times), then, surely, it must still be capable of engaging with social and cultural contexts of today in its desire to serve the *missio Dei*. No matter how 'substantial unity' is defined, it must always be in view of transmitting a living salvific reality through sacramental encounter.

But there is another level on which reform of liturgy must be understood to serve reform of Church. The reference in SC 10 to liturgy being both the *culmen* and *fons* of the life of the Church must also be understood in terms of reform. If Church reform requires liturgical reform, it is because liturgy puts the Church in touch with the source (*fons*) of its very life and being: the Paschal Mystery of Christ. In this sense we can say that liturgy needs to be reformed by the Church so that, in turn, liturgy will become the graced ontological environment within which reform of Church and of Christians will be enabled.[79]

Church reform, therefore, conspires to work towards the self-realisation of the 'christian project' in Christ. This project will only find its fulfilment at the second coming (*parousia*) which means that, in these eschatological times between the two comings of Christ in which we live, the ecclesial Body of Christ must engage in a continual 'act of becoming'. To achieve this, Church reform has always worked towards a return to Tradition [capital 'T'], often requiring that the way in which liturgy 'traditions' Tradition be adjusted so as to bear the weight of the greater ecclesial reform.[80] In traditioning Tradition, liturgy is revealed as the privileged source (*fons*) where the Paschal Mystery is encountered as salvation. Liturgical tradition, through its efficacious ritual and prayer, becomes the place where Tradition [capital 'T'] is experienced as a Spirit-induced contemporary reality that is rooted in the historical incarnation of Christ which projects us towards our salvific fullness in God.[81] All of liturgy (and not just certain moments) is *anamnetic*, making the salvation brought about for us by Christ in the Paschal Mystery a reality for us today. This *anamnesis* is not made, in the first place, in simple reference to creed or a moment of sacramental institution, but, efficaciously, to the salvific work of God for us in Christ. We say 'efficacious,' because of the transforming agency of the Spirit who makes 'actual' to us (= the *hodie* of liturgy) the saving work of God in Christ. The encounter in liturgy between our *hodie* and that of Christ permits a transaction to take place between salvation and our political, economic and cultural contexts. This is the arena in which Tradition shapes our 'becoming church' and which in turn cannot but give to Tradition new forms of expression. It is in this 'becoming' that Mystery directs us to our eschatological climax in God. It is the eschatological that gives meaning to *anamnesis-epiclesis* as an activity of the present that is rooted in God's 'past' (throughout both Testaments).[82]

When the Church considers reform, it is in view of its desire to 'profoundly re-think its own identity' (Grillo) and role in the world. This has profound implications for how we understand 'meaning' in liturgy. The meaning that is generated in a liturgical event takes shape in the assembly because of a collectivity of ritual activities and texts (be these biblical or euchological). In this sense meaning cannot be predetermined or controlled, but is generated by a complexity of movements, some of which are extra-liturgical.[83] This means that, in the quest to uncover 'tradition' (at both second and third levels) a sense of the origins and provenance of different elements is essential. However, this exercise does not produce meaning, which is a contemporary experience, but history. It must be recognised that to the extent that ritual and textual elements of worship are accepted or modified throughout the various liturgy reforms of history, their original referents that helped to create their former meaning(s) have also been changed – sometimes unrecognisably so. If the reform of liturgy is part of the larger desire to 'profoundly re-think its identity' in view of contemporary needs to witness to the Gospel, then this has the effect – often unintended and unconscious – of imbuing old rites with different and new meaning.

Liturgical reform is in view of enabling the conversion of the local Church so that its adjustment in faith will return the Church to its original identity as believers who bear witness in their lifestyle and conduct to the self-giving Passion and Resurrection of Christ whose Spirit enables. If the Church grew from mission – mission is also its very raison d'être – then the realisation of the *missio Dei* must be the fundamental goal of the liturgy. The reform of liturgy sets out to achieve this and does so in fidelity with Tradition, and with how Tradition is traditioned liturgically. Liturgical reform that is occasioned by Church reform remains the primary criterion for evaluating liturgical tradition. Essential to this process is that it happens *in ecclesia*, wherein rests the authority for such a reform.

4. CONCLUSION

This essay offers no more than an initial exploration of an issue that is important and pertains to both 'fundamental' liturgical theology as well as to liturgical methodology. Criteria and processes of discernment are needed in order that liturgical theology will interpret liturgical history so that Tradition will be served in its task of aligning believers with the foundations of God's saving interaction in human history, culminating with the loving embrace of Christ which reaches out to all.

History remains important – the peripheral more so than the centre, and the marginal in preference to the privileged. So much of liturgical history seems to concentrate on the cathedral and the large monastic centres, understandable in that these were the places that supplied, for the most part, the important manuscript sources, and which in turn influenced local worship practices of their time. As important as these were, they came to be deemed formative and representative in a way that current historical research belies. To the extent that the 'silent' participant in worship throughout the centuries effected change (sometimes deemed to be irregular, forbidden or unapproved by local Church authorities), these must be read theologically as expressions of local churches and their authentic desire to offer prayers and praise to God.[84] Just as the victors rather than victims write social and political history, so too has the scholarship of manuscripts and episcopal edicts created a narrative of the 'development' of liturgy, particularly of the Latin West.[85] They form part of liturgical 'tradition(s),' but need to be read and re-read against how liturgy came to 'tradition Tradition.'

Christian Tradition, as a living entity, seeks to understand the contemporary context of faith as it is expressed in the shifting reality that is composed of complex and sometimes opposing movements in politics, sociology, economics, and environment –

as well as how the global and the local compete as legitimate arenas for the generation of 'meaning'. To do this requires a keen sense of the past – not just in terms of history but in terms of what past generations deemed to be 'essential' and important. But history will show that Tradition [capital 'T'] is always read and interpreted 'from where we are,' and that various eras will emphasise one or other aspect of the christian belief over another, in response to pastoral needs of the time. There is nothing arbitrary happening here. In order that it remains a living entity which frames 'meaning' for those who subscribe to it and so as to place an assembly in touch with its origins, Tradition must be capable of restatement which employs fresh language and concepts as well as diverse cultural referents (as has *always* been the case). And, for christians, the root metaphor which best describes these origins is Paschal Mystery. But the reason for referencing the past is always in view of the present so that it might have a future that is deemed to be in continuity with its origins.

To the extent that deep structures of liturgy (not just in terms of ritual shape but also as these influence the structure of christian living) relate to the liturgical traditioning of Tradition, they must be respected. But the patterns of christian existence must be continually served by rites and prayers which will help form christian belief and practice in fidelity to tradition. It is in this that the 'future orientation' of Tradition resides. The salvific and graced nature of liturgical Tradition is available through the liturgical action of the local assembly, and this also serves the Church's renewal and its consequent requirement that liturgy, as an embodiment of tradition [small 't'], be adapted to facilitate such a renewal.

The criterion of 'ecclesial reform' is important. Its authority does not come, in the first place, from Church authorities but from the reform that happens *in ecclesia* which is ratified and 'confirmed' by Church authority (at the levels of Rome, or Episcopal Conference, or local Ordinary, as appropriate). Some traditions must change, irrespective as to their age and ubiquity, particularly if these block the deeper reform of Church. Here one thinks of, for instance, the clericalisation of the liturgy and ministry[86] and the privatisation of worship because these betray the Kingdom intention of Jesus and also compromise the transmission and experience of Christian 'becoming' – the protection of which is the purpose of Tradition, a living expression of God's saving outreach to us. Ecclesial reform always moves from pastoral concerns and from a sense that current ecclesial practices and expressions of biblical faith may need to be re-presented in a way that enables those whose faith-identity is centred on the Paschal Mystery of Christ to be refreshed and re-orientated in how they live their Christian lives. It would seem that all Church reforms in history have either directly included liturgy reform or, at least, had serious implications for liturgy.

Let me end where I began: weekday parish worship when there is no Mass. In the search for a pastoral solution, reflection needs to consider the various practices for weekday worship throughout history in a theological key, as well as seek reasons why daily Communion and later, daily Mass, came to be considered normal. To get in touch with liturgical Tradition [capital 'T'] such considerations need to include a review of how Eastern churches worship daily. These need to be critically evaluated in terms of a movement of practice and thought over two millennia. Whatever ritual forms of worship are proposed must sit comfortably with the ecclesiology found in the pages of the sixteen documents of Vatican Two and must be underpinned by the theological vision of liturgy that is found in SC. The ecclesial reform proposed at the Council can only be brought to fruition if it is served by appropriate reform of how we understand our worshipful relationship with the God of Jesus Christ, and of how the Spirit will lead us towards fresh ways to embody our 'act of becoming' in ecclesial, ministerial and liturgical ways that fulfil the reform aspirations of SC 1. In this way we might have reason to aspire to bring ever greater vigour to Christian life today in local churches and parishes, to nourish them in their outreach to those on the margins of society.

Notes

1. See Daniel Callam, 'The Frequency of Mass in the Latin Church ca. 400', *Theological Studies* 45 (1984), 613–50.

2. See a number of essays in Paul F. Bradshaw, *Reconstructing Early Christian Worship* (London: SPCK, 2009), along with his many writings on early eucharistic practices as well as daily praying of the 'Hours'.

3. See Robert Taft, 'The Frequency of the Eucharist throughout History', *Beyond East and West Problems in Liturgical Understanding* (Washington, DC: Pastoral Press, 1984), 61–80.

4. See John F. Baldovin, 'Reflections on the Frequency of Eucharistic Celebration', *Worship: City, Church and Renewal* (Washington, DC: Pastoral Press, 1991), 99–113.

5. Anecdotal evidence suggests that no attempt is made by those who appeal to 'tradition' to interpret earlier practices in their historical, ecclesial or theological contexts, such as is done by the authors of the articles referred to in previous footnotes.

6. An introduction to the discussion is proposed in Thomas R. Whelan, 'No Mass on Weekdays: Some Reflections from Theology', *The Furrow* 65 (2014), 233–41; 297–304 [also available on www.liturgy-ireland.ie/resources.html].

7. This is not a uniquely Catholic problem, and each worship tradition is informed from within its own ecclesial practices over the centuries as to how it can best engage with history and tradition. While very little has been written that directly relates to the topic, the following are relevant: Louis-Marie Chauvet, 'La notion de "tradition"', *La Maison-Dieu* 178 (1989), 7–46; Pierre-Marie Gy, 'Tradition vivante, réforme liturgique et identité ecclésiale', *La Maison-Dieu* 178 (1989), 93–106; Geoffrey Wainwright, 'Tradition as a Liturgical Act', *Worship with One Accord: Where Liturgy and Ecumenism Embrace* (Oxford: Oxford University Press, 1997), 45–64; and Martin Klöckener, 'La tension entre tradition et renouvellement dans la liturgie de l'église catholique', *La Maison-Dieu* 275 (2013), 135–72.

8. The approach here will be 'classical'. A more complete study than this would need to include a serious consideration of contemporary cultural studies and how trends and 'movements' influence the interpretation of history, tradition and pastoral practice. For instance, an appeal to tradition is difficult to sustain in a society that challenges the validity of an expansive or all-embracing narrative that goes beyond the subjective, or that situates 'authority' in the self and one's own experience, or that places the immediate and local as primary referents for the generation of meaning or relevance.

9. How I employ the term in this essay is not uninfluenced by the final Report from a meeting of the Faith and Order section of the World Council of Churches in 1963 at which the question of tradition was discussed. In Section II (# 39) the Report proposed that *Tradition* [capital 'T'] refers to 'the Gospel itself, transmitted from generation to generation in and by the Church, Christ himself present in the life of the Church'. Elsewhere it described the Tradition of the Gospel as the *parádosis* of the *kerygma* (# 45). No 39 continued to speak of *tradition* [small 't'] as the 'traditionary process'; and proposed that *traditions* is used to refer to the 'diversity of forms of expression' (as confessional traditions) as well as to cultural traditions. See *The Fourth World Conference on Faith and Order, Montreal 1963*, Faith and Order Paper no. 42, P. C. Roger and L. Vischer, eds. (London: SCM Press, 1964), 50, 52. Some similarities of thought can be seen in *Dei verbum* of Vatican II which was published in late 1965.

10. Robert F. Taft says that liturgical history does not deal with the past, 'but with tradition, which is a *genetic vision of the present*, a present conditioned by its understanding of its roots': 'The Structural Analysis of Liturgical Units', *Beyond East and West*, 151–64, at 153 (emphasis in original).

11. One thinks of, for example, St Paul in 1 Corinthians 11:2, 23-26; 15:3-11; as well as 2 Thessalonians 1: 12, 14; 2:15; 3:6 and Jude 1:3.

12. This refers to a movement in recent decades which holds that the reforms which took place after the Council misunderstood its intentions and ought to be corrected. See the contributions by John F. Baldovin and Liam G. Walsh in this volume which deal with concerns which arise from this movement.

13. The Latin word appears some twenty times in the Constitution, its principal occurrences being, SC 4; 23; 24; 40 (1) which interestingly refers to the 'traditions and cultures' of people (not in texts) in the context of its discussion of a more radical form of liturgical inculturation, as does SC 81 with regard to funeral rites, and SC 119 in relation to indigenous music; 65; 89 (a); 91; 101 in relation to the Liturgy of the Hours; 106 in reference to the liturgical year; 109 (a); 111; 112 and 120 with regard to music.

14. The notion of 'sound tradition' is explored in Klöckener, 'La tension entre tradition et renouvellement', esp. 165–71.

15. While this statement is not wrong, it is broad-sweeping and would need to be modified by a more detailed and nuanced survey of criteria which developed in the process of preparation of the post-Conciliar liturgy. A good starting point for such an overview is Annibale Bugnini, *The Reform of the Liturgy 1948–1975* (Collegeville, MN: Liturgical Press, 1990).

16. Faith and Order Paper 42 (see note 9, above) also presents Tradition as a living entity, noting that Scripture needs 'to be interpreted by the Church in every new situations' (# 50).

17. Theologians and biblical scholars sometimes confuse participation in the salvific mission of Christ and its enactment – which is at the core of these two sacraments and actualized through efficacious memory in liturgy (*anamnesis*) – with imitation (*mimesis*), expecting some of their ritual dimensions as recorded in Scripture to be replicated in modern rituals. A two thousand year liturgical tradition [small 't'] demonstrates little consistency regarding the details of how churches kept the memory of Jesus in ritual form. The (liturgical) Tradition [capital 'T'] in relation to baptism, one can argue, relates only to the water rites and a Trinitarian creedal profession of belief, even if both of these elements are not always clear. One thinks, for instance, of the possible use of foot-washing in the some early churches as constitutive of the water rite of baptism rather than forms of immersion or submersion (see Martin F. Connell, '*Nisi pedes*, Except for the Feet: Footwashing in the Community of St John's Gospel', *Worship* 70 [1996], 517–31); or the absence of an Institution Narrative in the Anaphora of Addai and Mari for approximately nine hundred years (see Robert Taft, 'Mass Without the Consecration? The Historic Agreement on the Eucharist between the Catholic Church and the Assyrian Church of the East Promulgated on 26 October 2001', *Worship* 77 [2003], 482–509).

18. This question is justifiable if we hold, as I do, that liturgy can be legitimately referred to as *theologia prima*. In her article 'Toward a Ricoeurian Hermeneutics of Liturgy', *Worship* 86 (2012), 482–506, Crina Gschwandtner uses Ricoeur's later writings on biblical interpretation to argue that the liturgical event is a primary or first order expression of faith and thus a source for the second order reflection of systematic theology. Some of what follows reflects the line of argument developed by Achille M. Triacca, '"Liturgia" locus theologicus, o "Theologia" locus liturgicus? Da un dilemma verso una sintesi', in *Paschale Mysterium: Studi in Memoria dell'Abate Prof. Salvatore Marsili (1910–1983)*, Giustino Farnedi, ed., Studia Anselma 91, Analecta Liturgica 10 (Rome: Pontificio Ateneo S. Anselmo, 1986), 193–233.

19. It needs to be noted that the first section of SC 7 speaks of the many modes of the (real) presence of Christ in the liturgy that enable it to be an enactment of the Paschal Mystery. These are founded on the real presence of Christ in the assembly that gathers; in the ministry of the Church; in the Word proclaimed; and especially in the Eucharist. SC 7 uses the same words, 'praesens adest' ('he is present

to') to introduce each of these four modes. Therefore something more than a static presence or ontology of substance is intended here. The 'presence' of Christ is described as 'present to/being for', and is therefore relational, intentional and dynamic. For a discussion of SC 7, see Michael G. Witczak, 'The Manifold Presence of Christ in the Liturgy', *Theological Studies* 59 (1998), 680–702; and Bruce T. Morrill, *Encountering Christ in the Eucharist: The Paschal Mystery in People, Word, and Sacrament* (New York/Mahwah, NJ: Paulist Press, 2012).

20. See Triacca, '"Liturgia" locus theologicus, o "Theologia" locus liturgicus?' 212–16.
21. There is nothing new here. The medieval theological world saw liturgy as one of the 'authorities' for authentic Church teaching, so, the liturgical event does not simply translate (sacred) Tradition into rite and prayer, but is in itself, and on its own terms, an 'auctoritas' (although I will nuance this claim later). See Yves M.-J. Congar, *Tradition and Traditions: An Historical and a Theological Essay* (London: Burns and Oates, 1966), esp. 354–61; 427–35; and Cyprian Vagaggini, *Theological Dimensions of the Liturgy: A General Treatise on the Theology of the Liturgy* (Collegeville, MN: Liturgical Press, 1976), esp. 582–89.
22. A summary of the theology of Salvatore Marsili can be found in his, 'Teologia liturgica', *Liturgia*, Domenico Sartore, Achille Maria Triacca, Carlo Cibien, eds. (Rome: Edizioni San Paolo, 2001), 2001–16. In an addendum Sartore claims that nobody has examined the relationship between liturgy and theology with the same degree of depth and profundity as has Marsili: see Idem, p. 2016. See also the entire issue of *Rivista Liturgica* 95/3 (2008) which is dedicated to presenting heretofore unpublished material of Marsili: 'Padre Salvatore Marsili OSB: Attualità di una mistagogia'.
23. In the words of Congar: 'The liturgy acts according to the general manner of Tradition, and since it is endowed with the genius of Tradition, it fills Tradition's role in a superlative way. Speaking about the liturgy, and describing its activity, I have felt myself to be speaking of Tradition itself and describing *its* work' (*Tradition and Traditions*, 435).
24. This is conditioned by the nature of the engagement of members of the assembly, what medieval theology referred to as *ex opere operantis*, described by SC 61 as the 'well-disposed members of the faithful'.
25. This does not mean that we strive to seek origins in biblical texts for the central signs and so-called 'sacramental words' or actions. It was a late medieval synthesis in the thirteenth century (expressed

formally for the first time at the Second Council of Lyons in 1274, followed by the Council of Florence in 1439) that speaks of there being seven sacraments, all of which had to find their institution in the deeds and actions of the earthly Jesus. Before that, both East and West had, at various moments, other reckonings as to how many sacraments there were (and often not considering this to be an important point in theological debate). Reaching back to patristic and biblical insights, the Liturgy Constitution, by applying the language of sacrament to 'Church' (see SC 5, 26; and eucharistically, in SC 41-42; later developed in LG 1, 9, 48; AG 1, 5; and GS 45), shifted the focus from seven ritual moments bound up with sometimes arbitrary biblical precedents, to the salvific working of God through Christ in the ministry of the Church. Sacramental numerology, *per se*, has no place in theological discourse today. The origination of 'individual' sacraments is no longer understood in terms of 'institution' by Christ in the historical sense but rather as flowing from Church as the living sacrament of Christ's saving work. Christ is the primordial sacrament of the saving Triune God (see SC 5).

26. Increasingly over the past fifty years or so liturgical scholars have examined the self-implicatory nature of worship. See the contribution of Julie Kavanagh in this volume, and also Siobhán Garrigan, 'Ethics', in *The Study of Liturgy and Worship*, An Alcuin Guide, Juliette Day and Benjamin Gordon-Taylor, eds. (London: SPCK, 2013), 193–201.

27. An earlier stratum in many local traditions had candidates aspersed or immersed in baptismal water as they responded to a creedal interrogation relating to the Persons of the Trinity, or, as in the case of what is probably witnessed to in the early ninth century Irish Stowe Missal (representing a Irish practice which predates the manuscript by approximately one hundred years, and probably borrowed from Spain), of the candidate being immersed three times in water silently after having responded to a creedal interrogation. A Roman practice, witnessed to in the early Sacramentaries, involved a *traditio symbolii* – a formal ritualisation of the handing over of the Creed, to be followed some weeks later with the *redditio symbolii*, the 'return' of the Creed. The transmission and return of the Creed find a place today in the Order of Christian Initiation of Adults.

28. See Wainwright, 'Tradition as a Liturgical Act', 53–56. The understanding implied here is that the 'return' to God at the heart of God's mission is for 'worship,' that is, in order that God be glorified in and through the new creation that has been restored to God's image and likeness. Liturgy serves worship. Thus, being 'destined for

cult' is not, in biblical terms, a 'churchy' matter but rather implicates the christian in an alignment with the poor and those on the margins. Paul applied the language of cult to his ministry and to the lifestyle of believers. See Thomas R. Whelan, '"The Liturgy is Missionary": Elements of a Fundamental Liturgical Theology of Mission', in *Faithful Witness: Glimpses of the Kingdom. Essays in Honour of M. Anthony Geoghegan and Vincent MacNamara*, Joe Egan and Brendan McConvery, eds. (Dublin: Milltown Institute of Theology and Philosophy, 2005), 357–75, esp. 366–69.

29. Wainwright refers to 1 Corinthians 6:19-20; 2 Corinthians 6:16-7:1; and Romans 12:1-2.
30. Wainwright, 'Tradition as a Liturgical Act', 53.
31. The ritual expression of Tradition (second level) – that of the 'Ordo/Order' – is consistent across the churches. The basic ritual elements, including their ordering, regarding Eucharist, for example, are: biblical word, incorporating or followed by intercession, a lengthy prayer of Thanksgiving which pronounced over the gifts of bread and wine in reference to what Jesus did the night before he died, followed by Communion. This same 'deep structure' is found across all churches (Orthodox, Oriental, Post-Reformation and Catholic). Other ritual elements (e.g., a penitential 'moment', litanies, the placement of the Lord's Prayer, the giving of 'peace', whether leavened or unleavened bread is used, styles of prayer, ministries, etc.) pertain to the third or 'surface' level and vary among the churches. Given the strength of ritual as a primordial form of expression, people always identify with this surface level of ritual and some can become disturbed by modifications that are made to it through reform, wrongly believing that it undermines the core of Tradition.
32. By way of an example, we can take the Lord's Prayer, an element found in diverse liturgies East and West from the third century onwards, and an element which had a rather bumpy ritual history before it became more or less established in all liturgical traditions by approximately the seventh century. For a discussion on this and how the Dominical prayer has been variously interpreted in the churches, see Kenneth Stevenson, 'The Lord's Prayer in Tradition', *Liturgy and Interpretation*, SCM Studies in Worship and Liturgy (London: SCM, 2011), 3–22.
33. Christmas and Easter obviously belong to the second level ('liturgy traditioning Tradition'), although the salvific reality of the Paschal Mystery to which these refer is clearly part of the liturgical Tradition [capital 'T'] (first level). A study of liturgical history and the practices of churches East and West show that Advent and Lent (which relate

to Christmas and Easter) are not celebrated uniformly across the churches and therefore represent, it could be argued, more localised traditions – however old or 'fixed' they may be now considered by the various churches.

34. The study by Liam M. Tracey in this volume demonstrates that this criterion was operative in the post-Conciliar reform, even if the historical data was not as secure as was originally thought.

35. Chauvet ('La notion de "tradition"', 23–27) refers to three levels of legitimization of tradition: normativity, value of exemplarity, and precedent. What I offer here is a somewhat different approach.

36. Wainwright, 'Tradition as a Liturgical Act', 45; emphases in the original.

37. Geoffrey Wainwright offers a survey of some of these texts in his *Doxology: The Praise of God in Worship, Doctrine, and Life. A Systematic Theology* (New York: Oxford University Press, 1980), 151–63.

38. See DV 8: '... the Church, in her doctrine, life *and worship*, perpetuates and transmits to every generation all that she herself is, all that she believes' (emphasis added).

39. Scriptural Tradition [capital 'T'] communicates the salvific content of the Paschal Mystery which is Trinitarian both in origins and economic expression: see SC 5-8. A lower case 't' must be employed for the scriptural tradition that transmits the ritual practices because [a] rites, in and of themselves, cannot be attributed with salvific weight except insofar as these are considered in anthropological terms to be enactments of the Paschal Mystery which unfold in the midst of the community of faith; and [b] the history of the development of liturgical practices in various churches witnesses to *variations* of rites and words that must nonetheless be deemed to be valid, grace-filled, and efficacious ritual expressions in line with biblical tradition even if not always imitating these through ritual acts (*mimesis*). These anthropological and historical assertions must be read in the light of the primacy of those events of Jesus which form the irreducible and non-negotiable basis of liturgical ritual actions throughout the liturgical tradition of the Church.

40. See Philippe Béguerie, 'La Bible née de la liturgie', *La Maison-Dieu* 126 (1976), 108–116. See the overview of Renato De Zan, 'Bible and Liturgy', *Handbook for Liturgical Studies*, Vol. 1, *Introduction to the Liturgy*, Anscar J. Chupungco, ed. (Collegeville, MN: Liturgical Press, 1997), 33–51.

41. Congar (*Tradition and Traditions*, 431) said that 'Scripture finds its fullest meaning in liturgy'. The importance of liturgy for the interpretation of Scripture is affirmed by Pope Benedict in his post-

Synodal Exhortation, *Verbum domini,* 52, in which he states that 'the liturgy is the privileged setting in which God speaks to us in the midst of our lives'. See also no. 53.

42. The Introduction to the *Lectionary for Mass* (1982), no. 4, states, 'the word of God unceasingly calls to mind and extends the plan of salvation, which achieves its fullest expression in the liturgy. The liturgical celebration becomes therefore the continuing, complete, and effective presentation of God's word.' The hermeneutical world must extend beyond the normal 'reader-text' relationship to take into account the performative acts that come into play when biblical (and other) text is employed in worship. See Bridget Nichols, 'The Bible and the Liturgy: A Hermeneutical Discussion of Faith and Language', *Studia Liturgica* 27 (1997), 200–16. The complexity of liturgical textual interpretation is studied by Juliette J. Day, *Reading the Liturgy: An Exploration of Texts in Christian Worship* (London: Bloomsbury T&T Clark, 2014).

43. Louis-Marie Chauvet speaks of the sacraments as being the 'precipitate of the Christian Scriptures' (*Symbol and Sacrament: A Sacramental Reinterpretation of Christian Existence* [Collegeville, MN: Liturgical Press, 1995], 221; see also 220–27).

44. See the Introduction to the *Lectionary for Mass,* no 3: '... the liturgical celebration, based primarily on the word of God and sustained by it, becomes a new event and enriches the word itself with new meaning and power'.

45. Robert F. Taft, *The Liturgy of the Hours in East and West: The Origins of the Divine Office and Its Meaning for Today* (Collegeville, MN: Liturgical Press, 1993), 336.

46. 'Whatever we say of the one, we can in turn say of the other, because each recalls the mystery of Christ and each in its own way causes that mystery to be ever present' (Introduction to the *Lectionary for Mass,* no 5). A good overview of this topic is given in Liam M. Tracey, 'Word and Sacrament', *The Study of Liturgy and Worship,* 53–62.

47. '... ut legem credendi lex statuat supplicandi' (*Indiculus de gratia Dei,* VIII [PL 51: 209]), attributed to Prosper. A fine exposition and analysis of this text can be found in Paul De Clerck, '"Lex orandi, lex credendi": The Original Sense and Historical Avatars of the Equivocal Adage', *Studia Liturgica* 24 (1994), 178–200; and Idem, '*Lex orandi, lex credendi*: Un principe heuristique', *La Maison-Dieu* 222 (2000), 61–78.

48. A good overview of this problem is presented by Maxwell Johnson, 'Liturgy and Theology', *Liturgy in Dialogue,* Paul Bradshaw and Bryan Spinks, eds. (London, SPCK, 1993), 202–25, although its

conclusion does not respect the balance and tension of Prosper's original dictum that is required for its more contoured application.

49. See, for example, Alexander Schmemann, *Introduction to Liturgical Theology* (Crestwood, NY: St. Vladimir's Seminary Press, 1986); and *Liturgy and Tradition: Theological Reflections of Alexander Schmemann*, Thomas Fisch, ed. (New York: St. Vladimir's Seminary Press, 1990). This principle is also applied by Orthodox theologians to an understanding that the 'mission activity' of the Church is fulfilled in the liturgy as it is here that the wonders of God in Christ are most clearly proclaimed. Of the many references to this that could be given, see Maurice Assad, 'Mission in the Coptic Orthodox Church – Perspective, Doctrine and Practice', *International Review of Missions* 80 (1991), 251–60. A Roman Catholic, Kevin W. Irwin, dialogues between the theological positions of the churches in, 'Liturgical Theology: What Do the East and West Have to Say to Each Other?' *Studia Liturgica* 30 (2000), 94–111.

50. By far the best expression of this is to be found in the important text of (the Methodist) Geoffrey Wainwright, *Doxology* [see note 37, above], esp. chapters 7 and 8, pp. 218–83. However, in more recent years there is a growing movement among liturgical theologians of different churches to re-evaluate how the liturgical celebration (both ritually and textually) shapes at least the operative theology of various churches if not its more formal articulations, as well as the pastoral 'formation' of worshippers. The literature here is extensive: see, for example, *Holy Things: A Liturgical Theology*, Gordon Lathrop (Minneapolis: Fortress Press, 1993).

51. The 'lex orandi' axiom (in its original Prosperian sense) informed the characterisation of liturgy in medieval discussion as an 'auctoritas'. Pope Sixtus V, when setting up the Congregation for Sacred Rites and Ceremonies in 1587, referred to liturgy as providing 'a protestation of the true faith (*verae fidei protestatio*)'. In the nineteenth century we find Prosper Guéranger appealing to the concept in his writings and it is suggested that he influenced Pius IX to introduce the adage in the bull *Ineffabilis deus* (1854) which declared the dogma of the Immaculate Conception. In its shortened form, the adage finds expression for the first time in Pius XII in his encyclical on the study of Scripture (*Divino afflante* of 1943) in the variant, 'lex precandi lex credendi est'.

52. See, especially, GIRM 2; 10; and 397. It should be noted that GIRM 2 and 10 were not part of the very first edition of GIRM in 1969 but were added to that of 1970 (which appeared in the first edition of the *Roman Missal*) so as to address accusations from Archbishop Marcel Lefebvre and his followers that the reformed liturgy was 'protestant'

and broke away from tradition. However we should note the important assertion of GIRM 10, echoing the Liturgy Constitution, that the norm of prayer is also 'open to legitimate progress' (SC 23).

53. See John Paul II, Apostolic Letter, *Vicesimus quintus annus* (1988), no. 10, marking the 25th Anniversary of the Liturgy Constitution.

54. Many commentators see here an affirmation by Rome of its authority over the work of liturgical translation.

55. The literature on this is enormous but mention must be made of the study of Kevin W. Irwin, *Context and Text: Method in Liturgical Theology* (Collegeville, MN: Liturgical Press, 1994), as well as David N. Power, 'Cult to Culture: The Mediating Role of Theology', *Worship: Culture and Theology* (Washington, DC: The Pastoral Press, 1990), 3–24. Although not beyond critique, the early text of Aidan Kavanagh (*On Liturgical Theology* [New York: Pueblo Publishing Company, 1984]) remains influential.

56. There is a general convergence of theological opinion on the priority of the liturgical act (ritual, prayer, including the space and social context in which these unfold) as a *locus theologicus*. See, for example, Paul V. Marshall, 'Reconsidering "Liturgical Theology": Is there a *Lex Orandi* for All Christians?', *Studia Liturgica* 25 (1995), 129–51; Siobhán Garrigan, *The Real Peace Process: Worship, Politics and the End of Sectarianism* (London: Equinox, 2010) who understands the worship environment to be important for theological reflection; Maxwell E. Johnson, *Praying and Believing in Early Christianity: The Interplay between Christian Worship and Doctrine* (Collegeville, MN: Liturgical Press, 2013); and Thomas R. Whelan, 'The Liturgical Axiom of Proper of Aquitaine: Text and Interpretation', *Lex Orandi, Lex Credendi, Lex Agendi: Patristic Writings*, Juliette Day and Gunnar af Hällström, eds., Studia Traditionis Theologiae (Turnhout: Brepols, 2015 – *in print*).

57. In Prosper's original aphorism, the term 'lex supplicandi' must be seen to include also the intercessions of believers that take place daily outside of liturgy.

58. The full axiom is always to be preferred to the binomial, except in those contexts in which the latter is understood in both the semantic and theological senses of the former.

59. This is not the place to speak of how methods are explored which allow us to expand the *lex orandi* to include its social and cultural contexts, as these also impinge on how 'meaning' is perceived and framed in worship.

60. On the place of historical research in liturgical studies, see especially Robert Taft, 'Historicism Revisited', *Beyond East and West*, 15–30;

Robert Cabié, 'La place de l'histoire dans les études liturgiques', *Ecclesia Orans* 23 (2006), 321–35; John F. Baldovin, 'The Uses of Liturgical History', *Worship* 82 (2008), 2–18; and Paul F. Bradshaw, 'The Relationship between Historical Research and Modern Liturgical Practice', *A Living Tradition: On the Intersection of Liturgical History and Pastoral Practice. Essays in Honor of Maxwell E. Johnson*, David A. Pitt, Stefanos Alexopoulos and Christian McConnell, eds. (Collegeville, MN: Liturgical Press, 2012), 3–18.

61. By this statement I do not wish to deny that what happens on the periphery and at the margins of history are of great importance and cannot therefore be dismissed. However, the statement does point to the need for criteria to help evaluate history and any claim it has to inform liturgical practices of today.

62. See Bradshaw, 'The Relationship between Historical Research and Modern Liturgical Practice', 11; see also 16–18. Bradshaw's article is complemented by that of Baldovin (note 60, above) who demonstrates how the ongoing work of historians continues to serve a deepening of the reform.

63. Cabié, 'La place de l'histoire dans les études liturgiques', 329.

64. See Cabié, 'La place de l'histoire dans les études liturgiques', 331.

65. Understood here to mean the mode of ritual enactment of the Paschal Mystery that is shared by the churches over two thousand years in fidelity to Scripture and that is experienced in every generation as a living encounter with Christ.

66. Clarifications and restatements of Tradition have always been and remain an important task of Conciliar and ecumenical discussion in the exercise of an authoritative/magisterial ecclesial leadership. The role of the *ecclesia* in determining liturgical tradition [small 't'] will be addressed in the third part of this essay.

67. An oft used criterion in antiquity, it is found in Cicero, *Tusculanae Disputationes* Book 1, xv, 35 (written around 45 BCE).

68. Vincent of Lérins, 'Id teneamus quod ubique, quod semper, quod ab omnibus creditum est', *Commonitorium adversus haereses* 2 [PL 50: 639]. The same criterion is appealed to in Prosper of Aquitaine as a justification for his axiom: 'that which has been handed on by the apostles [antiquity], and uniformly celebrated [universality] in every catholic Church and in the whole world [unanimity], so that the law of supplicating may establish the law of beliving' ('quae ab apostolis tradita, in toto mundo atque in omni catholica Ecclesia uniformiter celebrantur, ut legem credendi lex statuat supplicandi': *Indiculus* VIII [PL 51: 209]). An almost identical idea is found in Irenaeus, *Adversus Haereses* III, 3, 2 (see also 5, 1; and 2, 3).

69. Chauvet adds a fourth element (*auctoritas*) and discusses these as 'objective factors of "traditionality"' ('La notion de "tradition"', 27–36).

70. We need to note that *Dei verbum* sought to move from a dualistic sense of 'Scripture' and 'tradition' to one which sees each in continuity with the other.

71. The fundamental driver in the argument of Andrea Grillo is that Church reform requires liturgical reform: *Beyond Pius V: Conflicting Interpretations of the Liturgical Reform* (Collegeville, MN: Liturgical Press, 2013).

72. A 'modified' *lex credendi* refers, for example, to the priority that the Conciliar documents gave to the recovery of the sense that we are saved 'as a people' and not primarily as individuals (LG 9); or that soteriology is better understood in the biblical and patristic sense to include the Resurrection at its core (rather than being principally constituted by the Passion and cross); or to the explicit ecumenical agenda that has coloured how post-Conciliar theology has developed. These are examples of how *ressourcement* serves contemporary reform. On this last point see Grillo, *Beyond Pius V*, 55–8.

73. See the excellent overview of this topic by Martin Klöckener, 'Liturgiereformen in der Geschichte', *Liturgiereformen in den Kirchen: 50 Jahre nach Sacrosanctum Concilium. [Akten des Kongresses der Societas Liturgica, Würzburg 2013]*, Gordon Lathrop and Martin Stuflesser, eds, Theologie der Liturgie 5 (Regensburg, 2013), 57–79.

74. Paul De Clerck observed that the Prosperian dictum has been employed in two different ways throughout history. In a time of fixed liturgy, of little formal change, when 'liturgy tends to be considered as a closed and well-defined ensemble', euchology is likely to be used as a source by which the faith of the Church is revealed. However, in a period of liturgical reform, the opposite is often the case: 'The very idea of reform gives primacy to the content of the faith' above all else. See De Clerck, '"Lex orandi, lex credendi": The Original Sense and Historical Avatars of the Equivocal Adage', 179.

75. De Clerck, '"Lex orandi, lex credendi": The Original Sense and Historical Avatars of the Equivocal Adage', 179, note 3.

76. On this relationship, see Franco Brovelli, 'Fede e Liturgia', *Nuovo Dizionario di Liturgia*, eds. Domenico Sartore and Achille M. Triacca (Milano/Torino: San Paolo, 1995, sixth edition), 506–17.

77. The Fourth Instruction on the Proper Implementation of *Sacrosanctum Concilium*, 37–40, *Varietatis legitimae*, no. 36, issued by CDWDS in 1994, describes 'substantial unity' as being found principally in the liturgical books. The somewhat conflicted sense of

the Roman Rite existing in both ordinary form and extraordinary form, the reformed Roman Rite alongside the version that this purports to reform, adds an even greater challenge to the task of unpacking what the term 'substantial unity' might mean. See Benedict XVI, Apostolic Letter, *Summorum pontificum*, issued *motu proprio* (2007), with the accompanying Letter from Pope Benedict; and the Pontifical Commission, *Ecclesia dei*, Instruction *Universae ecclesiae* (2011), no. 7.

78. See the helpful commentary on this by Mark R. Francis, 'Another Look at the Constitution on the Sacred Liturgy and the Substantial Unity of the Roman Rite', *Worship* 88 (2014), 239–254.

79. See Grillo, *Beyond Pius V*, esp. 59–65.

80. The traditioning of Tradition continues to be understood, as set out above, as happening in biblical word proclaimed in the midst of the assembly, as well as in sacrament. Outside of these living contexts of word and sacrament, Tradition no longer functions and it is reduced to becoming little more than a study of history and a record of magisterial statements.

81. George Tavard speaks of Tradition being structured as 'memory', 'presence' and 'hope': 'Tradition as Koinonia in Historical Perspective', *One in Christ* 24 (1988), 97–111; esp. 105–10.

82. The Paschal Mystery which is actualised in liturgy cannot be broken into discrete moments, representing the final acts of Christ. The Paschal Mystery begins in the incarnation and finds its completion when Christ 'returns again in glory at the end of time.' As a baptised people we live in the ontological environment of the Paschal Mystery. The various historical moments of cross, Resurrection, and Pentecost, for instance, are but intense and real expressions of the single paschal sacrifice of Christ, no one moment of which can be understood in faith apart from the other. Paschal Mystery reveals the grammar of the inner workings of God: self-emptying (*kenosis*) is central to salvation, as is the healing and reconciliation that flows from this Mystery – revealing the profound Love which describes the very outreach and salvific intention of the Triune God. The *hodie* of liturgy, expressed in liturgical prayer, makes sense of the present only because of the eschatological nature of the Paschal Mystery. It is for this reason that liturgical theology considers it somewhat fatuous to consider *anamnesis* as not embracing eschatology and the *hodie* – none of which can be conceived of without the *epiclesis* of the Spirit which makes of the liturgical act a moment of sacramental encounter.

83. See the important insights given in Laurence A. Hoffman, 'How Ritual Means: Ritual Circumcision in Rabbinic Culture and Today', *Studia Liturgica* 23 (1993), 78–97.

84. A student of liturgical Tradition must be prepared to consider the sacramental validity of worship practices for christians, deemed to be irregular, at least, if not subsequently forbidden (for example, eucharistic elements other than bread and wine, irregular reception of sacraments, Masses with monastic nuns which may have been presided over by the Abbess, etc.), when these were celebrated with faith and with the intention of doing what the Church intends to do on these occasions. See, for example, the study of Celia Chazelle, 'The Eucharist in Early Medieval Europe', *A Companion to the Eucharist in the Middle Ages*, Ian Christopher Levy, *et al.*, eds, Brill's Companions to the Christian Tradition, 26 (Leiden: Brill, 2012), 205–49.

85. See some recent attempts at a social history of liturgy by Martin D. Stinger, *A Sociological History of Christian Worship* (Cambridge: Cambridge University Press, 2005), Frank C. Senn, *The People's Work: A Social History of the Liturgy* (Minnesota: Fortress Press, 2006), and Teresa Berger, *Gender Differences and the Making of Liturgical History: Lifting a Veil on Liturgy's Past* (Farnham, Surrey: Ashgate, 2011).

86. This is addressed in, Thomas R. Whelan, 'Culture of Clericalism: Towards a Theological Deconstruction', *Broken Faith: Why Hope Matters*, Joe Egan, Patrick Claffey and Marie Keenan, eds, *Studies in Theology Society and Culture* 10 (Oxford: Peter Lang, 2013), 175–212.

IMPLICATIONS
FOR LIFE

READING JOHN 6:1-14 FROM AN ECOLOGICAL PERSPECTIVE

᠈ᢁ ᠈ᢁ ᠈ᢁ

MARGARET DALY-DENTON

In recent years there has been a strong impulse among the religions of the world to take a new look at their traditions and see if they might contain earth-respecting values that would have potential to inspire people of faith to see ecological responsibility as a constitutive part of their ethics. In Judaism and Christianity this has involved developing ways of reading the Bible from an ecological perspective. The 'Earth Bible' project at Flinders University, published in a five-volume collection of essays, was a significant early twenty-first century attempt on the part of a team of biblical scholars to read various passages from the Scriptures in light of a set of eco-justice principles devised in consultation with scientists and ecologists.[1] The benefit of doing such hermeneutical work in conversation with parallel developments in the emerging disciplines of eco-theology and eco-feminism is evident in another important initiative: a series of international and inter-faith colloquia held at Harvard University, the proceedings of which are published in a series of essay collections, 'Religions of the World and Ecology'.[2] Since then, the on-going ecological hermeneutics seminar at the annual meetings of the Society of Biblical Literature (SBL)[3] and the Exeter Project on 'Uses of the Bible in Environmental Ethics'[4] have been major players in the task of honing hermeneutical methodologies apt for this challenge, for example, by adapting the feminist critical approach of 'suspicion, identification and retrieval', an approach with considerable potential to highlight ecologically significant features in a biblical text that have been previously ignored. The aim, as articulated by the Exeter researchers, is to develop interpretive strategies positioned between readings of recovery (that attempt to claim that the Bible is consistently 'ecological') and readings of resistance (that acknowledge that the Bible itself – and not always just the way it has been read – may well be part of the problem).[5] What is needed is a many-faceted hermeneutic that will be adequate to the challenge facing today's ecologically alert readers of the Bible. This brief presentation is part of its author's on-going work on a reading of the Fourth Gospel from an ecological perspective for the Earth Bible Commentary, a multi-volume series taking the Earth Bible Project a step further, and now gradually appearing from Sheffield Phoenix Press.[6] It focuses on the one miracle of Jesus reported in all four Gospels, as told by the Fourth Evangelist: the multiplication of the loaves and fishes. It is the author's hope that her attempt to view a Gospel scene with such strong liturgical resonances from an ecological perspective may be a fitting tribute to Fr Paddy Jones who has for so many years dedicated his energies to the worthy celebration of the Eucharist.

How does one go about doing an eco-hermeneutical reading of the Fourth Gospel? A comprehensive methodological presentation would be disproportionate here, so we will limit the explanations to the strategies used in this reading of John 6:1-14. Guided by the aforementioned initiatives, we are attempting to listen to the Johannine portrayal of Jesus in our present global situation – an ecologically deteriorating planet – and more specifically from our situation in the one-third world, the so-called developed world. We may not be professional scientists, but we have enough basic facts and figures about the current ecological crisis to know that our excess – the most voracious lifestyle the earth has ever been expected to provide for – is largely responsible for it. So as we read the Gospel, we try to use our awareness of our planet's predicament as a 'hermeneutical lens' through which we might see things that we never noticed before. We look out for the impact of socio-economic realities on the natural world as portrayed in the text. We attend to the ways in which features of the natural world figure in the narrative world of the Gospel, foregrounding them, instead of regarding them as mere background or 'props', somehow showing them the regard and respect that we are trying to develop in our everyday lives. We try to change our anthropocentric reading habits into more earth-centred approaches. We recognise that it is not only the ecologies of the narrative world – early first century Galilee and Jerusalem – that have shaped the text, but also the ecology of the intended audience's world – a city (Ephesus?) of the late first century Greco Roman world. We purposefully allow the ecology of our own world to affect our reading, keeping our eyes open for parallels between Fourth Gospel passages and current environmental discourse.

We also remember that the New Testament presupposes the Old, what the Gospel calls simply 'the Scriptures'. The Fourth Evangelist locates Jesus' story inter-textually within Israel's great story that tells in narrative, poem, song and vision of God's 'master plan' for the creation, a plan which was eventually to include, as the Evangelist will claim, the creating and sustaining 'Word' becoming flesh. This meta-narrative – an over-arching myth giving a comprehensive explanation of the world and everything in it – has profoundly shaped the Johannine portrayal of Jesus. This is the myth that Jesus lived by and the way in which he did challenges quite a few of the myths we live by today. Two examples could be offered: the notion that the natural world exists purely for the benefit of humankind; and the myth of the omni-competence of science, the presumption that just because we have the technology to modify natural processes, we have the right to do so.[7]

As John 6 begins, the scene moves from Jerusalem to beyond or on the other side (the eastern side?) of 'the Sea of Galilee of Tiberias', which, of course, is actually a lake. Presumably the ancients, many of whom had never seen the ocean, perceived a large body of water as a 'sea'. John is the only Evangelist (also in 21:1) to use the colonial name that linked the lake with Tiberias, the new capital city on the west side of the lake that the tetrarch Herod Antipas founded around 20CE as a centre of Roman administration and named in honour of the Emperor reigning at the time. It would seem that from then on people, or at least those more accepting of this policy of ingratiation, started calling the Sea of Galilee the 'Tiberian' sea, possibly even recognising the etymological 'homage' to the Tiber (Latin and Greek: *Tiberis*), the great navigable river that brought the tribute of subject peoples flowing into Rome – their grain, oil, wine, timber, et cetera. Antipas and his elite retainers would certainly have seen political and economic advantage in including the lake in this dedication of territory to their Roman overlord. The building of Tiberias and the rebuilding of Sepphoris nearby would have impacted seriously on the landscape, demographics and economy of this part of Galilee, in ways not dissimilar to today's massive conversion of family-based farming economies to 'agribusiness', forcing the landless poor to crowd into cities. Ellen F. Davis would count this process among 'the acts of contempt for the work of God's hands' that are at the root of present ecological destruction.[8] Whatever the Evangelist's reason for adding 'of Tiberias', for us today it underscores the hubris of the imperial claim to ownership of the entire (known) world's natural resources, in this case, a lake whose waters teemed with potential for tribute and tax revenue. The similarities with corporate colonialisation in our world today would not be lost on ecologically alert readers.

The crowd that has been following Jesus (the imperfect tense indicating duration) is identified at first as people who have seen 'the signs', the life-giving effects of his impact on the sick, *epitōnasthenountōn*. In the Fourth Gospel, illness is never attributed to evil spirits. The verb *astheneō* is used in all three Johannine references to sickness (6:1; 5:7 and 11:1). The cognate noun *asthenia*, usually translated 'illness', actually means weakness or feebleness, lack of strength. *Asthenia* can also be used metaphorically to suggest neediness, social insignificance, or poverty, all conditions that diminish life and result in marginalisation. This would certainly have been the case for the vast majority of those in this scene: impoverished people, many unable to get more than occasional work as day labourers, among whom the better-off earned a bare subsistence living as farm workers, artisans, fishermen; people beset by disease caused by poor food supply, contagion and ignorance; non-elite people who cannot afford to attend the Passover Festival in Jerusalem which the Evangelist tells us is at hand. The burden of taxation by both Rome and the local client king, temple tithes and rents make that impossible. But Jesus is about to put on for them 'a counter-Passover: without money, without sacral slaughter and without the Jerusalem priesthood that oversees the exchange of one for the other.'[9] As Jesus acts out God's intention that everyone should have ample food to sustain life, *asthenia* gives way to *zoē,* the abundant life that he has come into the *cosmos* to bring: a fullness of life to be lived, not in some future age, not in another 'better' world, but in the earthly materiality of the here and now (10:10). The use of the word *zoē* throughout the Fourth Gospel will actually peak in John 6 where the word occurs eighteen times.

Awareness of the agricultural origins of the festivals around which the Fourth Gospel narrative is entwined can enhance an ecological reading. Passover is redolent of spring renewal. This celebration of Israel's liberation from slavery coincides with the time when the rains are over and the grain is beginning to ripen. To this day, around Passover time, the hills sloping down to the Sea of Galilee are covered in lush green grass, flecked with delicate wild flowers. This grass does not last long, as spring quickly gives way to the scorching heat of summer, so the Fourth Evangelist's reference to it is a delightfully authentic touch, placing this scene in the exact phase of nature's annual cycle that corresponds to 'the Passover, the festival of the Jews' being at hand (6:4). It is from his vantage point sitting with his disciples on one of these swards of spring grass that Jesus can see how large the crowd that is coming towards him – both literally and metaphorically – actually is. Keenly aware of their neediness, their *asthenia,* he puts what the Evangelist tells us is a test question to Philip. The RSV renders it, 'How are we to buy bread so that these people may eat?'

The test that Philip is being set up by the Evangelist to fail hinges on that distinction between the literal and the metaphorical that, earlier in the narrative, Nicodemus also failed to grasp (3:12). Ecologically minded readers tend to throw up their hands in horror at what they perceive as Johannine dualism, as if the physicality of Earth is being denigrated as somehow inferior to 'spiritual' realities accessible only in another life above and beyond life on Earth. However, the Johannine contrasts between 'flesh' and 'spirit', 'above' and 'below', 'heavenly' and 'earthly' (3:6; 12; 31) are not so much reflections of 'dualism proper in the religio-historical and phenomenological sense', as dualities drawing on natural symbols, 'the simple contrasting of good and evil, life and death, light and darkness, and so on [that] is in fact coextensive with religion itself'.[10] The use of these dualities is part of the Fourth Evangelist's literary technique of *double entendre.* Just as the people are 'coming' to Jesus by climbing up the grassy hillside to where he is sitting with his disciples, they are also coming to him on a spiritual quest. The significance of the literal hill climb is not in any way diminished, just because it also functions as a symbol. Similarly, the fact that Jesus' provision of sustenance for natural life points metaphorically to his provision of the sustenance for *zoēaiōnios* (usually quite inadequately translated as 'eternal life') in no way makes the actual bread and fish inconsequential. In fact, the significance of the food's materiality is actually emphasised in the Fourth Gospel account of this scene, precisely because of the Fourth Gospel's insistence on the 'here-and-now-ness' of the life that Jesus gives. The bread and fish received from Jesus' hand sustain bodies of flesh and blood. In doing that they point to the food that Jesus really wants to give, 'the food that endures to *zoēaiōnios*' (6:27). And this 'life of the aeon' (*aiōnios* being the cognate adjective of *aiōn* meaning age, era, epoch), the flourishing that God intends for all creation, that people thought would not happen until a new 'golden age' dawned, is not actually some future other-worldly existence. It is a new way of living on earth now, a way of living that is in harmony with the energy sustaining the creation that the Evangelist has earlier told us is enfleshed in Jesus (1:14).

Returning to Jesus' test question to Philip, the Greek adverb *pothen*, translated 'how' in the RSV, can also function as an interrogative of place. The NRSV revisers have changed 'how' to 'where', thereby giving quite a different slant to the question. Later in the Gospel (12:5-8 and 13:29) we will learn that the disciples have a common fund from which they regularly donate to the poor. Jesus, if understood at the literal level, would seem to intend that his group use this fund to provide food for the crowd and is asking – with characteristic Johannine irony – where in the vicinity of this hill that they have just climbed, there might possibly be a market where bread could be bought. The verb *agorazo* means to buy in the market, the *agora*. The test seems to be whether Philip will respond at this 'earthly' level or whether he might sense that the crowd's real hunger is far deeper than a craving for bread that can be bought in an *agora*. Predictably Philip walks into the 'trap' with what Robert J. Karris calls his 'business manager's answer: we have money, but not the amount it would take to feed this crowd'.[11]

Andrew has spotted a young lad there who has five loaves and two fish. The Fourth Gospel is unique in specifying that the loaves were made of barley flour. This detail accentuates the reminiscence of a scene where a man brings the prophet Elisha a gift of twenty barley loaves for his hungry followers. When ordered to distribute them, Elisha's servant objects that twenty loaves could not possibly satisfy one hundred men. All eat their fill, however, and there is even some left over, 'according to the word of the Lord' (2 Kings 4:42-44). While this Elisha echo is part of the Evangelist's project of telling us who Jesus is, or even who he surpasses, an ecological reading would zoom in on the barley loaves, resisting a 'spiritualising' tendency to dismiss them as a mere husk that we can strip away to reveal something more profound, as if the real import of John 6:1-15 is christological. As we will see, there are indications in the Fourth Gospel that, at least for some Johannine Christians, the bread that believers share to express their belonging to Jesus is not identified as something else – Jesus body. It is not bread of special significance because it represents something more 'spiritual'. It is simply bread in all its materiality, the staff of human life on Earth, but bread shared by those who belong to Jesus that they may have *zoeaionios* because of him (6:57).

An ecological perspective on the barley loaves would attend to the soil's productivity, to the human agricultural activity that produced the barley and to the work of women who ground the grain, kneaded the dough and baked the loaves. Barley was sown once the early autumn rains had softened the ground to allow ploughing. The first cereal crop to ripen, barley was brought to the temple on the second day of Passover as an offering of the 'first fruits' of the year's new grain harvest. Able to grow in poor soil and resistant to heat and drought, barley was the food of the poor (three times cheaper than wheat in Revelation 6:6). 'Because of the gluten content of cereals, wheat makes the best leavened bread, rye is second best, and barley can only be used for unleavened bread'.[12] The boy's five loaves (*artoi*) are the produce of a village woman baking on a daily basis in a communal oven. *Artos* refers to 'a relatively small and generally round loaf of bread (considerably smaller than present-day typical loaves of bread and thus more like "rolls" or "buns")'.[13] In this case they would have been flat, unleavened cakes of bread, possibly containing millet, spelt or pea meal mixed with barley.[14]

With regard to the two fish, the Greek text does not let us know which of the eighteen species indigenous to the lake these might have been. A couple of sardines, the most plentiful fish in the lake, possibly even dried sardines, would be a typical 'lunch' that a Galilean peasant mother might pack for her son. Even though the lake teemed with sardines and other larger fish (biny and musht), by the time fishermen had paid for fishing rights, compensated their helpers, observed the purity laws by sorting 'clean' from 'unclean' fish (see Leviticus 11:9-12), and handed over a sizeable proportion of their haul in a hefty tax or tribute to an official waiting on the shore, there was not much left to sustain a family. So no doubt, fish had to be carefully rationed.

Andrew's reaction to the young lad's willingness to share his portion of bread and fish is another example of literal thinking. If even two hundred days' wages worth of bread would be insufficient, how derisory do five loaves and two fish seem! 'What are they among so many?' Yet Jesus simply asks the disciples to get the people (*hoi anthrōpoi*) to recline, in other words, to prepare to eat. An eco-feminist reader would see a familiar pattern in the fact that it is the men folk (*hoi andres*) who promptly stretch out on the grass in expectation of a free meal being handed to them, no less than five thousand of them! By mentioning the verdant green grass on which they lie down, the Evangelist alludes to another scriptural passage, Psalm 23 (LXX Psalm 22). Activating this resonance highlights the role of the natural world in this scene. The people are about to experience that in Jesus God is shepherding them, that they lack nothing, that God is inviting them to abide (LXX: *kataskēnoō*) in a place that is bright green (LXX: *chloē*) with the early shoots of spring grass, that they are about to be nourished there beside the restful waters of the lake. This intimation of Jesus' role as the ideal or model shepherd prepares for a more extended treatment later in the gospel (10:11-18).

In taking the loaves and the fish, Jesus is receiving them from a young boy who is willing to give the little that he has. In giving thanks, Jesus uses the Jewish *Berakah* form of prayer that blesses God who is the cause of the land's fruitfulness and the lake's bounty. The verbs 'took', 'gave thanks' and 'gave' (*diadidomi*, meaning 'distribute', is a cognate of *didomai*, to give) cannot but remind a Christian audience of Jesus' interpretive words over the bread and cup at the Last Supper, so familiar because of their liturgical significance. It is important, though, to remember that the Fourth Gospel does not contain these interpretive words, and to take this divergence from 1 Corinthians 11:23-25 and the synoptic 'Last

Supper' accounts as seriously as we do, other instances of the Fourth Gospel's distinctiveness need to come into play. The Fourth Gospel attests the diversity of eucharistic origins, showing that there was a strand of the early Jesus movement where what made the community's meal an occasion of communion with Jesus was not the identification of bread and wine as his body and blood, but the practice of washing one another's feet (13:8; 14-15). This strand is still represented in the Gospel, coexisting with the redactional passage about eating Jesus' flesh and drinking his blood (6:51c-56) which reflects the form of eucharistic understanding and practice that was eventually to 'win out'.[15]

John is also distinctive, compared with the synoptics, in insisting that Jesus himself – not the disciples – hands the food to the people reclining on the grass, giving them as much as they want. This is part of the Fourth Gospel's emphasis on each believer's direct relationship with Jesus, shown, for example, in the absence of any distinction between an inner circle of 'apostles' and a larger group of 'disciples'. Another unique feature in John's presentation of this scene is the use of the verb *empimplēmi* (to fill to the full) in 6:12. The synoptics all use forms of the verb *chortazō* (to eat to the full, to be satisfied) as John does in a retrospective reference to the feeding in 6:26. The verb *empimplēmi* stresses Jesus' agency in filling hungry stomachs, while also echoing a psalm that will be an important scriptural witness to him, particularly in the account of his laying down of his life, at the moment when his garments are shared out among his executioners (19:23-24, citing Psalm 22:18). Psalm 22 (LXX Psalm 21) includes the lines:

> The poor shall eat and be filled (*emplēsthēsontai*)
> and they shall praise the Lord that seek him:
> their heart shall live for ever.

So the reader who is alert to the echoed passage with its 'Johannine' motifs – seeking the Lord, being gifted with *zoēaiōnios* – is reminded of the cost for Jesus of what this 'sign' (6:14) represents.

All four Gospels tell of the twelve baskets of leftover food. John's word *kophinos* gives us no help in determining the size or type of basket. The most the Greek text allows us to say is that a *kophinos* is 'a relatively large basket used primarily for food or produce'.[16] Wicker baskets were commonplace as they were also used as fish traps. The description of the remaining food as 'left over' (RSV) is actually quite a weak translation of the word *perissousanta* (also used in Matthew's and Luke's telling of this story) which conveys a sense of extraordinary, overflowing abundance. The surplus remaining after the crowd has been 'filled' to satiety is even more remarkable when set within the context of the tributary economy in which most of the crowd would have struggled to survive, with a powerful and distant elite taking for their own consumption what they deemed to be 'surplus'. Warren Carter, writing with a consciousness of the Roman Empire as a pervading presence in both the Palestine of Jesus' time and the urban Mediterranean world of the intended audience suggests that in this scene Jesus may well be 'trumping' the occasional distribution of free food that was part of the propaganda intended to portray the Emperor, or his representative, as a munificent benefactor.[17]

There are two distinctive details in John's report of the surplus. First, Jesus takes the initiative in telling the disciples to gather up the leftover fragments. Second, Jesus explains why: 'that nothing may be lost'. Commentators who see in this scene a prefiguration of the Eucharist draw attention to the *Didache*'s insistence that the fragments (*klasmata*, the word also used in John 6:12) left over after the Christian ritual meal should be carefully collected (*Didache* 10). Our liturgical experience conditions us to think in terms of respect for the consecrated bread of the Eucharist. An ecological reading pursues quite a different line. Jesus' twenty-first-century disciples who live in a world where food is wasted by a privileged minority while the majority starve, where, for example, surplus fish catches are dumped lest they exceed fishing quotas, might find themselves reproached by this command of Jesus to gather up the surplus that nothing may be lost. Maybe too from our location in a world so often disfigured by the 'leftovers' from human consumption – ranging from litter to large-scale industrial waste – we might note that the disciples cleaned up after the meal, restoring the landscape and repairing whatever damage had been done. Perhaps the Johannine Jesus' words 'that nothing may be lost' might also inspire his followers to see recycling of waste as part of their discipleship, like the Anglican congregation in England that has set up story boards giving instructions for composting in a side aisle of their church. Or like the UK food company *Pret a Manger* whose packaging declares under the heading 'Give & Take':

> At the end of each day we take our delicious handmade food to hostels, shelters and charities all over the country. We've always done this. The Pret Foundation Trust (PFT) helps provide the people and vans that make all this possible. We absolutely don't do this because we are 'nice' people. We do it because wasting good food and hard work is madness.

The Johannine Jesus would surely approve.

The Greek verb *agorazo*, used in Jesus' test question to Philip (6:5), can also mean frequenting the *agora*, hanging around the market. Perhaps a contemporary translation might be 'indulging in retail therapy'. In the cities of the privileged one-third world, it is commonplace for dwindling Church congregations to remark that shopping malls have become the new cathedrals and that the Christian Sunday has changed from a day of worship, hospitality and enjoyment of the natural world to a day for shopping, the day when the consumerism responsible for so much ecological damage may even reach its weekly peak. Viewing this Gospel scene from our location on our critically damaged earth home, there are parallels between the crowd's main preoccupation of eating their fill and our thinking that our hunger for fulfilment can be satisfied by more and more consumption. As the Johannine narrative progresses, Jesus will address precisely this issue. 'Do not work for the food that perishes, but for the food that endures to *zoēaiōnios* which the Son of Man will give you' (6:27).

When the crowd sees the sign, they conclude that Jesus must be the 'prophet' expected to come into the 'world'. This refers to the expected prophet like Moses (Deuteronomy 18:18) who, it was believed, would repeat the miracle of the manna (Exodus 16). However, as before in the Gospel, to speak of Jesus as coming into the *cosmos* (11:27) is to hint at where he has come from: 'from God' (6:46; 13:3; 16:30). From our ecological perspective, we can certainly think of his coming as not just into human society, but into the wider earth community of both the human and the more-than-human. This is where the Word becomes 'flesh' in all its materiality and interconnectedness with and dependence upon other living things. This harks back to the Gospel's prologue where the Fourth Evangelist spins that rich web of scriptural allusion to intimate that Jesus embodies the Word, the creative energy that sustains the world, that divine wisdom continually at work in the creation, 'holding all things together' (Wisdom 1:7).

In conclusion, the all-important question: What is the point of reading the Fourth Gospel from an ecological perspective? First of all, this is an engaged reading undertaken by believers who look to the memories and interpretations of Jesus preserved in the Gospel as a guide for their everyday life. As disciples of Jesus, we are sent by him to do the works that he did, and even greater works (14:12). As God has sent him, so he sends us (20:21). We are people on a learning curve: discovering – mainly through the damage that we cause – that we are part of an intricately interconnected biosphere, the community of living things in which we find our home, our *oikos*. The remedy to the ecological crisis has to do with our sense of that community. In fact, it may be summed up in the one word, love. As agnostic scientist, Stephen Jay puts it:

> We cannot win this battle to save species and environment without forging an emotional bond between ourselves and nature as well – for we will not fight to save what we do not love ... we must have visceral contact in order to love. We really must make room for nature in our hearts.[18]

We must surely extend the one explicit ethical command of Jesus in the Fourth Gospel, 'Love one another as I have loved you' (13:34), to include all of earthkind – our own 'kin', as the geneticists have shown us, from whom we must not turn away (Isaiah 58:7). This is not to suggest that either Jesus or the Fourth Evangelist had ecology in mind. It is to tap into the on-going generativity of our Scriptures, their capacity to create new meanings in new contexts, something that the Johannine strand of early Christianity understood well with its teaching about the Paraclete whose guidance of Jesus' disciples goes beyond what Jesus actually said to them (14:26; 16:12-13). As people on a mission, as Jesus was, to give life to a world beset by *asthenia*, we must be imaginative, resourceful and creative, continually finding ways to heal and sustain the earth. Like Andrew, we admit the scantiness of the lifestyle changes we are only now beginning to make, compared with the vastness and complexity of the problem. We acknowledge our need for a wisdom far beyond what we have demonstrated so far. For believers in Jesus, the surest way forward is to align our ways of thinking and acting with those of Jesus, because he reveals the sustaining source of all life, 'reaching mightily from one end of the earth to the other, ordering all things well' (Wisdom 8:1).

Notes

1. Norman C. Habel, ed., *Readings from the Perspective of Earth*, The Earth Bible [EB] 1 (Sheffield: Sheffield Academic Press, 2000); Norman C. Habel and Shirley Wurst, eds., *The Earth Story in Genesis*, EB 2 (Sheffield: Sheffield Academic Press, 2000); Norman C. Habel and Shirley Wurst, eds., *The Earth Story in Wisdom Traditions*, EB 3 (Sheffield: Sheffield Academic Press, 2001);

Norman C. Habel, ed., *The Earth Story in the Psalms and the Prophets*, EB 4 (Sheffield: Sheffield Academic Press, 2001); Norman C. Habel and Vicky Balabanski, eds, *The Earth Story in the New Testament*, EB 5 (Sheffield: Sheffield Academic Press, 2002).

2. See Dieter T. Hessel and Rosemary Radford Ruether, eds., *Christianity and Ecology: Seeking the Well-Being of Earth and Humans* (Cambridge, Mass: Harvard University Press, 2000); Hava Tiresh Samuelson, ed., *Judaism and Ecology: Created World, Revealed Word* (Cambridge, Mass.: Harvard University Press, 2003).

3. See Norman C. Habel and Peter Trudinger, eds, *Exploring Ecological Hermeneutics*, Society of Biblical Literature Symposium Series 46 (Atlanta: Society of Biblical Literature, 2008).

4. See David G. Horrell, et al. eds, *Ecological Hermeneutics: Biblical, Historical and Theological* Perspectives (London: T.&T. Clark, 2010); David G. Horrell, et al., *Greening Paul: Rereading the Apostle in a Time of Ecological Crisis* (Waco, TX: Baylor, 2010).

5. See also Norman C. Habel, *An Inconvenient Text: Is a Green Reading of the Bible Possible?* (Adelaide: Australasian Theological Forum Press, 2009).

6. At the time of writing, two volumes have appeared: Norman C. Habel, *The Birth, the Curse and the Greening of Earth: An Ecological Reading of Genesis 1-11* (Sheffield: Sheffield Phoenix, 2011); and Michael Trainor, *About Earth's Child: An Ecological Listening to the Gospel of Luke* (Sheffield: Sheffield Phoenix, 2012).

7. See Mary Midgley, *The Myths We Live By* (London: Routledge, 2003).

8. Ellen F. Davis, *Scripture, Culture, and Agriculture: An Agrarian Reading of the Bible* (Cambridge: Cambridge University Press, 2009), 13.

9. Allen D. Callahan, *A Love Supreme: A History of the Johannine Tradition* (Minneapolis: Fortress, 2005), 61–2.

10. Stephen C. Barton, 'Johannine Dualism and Contemporary Pluralism', *The Gospel of John and Christian Theology*, Richard Bauckham and Carl Mosser, eds., (Grand Rapids: Eerdmans, 2008), 3–18, at 7.

11. Robert J. Karris, *Jesus and the Marginalized in John's Gospel* (Collegeville, MN: Liturgical Press, 1990), 31.

12. Stephen A. Reed, 'Bread', *The Anchor Bible Dictionary* [=ABD] David N. Freedman, ed. (New York: Doubleday, 2007), I, 777–80.

13. J.P. Louw and E.A. Nida, *Greek English Lexicon of the New Testament in Semantic Domains* (New York: United Bible Societies, 1988), 50.

14. Irene and Walter Jacob, 'Flora', *ABD*, II, 808–9.
15. John Dominic Crossan, *The Historical Jesus: The Life of a Mediterranean Jewish Peasant* (New York: HarperSanFrancisco, 1991), 360–7, proposes six different nuances of eucharistic understanding in the early Jesus movement. Bruce Chilton, *A Feast of Meanings: Eucharistic Theologies from Jesus through Johannine Circles* (Leiden: E. J. Brill, 1994) proposes seven. See also Paul F. Bradshaw, *Eucharistic Origins* (London: SPCK, 2004), 1–15. For a summary of the issues, see Margaret Daly-Denton, 'Looking Beyond the Upper Room: Eucharistic Origins in Contemporary Research', *Search* 31/1 (2008), 3–15.
16. Louw and Nida, *Greek English Lexicon*, I, 71–2.
17. Warren Carter, *John and Empire: Initial Explorations* (London: T&T Clark, 2008), 226.
18. Stephen Jay Gould, *Eight Little Piggies: Reflections in Natural History* (New York: Norton Paperback, 1993), 40.

THE EUCHARIST AS WEAPON

⁊ ⁊ ⁊

PATRICK HANNON

The title of this piece looks tendentious and it may seem that the writer sees denial of Holy Communion in the terms the title sets, and that what follows is angled in a particular and predictable direction. I hope it will emerge that this isn't so, and that these reflections do some justice to the multiple layers of our theme. There are several contexts in which the question of exclusion from Communion can arise: inter-Church worship for example, or the case of Catholics who have divorced and remarried civilly without a canonical annulment or dissolution, and the situation of a Catholic vis-à-vis political platforms or programmes that include elements at variance with Catholic moral teaching. Each of these merits extended treatment, and in selecting the third I have in mind that the first two are currently under active consideration at the highest levels as to underlying principle and present and future practice, and that, whatever the outcome, the lines of an approach to them are likely to be clear. Not so in the case of the third context, in many ways the most difficult of the three on which to gain clarity, for reasons that will appear.

But why the title? No deeper reason, it must immediately be conceded, than that I couldn't think of any better. The reader may be reminded of Dr Johnson's reply to the lady who wanted to know how it was that he'd mistakenly defined the word pastern in his dictionary: 'Ignorance, Madam. Pure ignorance';

though one needn't, I think, be entirely diffident as regards the choice of title here. For it is as a weapon that exclusion from Communion is commonly regarded in public discussion of Catholics and politics and, however much this is to be deplored, it needs to be met by argument, not by anxious hand-wringing about public ignorance. The argument is not made any easier if the public mind includes a memory of instances where denial of the Eucharist could hardly be seen as other than improperly coercive or even punitive.

Exclusion from Holy Communion can be discussed in terms of canon law, for there are a number of canons and other official instruments that express and shape a Church approach. An essay in canon law would be a rash undertaking for a non-specialist, but the interpretation and application of relevant law raises questions for moral theology, and it is these questions that are foremost in what follows here. The theological issues are best reached by way of pertinent canons though, and it is possible to look at them without becoming unduly involved in complex questions of canonical interpretation. In any case it happens that a useful point of entry for our reflections is provided by CIC canon 915, which can help us focus precisely on our topic, distinguishing it from one with which it is often unhelpfully confused.

The canon reads: 'Those who have been excommunicated or interdicted after the imposition or declaration of the penalty and others obstinately persevering in manifest grave sin are not to be admitted to Holy Communion'. It is important to notice that exclusion from Communion is not the same as excommunication: people who are excommunicated are denied access to all the sacraments and sacramentals, those who obstinately persevere in grave sin stand to be refused admittance to Holy Communion only; and it is the latter category that will occupy us. The choice was motivated in part by the fact that the refusal of Holy Communion is more commonly and more plausibly the question in the context we're considering, but partly also because reflection on it must bring our thinking in the direction of sacramental theology and the meaning of liturgy, and this seemed appropriate in a contribution to a volume honouring the work of Patrick Jones.

In the context we're considering – a Catholic's engagement in civic life – the clearest illustration of the problematic is the case of a candidate for office who is a Catholic, and who goes forward on a platform involving support for or acquiescence in policies at variance with Catholic teaching on a moral issue. The question, how is a Catholic expected to vote on legislation which sanctions behaviour that Catholic teaching considers immoral?, has during the past few decades become prominent in many countries, including our own. But the problems that typically and recurrently surface in the western world are most vividly illustrated in the United States, in state and federal elections campaigns, and especially in campaigns for elections to the presidency. The US experience – here necessarily briefly told and therefore simplified – can be instructive for a general understanding of the main problems which an answer to the question must face.

In the United States, fears and prejudices regarding Catholicism ensured the failure of the first Catholic to run for the presidency, New York Governor Al Smith, in 1929, and the same prejudices and fears lay in the way of the election of Senator John F. Kennedy in 1960. Put in the language of US constitutional law, the key issue was whether a Catholic could be counted upon to uphold the separation of Church and state guaranteed by the First Amendment to the Constitution. In more mundane terms the fear was that a Catholic president must take his orders from Rome and would try to impose Catholic values on a religiously diverse people. Kennedy confronted the problem directly when he addressed southern Baptist leaders in a speech in which he pledged that no authority other than his own conscience would dictate the decisions of his presidency; that Americans of every persuasion could be assured that he would never seek to impose a tenet of his faith on people not of that faith; and that should there ever be a conflict between his religio-moral convictions and his responsibilities under the Constitution he would resign.[1] This declaration allayed the fears of a sufficient number of voters among people who didn't share his faith, and it was acceptable also to the Catholic hierarchy of the time. The implied disjunction between private personal credo and public civic obligations has been invoked by Catholic candidates for various high offices since then, but recognition of its validity by the Catholic hierarchy has gradually attenuated to the point of explicit rejection in Church interventions in recent public political debate.[2]

Of course a candidate's dilemma is shared by the citizen who is asked to vote for someone, Catholic or not, whose programme includes policies that are at odds with Catholic teaching. Numerous issues have come to the fore over the years,[3] but a central preoccupation has been with the sacredness of human life from conception to natural death, with particular emphasis on Catholic teaching on abortion. Abortion has been a core concern since 1973, when the US Supreme Court declared unconstitutional any law which purported to abridge what came to be called a woman's right to choose to have an abortion or not;[4] and indeed a candidate's position on that finding has become a test of his or her commitment to Catholic moral doctrine and life. Obviously this presents a dilemma for a Catholic voter and for a Catholic seeking office: what to do if one's party espouses a policy which is pro-choice.

An approach to this kind of dilemma has been developed over the past four decades by the US Conference of Catholic Bishops: in each presidential election year since 1976 the Conference has issued a document, now entitled *Forming Consciences for Faithful Citizenship*, which sets out comprehensively the civic responsibilities of Catholics, and highlights matters of particular concern as they emerge. Whilst affirming Church teaching on substantive moral principle, the Conference avers that it doesn't wish to tell people how to vote but to set down markers for the guidance of Catholics regarding their responsibilities in the public square. It recognises that the spheres of law and morality though related are different, and not every infraction of a moral code should be made a crime, and nor is everything that's legal necessarily morally right; but it insists on the 'intrinsic immorality' of certain acts, most notably 'procured' or 'direct' abortion. It teaches that voters should attend to a candidate's overall commitments, not just to a single issue; that there are principles to help decide how far one may morally plausibly go in cooperating in what Catholic teaching regards as the wrongdoing of another; that in the end, having due regard to all relevant principles of Church teaching, and following prayerful reflection, a candidate or voter must act according to conscience.[5]

A major moment in the evolution of the Conference's approach occurred in the run-up to the presidential election of 2004 when Senator John Kerry, a practising Catholic, emerged as the Democratic candidate. Early in the contest Kerry began to be questioned about his moral beliefs and inevitably – the Democratic Party platform having become unmistakably 'pro-choice' – his position regarding abortion law became the object of media attention. Early in the contest, too, some bishops began to indicate that Catholics were obliged not to vote for him, and soon it was being asked whether Kerry might not be excommunicated, or at least denied access to the Eucharist. It was at this point that canon 915 came into sharp focus, especially its provision that Catholics 'obstinately persevering in manifest grave sin are not to be admitted to Holy Communion'.

It should be remarked that the framework proposed in *Faithful Citizenship* remained the position of the Bishops' Conference and that the great majority of the bishops was content to let it stand as the official guide, as it still does.[6] The attribution of sinfulness to John Kerry's candidacy by some individual bishops – and the extension of that verdict to support for Kerry at the polls – resulted from a particular interpretation of moral theology principles regarding cooperation in the wrongdoing of another. But that interpretation wasn't conclusive for the Conference when at its meeting in June it decided to issue a short document entitled *Catholics in Political Life*. This explicitly addressed the question 'whether the denial of Holy Communion to some Catholics in political life is necessary because of their public support for abortion on demand'. The Conference's reply was: 'Given the wide range of circumstances involved in arriving at a prudential judgment on a matter of this seriousness, we recognise that such decisions rest with the individual bishop in accord with the established canonical and pastoral principles. Bishops can legitimately make different judgments on the most prudent course of pastoral action'.[7]

The concept of 'prudential judgment' is of the utmost significance, and a satisfactory treatment of it would need more space than we have. It must suffice for now to borrow a brief account from the *Compendium of the Social Doctrine of the Church*:

> Prudence makes it possible to make decisions that are consistent, and to make them with realism and a sense of responsibility for the consequences of one's action. The rather widespread opinion that equates prudence with shrewdness, with utilitarian calculations, with diffidence or with timidity or indecision, is far from the correct understanding of this virtue. It is a characteristic of practical reason and offers assistance in deciding with wisdom and courage the course of action that should be followed, becoming the measure of the other virtues. Prudence affirms the good as a duty and shows in what manner the person should accomplish it. In the final analysis, it is a virtue that requires the mature exercise of thought and responsibility in an objective understanding of a specific situation and in making decisions according to a correct will.[8]

We should notice an apparent ambiguity in *Catholics and Political Life*: one could ask whether the first reference to prudential judgment applies to politicians as well as to the bishops; whether indeed the fact that bishops can make different judgments is in part a consequence of the fact that politicians can.

It transpired later that Cardinal Theodore McCarrick, head of a working group charged with guiding the Conference's response, had received a memorandum entitled 'Worthiness to Receive Holy Communion: General Principles' from the then Prefect of the Congregation for the Doctrine of the Faith, Cardinal Josef Ratzinger. Cardinal McCarrick sent a copy of *Catholics in Political Life* to Cardinal Ratzinger who in a reply dated 9 July said: 'The statement is very much in harmony with the general principles "Worthiness to Receive Holy Communion", sent as a fraternal service – to clarify the doctrine of the Church on this specific issue – in order to assist the American bishops in their related discussion and determinations'.[9]

The Conference's position on withholding Communion is set in a statement that takes care to reaffirm Catholic teaching regarding abortion, and insists on the duty of office-holders and of every Catholic to resist permissive laws and policies. The Ratzinger memorandum is similarly trenchant in these respects, and four of the six principles it offers concern directly the application of canon 915 to Catholic politicians. But as regards the withholding of Holy Communion, the take-away point for now is the recognition that a decision to do so is a matter of prudential judgment.[10]

Our interest here, as mentioned at the outset, is in some theological questions associated with exclusion from Communion. But the application of relevant canon law is where these are in practice encountered, and we have already seen that canon 915 is an important point of entry to the discussion. How to interpret the phrase 'others obstinately persevering in manifest grave sin' is obviously a critical question, and we'll return to it soon. Before doing so we might notice three other canons that have a bearing. First is the leading canon in the section entitled 'Participation in the Most Holy Eucharist', canon 912: 'Any baptised person not prohibited by law can and must be admitted to holy communion'. This may be read as a specification of canon 213: 'The Christian faithful have the right to receive assistance from the sacred pastors out of the spiritual goods of the Church, especially the word of God and the sacraments'. And since denial of Communion is a restriction of the exercise of a right, it is governed by canon 18: 'Laws which establish a penalty, restrict the free exercise of rights, or contain an exception from the law are subject to strict interpretation'.[11]

The cumulative import of these provisions is that the right of a baptised person to be admitted to Communion is in possession, and a minister of the Eucharist is *prima facie* obliged not to refuse. Should the question arise whether the would-be communicant is prohibited from receiving the Eucharist, a purported prohibition must be strictly scrutinised, and admittance must be granted unless it is plain that the law forbids it. At this point arises the question of the meaning and reach of the phrase 'others obstinately persevering in manifest grave sin'.

Canonists have parsed this phrase closely in connection with the situation of politicians and other public officials in the US, and it has been central in the interventions of bishops. All agree on the gravity of the sin of abortion, but there is always disagreement as regards each of the other terms of the description. Of these the crucial term involves the attribution of sinfulness, for if there is no sin the other terms needn't be discussed. Now, in Catholic theology grave or mortal sin requires not just gravity of matter but also 'full knowledge' and 'full consent' on the part of the person acting – internal factors that cannot be known with certainty by an outsider, that are, as we say colloquially, between the doer and God. The matter is complicated by the fact that though in Catholic doctrine to procure an abortion is gravely wrong, this isn't the issue in the case of parties other than the woman who seeks an abortion and the person who performs the procedure. The moral status of everyone else is evaluated by reference to the principles regarding cooperation in another's wrongdoing, mentioned above.[12]

These principles were evolved in the manual tradition in Catholic moral theology and have been found helpful in other contexts, notably in the field of medical ethics. In rough summary their sense is: it is wrong to cooperate in wrongdoing if cooperation means backing an action or omission or state of affairs because you want/intend the evil outcome – this is called *formal* cooperation. If you don't want it but are prepared to go along with it, the cooperation is said to be *material*; and whether it is justified or not depends both on the closeness of one's involvement and on the reasons for being involved at all. The question to be asked regarding a Catholic's involvement, as citizen or public official, is whether it is *formal* and therefore necessarily sinful, or *material*, in which case its morality is evaluated by reference also to the reason for any involvement, and by how close to the wrongful act the involvement is. Closeness is estimated by asking whether the involvement is – in the technical terminology – 'proximate' or 'remote', and whether it is 'immediate' or 'mediate'; and the reason for involvement must be – again a technical term – 'proportionate'.[13]

At this point one might ask, who is the judge of anyone's sinfulness? Some commentators say that the answer to this is in canon 916, which imposes an obligation on the communicant: 'A person who is conscious of grave sin is not to ... receive the body of the Lord without previous sacramental confession unless there is a grave reason and there is no opportunity to confess; in this case the person is to remember the obligation to make an act of perfect contrition which includes the resolution of confessing as soon as possible'. If this is the governing principle it must seem that Communion ought never to be denied to any baptised person not excluded by excommunication or interdict 'after the imposition or declaration of the penalty'.[14] But that would deprive the phrase 'obstinately persevering in manifest grave sin' of any significance; and it overlooks the fact that canon 915 places an obligation on the minister. Here I shall assume that a minister may be faced with the question whether to exclude, and that in a matter of the sort we are considering, a bishop or other competent authority is likely to have had to intervene.

So there remains the question, how can any outsider know the interior dispositions, the state of a communicant's soul? According to the principles formulated by Cardinal Ratzinger for the guidance of the US Conference this might seem to be beside the point, for in the circumstances envisaged by canon 915, a minister of the Eucharist – or, it may be inferred, a competent authority – is not 'passing judgment on the person's subjective guilt, but rather is reacting to the person's public unworthiness to receive Holy Communion due to an objective situation of sin'. But this verdict refers to *formal* cooperation on the communicant's part, it seems clear from the context, and it doesn't obviate the need to evaluate the degree of *material* cooperation of citizen or voter in terms of its relationship to procuring an abortion – whether it is remote or proximate, immediate or mediate – or of the proportionality of the reason for cooperating at all.[15]

The US experience is used here only as an example of how exclusion from Communion can arise in the context of Catholic engagement in civic life, hence I won't attempt to discuss the applicability of these tests to John Kerry or any other of the public figures whose situations have been debated in the United States. But some general considerations shed light on the reasons for a difference of viewpoint among canonists and among members of the Bishops' Conference, leading the Conference to the conclusion that '[b]ishops can legitimately make different judgments on the most prudent course of pastoral action', a conclusion not challenged in Cardinal Ratzinger's response to *Catholics in Political Life*. These considerations are important should the question of denying Communion come up in a comparable context in communities closer to home.

The first question is whether the stance of a politician or voter amounts to sinful material cooperation. Help toward answering this is found in the current most authoritative expression of Magisterium, the encyclical *Evangelium vitae*, issued in 1995 by John Paul II. For our concerns, article no. 73 is directly on point and is best quoted verbatim, slightly abridged:

Abortion and euthanasia are ... crimes which no human law can claim to legitimise. There is no obligation in conscience to obey such laws; instead there is a grave and clear obligation to oppose them by conscientious objection ... In the case of an intrinsically unjust law, such as a law permitting abortion or euthanasia, it is ... never licit to obey it, or to 'take part in a propaganda campaign in favour of such a law, or vote for it'.

A particular problem of conscience can arise in cases where a legislative vote would be decisive for the passage of a more restrictive law, aimed at limiting the number of authorised abortions, in place of a more permissive law already passed or ready to be voted on ... In a case like the one just mentioned, when it is not possible to overturn or completely abrogate a pro-abortion law, an elected official, whose absolute personal opposition to procured abortion was well known, could licitly support proposals aimed at limiting the harm done by such a law and at lessening its negative consequences at the level of general opinion and public morality. This does not in fact represent an illicit cooperation with an unjust law, but rather a legitimate and proper attempt to limit its evil aspects.[16]

The first paragraph seems primarily to have in mind any medical personnel requested to carry out an abortion when it says 'There is no obligation in conscience to obey such laws; instead there is a grave and clear obligation to oppose them by conscientious objection ... In the case of an intrinsically unjust law, such as a law permitting abortion or euthanasia, it is ... never licit to obey it'. But it explicitly addresses the politician and voter in the phrase 'take part in a propaganda campaign in favour of such a law, or vote for it'; and the politician in office is also directly in view in the second paragraph. Here the key sentence is 'when it is not possible to overturn or completely abrogate a pro-abortion law, an elected official, whose absolute personal opposition was well known, could licitly support proposals aimed at limiting the harm done by such a law and at lessening its negative consequences at the level of general opinion and public morality'. As the paragraph concludes, 'This does not in fact represent an illicit cooperation with an unjust law, but rather a legitimate and proper attempt to limit its evil aspects'.

In the language of the principles regarding cooperation in evil, what is in question here is material cooperation which is neither proximate nor immediate, and which engages the official for a proportionate reason. It requires little reflection to see that the application of these principles in any given case depends on the facts and circumstances of the case. The principles have to be applied in the first place by the politician himself or herself, which is why I referred earlier to an ambiguity in *Catholics in Political Life* that can be resolved only by postulating that there were two points at which a prudential judgment was called for: first, when a candidate decided to go forward for election; second, when the bishops came to decide whether the Conference should make a general rule. Given the difficulty of assessing the correctness of the judgment at the first point – 'given the wide range of circumstances involved in arriving at a prudential judgment on a matter of this seriousness', as the document puts it – it was surely only prudent to conclude that 'such decisions rest with the individual bishop in accord with the established canonical and pastoral principles. Bishops can legitimately make different judgments on the most prudent course of pastoral action'.

And this leads to a different question: why would bishops entertain the idea that exclusion from Holy Communion is called for in the context of the duties of a Catholic in the public square? One answer was given by Cardinal Avery Dulles: 'In imposing penalties, the Church is trying to protect the sacraments against the profanation that occurs when they are received by people without the proper dispositions. Dissenting politicians often want to receive Communion as a way of showing that they are still "good Catholics", when in fact they are choosing their political party over their faith'.[17] Also often given as a reason is a bishop's responsibility as teacher of the faith and morals which Catholics profess. In this connection it is sometimes maintained that the clarity of moral teaching is jeopardised if its public contravention appears to be tolerated by Church authority. And, relatedly, it is said that if Church authorities are not seen to take effective action in such circumstances, scandal is given, both inside and outside the Church.

In the interview already cited Cardinal Dulles offered the makings of a reply to these contentions, pointing out that the imposition of penalties involves at least three risks. 'In the first place, the bishop may be accused, however unfairly, of trying to coerce the politician's conscience. Secondly, people can easily accuse the Church of trying to meddle in the political process, which in this country depends on the free consent of the governed. And finally, the Church incurs a danger of alienating judges, legislators and public administrators whose good will is needed for other good programmes, such as the support of Catholic education and the care of the poor'. 'The Church's prime responsibility is to teach and to persuade', Dulles added; '[s]he tries to convince citizens to engage in the political process with a well-informed conscience'.[18]

'To teach and to persuade': the phrase evokes a memorable dictum of John Courtney Murray SJ when he spoke of the role of Church leadership in matters of the public square, saying that the appropriate tools are 'persuasion and pacific argument'. Teachers know that effective education is not achieved by diktat and in the absence of a mutual trust and respect, and any other approach is especially out of place when those to be taught are adults. This doesn't bespeak indiscipline, or a naiveté about human waywardness. It does suggest that an attitude to the teaching role which regards those to be taught as invariably wayward and undeserving of trust is bound to fail. Of course Church leaders must teach and teach clearly, but when their teaching is not taking hold among their hearers, it must be time to ask whether there isn't another way.

That is one reason why the reticence of the US Conference as regards exclusion from Holy Communion is, I think, the better way. But what of the point that canon 915 is meant to ensure that the Eucharist is not profaned? In these reflections I've cited in the main what seemed most relevant in official Church teaching, and the views of prelates known also as professional theologians, but the last word may be left to a canonist. John Beal, in an article which notes that the approach to the framing of canon 915 by the Commission for the Revision of the Code quite deliberately pointed toward a strict interpretation, wrote: 'By making it difficult for Church authorities to refuse admission to holy Communion to politicians whose public records arguably cannot be squared with Church teaching, a necessarily strict interpretation of canon 915 serves as a brake on the temptation to politicise the Eucharist by allowing the sacrament that signifies and effects the union of love between Christ and the Church to become a sacrament that signifies and brings about disunity. Zeal to protect the Eucharist from profanation by sinners can unwittingly lead to an even greater profanation by transforming the eucharistic celebration into a continuation of politics by liturgical means'.[19] Could there be a better reason for seeking to ensure that the Eucharist is never perceived as a weapon?

Notes

1. 'I am not the Catholic candidate for president. I am the Democratic Party's candidate for president, who happens also to be a Catholic. I do not speak for my Church on public matters, and the Church does not speak for me.

   'Whatever issue may come before me as president – on birth control, divorce, censorship, gambling or any other subject – I will make my decision in accordance with these views, in accordance with what my conscience tells me to be the national interest, and without regard to outside religious pressures or dictates. And no power or threat of punishment could cause me to decide otherwise'. Podcast and transcript at www.npr.org/templates/story/story.php?storyId=16920600 (accessed 7 June 2014).

2. Interventions by Church leaders and theologians have rightly pointed out that, as the saying goes, a lawmaker can't leave conscience at the door of the legislative chamber. But a lawmaker might reply that it is not a matter of leaving conscience at the door, but of trying to discern what conscience requires in his or her position and circumstances. This would not be a sufficient reply if what the legislator is contemplating is in direct contravention of an exceptionless moral norm; it does merit respect, however, when what's in question is a prudential judgment as to how a moral principle is to be applied in a complex situation.

3. Most recently – in addition to abortion and euthanasia – warfare, capital punishment, embryonic stem-cell research, same-sex unions, immigration policy, poverty, and religious freedom.

4. *Roe v. Wade*, 410 U.S. 113 (1973).

5. Text at www.usccb.org/issues-and-action/faithful-citizenship (accessed 8 June 2014).

6. Its full title is *Forming Consciences for Faithful Citizenship: The U.S. Bishops' Reflection on Catholic Teaching and Political Life*. The document is to be updated following the Conference's meeting in June 2014.

7. Text at www.usccb.org/issues-and-action/faithful-citizenship/ Church-teaching/catholics-in-political-life.cfm (accessed 8 June 2014).

8. Par 548. ET: www.vatican.va/roman_curia/pontifical_councils/ justpeace/documents/ (accessed 23 June 2014). A translation has been published also by Veritas (2005).

9. Text at popebenedictxvi.blogspot.ie/The Ratzinger Archives (accessed 14 June 2014).

10. *Catholics in Political Life,* and especially its view of Canon 915, was severely criticised by Archbishop Raymond Burke (now Cardinal and Prefect of the Signatura) in the course of an article entitled, 'The discipline regarding the denial of Holy Communion to those obstinately persevering in grave sin', *Periodica* 96 (2007), 3–58. Needless to say, the critique must be taken very seriously, and only a canonist with comparable expertise could properly engage with the argument. From the field of moral theology, though, one might, *salva reverentia*, venture an observation and a question. The article establishes beyond all doubt that the Eucharist must be refused to one who cooperates *formally* in abortion; but does it answer to the situation of a politician or voter whose cooperation is *material*? The point of the question should emerge when later we look at the principles regarding cooperation which have evolved in moral theology over the centuries, and at Cardinal Ratzinger's memorandum for the guidance of the US bishops.

11. Canon 213 is one of a number of canons sometimes referred to by commentators as constituting a charter of fundamental rights.

12. It should be mentioned – difficult as the situation may be to imagine – that someone who ordered or commanded an abortion to be procured is also *ipso facto* guilty of grave sin.

13. For a detailed note, see www.ncbcenter.org/, website of the National Catholic Bioethics Center which, as may be inferred from the membership of its board of directors, has a quasi-official standing in the US.

14. The allusion is to the distinction between penalties *ferendae sententiae* and *latae sententiae*, respectively, those that require to be imposed by competent authority and those incurred automatically. The former may be imposed only after due process, and for the purposes of canon 915 must have been publicly notified; and the latter must be declared to have been incurred.

15. The relevant sections of the memorandum are:

    5. Regarding the grave sin of abortion or euthanasia, when a person's formal cooperation becomes manifest (understood, in the case of a Catholic politician, as his consistently campaigning and voting for permissive abortion and euthanasia laws), his pastor should meet with him, instructing him about the Church's teaching, informing him that he is not to present himself for Holy Communion until he brings to an end the objective situation of sin, and warning him that he will otherwise be denied the Eucharist.

    6. When 'these precautionary measures have not had their effect or in which they were not possible', and the person in question, with obstinate persistence, still presents himself to receive the Holy Eucharist, 'the minister of Holy Communion must refuse to distribute it' (see Pontifical Council for Legislative Texts Declaration 'Holy Communion and Divorced, Civilly Remarried Catholics' [2002], nos. 34). This decision, properly speaking, is not a sanction or a penalty. Nor is the minister of Holy Communion passing judgment on the person's subjective guilt, but rather is reacting to the person's public unworthiness to receive Holy Communion due to an objective situation of sin.

16. The quotation in *Evangelium vitae* is from a *Declaration on Procured Abortion* by the Congregation or the Doctrine of the Faith on 18 November 1974. At first sight this may be thought inapplicable to the US situation, where the impossibility of overturning the law is owing to the fact that the law is a product of a Supreme Court interpretation of the Constitution, which can be changed only by another decision of the Supreme Court or by public referendum. But that doesn't preclude the introduction of policy

programmes and legislation 'aimed at limiting the harm done by such a law and at lessening its negative consequences at the level of general opinion and public morality', and is therefore 'a legitimate and proper attempt to limit its evil aspects'. And of course the encyclical's words are directly applicable in countries in which the law is a product of ordinary legislation.

17. Interview with *Zenit*, 29 June 2004. Text at www.zenit.org/en/articles/cardinal-dulles-on-communion-and-pro-abortion-politicians (accessed 8 June 2014).

18. A similar view was expressed by Cardinal George of Chicago in an interview with John Allen, then Vatican correspondent for the National Catholic Reporter. Allen asked: 'is there room for a diversity of opinion on political strategy – whether it is legislative, judicial or cultural – as long as the moral point is clear that no just society can tolerate abortion?' George agreed, adding 'The question is, how do we limit it most effectively? Those are questions of prudential judgment around which there can be many discussions. The Church has not taken a position on which of those strategies is to be preferred, and I don't think we should'.

19. *America*, 21–28 June 2004, 16–18.

PROCLAIMING AND REHEARSING JUSTICE IN THE EUCHARIST

꒳ ꒳ ꒳

JULIE KAVANAGH

The working premise of this essay is that in the ritual celebration of Eucharist the gathered Church at once proclaims and rehearses justice to and for the world. An authentic worship of our God requires that we open ourselves up to both the vision of the kingdom of God as expressed in the Eucharist and to the change that such a vision works upon us. An authentic worship demands an embodiment of the ways of justice within and outside the liturgical experience. It assumes a belief and expectation that 'genuine participation in the Sunday Eucharist can actually change the way we live'.[1] Behind this premise are presuppositions about the nature of justice and of liturgy and, in particular, the Eucharistic liturgy. If what is asserted holds true, then there are, in turn, implications for the ritual celebration itself and for the ritual participants beyond the liturgical rite. Both the presuppositions and the implications will frame the exploration that follows.

Context
We live in a world that is deeply scarred and wounded by injustice. The twenty-first century continues to give witness to poverty, hunger, war and discrimination. This century bears the dark shadow of terrorism, chemical warfare, the devastating impact of climate change and the forced displacement of people from their homeland. Millions throughout the world live in

circumstances of inequality, unemployment, under the threat of violence in their neighbourhood or in their very home.

As Christians we cannot ignore these situations. We are mandated to bring God's justice to these places of injustice, to work to bring God's healing, peace and compassion to the people of this world. But what has this to do with liturgy? What does liturgy have to offer to heal our world? Rita Ferrone, in an address to the monks of St John's Abbey in Minnesota, reminded them that Virgil Michel, one of their own and one of the twentieth century founders of liturgical renewal in the United States, would answer: It has Christ.[2] In our liturgical celebrations we encounter Christ and, indeed, are called to become the Body of Christ. This is the gift that the liturgy offers us, the gift of Christ who overcomes all barriers, all sin, all injustice; this is the gift whom we are called to carry beyond the liturgy. Leo the Great preached that 'What was to be seen of our Redeemer has passed over into the sacraments.'[3] The task of all who celebrate these mysteries is, in turn, to make Christ visible in the world.

History and contemporary times have borne witness to many people who celebrate Eucharist and who commit terrible injustices. There are also many people who have and do work tirelessly for justice but who genuinely see no practical relationship between what they do and what is celebrated in a church on a Sunday. There is a tremendous dissonance between both these scenarios and this demands an honest evaluation and understanding of what we are called to when we gather to enact Eucharist, and of how we go about that enactment. In an era that has seen much focus and energy on the language of our liturgical prayer, perhaps the time is overdue to remember the intrinsic relationship between justice and liturgy and to consciously reflect on the Eucharistic liturgy from the perspective of justice.

Presuppositions
The Meaning of Justice
The justice we speak of is not about legal redress, restitution or law-keeping but rather it is about living in right relationship and

harmony with ourselves, our God and our neighbour. It is a justice founded in God and God's covenantal relationship with us. We are a people called by God into right relationship and to the ways of right relationship. We live in justice when we live in harmony, mutual respect, unity and equity. Justice is about wanting for our neighbour what God wants for us; that which Jesus proclaimed as his mission and purpose: 'I came that they may have life, and have it abundantly' (John 10:10). Justice, therefore, has to do with human flourishing. As Christians we recognise that such flourishing comes about through our on-going relationship with Christ and his Gospel message of the Kingdom of God. Justice is the life we are called to in response to this Gospel message; human flourishing is its fruit.

Scripture, Justice and Worship

It is very evident from Scripture that we cannot turn to God in worship without also practising justice. Time and time again in the prophetic tradition we find the people being admonished for worship that ignores justice. Amos tells the people:

> The Lord says this ... I hate, I despise your festivals, and I take no delight in your solemn assemblies. Even though you offer me your burnt offerings and grain offerings, I will not accept them; and the offerings of well-being of your fatted animals I will not look upon. Take away from me the noise of your songs; I will not listen to the melody of your harps. But let justice roll down like waters, and righteousness like an ever-flowing stream. (5:21-25)

Hosea reminds the people of their priorities, saying

> For I desire steadfast love and not sacrifice, the knowledge of God rather than burnt offerings. (6:6)

Isaiah also has strong words to say about worthless offerings and the need to learn to do good and to search for justice (see Isaiah 1:11-17). Later on in his ministry the prophet has to remind the people of God that justice and concern for the poor are essential to the way they worship. He does so in response to their anger when their fasting does not appear to have met with God's approval. But their fasting, which Isaiah implies has resulted in quarrelling and oppressive treatment of workers, is not the kind of fasting that God wants. Rather, he asks, is not the fast that God desires

> to loose the bonds of injustice, to undo the thongs of the yoke, to let the oppressed go free, and to break every yoke? Is it not to share your bread with the hungry, and bring the homeless poor into your house; when you see the naked, to cover them, and not to hide yourself from your own kin? (Isaiah 58:6-7)

The essential link between worship and the call to justice is continued in the New Testament. The ethical demands of worship are solidly placed before us in the words and actions of Jesus. In Matthew 5 Jesus clearly outlines for the disciples the need to be reconciled with one's brother and sister before coming to the altar of God. Cultic practice must be matched by human interactions of right relationship. Again in Matthew, Jesus addresses the Pharisees and reminds them of the words of Hosea (6:6): 'Go and learn what this means, "I desire mercy not sacrifice"' (Matthew 9:13). In the scriptures it is quite clear that the people of God are called to join their liturgy to lives of justice.

Perhaps the greatest illustration of this point is to be found in the Gospel of John and the account of Jesus' washing of the feet of the disciples (see John 13:1-14). This has come to be viewed as a deliberate substitution for the Institution Narrative by John. By so doing, John is making a definite link between Eucharist and service. The washing of feet, according to Dermot Lane, '... is an explanation of what the Eucharist is really all about; it is a type of symbolic commentary on the deeper meaning of the Eucharist provided by Jesus'.[4]

Early Church writing continues to link worship with justice practices. Paul, writing to the Corinthians, is quick to remind them of the ethical demands that come with choosing to sit at the Eucharistic table (see 1 Corinthians 11:17-27). Indeed, rather than embodying this link the community in Corinth appear to be falling so far short of it as to be calling into question whether theirs is the Lord's Supper at all. For when they come to the table they do so with divisions and distinctions, where some have a place and others do not, where some are hungry and others are drunk. Here the lack of internal justice in the liturgy is a condemnation of themselves and a threat to their very identity as Church. Justice, then, needs to be exercised in the assembly of worship as well as in community life. This is echoed in James 2:2-4 where the community is warned not to make distinctions between poor and rich in the assembly. Finally, the community depicted in Acts 2:42-47 presents us with an image of harmonious and just living where eucharistic sharing is coupled with a real and responsive concern and care for the poor and needy.

Some Understandings about Liturgy

Before looking specifically to justice in the liturgical enactment of Eucharist it will be beneficial to highlight some key understandings about liturgy. Together they provide a particular lens for our subsequent exploration.

Liturgy is an encounter with Christ. When we gather in prayer in the name of Christ, Christ is present in our midst (see Matthew 18:20). When we engage in liturgical prayer the Paschal Mystery of Christ's living, dying and rising is proclaimed and made present to us in the very heart of the celebration. The One who has promised to be with us always, comes to us in the liturgy and continues to act upon us in love, care, compassion, healing and graciousness. In the liturgy we encounter in a real way the person of Christ today. We affirm our commitment to live in relationship with this Christ, an on-going relationship which opens us up to be changed and to live the consequences of life in Christ.

Liturgy at once expresses and shapes our faith. Through the actions, signs, and words of the liturgy we hear and express our faith in the risen Lord. By so doing we renew and deepen that faith and our commitment to it. Liturgy is both proclamation and rehearsal. What we proclaim and practice in the liturgy we are called to live beyond the liturgy. This calls for an active engagement in and attentiveness to the liturgy, its words and actions, and an openness to discern the implications of our worship for daily living. We do not shape and form liturgy: liturgy shapes and forms us.

Liturgy gives us a vision of the kingdom of God. While liturgy is celebrated in the cultural context of a particular worshipping community, it rises above culture to place us within an experience of the kingdom. It holds before us in practice and proclamation a vision of kingdom attitudes, bearing witness to kingdom relationships. In the liturgy we insert ourselves into the vision of this kingdom and commit ourselves to its practice beyond the liturgy. 'Into the liturgy the people bring their entire existence so that it may be gathered up in praise. From the liturgy the people depart with a renewed vision of the value-patterns of God's kingdom, by the more effective practice of which they intend to glorify God in their whole life'.[5]

Liturgy is corporate. It is an action of the Body of Christ in union with its head, Christ. As such it is a collective endeavour. We go to God together, at God's initiative. We are not a random grouping of individuals. We are a people, a Church called into being by God. The doing of liturgy itself proclaims and rehearses this identity. United in our common Baptism, liturgy reminds us of and calls us to our corporate identity as the Body of Christ. If we can experience ourselves as the Body of Christ in the liturgy we are surely compelled to go out in solidarity with one another to be the Body of Christ in the world. The corporate nature of liturgy is itself a statement to the world that we are called to look beyond the individual and to live in justice and harmony with one another.

Liturgy is embodied ritual. In the liturgy we engage in repeated, predictable, patterned behaviours and actions of worship through the medium of our bodies. Among the components of ritual language of liturgy are symbol and signs, word, gesture, music, posture, environment and silence. These elements work together and demand an inner-coherency that collectively gives them their capacity to act upon us. The symbolic action of the liturgy ought to engage us bodily, taking up and engaging all our senses, memories, hopes and dispositions into the active liturgical experience with all its capacities.

Liturgy is an art of performed communication. All that we do in the liturgy reveals an understanding of ourselves as Church and of our God. It is the whole experience that communicates this meaning. While we can break the liturgy down to its various parts and offer commentary on the meaning and aspirations of these parts, the full meaning is always greater than the sum of those individual parts. Indeed, outside of the immediate act of liturgy itself, all is commentary rather than communication. Communication works upon us in the liturgical experience as an exchange between God and the active participants at the liturgy. Through this exchange God continues to call us, to love us and shape us into being. For those called to prepare liturgy, an essential part of their task is allowing this communication to breathe in the midst of the assembly, facilitating the ritual language as art to bear the weight of its own mystery. The story is told of the dancer Isadora Duncan who, on being asked by a group of journalists the meaning of a particular dance, replied: 'If I could have told you what it meant, darlings, I wouldn't have had to dance it!' As an art of communication, liturgy finds its voice in its doing. It is, therefore, unashamedly performative. In the ritual performance of liturgy we engage in an action '... in which meanings and values can be communicated, created and transformed'.[6] In the liturgy we perform those beliefs, values, memories and hopes that we seek to carry out with us beyond the liturgy to perform in our lives. And yet precisely because of this performative characteristic, we know from our own experience that 'the same liturgical books used in different assemblies can result in very different ritual performances'.[7] The ritual performance itself runs the risk of distorting or altering the intended communication. This is why the US bishops could make the bold and sobering statement: 'Faith grows when it is well expressed in celebration. Good celebrations can foster and nourish faith. Poor celebrations may weaken it'.[8] The consideration of performance in the liturgy is never about making liturgy relevant or interesting or entertaining; performance in liturgy needs to be understood from the point of view of the power of performed ritual to shape and form people into the values and beliefs expressed – whether or not they are the intended values and beliefs.

The liturgy and its expression of justice. The dynamic nature of liturgy is hopefully very evident in what has been articulated so far. Liturgy is never about getting through the rubrics and prayers, saying the black and doing the red in order to fulfil a perceived obligation to God. Enacted liturgy proclaims and rehearses who we are called to be in the world in light of our encounter with Christ and the vision of the reign of God as articulated in the whole communication of the liturgy.

Such an understanding must surely impact how we approach the celebration of liturgy, how we prepare the 'given' liturgy, how we engage with its enactment, and our commitment to what and who and where the liturgy sends us. Such an understanding impacts upon our expectations of both the liturgy itself and of ourselves.

Implications: Justice in the Eucharistic Liturgy

As we begin to identify how the vision of the kingdom of God is expressed in the liturgy, a note of caution is necessary. Justice is indeed intrinsic to the liturgy because the liturgy is of God. However, as alluded to above, we cannot presume in the ritual experience that justice is self-evident. This is where dissonance can occur. *Because* we have said it, doesn't make it so.

Theological commentary and liturgical enactment do not always coincide. We need to consciously enact the ritual mindful of its expressions of justice and willing to be challenged and invited to embody that justice in the very practices of the liturgy itself. We need to also be prepared to name where our liturgical practices may fall short and actually express values that are not of the kingdom.

Gathering

The first action of the eucharistic liturgy, gathering, is an intentional and purposeful act. Through the very action of our gathering Christ is in our midst. This Christ is revealed in the assembly itself who are now constituted as the Body of Christ. This is the Christ who in his earthly ministry exercised an indiscriminate welcome; who in his table fellowship demonstrated a hospitality that tolerated no distinctions of class, age, sexual orientation, race, gender or creed; who practised a welcome that actively sought out the marginalised and outcast of society. Jesus demonstrated for us how to gather as the Body of Christ. It is to welcome the stranger, to reach out to the 'little ones' of the community. It is to gather in a manner that actively seeks out rather than passively tolerates the 'other' – whoever the other is. In Christ there is no room for exclusivity or prestige or division, for 'where Christ is present, human barriers are being broken'.[9] Our celebrations of Eucharist must be an active proclamation of this truth. Welcome and hospitality are core attitudes of justice that must permeate the whole liturgical experience. Just as liturgy flourishes in a climate of hospitality[10] so do those who gather flourish when they experience that there is a place, a welcome for them at the table of the Eucharist. Given the particular circumstances and contexts of our own local celebrations, we need to ask whether or not our enactment of the Eucharist is an adequate proclamation and rehearsal of the kingdom hospitality and welcome to which being the Body of Christ in the world calls us. Who are the 'little ones' of our worship community? Surely these include the homeless, people with a disability, people living with mental illness, foreigners, the economically underprivileged. Who else might we name? Are they actively welcomed in our gathering as equal participants? Do they feel they have a rightful place? In turn, if we are willing to recognise and welcome Christ in the gathered community at Eucharist, we must be willing to welcome Christ in the world where we encounter him in the hungry, thirsty, naked, imprisoned, sick and unwelcome (see Matthew 25).

The Liturgy of the Word

In the Liturgy of the Word Christ speaks to us today. We are not simply sharing stories of a past tradition. Through the *proclamation of the Word of God* the reality of our on-going covenantal relationship with God is present to us. In God's word to us we are reminded of and drawn into the practices and values of the kingdom. We are called to renew and deepen our understanding of what it means to be in relationship with God, of what it means as Christians to share in the task of making the practices, attitudes and values of the kingdom of God operative in our world. The Word of God is poured out upon our very selves; it is poured out upon us in the context of the culture in which we are immersed, in the context of the human tragedies and joys of our times, of the conflicts and struggles of our daily living. The *Homily* seeks to literally break open the Word into the circumstances of our lives, to weave it into the fabric of our individual and collective being, so that the proclaimed Word can find a responsive listening on our part.

The quality of our proclamation, of our listening and of our homilies in the celebration will help or hinder how we go out and live this Word in the world. This is justice – authentically living and acting in response to the Gospel message of the kingdom we have received.

The Liturgy of the Word concludes with the Prayer of the Faithful or Universal Prayer. This latter title reminds us that local celebrations of liturgy cannot remain isolated from the wider context of Church and world. We bring the whole world with us into the Eucharist. This prayer is a very conscious moment of looking beyond ourselves. In our prayer we seek the fruits of right relationship and justice for our world and its people. We remember in particular the most vulnerable in our societies. We demonstrate explicitly that 'the joys and the hopes, the griefs and the anxieties of the [people] of this age, especially those who are poor or in any way afflicted, these are the joys and hopes, the griefs and anxieties of the followers of Christ' (GS 1). And as true disciples, if we pray for justice we must be willing to do justice.

Liturgy of the Eucharist

Gathering of Gifts for the Poor

In the contemporary experience of worship we seem to have an uneasy relationship with what is commonly referred to as 'the collection'. It is an action we seem to want to get over with because it is an apparently necessary yet almost embarrassing task to be done within the rite. One explanation for this unease is that we have forgotten the history and purpose of this action. We need to go back to scriptures and the early Church communities and remember that in this action these Christian communities demonstrated the intrinsic link between worship and justice.

Referring to a collection being organised for the poor churches of Judea, St Paul reminds the Corinthians that 'On the first day of the week, each of you is to put aside and save whatever extra you earn' (1 Corinthians 16:2). In commentating on this passage, Pope John Paul II wrote: 'Far from trying to create a narrow "gift" mentality, Paul calls rather for a demanding *culture of sharing*, to be lived not only among the members of the community itself but also in society as a whole'.[11] Saint Justin in his *Apologia* offers the following instruction: '... those who are well-to-do and willing give as they choose, as each one so desires. The collection is then deposited with the presider who uses it on behalf of orphans, widows, those who are needy due to sickness or any other cause, prisoners, strangers who are travelling; in short, he assists all who are in need'.[12] Justin is clearly demonstrating for us, like Jesus in his earthly ministry did, what it means to authentically celebrate the Eucharist. This collection is an explicit expression of the intrinsic link between liturgy and justice. It expresses the solidarity of the worshipping community with the poor; solidarity that, in a *culture of sharing*, speaks of mutuality and relationship.

For the moment, in many of our communities, we appear to have disempowered this element of our celebration. In an Irish context, the returning of Lenten Trócaire boxes to the church on Holy Thursday or specific Trócaire emergency appeals are perhaps the only times parishioners witness this particular action of justice within the liturgy. For many the collection is perceived as simply being about paying the church light bill or the school mortgage. Yet, while in our stewardship of the parish we have to ensure the payment of bills, this action obviously could be so much more. It is an opportunity to explicitly proclaim and rehearse practical solidarity with those in need.

Presentation of the Gifts

Through this action we proclaim that all of God's creation is taken up by Christ to be affirmed and transformed. 'In this way we also bring to the altar all the pain and suffering of the world, in the certainty that everything has value in God's eyes'.[13] We do not bring wheat or grapes but rather bread and wine, the fruit of God's creation *and* our human labour. We bring our gifts for the needs of the poor and the Church. In this action we proclaim our just stewardship of God's creation, our participation in God's work and our belief that all, not least ourselves, is transformed in God. Such transformation takes us beyond the liturgy where 'we are challenged to promote this harmony between humans and the rest of creation by the way we live our lives'.[14] Within this humble gesture we find, therefore, global, environmental and interpersonal dimensions.[15] The communication of these dimensions is reliant on the local performance of this phase of the liturgical action of the Eucharist. There is a distortion in our communication when our monetary gifts 'discretely' disappear into a sacristy and our gifts of bread and wine suddenly appear from a convenient side table in the sanctuary and when, indeed, these gifts are not readily identifiable as fruit of the vine and work of human hands.

Eucharistic Prayer

As a prayer of thanksgiving, this prayer reminds us that a truly eucharistic, Christian stance to life is one of joy and thanksgiving, gratitude and deep appreciation. The promise of justice, right relationship, human flourishing for all people in God evokes our prayer of thanks. Through this prayer we place solidly before us the good news of our salvation in Christ. The once and for all sacrifice of the cross is present to us today in our prayers and actions of remembrance, reconciling us with and in God and seeking to accomplish in us the fruits of our redemption: 'a kingdom of truth and life, a kingdom of holiness and grace, a kingdom of justice, love and peace'.[16]

Our Father

The Our Father reminds us that the kingdom of God is not some future reality; the kingdom of God is already operative in our world today when we do the will of the One we call Father. As children of God, as those who can *dare* to call our God Father, we are invited to become kingdom builders by discerning God's will. To carry out this divine task we receive the grace of the physical and spiritual nourishment of the Body of Christ, the Bread of Life.

When we pray the Our Father at this stage of the Mass we are once more placing before us the call to practice the ways of God's kingdom, the call to justice and right relationship. With its core themes of kingdom, daily bread and mutual forgiveness it is a most appropriate prayer of preparation for the reception of Communion.

Sign of Peace

While a preparatory rite for receiving communion, this action is an important reminder to the community of integrity of practice. We cannot gather around the table of reconciliation, peace and communion without being willing to bring these realities to the world around us. This gesture is a proclamation not only to ourselves but to the world around us, a world fraught and fractured with fear and conflict, that Christ is our peace. Living in Christ, ours is the privilege and task of bringing this peace to the circumstances of our lives. Sadly, again this is an action with which many feel uncomfortable. Indeed, there is among some an active welcoming of the opportunity that medical epidemics present for jettisoning this action from the liturgy. This highlights a serious need of formation for the faithful who gather. We must be mindful of the call to authentically rehearse in the liturgy these gestures of peace and reconciliation in order to exercise them outside of the liturgy.

Communion Sharing

The action of drinking and eating in common around the holy table is one of the strongest enactments of justice in our liturgy. At the table of the Lord we are fed and nourished by the Body and Blood of Christ. In the greatest action of solidarity and love, just as those who gather *around* the table come with their own brokenness, the One *on* the table is broken and poured out for us. 'It is the broken host that carries the broken but healing Jesus. It takes a Crucified Jesus to love deeply "crucified" people'.[17] The *fraction rite* is a powerful enactment of God's love of God's people. Through this action the one Body of Christ is physically broken down in order that it may be shared with the faithful, who in turn are made one, are made whole.[18] The frequently observed practice of a priest-celebrant breaking a host and consuming it in its entirety is a distortion of this ritual action.

This distortion is compounded by a routine use of ciboria taken from the tabernacle rather than the use of hosts consecrated in the particular liturgy being celebrated.[19] This practice greatly diminishes the communication of one of the central gifts of our liturgical experience: we receive back what we ourselves have initially given, only now transformed through the grace of God, just as we are being transformed. And we are invited to receive back not only our transformed humble gift of bread but also our transformed gift of wine. Take and eat; take and drink. And yet our common response to this invitation is to 'clericalise' the chalice, thereby introducing distinctions within communion sharing that appear contradictory to the table fellowship exercised by Jesus.[20] As proclamation and rehearsal, this is a practice that needs reflection.

As a pilgrim people we come to the altar of our God, together. The *communion procession* can be a powerful proclamation and rehearsal of our solidarity with one another on our common baptismal journey.

And ultimately, as St Augustine is oft repeated as saying, we are to become what we receive (see his Homily 272). This represents, perhaps, the greatest mandate to right relationship and justice in the liturgy. We have encountered and received Christ in the Eucharist, we are now sent to be the Body of Christ beyond the Eucharist. Returning to the vision of Virgil Michel: what does the liturgy have to offer the world? It has Christ. We are the bearers of Christ to and for the world. And in this world beyond the Eucharist, 'by our mutual love and, in particular, by our concern for those in need we will be recognised as true followers of Christ. This will be the criterion by which the authenticity of our eucharistic celebrations is judged'.[21]

Dismissal

Every liturgy demands an exodus. Jean Corbon has written, 'The people of God who gather in a church are only pausing there on their exodus journey'.[22] We must move from proclamation and rehearsal to live, as termed in the Orthodox tradition, 'the liturgy after the liturgy', bringing what we do in our worship to our lives beyond it, making present in the world 'a visible Christian fellowship which overcomes human barriers against justice, freedom and unity'.[23] The Dismissal is our negotiation of this exit point from the liturgy. We depart with the blessing of God; we have the on-going love and support of our Creator who sustains us and is with us in all our actions. We are called to go and announce in our lives the good news of the kingdom, to embody the kingdom attitudes and practices that we have rehearsed in the Eucharist. Pope Benedict XVI wrote that, 'These few words succinctly express the missionary nature of the Church'.[24] As members of the Body of Christ, as we leave our places of worship, hopefully, we have heard the call and mandate to actively share in the mission and task of the Church; to bring Christ, in whom we find life in abundance, to the world.

This essay has sought to demonstrate that the eucharistic liturgy is a locus of both the proclamation and rehearsal of justice. In our worship we celebrate the already present reign of God even as we await its final consummation, offering ourselves and the world an embodied, enacted vision of how life might be ordered and lived in God's justice.

The reform of the liturgy continues. Words and actions, symbols and gestures are of profound importance. We must never lose sight, however, of the area of liturgy in need of greatest reform: the liturgical subjects. When we look to the Eucharist through the lens of proclamation and rehearsal of God's justice, we may well come to worship open to having God's change wrought upon us so that not only liturgy but our lives can become a foretaste of the reign of God's justice. The challenge and the invitation for local celebrations of the Eucharist is to allow God's Spirit to richly and deeply breath in the liturgy so that they can truly be experienced as both proclamation and rehearsal, sign and instrument of the kingdom of God in our midst.

Notes

1. Irish Catholic Bishops' Conference, *O Sacred Banquet: Revitalising the Sunday Celebration of the Eucharist* (Dublin: Veritas, 2011), no. 9.
2. Rita Ferrone, 'Sunday at the Abbey' Conference: *Liturgy and Social Justice: Fresh Challenges for Today in Virgil Michel's Legacy.* Chapter House, St John's Abbey, Collegeville, Minnesota, 7 April 2013, p. 7. PDF of text at www.praytellblog.com/wp-content/uploads/20/ [accessed 22 August 2013].

3. St Leo the Great, *Sermon 74*, 2 [PL 54, 398]: ET, *St Leo the Great: Sermons*, Jane Patricia Freeland and Agnes Josephine Conway, trans., The Fathers of the Church, 93 (Washington, DC: Catholic University of America Press, 1996), 326.

4. Dermot Lane, 'Eucharist and Social Justice', *Eucharist for a New World; Select Addresses, Homilies and Conferences from the 42nd International Eucharistic Congress, Lourdes, 1981*, Seán Swayne, ed. (Carlow: Irish Institute of Pastoral Liturgy, 1981), 55–68, at 60.

5. Geoffrey Wainwright, *Doxology: The Praise of God in Worship, Doctrine and Life. A Systematic Theology* (New York: Oxford University Press, 1980), 8.

6. Margaret Mary Kelleher, 'Ritual Studies and the Eucharist: Paying Attention to Performance', *Eucharist: Toward the Third Millennium*, Martin F. Connell, ed. (Chicago: Liturgy Training Publications, 1997), 51–69, at 54.

7. Kelleher, 'Ritual Studies and the Eucharist', 59.

8. United States Conference of Catholic Bishops, *Sing to the Lord: Music in Divine Worship*, [2007], no. 5. Full text at nccbuscc.org/liturgy/SingToTheLord.pdf (accessed 24 August 2013).

9. 'Ministry', no. 18, in *Baptism, Eucharist and Ministry*, Faith and Order Paper No. 111 (Geneva: World Council of Churches, 1982), 23.

10. See [US] National Conference of Catholic Bishops, Bishops' Committee on the Liturgy, *Environment and Art in Catholic Worship* [1978], no. 11, in *The Liturgy Documents: A Parish Resource*, Vol. 1, 3rd ed. (Chicago: Liturgy Training Publications, 1991), 320.

11. John Paul II, Apostolic Letter, *Dies domini*, On Keeping the Lord's Day Holy, 70, in *The Liturgy Documents: A Parish Resource*, Vol. 2 (Chicago: Liturgy Training Publications, 1999), 9–49, at 38.

12. St Justin Martyr, *Apologia* I, 67, 6 [PG 6, 430]. ET, Lawrence J. Johnson, *Worship in the Early Church: An Anthology of Historical Sources* (Collegeville, MN: Liturgical Press, 2009), Vol. 1, no. 246, 68.

13. Benedict XVI, Post Synodal Apostolic Exhortation (on the Eucharist), *Sacramentum caritatis*, [2007], 47.

14. Irish Catholic Bishops' Conference, *The Cry of the Earth*, Pastoral Reflection on Climate Change (Dublin: Veritas, 2009), 17.

15. See *O Sacred Banquet*, 26.

16. *Roman Missal*: Preface from Solemnity of Our Lord Jesus Christ, King of the Universe.

17. Aidan Troy, 'Solidarity', *At the Breaking of Bread: Homilies on the Eucharist*, Patrick Jones, ed. (Dublin: Veritas, 2005), 29–32, at 31.

18. See *General Instruction of the Roman Missal* [= GIRM] 321.
19. This practice is also discouraged by GIRM 85: 'It is most desirable that the faithful, just as the Priest himself is bound to do, receive the Lord's Body from hosts consecrated at the same Mass ...'.
20. GIRM 281 states, 'Holy Communion has a fuller form as a sign when it takes place under both kinds'; and GIRM 282, '... the faithful should be instructed to participate more readily in this sacred rite [communion under both kinds], by which the sign of the Eucharistic banquet is more fully evident'. See also GIRM 85.
21. John Paul II, Apostolic Letter, *Mane nobiscum domine*, 28.
22. Jean Corbon, *The Wellsprings of Worship*, Matthew J. O'Connell, trans. (New York/Mahwah: Paulist Press, 1988), 133.
23. Ion Bria, 'The Liturgy after the Liturgy', *Martyria/Mission: The Witness of the Orthodox Churches Today*, Ion Bria, ed. (Geneva: World Council of Churches, 1980), 66–71, at 70.
24. *Sacramentum caritatis*, 51.

LITURGY AND FORMATION TO CARMELITE LIFE:
A PASTORAL COMMENTARY ON THE CARMELITE ORDER'S FORMATION DOCUMENT (2013)

➷ ➷ ➷

JOHN KEATING OCARM

This chapter offers a pastoral reflection on that part of the Carmelite Order's international formation document, now in its third edition, which pertains to liturgical formation: the *Ratio Institutionis Vitae Carmelitanae* [= RIVC].[1] Here my intention is to underline some aspects of the importance of liturgical formation for religious life and for priestly ministry as these are outlined by the *Ratio*.[2] Much of our reflection is drawn from the following article (RIVC 39):

> The Rule of Carmel puts liturgical life at the centre of our community life both practically and symbolically. The oratory is at the 'centre' not just architecturally but identifies it as central to who we are, and it becomes the place of the visible 'assembly' of all the brethren where possible. We are reminded that the liturgy is the most outstanding means by which we express in our community the mystery of Christ. For it is through the liturgy that 'the work of our redemption is accomplished' (SC 2). The Rule speaks of daily Eucharist and the celebration of the Liturgy of the Hours as constitutive of the nature of our Carmelite community. This ought not to be merely routine or obligation but a truly contemplative action. Liturgy is the Church at common prayer – it is moreover the visible sign of the Order at prayer. People

are formed and grow in faith through good liturgy. The presence of the Living God in Word, in Sacrament, in ritual, in silence, in gesture and in song is transformative – it changes the nature of our being community. The Word is addressed to us in *lectio divina* alone and as a community, and the bread is broken and shared, not just symbolically but as a sign of the sharing in the mystery of God and with the community of those in need. Good liturgical formation in community marks us for life. Through spiritual preparation, 'meditating day and night on the law of the Lord', we recognise the presence of Christ among us; through living out the Paschal Mystery in our lives we come to celebrate the death and Resurrection of the Risen One. It builds us into a holy temple of God. The Resurrection celebration formed the identity of our Order over centuries through the Carmelite Rite. Thus liturgical practice and formation ought to be life-giving and life celebrating, following the Liturgical Year in all its richness and diversity. Formation in liturgy is not just about liturgical studies for ministry or knowledge of the rubrics, but about a fraternal celebration of who we Carmelites are. Our formation communities are built up in the following of Christ and missioned to go in peace to serve the Lord, nourished by the Bread of Life and the Word of the Lord.

A third edition of the RIVC was undertaken by the International Formation Commission of the Order following a questionnaire sent to provincials and formators, and a section on the role of liturgy in the process of formation was drafted and published. My pastoral reflection is an attempt to draw together a number of factors pertaining to the liturgy and to Carmelite life.

I am well aware that liturgical expression and style can be quite diverse within the Order, so what I write needs to be read within the context of cultural adaptation. It is true that today there has been a certain tendency to return to a pre-Vatican II agenda in certain places.[3] My work in the area of liturgical studies has been mainly from the perspective of spirituality, rather than the technicalities of liturgical law and rubrics. In this context liturgical formation must be part of the overall spiritual and prayer formation of the *formandi*. I see the more technical aspects assisting the common prayer of God's people, rather than as a means to control freedom of prayerful expression and worship. Rubrics read in the right context facilitate good worship practice. They need also to be understood in a theological and ecclesial context. The *Ratio* (RIVC) carries the secondary title of 'A Journey of Transformation'. Sadly, sometimes in formation ministry we forget the power of liturgy to change lives.

In this presentation I would like to address just five elements one finds in article 39 of the RIVC, cited above.

1. A Carmelite Way – A Visible Liturgical Assembly

The Rule of Carmel puts liturgical life at the centre of our community life both practically and symbolically. The oratory is at the 'centre' not just architecturally but identifies it as central to who we are, and it becomes the place of the visible 'assembly' of all the brethren where possible. (RIVC 39)

a) Historical Understanding

I am not an expert in Carmelite liturgical history and its development, and rely on the research of the late American Carmelite, Fr James Boyce.[4] What follows depends greatly on his writings and especially on his contribution to the Congress on the Carmelite Rule in Lisieux in 2005.[5] Boyce suggests that the very early sources regarding liturgy are 'minimal'.[6] Yet, there are a number of elements that stand out in the Carmelite tradition and these can be noted as follows: a daily Eucharist where possible; the liturgy as part of the early Carmelites self-understanding and expression; with the approved text of Pope Innocent IV,[7] the hermit community on Mount Carmel is set firmly within the liturgical life of the Latin Kingdom of the Holy Land; the place of the oratory is central; the liturgical practice of these hermits relates to the liturgy of the Holy Sepulchre;[8] and the oratory is a place of reference for all the community and is at its very centre.

Thus, we find three fundamental and basic key elements from the earliest times and they remain constant: the oratory with its Eucharist at the centre; the Hours; and silence. The change from the ermitical to the mendicant way of life, adopted by the hermits on arrival in Europe in the mid-thirteenth century, brought with it a process of change leading them into the formal approved custom.[9] Silence is very important and the time of silence is governed by the times of the liturgical Hours.[10]

At the beginning of the fourteenth century the *Ordinal* of Sibert de Beka (1312) brings uniformity throughout the Order in Carmelite liturgy, with certain variations. Boyce states, 'the implementation of Sibert's *Ordinal* suggests that liturgical observance continued to exercise unusual importance in the life of Carmelites: this *Ordinal* defined their status as mendicants and shaped their unique contribution to the life of the Church'.[11] This has had a lasting effect on the identity of Carmelites. Recent studies have identified the further research needed in this area of liturgical practice with regard to the formation of Carmelite identity over the past eight hundred years. The present article of the RIVC attempts to address this history in the context of present day liturgical terminology.

b) The 'Assembly'

The word 'assembly' is both ancient and modern. Post-Vatican II scholarship refers to the re-discovery of the notion of assembly.[12] In many ways the walls of division between people and sanctuary are broken down. The gathering is not a divided body but one unified in a visible reality. As the early Christian community understood, the great assemblies of Israel were now visible in their new assemblies. Putting it succinctly: Church is Church when it is gathered. Community is visible as community and as a liturgical community when it is gathered at its centre. As A.G. Martimort has said, 'The actual assembly of Christians renders visible the gathering of humankind that Christ has accomplished; the grace that effects this gathering is mysteriously at work in every liturgical celebration'.[13] The visible reality of the Carmelite community at worship is also a sign of that deeper reality to which we are all called. In a recent letter to the Carmelites, Pope Francis states:

> As you approach the eight centenary of the death of Albert, Patriarch of Jerusalem in 1214 you will recall that he formulated 'a way of life', a space that enables you to live a spirituality that is totally orientated towards Christ. He outlines both external and internal elements, a physical ecology of space and the spiritual armour needed in order to fulfil one's vocation and mission.[14]

At the heart of the mystical space of Carmel is the physical reality of a chapel in the middle of the hermits' cells.[15] It is a symbol of unity when they are focused on Christ whom Carmelites seek to follow. The gathering is therefore a truly significant element in the formation of young Carmelites. For in the assembly Christ, who is present, is mysteriously at work forming and transforming (see SC 7).

2. A Theological Understanding of Liturgy in the Context of Community Life

> We are reminded that the liturgy is the most outstanding means by which we express in our community the mystery of Christ. For it is through the liturgy that 'the work of our redemption is accomplished' (SC 2). The Rule speaks of daily Eucharist and the celebration of the Liturgy of the Hours as constitutive of the nature of our Carmelite community. This ought not to be merely routine or obligation but a truly contemplative action. (RIVC 39)

a) Participation

We know that there are many usages of the word 'participation', most often popularly interpreted as 'having a ministerial role' or doing something during a liturgy – a type of popular buzzword. But there is the deeper significance that relates to something more profound. It is the participation in the very mystery of Christ himself. Put another way, the liturgy becomes the outstanding means by which we, as followers of Christ and as Carmelites, celebrate the paschal journey being acted out in the reality of our lives – a journey of transformation. Liturgical participation will not always require that those in the life-long formation process 'have something to do' in the liturgy, but it will require their participation in the life of faith, in a community of faith, in living their Gospel call, proclaimed every day at the central space within their religious environment.[16] Liturgical participation requires Christian life participation. There can be no dichotomy. Liturgy is in the broadest context, the Christian life lived in relation to Jesus Christ. The liturgical life of the community is thus doxological: in, with and through Christ, and is truly a celebratory action of the reality of Christ united to his body the Church.

What is happening in this process of formation is a deeper penetration into the mystery of Christ. The liturgy of the formation community ought to celebrate this, in all its expressions. The liturgical life of the formation community celebrates Christ at its centre. The approach is 'mystagogical'.[17] The itinerary is set out, the feasts are designed to draw us deeper every day into Christ, the identity is being formed, nourished, enlightened, healed, reconciled ... It is the moment when the community fixes its gaze on God. Von Balthasar says, 'In this sacred service the Church *fixes its gaze* on God: its service is spiritual, marked by insight and understanding (Romans 12:1). It *contemplates* God's truth and opens itself to his word.'[18]

b) Cell and Celebration

The 'meditation of the Law of the Lord day and night' within the cell[19] breaks forth into the light when it is celebrated in community. The communion with the Lord achieved in privacy of 'one's room with the door shut' (Matthew 6:6) is celebrated and ritually enacted in public. The God who speaks within the privacy of the 'cell of the heart' is recognised and acclaimed in public gathering all into one. The Word of God that whispers in the hermit's cave, breaks forth into praise and song in the midst of our brothers and sisters. This link is vital to the process of liturgical formation, if it is to be source and summit of their lives as consecrated religious. The word used by the Constitution on the Sacred Liturgy (83) to describe the Liturgy of the Hours is the word 'hymn' or 'song': 'Jesus Christ, the high priest of the new and eternal covenant, taking human nature, introduced into this earthly exile that *hymn* which is *sung* throughout all ages in the realms above.' The early hermit on Mount Carmel might ponder the psalms in private in his cell but then joyfully make their proclamation in community. Through the liturgy the community is 'ceaselessly engaged in praising the Lord, and interceding for the salvation of the whole world' (SC 83).

This might be a response to the oft heard questions, why is it so boring and tedious at times? Why do we have to put so much effort into 'making it happen'? The liturgy has been described as our privileged way of praising God. Liturgical formation, and especially with reference growth and transformation, is not just about developing community, or ensuring sound doctrine, or learning to do the rubrics right, it is about offering the praise of this community and with the gifts and limitations, through Christ, to the eternal and almighty One. It is the meeting place between mystery and life. An image from the Liturgy of the Hours might help us to understand our formation community as the body of believers together united with Christ their head ceaselessly 'singing a hymn of praise' to the Father. Liturgy is above all an activity of praise and thanksgiving to the One who has given us life in the beloved One, Jesus Christ. This deserves the best possible response from us. Our liturgical communities are being shaped (formed) by the mystery of God, learning to surrender to God while being shaped by God through the rhythms of the time and space within the liturgical year. The shape and form of the liturgy is itself formative.

Yes, we often do our best and sometimes it is not the most perfect liturgy in the world. Liturgy can demonstrate also the worst and best elements of community; its poverty, its lack of talents, its conflicts and diversity, its weaknesses seen in the absence of brethren who find other excuses not to be present, or who have difficulty for one reason or another. In dialogue and a common search within the formation community, we come to understand the true nature of our worshipful formation communities finding a way that transcends division, through surrender and praise. In community we ought to discover that liturgy is a corporate action.[20] It should lead us to giving our allegiance to the very heart of the Christian life. Our worship is about uniting rather than dividing.[21]

3. Liturgy as Prayer – A Spirituality of Liturgy

Liturgy is the Church at common prayer – it is moreover the visible sign of the Order at prayer. People are formed and grow in faith through good liturgy. The presence of the Living God in Word, in Sacrament, in ritual, in silence, in gesture and in song is transformative – it changes the nature of our being community. (RIVC 39)

a) Prayer

One religious who spent his life in liturgical ministry never ceased to say that where people are praying there is always good liturgy, for liturgy is our common prayer. Our spirituality is our personal relationship with Christ; our common worship is *the assembly of believer's personal relationship with Christ*, precisely as his Body. The spiritual life of the individual and the public worship of the Church are one. The liturgy expresses the spirituality of the community as community. 'For in her public worship it is precisely this work of spiritual formation that the Church carries on'.[22] Liturgical prayer shapes our individual prayer, and our private prayer ought to find its expression in the common prayer of the Church. The person in formation is formed at the Church's school of prayer, which is the liturgy. It ought to purify and teach, gathering the formation community into a common exercise of prayer. We encounter Christ in these moments and he is our teacher.[23] In the Catholic tradition the form is given, handed down through centuries of community experience of prayer. The community of faith is not just the members present here and now, but all the generations of believers including our many holy Carmelite men and women, heaven and earth united in common song, echoing Mary's song: 'for the Mighty One has done great things for me, and holy is his name' (Luke 1:49).

b) Transformation

The RIVC speaks of the journey of formation as a process of transformation. The actual *form* of the liturgy does not just teach us but also forms us into Christ himself. The Word proclaimed over and over again in the liturgical assembly is calling us to constant conversion. The actual form of the ancient structure is leading the human heart from listening to praising, from hearing to speaking, to an obedience of faith. Saint Paul begins his Letter to the Romans with a reference to 'the obedience of faith' (1:5) and ends it with a key text:

> Now to God, who is able to *strengthen* you according to my gospel and the *proclamation* of Jesus Christ, according to the *revelation of the mystery* that was kept secret for long ages but is *now disclosed*, and through the prophetic writings is made known to all the Gentiles, according to the command of the eternal God, *to bring about the obedience of faith* – to the only wise God, through Jesus Christ, to whom be the glory forever! Amen. (16:25-27)

The liturgy constantly calls us to obedience – to say 'yes' to God. It reinforces the choices we make regarding our vocation. It is essential for the formation programme, not to make of mendicants 'little monks' but in order to hear the Word disclosed, the mystery revealed and celebrated, along with the invitation to respond unceasingly to the living God. Liturgical prayer structure invites us to obedience and the affirmation of that faith – 'Amen'.

4. Contemplative Fraternity – Word-centred Life Expressed in the Liturgy

> The Word is addressed to us in *lectio divina* alone and as a community, and the bread is broken and shared, not just symbolically but as a sign of the sharing in the mystery of God and with the community of those in need. Good liturgical formation in community marks us for life. Through spiritual preparation, 'meditating day and night on the law of the Lord', we recognise the presence of Christ among us; through living out the Paschal mystery in our lives we come to celebrate the death and Resurrection of the Risen One. It builds us into a holy temple of God. The Resurrection celebration formed the identity of our Order over centuries through the Carmelite Rite. (RIVC 39)

a) Good Liturgical Formation

Liturgical formation is not just learning about liturgy or being told how to 'do the ceremonies well'. It is an exercise in love. In the context of the Carmelite tradition it too is a contemplative experience, requiring time and indeed interior silence.[24] So much of ministerial life is centred around the liturgical life of the Church. In formation communities, if the liturgy is celebrated well it marks the members of that community for life. Learning to love liturgical life in community will have immense repercussions way beyond our feeble efforts to celebrate well. We have no idea what God is doing during the liturgy. Only God can see into the hearts of the worshippers. What good liturgical training does is to release through celebration the power of God, so that his Word is heard and communion takes place. After many years, I have discovered that often we may think that the liturgy is one thing, but God has other ways of acting within our liturgical enactment beyond anything we might imagine. Hence, the time of liturgical prayer within formation communities is never a mere formality. It is formation itself. The Lord is not just the *Liturgist* (see Hebrews 8:6) but the *Supreme Formator* at that moment, and we are formed by the community liturgical practice we adopt.

b) *Being Lifted Up*

In recent years Carmelites have once again been talking about the influence of the Rite of the Holy Sepulchre, carried with them from the Holy Land to Europe. The Carmelite Rite used by the Order until the Second Vatican Council can offer elements specific to the Order and its charism. The emphasis on the Resurrection in that Rite is one of joy, of mystery, of incarnation and redemption. The languages used in liturgy are diverse: word as spoken or sung, symbol in silence or with a liturgical text, stillness and silence as they resonate with a deeper mystical 'soundings'. Our liturgical rites are deeply rooted in human experience. Like all ritual they are profoundly rooted in the sacred. The liturgical space, the use of light and darkness, the language of emotion expressed in musical notation, all enhance our worship experience. Early Carmelites had some idea of these things. In a contemporary situation and after decades of experience with the Roman Rite since the Second Vatican Council, that involved leaving behind the Carmelite Rite, some are wondering what might be gleaned from the past but in harmony with the future. Kallenberg says, ' ... the most characteristic traits of the Rite of the Holy Sepulchre, and consequently also of the early liturgy of the Carmelites, was the feast of the Solemn Commemoration of the *Resurrectio Dominica*, the Resurrection of the Lord which were celebrated throughout the year by way of votive masses (e.g. a Carmelite Missal of Tours of 1461/1478, fol. 20) and the almost daily prayers and antiphons at vespers and matins in the period from Easter to Advent'.[25] Also arising from his reflections of the *Ordinale* of Sibert de Beka, Paul Chandler lists a number of possible elements from our past traditions that sit well within the present liturgical form of today: the splendour of beauty, discretion and balance between feast and other moments, restoration of procession into the place of assembly, etc.[26] Attention to both tradition and beauty mark the Carmelite tradition of earlier times. In the liturgy, the Lord who passes by must also be allowed to sacramentally lift us up.

5. Liturgical Life of the Community as Life-giving

Thus liturgical practice and formation ought to be life-giving and life celebrating, following the Liturgical Year in all its richness and diversity. Formation in liturgy is not just about liturgical studies for ministry or knowledge of the rubrics, but about a fraternal celebration of who we Carmelites are. Our formation communities are built up in the following of Christ and missioned to go in peace to serve the Lord, nourished by the Bread of Life and the Word of the Lord. (RIVC 39)

a) Celebration

Liturgy is work, an action and it is a celebration. It just does not happen, it has to be done. It requires our commitment and dedication. It does not have to be invented every day. The rhythms and traditions have been handed down and stretch right back through both testaments. This is an important moment for the life of any community because at this celebratory moment our assembly can become one – a communion.[27] That, I suppose, is why people get so up tight about it at times. We tend to take ownership of it: 'my Mass', 'my wedding', 'my ordination' or 'my profession'.

The liturgy carries the values of the Christian community down through the generations, so it cannot be viewed solely in terms of 'ceremonies'. It holds our values and conveys the deeper meaning of who we are, including who we are as members of religious families. Ultimately the liturgy conveys the eternal truth that the final word rests not with us but with the transcendent God. This God is addressed directly through the liturgy. The liturgy therefore calls the formation community together at special times and moments, and in special ways to acknowledge who we are and to celebrate that relationship with festivity. Perhaps one of the lessons we can learn from our liturgical history is that feast and festivity go together. Contemporary society forces a divide between these. Secular holidays become separated celebrations from the notion of feast. The loss of Sabbath rest is perhaps the clearest expression of that fact. A religious community might hold fast to this notion of a day of rest. It makes a statement and gives balance to different aspects of life. Donna Orsuto has linked keeping the Sunday with the call to holiness:

> Celebrating Sunday is more than simply keeping the commandment to honour the Lord. It defines our Christian identity and helps us to live out the call to holiness. When the Sunday becomes just another day, we lose a sense of celebration which is at the heart of the Christian faith. By integrating a theology of festival with a theology of work, we will recover an equilibrium which is essential for holy living.[28]

Feast, festivity, refraining from our usual work activities is necessary if we are truly to understand the nature of feast day. Feast requires 'assembly' in order to celebrate the relationship of the community with God in a covenant act – indicating clearly who we are by what we are doing. The attention to festive gathering is a witness to those in formation. It clearly identifies what type of community we are and the values we treasure in our vocation as Christians and indeed as Carmelites.

b) Mission
Finally, we see that hearing and 'missioning' go together. The natural movement of the liturgy moves us beyond the celebration. We take the experience into the marketplace of ordinary life. Liturgy is lived in real living and not 'a precious activity' that separates us from the real human encounters in which it is located. The Gospel can be brutally clear in this regard: 'so when you are offering your gift at the altar, if you remember that your brother or sister has something against you, leave your gift there before the altar and go; first be reconciled to your brother or sister, and then come and offer your gift' (Matthew 5:23-24).

Liturgical formation in religious community is about establishing a pattern that will guide one throughout one's life.

Formation calls upon each Order or Congregation to locate its tradition within the liturgy of the Church. In his letter to Carmelites Pope Francis writes regarding the vocation to Carmel:

> It is a continuous call to follow Christ and be conformed to him. This is of vital importance in our world so disoriented, 'for once the flame of faith dies out, all other lights begin to dim' (*Lumen fidei*, 4). Christ is present in your fraternity, your common worship and in the ministry entrusted to you: renew the allegiance of your whole life![29]

6. Some Applications and Conclusions

What might the application of these very Carmelite ideas be to formation communities of other religious, or perhaps seminary communities? Briefly, I would like to indicate some possible avenues for reflection.

First, liturgy and community life are not separate realities, but very closely interconnected. Using a model from Kevin Irwin,[30] formation in community must be seen in the context of the identity, charism and spirituality of a religious order or congregation. The formulation of any aspects of liturgical formation can be enriched through dialogue between identity and praxis (past and present).

Second, being in community reverses tendencies for individualism and runs against the tide of some contemporary cultures. It calls for a certain surrender and unity, heart and mind, so as to break down walls of division that could lead to any pastoral liturgical rigidity. In community one learns what celebrating a truly 'community liturgy' involves.

Third, good liturgical formation ought to relate to the 'internal' and 'external' spiritual journey, bridging the gap between 'cell' and 'celebration' – thus, helping *formandi* to move towards an integrated harmony.

Fourth, when there is good liturgical proclamation in community a constant daily *disclosure*[31] of wisdom is taking place so as to guide those seeking to follow a vocation to the priesthood or religious. This is indeed solid spiritual direction, and recognises that God speaks in the midst of our assemblies.

Lastly, emphasis on a place and space, no matter how poor or humble that place might be, is important. Personally, when I see some formation communities having retired to private oratories away from visibly praying with others, I feel something has gone wrong. The public prayer of the Church is better celebrated in the midst of our people. Some newer communities formed over the past decades can teach older communities how to pray among the people.[32]

The Lord is at work when we are gathered in his name. It is for us we create a space for the Lord to speak, to touch, to anoint, to heal, to restore, to forgive – a contemplative space where liturgy is not separate from the deeper reality of the Christian life but at its very heart and centre.

꒰ ꒰ ꒰

Notes

1. The third edition was published in Rome by the General Curia [of the Carmelites] in 2013.

2. Liturgical formation has been an important part of Carmelite life in Ireland, as elsewhere. For over twenty years the Conference and Retreat Centre of the Irish Carmelites at Gort Muire, Dublin, was a place of liturgical ministry and renewal. This community had been a formation house of the Irish Province since 1944. The liturgical ministry that began there from its opening as a Centre in 1975, brought the Carmelite community into direct contact with the liturgical reform that followed on from the Second Vatican Council. It also forged links with the Irish Institute of Pastoral Liturgy (Portarlington/Carlow; which later became the National Centre for Liturgy in Maynooth), Glenstal Abbey and other places. A network of collaboration and friendship was established with those leading the liturgical renewal in Ireland and overseas. For more on this, see Seán Swayne, 'Liturgical Renewal in Ireland 1963–1983', New Liturgy 40–41 (1983–1984), 12–29, at 24; and Edmond Gerard Cullinan, The Story of the Liturgy in Ireland (Dublin: Columba Press, 2010), 102.

3. On this, see Massimo Faggioli, True Reform: Liturgy and Ecclesiology in Sacrosanctum Concilium (Collegeville, MN: Liturgical Press, 2012), 161–2.

4. James Boyce OCarm received his PhD from New York University in 1984 on Historical Musicology and he was Associate Professor of Music and Chair of the Department of Art History and Music at Fordham University (NY). One of his most important works in Carmelite studies was entitled *Carmelite Liturgy and Spiritual Identity: The Choir Books of Kraków* (Turnhout: Brepols, 2008). James Boyce died of cancer in 2010 at the age of sixty-one.

5. See James Boyce, 'The Liturgical Life of the Early Carmelites', *The Carmelite Rule 1207–2007: Proceedings of the Lisieux Conference 4–7 July 2005*, Institutum Carmelitanum, Textus et Studia Historica Carmelitana, 28, Evaldo Xavier Gomes, et al., eds. (Rome: Edizioni Carmelitane, 2008), 359–79. For an overview of studies on the Carmelite Rite, see, Giuseppe Midili, 'Il rito carmelitano: *Status questionis*', *Ecclesia Orans* 22 (2005), 199–208.

6. See Boyce, 'The Liturgical Life of the Early Carmelites', 359.

7. 'Albert Avagardro, Patriarch of Jerusalem, at a date which may be set as sometime between 1206 and 1214 gave a formula of life to a group of Latin hermits on Mount Carmel. This formula of life was first approved on 30 January 1226 by Pope Honorius III; it was then confirmed by Gregory IX on 6 April 1229, and again by Innocent IV on 8 June 1247. This last mentioned pope approved it finally, definitively, and solemnly as a true and proper rule (*regula bullata*) on 1 October 1247, with adaptations to Western conditions of life.' From the brief introduction to the English text of the *Rule* (Rome: Edizioni Carmelitane, 2007).

8. See Arie G. Kallenberg, 'From Gallican, to Sepulchre, to Carmelite Rite: A Short Reflection on the Origins of the Carmelite Liturgy', *Fons et culmen vitae carmelitanae: Proceedings of the Carmelite Liturgical Seminar, S. Felice del Benaco, 13–16 June 2006*, Institutum Carmelitanum, Textus et Studia Historica Carmelitana, 30 (Roma: Edizioni Carmelitane, 2007), 55–73.

9. There was a change from recitation of the psalms to 'canonical hours' for those who were able to read.

10. Reading the *Rule*, there is a strong suggestion from Albert and Innocent 'that at least an implicit liturgical structure governed the day for the Carmelites and therefore both versions indicate the importance of liturgical observance to the Carmelite self-understanding from the outset'. See Boyce, 'The Liturgical Life of the Early Carmelites', 362.

11. Boyce also underlines this importance as follows: 'Provincials were required to correct and disseminate this ordinal to all the houses of the province under pain of removal from office'. See his 'The Liturgical Life of the Early Carmelites', 366.

12. See SC 6, 10, 26, 41, 42, 106; LG 11, 26; PO 5, 6.
13. A.G. Martimort, 'The Assembly', *The Church at Prayer*, Vol. 1: *Principles of Liturgy*, A.G. Martimort, ed. (London: Geoffrey Chapman, 1987), 91.
14. Pope Francis, *Letter to the Prior General of the Order of the Brothers of the Blessed Virgin Mary of Mount Carmel, General Chapter*, September 2013.
15. 'An oratory, as far as it can be done conveniently, is to be built in the midst of the cells (*in medio cellularum*), where you must come together every day in the morning to hear Mass where this can be done conveniently', *Carmelite Rule*, 14.
16. For a discussion of the importance of liturgical architecture in the Carmelite tradition, see Emanuele Boaga, 'L'architettura dei Carmelitani', *Fons et culmen vitae Carmelitane*, 195–206.
17. 'All genuine liturgical formation includes both doctrine and practice. As a 'mystagogical' formation, the practice is obtained first and mainly through the student's actual liturgical life, into which they are daily more deeply initiated through celebrating the liturgy together. Such a careful and practical initiation is the foundation of all further liturgical study and its possession is a prerequisite for the academic discussions of liturgical questions'. Sacred Congregation for Catholic Education, *Instruction on Liturgical Formation in Seminaries* (1979), no. 2; ET, *Documents on the Liturgy 1963–1979. Conciliar, Papal, and Curial Texts* [= DOL], International Commission on English in the Liturgy, ed. (Collegeville, MN.: Liturgical Press, 1982), 874.
18. Hans Urs von Balthasar, *Prayer* (San Francisco: Ignatius Press, 1986), 108.
19. *Carmelite Rule*, 10.
20. '... liturgical praying is first and foremost a *corporate* action rather than an individual act of devotion. God saves and acts on behalf of a people. We each draw our precious and personal baptismal identity from that primordial and communal grounding'. Paul A. Janowiak, *Standing Together in the Community of God: Liturgical Spirituality and the Presence of Christ* (Collegeville, MN: Liturgical Press, 2011), 3.
21. 'The celebration of the liturgy, as the prayer of the Church, embodies the very nature of the Church in such a way that the celebration itself moves all to a unity of voice and heart and it is at the same time a celebration that is fully communal and fully personal', SCCE, *Instruction on Liturgical Formation in Seminaries*, 10 §1 [= DOL, 875].
22. Robert F. Taft, *Beyond East and West: Problems in Liturgical Understanding*, 2nd ed. (Rome: Edizioni Orientalia Christiana, 1997), 166.

23. 'Carmelites feel drawn to the Lord Jesus Christ and invited to a deep, constant, personal and living relationship with him, to the point of taking on his spiritual qualities and personality. As they encounter Christ in prayer, in the Word and in the Eucharist, as well as in their brothers and sisters and in the events of daily life, Carmelites are transformed and motivated to witness to Christ and to proclaim him throughout the world' (RIVC 6).

24. The RIVC also make the connection between silence and the liturgy: 'Becoming silent in God's silent presence, we become anchored in God who is imageless and inexpressible. Silence allows God to do his work in us. The modern world teaches us never to be open to silence. The Liturgy constantly reminds us to "be still and know that I am God". But the silence that comes in the stillness will only happen when we create the space, the environment and the time for it, both in community and alone' (RIVC 36).

25. Kallenberg, 'From Gallican, to Sepulchre, to Carmelite Rite', 71.

26. Paul Chandler, *We Sing a Hymn of Glory to the Lord: Preparing to Celebrate Seven Hundred Years of Sibert de Beka's Ordinal 1312–2012*, Kevin Alban, ed. (Rome: Edizioni Carmelitane, 2010), 85–113.

27. See I.H. Dalmais, 'Theology of the Liturgical Celebration', *The Church at Prayer*, Vol. 1, 233.

28. Donna Orsuto, *Holiness* (London-New York: Continuum, 2006), 173.

29. Pope Francis, *Letter to the Prior General*.

30. See Kevin W. Irwin, *Context and Text: Method in Liturgical Theology* (Collegeville, MN: Liturgical Press, 1994).

31. Irwin, *Context and Text*, 324–29.

32. Just three examples might help: The Taizé community (France); Monks and Nuns of Jerusalem (Paris); S. Egidio Community (Rome).

THE CATHEDRAL AS A CENTRE OF PASTORAL AND LITURGICAL RENEWAL

⌖ ⌖ ⌖

HUGH P. KENNEDY

> All should hold in great esteem the liturgical life of the diocese centred around the bishop, especially in his cathedral church; they must be convinced that the pre-eminent manifestation of the Church consists in the full active participation of all God's holy people in these liturgical celebrations, especially in the same Eucharist, in a single prayer, at one altar, at which there presides the bishop surrounded by his college of priests and by his ministers. (SC 41)

When a bishop celebrates the liturgy in his cathedral, it should be clearly seen that this is not just as a liturgical celebration akin to any other church in the diocese, but rather becomes the living symbolism of the unity of the church community which is the local church. It is in this context that the bishop should be seen with an enhanced emphasis as the teacher, sanctifier and pastor of his church. Furthermore, the very form of the celebration in the cathedral should not only act as a catalyst for the liturgical life of the diocese, but also as a model for other churches in the diocese to follow. Therefore the liturgical life of the cathedral should be at the very heart of the pastoral and liturgical life of a diocese, precisely because it is the bishop's particular church, and becomes the ideal location where he is enabled in a particular way to fulfil his ministry, as pastor, sanctifier and teacher.

The *Directory for the Pastoral Ministry of Bishops* reads: 'Of all the churches in the diocese, the most important is the cathedral church, which is the sign of the unity of the particular Church'. And it further expands on the role of the cathedral for a bishop:

> It is here that diocesan life finds its fullest expression and it is here that the most sublime and sacred act of the Bishop's *munus sanctificandi* is accomplished, which, like the liturgy at which he presides, involves both the sanctification of the people and the worship and glorification of God.[1]

The Cathedral as the 'Church of the Local Bishop'

The late Richard Hurley, one of the most influential Irish architects of the past century, when asked to undertake a comprehensive re-ordering of the Cathedral of St Mary and St Anne, Cork, saw as his first task the need to promote a greater understanding of the significant role a cathedral should play in the life of its diocese. He offered his understanding of this role in these words:

> The cathedral is, for all the world, the bishop's church. The cathedral may be seen as the church among churches. Its ascribed definition as the bishop's seat requires that it reflects environmentally a sense of solemnity and the evocation of that continuity of apostolic succession, as well as accessibility for worship designed with particular episcopal rites in mind, the ordination of priests and deacons, Mass of the Chrism, Holy Week celebrations and adult Baptism and Confirmation. The cathedral is a seat of culture as well as cult. It is a place where great music may be performed and where drama proportionate to [humankind's] true stature, may be enacted.[2]

The first centuries of the Church saw the Christian community normally gravitating towards urban centres. There was little outreach to rural communities and therefore when the Church community following the Edict of Constantine was able to worship openly, the tendency was that the faithful would attend the bishop's liturgy which he celebrated with the local presbyteral community. Christians adopted the then main architectural place of meeting, namely the Basilica. The plan was that of a long rectangular hall with an apse at one end, containing the bishops *Cathedra* or Chair,[3] and, grouped either side of him, was the clergy comprising of presbyters, deacons and other ministers. The principal church of the bishop which contained the symbol of his teaching authority, namely the 'Chair', became the location for all major episcopal liturgies. In time, as the numbers increased, it became obvious that other church buildings would be required, especially as communities outside urban development also embraced Christianity. Whilst individual priests would serve these more isolated communities, the tradition remained that the major liturgies, such as Christian Initiation, would preserve a direct connection with the bishop's church. The Council of Aachen, held in 789, stipulated that the Cathedral Church was distinguished from all other churches in the diocese because it was the *principalis cathedrae.*

Cathedral Office

The importance of the cathedral as the focus of liturgical celebration is shown in the tradition of the *Cathedral Office.*

The tradition of praying throughout the day at various set hours was inherited from Jewish custom by the early Christians, as shown in the Acts of the Apostles. With the development of spirituality and liturgical traditions, two major locations of liturgical celebrations emerged.[4] The emergence of coenobitic communities in monastic life, particularly in the Western Church, brought about a development of a liturgy that reflected the contemplative life, while the liturgy celebrated by the bishop in union with his presbyters produced a more varied and inclusive style of liturgy that was open to the participation of clergy and laity together. The first form of the 'Hours' was obviously confined to the monasteries, the second was lodged in the liturgical life of the local cathedral.

The form of praying the Divine Office reflected these two different centres of liturgy. It should be recognised that these two diverse ways of celebrating the Divine Office were not seen as being in liturgical competition; rather, it was the local church adapting the manner of celebrating the liturgy in response to the practical situation in which the liturgy was being celebrated. A lesson that has perennial significance!

For obvious reasons, the 'Monastic Office' tended to be lengthier with a frequent schedule of Hours of the Office throughout the day and night. The 'Cathedral Office' celebrated the principal hours of Morning Prayer (*Lauds*) and Evening Prayer (*Vespers*). Further to this, on Sundays and Holy Days, the Office of Vigils was also celebrated.

The manner of the celebration of the Cathedral Office was presented as such to encourage the greater participation of a variety of ministries and included the congregation. Thus in a given celebration, the bishop, the presbytery and deacons would each have their liturgical roles, as would also readers, psalmist and cantor. This was achieved with the use of symbols and actions such as lights, incense and processions. The music tended to be more varied than that used in the Monastic Office, by the use of hymns, responses and antiphons. The Cathedral Office was a liturgy to be celebrated by all the community, bishop, clergy and lay people. It was very much the expression of public prayer by a liturgical community.

In time however, the congregational element in the celebration of the Divine Office declined. As ministries in the Church became more clerical and less associated with the laity, the liturgy came to be seen more as a clerical prerogative. This was intensified by associating the obligation of reciting the Divine Office with conferment of clerical orders. There was a shift from viewing the Divine Office as a celebration for the whole liturgical community to being associated with the duties of the clergy. The bishop was still encouraged to recite the Office with his clergy. However, in time, bishops absented themselves and delegated this task to a number of priests appointed to undertake this role in his cathedral as a Chapter of Canons. Gradually this practice was seen as a duty and or privilege to those authorised to do so and, as a result, the public recitation of the Cathedral Office was undertaken increasingly less often by the ordinary parish clergy.

By the Fourth Lateran Council in 1215, it was acknowledged that the majority of diocesan clergy were no longer reciting the Divine Office in public, and were, in most cases, reciting it alone rather than with their fellow clergy. Over the next few centuries the Office tended to be celebrated either in a monastic setting or, with the exception of collegiate bodies such as the Chapter of Canons, in private by the clergy.

In this historical context, it is interesting to note that St Malachy, as part of his effort to reform the Church in Ireland during the twelfth century, introduced the singing of the Divine Office in his cathedral, and he himself undertook to teach the singing of the psalms for the Office. (Is it any wonder that St Bernard of Clairvaux regarded him as model for reforming bishops?)[5]

Dom Lambert Beaudin proposed that the celebration of the Liturgy of the Hours, if it was truly to become recognised as the *Prayer of the Church*, should involve the participation of the laity. During the reform of the Divine Office following the Second Vatican Council, many liturgical scholars, particularly Canon Aimé Georges Martimort and Mgr Pierre Jounel, felt that a greater emphasis should have been placed on a renewal of the tradition of the 'Cathedral Office' so as to encourage both clergy and laity to publically pray the Divine Office together. Martimort in particular, as a peritus at the Second Vatican Council and as an advisor on the reform of the Divine Office, encouraged the concept of a 'rediscovery of the Office as prayer of the Christian People'.[6]

It is perhaps timely to renew this possibility for both clergy and laity, and to do so in our cathedrals as a public form of daily prayer.[7]

The Bishop, His Cathedral, and the Rite of Christian Initiation of Adults

During the early centuries of the Church, the bishop was intimately linked with the Rite of Christian Initiation, and naturally this was associated with his cathedral church.[8] To testify to this link we still have the monumental witnesses of the great baptisteries of St John Lateran, Florence, Ravenna and so many more and the texts of the early medieval Sacramentaries. In time, this link became broken and a 'travelling bishop' on Confirmation schedule became the last 'vestiges' of this practice. However, following the Second Vatican Council with the introduction of the Rite of Christian Initiation of Adults, the active role of the bishop in this Rite was once again emphasised.

The decision to adopt the RCIA in a diocese is ultimately the decision of the local bishop. It is anticipated that he will preside over the Lenten liturgy, particularly that of the Rite of Election on the First Sunday of Lent, when in the name of the local church, he welcomes those presenting themselves in the cathedral church.[9]

The Teaching Office of the Bishop in the Cathedral

A principal duty of the bishop is to preach the Gospel, and his cathedral should be seen as the primary location from which he should undertake this responsibility. A very potent example of a bishop using his cathedral as a platform for evangelisation was shown by the late Cardinal Martini in his Cathedral in Milan. During his time as Archbishop, Cardinal Martini, on the first Thursday of each month, conducted a session of *lectio divina* for up to three thousand young persons in the Cathedral of Milan. These encounters were to become so popular that even the vast Cathedral of Milan was not sufficiently large enough to hold the numbers attending, and cameras were installed which simultaneously transmitted these meetings to nearby churches. With the encouragement of the numbers attending these sessions, Cardinal Martini realised that there was a clear desire for a greater knowledge of the scriptures among the young people of his diocese, and so he then trained seventy of his priests to conduct *lectio* on similar lines. After his death they continue to serve another twelve thousand young people in other churches throughout the city of Milan.

The example of Cardinal Martini was to act as an encouragement for others to follow. One such example was the then Archbishop, now Cardinal, Thomas Collins, who shortly after he had been appointed Archbishop of Edmonton, Canada, visited Milan and spoke with some of the local priests of this experience of *lectio divina* in the cathedral. On returning to Canada, he introduced the practice in his own cathedral. Following his appointment as Archbishop of Toronto he continued the practice that on one Sunday evening each month, from September to June, he holds a *lectio divina* at St Michael's Cathedral. It begins with a celebration of Vespers starting at 7 p.m., followed by *lectio divina* from 7.30 to 8.15 p.m.

The celebration of Vespers is important to the cardinal because he feels strongly that the public celebration of the Liturgy of the Hours is a perfect preparation of prayer, and has directed that his seminarians attend the celebration and lead the congregation in the chanting of the psalms. Furthermore, he believes that *lectio divina* should be seen in the context of liturgical prayer in the cathedral and not be confused as a class in biblical study. In 2010, as part of the celebrations to mark the centenary of the Pontifical Biblical Institute in Rome, Cardinal Collins gave a talk of his experience as a bishop of sharing *lectio divina* in his cathedral:

> At the ordination of a bishop, the Book of the Gospels is held over the head of the newly ordained bishop during the prayer of consecration. I have often thought of that as signifying a fundamental dimension of the episcopal mission. As a bishop I am sent to preach the Gospel, and to assist those whom I serve to encounter the Word of God. By leading sessions of *Lectio Divina* in my cathedral I seek to fulfil my mission.[10]

The Cathedral: Centre of the Liturgical Life of the Diocese

With good reason, the cathedral church should be regarded as the centre of the liturgical life of the diocese.[11]

The *Ceremonial of Bishops* devotes a whole chapter to the role of the cathedral in the liturgical ministry of a bishop. It recommends that the cathedral should provide the impetus for the celebration of the liturgies in the other churches in a diocese, and should also provide a worthy and natural focus for the major occasions in the life of a diocese. Not for nothing, therefore, should the cathedral be recognised as the 'mother Church' of a diocese. On those occasions when diocesan liturgies occur in a cathedral, people coming from throughout the diocese should come with a sense of expectation that they are going to participate in a liturgy that will be truly uplifting. In the same fashion they should leave with a sense of enthusiasm to bring something of that experience back to their own parishes.

Cathedrals should therefore be endowed with the necessary resources to become a focal point and offer leadership in the liturgical renewal of a diocese. Jeremy Haselock has envisaged their potential: 'As liturgical laboratories, cathedrals are privileged to lead the way in the renewal of core forms of service, to pioneer new forms of worship and to model good practice'.[12]

All the constituent elements within such a cathedral liturgy should act as a catalyst, to encourage others in the diocese to work towards a true and authentic renewal of the liturgies within their own parishes. When it is celebrated well, so much can be learned of an understanding of liturgy, founded, as it should be, on a true appreciation of liturgical renewal. On a number of occasions, Pope John Paul II spoke how a liturgy that is celebrated with reverence and with a true understanding can enhance the faith of those present. The US Bishops took this a stage further and suggested that the opposite is also true: liturgy well celebrated can renew the faith; badly celebrated liturgy can so easily damage it.[13] In this I am reminded of a bishop in meeting with students of a VI Form College, asked why some no longer went to Mass, was met with the answer, 'I no longer go to Mass because I felt the priest no longer believed in what he was doing'.

We don't just teach liturgy, we celebrate it; it is a living action, and in a diocese, there is no other place better to realise this than in the bishop's own church, his cathedral. Rightly, therefore, it should be seen as a model for other diocesan liturgies, and indeed as the 'centre of the liturgical life of the diocese'. The way the liturgy is celebrated in a cathedral should be like a litmus test for the importance that the local bishop gives to the celebration of the liturgy in his own spiritual life, and in the pastoral and spiritual life of his diocese. Clearly this is reflected in determining the regularity by which a bishop celebrates the liturgy in his cathedral. This can be especially apparent as with the recent refurbishment of cathedral sanctuaries, and the bishop's Chair is often now placed in a more prominent place than hitherto. Before the Second Vatican Council, the chair (or episcopal throne) was generally placed along the chapter stalls – almost hidden – so that on certain occasions a faldstool was employed to ensure that the bishop was seen by the entire congregation. Now the bishop's chair is placed in a much more visible position. No one else can sit on it; no one else can liturgically preside from it. Because the chair is the symbol of the bishop as a focus for unity and the sign that he presides over the whole community in the liturgy, the 'vacant seat' on a too regular basis conveys to all present a sense of an 'absentee episcopal presider'.

The Importance of Music in the Liturgical Life of a Cathedral

In the Constitution on the Sacred Liturgy, the Council Fathers stressed the importance of Church music, and intimately linked the preservation of the musical heritage with that of cathedral liturgy.

> The treasure of sacred music is to be preserved and fostered with great care. Choirs must be diligently promoted, especially in cathedral churches. (SC 114)

The association of musical excellence and cathedral liturgy goes back well over one thousand years. As with the monastic tradition, cathedrals also celebrated the daily liturgies of the Eucharist and the Divine Office. However, the liturgies in the cathedrals naturally were able to draw upon a more varied number of ministries and this was reflected in its style of music adopted for the celebration of the liturgy. In this context therefore, the development of early polyphony originated in the cathedral liturgy while it would have been relatively unknown in that of the monastic tradition. In 975 Bishop Wolfgang of Regensburg established a 'choir school' to educate boys and young men who would be available to sing in his cathedral church. A thousand years later the *Regensburger Domspatzen* still fulfils this purpose.

In the late nineteenth century it was decided to build a cathedral in London to serve the growing Catholic population. For Cardinal Herbert Vaughan, the major purpose of building the cathedral was to provide a setting worthy for the celebration of the liturgy, and to achieve this goal he desired to establish a choral tradition there. Vaughan laid great emphasis on the beauty and integrity of the new cathedral's liturgy, and regarded a residential choir school as essential to the realisation of his vision. Daily sung Masses and Offices were immediately established when Westminster Cathedral opened in 1903, and have continued without interruption ever since.[14]

Vaughan also had the perception to appoint as the cathedral's first master of music, Sir Richard Terry, an exceptional choir director who, as a distinguished musicologist, revived the great works of the English and other European Renaissance composers. Much of this music had not been heard since the sixteenth and seventeenth centuries. The singing of this great musical heritage of the Catholic Church in its proper liturgical context remains the cornerstone of the Westminster Cathedral choir's activity. It is the model of a vision which can combine the beauty of the Church's liturgy with its rich heritage of music along with a fitting recognition of composers who, over the centuries, have offered their talents to the service of the Church and the praise of God in its liturgy.

The standards of excellence achieved by the cathedrals at Westminster or Regensburg are not feasible for the ordinary parish; however, to abandon this excellence completely means confining much of our musical heritage to the concert platform, and to greatly lessen the place of the aesthetic and the role of beauty in the celebration of the liturgical life of the Church and its potential to assist people in prayer. To permit this would be to run counter to those who are too often disenchanted by a celebration of the liturgy that can come across as unprepared, rushed and mediocre. Father Timothy Radcliffe addressed this tension in a talk given at Westminster Cathedral: 'We have to find an aesthetic which makes beauty speak today. Beauty is not the icing on the liturgical cake, it is the essence!'[15]

Equally, as the music in a cathedral should strive for excellence, so the cathedral choir has a function to encourage, support and nourish the work undertaken by choirs throughout the diocese. For major diocesan occasions, such as ordinations, the Mass of Chrism, the cathedral music should be inspirational, uplifting and convey to those present from different parishes a sense of diocesan unity. In these celebrations of the liturgy the choir, whilst presenting its usual repertoire, can offer music that encourages the whole congregation to participate with confidence, and share a common identity.

The recognition of the particular role of the Catholic cathedral choir is seen in the work undertaken by the Conference of Roman Catholic Cathedral Musicians (CRCCM). This is a gathering of musicians serving cathedral churches in the United States and Canada. This organisation provides resource exchange, mutual support and on-going professional development in the consideration of the musical-liturgical practice in settings unique to a cathedral, but accomplishes this by the understanding that the choral work in cathedrals is to be seen as a role model for the Church in the general.

The Cathedral as a Place of Cultural Outreach

The French Medieval Historian, Henri Daniel-Rops, regarded the great programme of building cathedrals in the eleventh and twelfth centuries as one of the major influences on European civilisation. The construction of the cathedrals led to enormous developments in the skills of architecture, sculpture, stained glass, music and even drama. The work of these artists was ultimately drawn from the celebration of the liturgy within the cathedral building.

> Everything in the cathedral was made with an eye to beauty. ... All the arts fostered by the cathedral shared in the living body of the liturgy, drawing substance from the Christian sap that rose from the thousand invisible roots of the building.[16]

The link between 'cult' and 'culture' therefore is very much found in the history of our cathedrals.[17] Both Pope John Paul II in his *Letter to Artists*, and Pope Benedict, speaking on the tenth anniversary of this letter, called for a renewal of the collaborative relationship between artists and the Church. Pope Paul VI in May 1964 spoke to a group of artists in a very forcible way that for the Church the work of artists was to be seen as intrinsic in the call to make know the message of God in the world.

> We need your collaboration in order to carry out our ministry, which consists, as you know, in preaching and rendering accessible and comprehensible to the minds and hearts of our people the things of the spirit, the invisible, the ineffable, the things of God himself.[18]

Therefore as the principal church within a diocese, the cathedral is an excellent place where the local church can engage with artists in a dialogue that is both respectful and fruitful.

The Cathedral as Place of a Bishop's Pastoral Outreach

In 1976, the diocese of Westminster was faced with a large deficit and forced to review its expenditure. For some, the existence of a Cathedral Choir School was seen as a luxury that could no longer be funded nor justified while others suggested that it was 'elitist', and therefore, with limited funds, the money could be better spent elsewhere. This was not the opinion of Cardinal Basil Hume who spoke with passion:

> I am determined to preserve the school, I believe in it. I believe in it because good music and pleasing singing is a help for many to raise their minds and hearts to glimpse something of the awesome and numinous character of the God they worship.[19]

He did endeavour to raise funds to maintain it. Yet for those who made the above criticisms of his motives, what was not known by many was that Hume was also only too well aware of the needs of so many disadvantaged young people within London and, with equal passion as an outlet from the cathedral community, sought to offer assistance for these young people. Today the *Cardinal Hume Centre* still supports homeless young people and badly housed families, alongside people from the local community in Westminster with little or no income, who face multiple challenges in turning their lives around. Among those who raised funds for this work were the boys of the Cathedral Choir School, with money raised from concerts and other activities. Both of these contrasting aspects of cathedral life complement each other and each in its own way reflects Basil Hume's vision of the work of a cathedral.

In today's diverse world employment often creates a multicultural environment, bringing people together in a foreign country. It can be an isolating experience and some arriving in a new county and a new city might find it difficult to become immediately associated with an individual parish. Often these people gravitate towards a cathedral for their worship. This factor was recognised by the younger members of the congregation of St Mary's Catholic Cathedral, Sydney. These young people recognising the isolation of so many immigrants in their city, decided to use the cathedral as a place of welcome. They have called this movement Embrace. The group consists of people from the ages of eighteen to thirty-five years from all over the world and of Australians with multicultural backgrounds. They meet every Sunday after the 6 p.m. Mass at St Mary's Cathedral House to support spiritual development and provide social and sporting activities. Thus in a special way the cathedral acts as the 'mother Church' for those new to the diocese.

In a similar fashion in Los Angeles, every third Tuesday of the month, the cathedral offers a night of spiritual development for young single adults, men and women, eighteen years of age or older who gather from all over the city to renew and rediscover their faith. Cathedrals therefore can become the very focus of a diocesan outreach to the needs of the isolated, the homeless, and those searching to deepen their faith.

As has been suggested, the members of the congregations who attend cathedral liturgies should not be seen as some form of 'liturgical refugees from surrounding churches'; rather they become links or bridges with the rest of the diocese.[20]

The Cathedral as a Place of Ecumenical Reconciliation
As the particular church of the bishop, the cathedral offers a special role as the symbol of the 'local church' reaching out to reconcile and working ecumenically with other members of the christian family.

On the night of 14 November 1940, the city of Coventry in England was devastated by bombs dropped by the Luftwaffe. The medieval cathedral burned with the city, having been hit by several incendiary devices. The following morning as both clergy and people inspected the ruins of their venerable cathedral church, the decision was made to rebuild. Rebuilding would not be an act of defiance, but rather a sign of faith, trust and hope for the future of the world. It was the vision of the Provost at the time, Richard Howard, which led the people of

Coventry away from feelings of bitterness and hatred. This has led to the Cathedral's Ministry of Peace and Reconciliation, an outreach to such places as the city of Dresden, but which also has provided spiritual and practical support in areas of conflict throughout the world. Shortly after the destruction, it was noticed that two of the charred medieval roof timbers had fallen in the shape of a cross. One of the workmen set them up in the ruins, where they were later placed on an altar of rubble with the moving words 'Father Forgive' inscribed on the Sanctuary wall. Another cross was fashioned from three medieval nails by local priest, the Reverend Arthur Wales. The Cross of Nails taken from the destroyed cathedral has become the symbol of Coventry's ministry of reconciliation.

A further example of cathedrals becoming symbols of reconciliation and ecumenical outreach is given by the example of the City of Liverpool. Liverpool as a result of the Industrial Revolution of the nineteenth century, had attracted immigrants who had brought with them sectarian tensions. In the 1970s the respective leaders of the Anglican and Catholic communities, namely Bishop David Shepherd and Archbishop Derek Worlock, sought to bring healing to these longstanding divisions. The Anglican Cathedral and the Catholic Metropolitan Cathedral stood at either end of the same thoroughfare. For some, this may have seemed as symbolic of the divided allegiances, yet both Church leaders recognised that the route that linked their cathedrals was appropriately called 'Hope Street'. Every second year on the feast of Pentecost, a service begins in one cathedral and ends in the other with the congregation, choirs and clergy processing along this street. Part way along, there is a sculpture depicting Bishop David Sheppard and great friend Derek Worlock.

In 1982 when John Paul II came to Liverpool in 1982 it seemed natural that he should attend a moving service of reconciliation in Liverpool's Catholic Metropolitan Cathedral, and he then went directly down Hope Street to participate in an ecumenical service in Liverpool Anglican Cathedral at which he was applauded all the way up the aisle. 'The applause which greeted the Holy Father', said Cardinal Hume, 'remains with me as the most earnest and insistent prayer for Christian unity that I have ever heard'.[21]

Sectarianism has also been endemic on the streets of Belfast, and so often religion has been blamed as the source of conflict and division. As with Liverpool, what seemed to be symbols of division became associated with that of reconciliation. In 1998, the then Dean of the Anglican Cathedral of St Anne with the Administrator of the Catholic Cathedral of St Peter formed the Belfast Cathedrals Partnership as a very public sign of hope and reconciliation. This partnership continues to grow and strengthen.

'Cathedrals: the Liturgical Laboratories of the Church?'

While the general trend for church attendance is on the decline, a recent survey for the Church of England has shown that the one place for growth in those attending worship are cathedrals. The Archbishops' Council for Research and Statistics has shown that, since the millennium, there has been a growth in numbers of people (as much as a 35 per cent rise in 2012 over figures for 2002) attending worship at cathedrals. Equally, volunteers offering their services at cathedrals had risen by 30 per cent.[22]

Cathedrals can offer the freedom and potential to minister to the spiritual needs of a wider group of people. The greatest increase in these numbers coming to cathedrals are those attending services mid-week, almost as if in the busiest part of their lives people feel the greater need for prayer and reflection.

Cathedrals have a unique position in any diocese: they are the 'mother Church' and thus a focus of unity for all the disparate parish communities, and, if given the proper resources they have the potential to offer people an experience of an excellence and a fullness of the celebration of liturgy and worthy music. It can be all of this even to the extent of accepting the challenge to become the 'liturgical laboratory' of a diocese and the model of good liturgical practice. By their very character cathedrals are the 'Bishop's Church', and thus can become the ideal place for the incarnation of the episcopal ministry in ecumenical reconciliation, social and cultural outreach, and focus for authentic pastoral renewal.

Notes

1. Congregation for Bishops, *Directory for the Pastoral Ministry of Bishops, Apostolorum Successores*, (2004), par. 155; emphasis in the original.

2. Architectural Presentation made by Richard Hurley on the commencement of the restoration of the Cathedral of St Mary and St Ann, Cork, in 1995: see www.rha.ie/cork.html [accessed, 23 November 2013]. For a full description of this re-ordering and restoration see, Richard Hurley, *Irish Church Architecture in the Era of Vatican II* (Dublin: Dominican Publications, 2001), 122–4.

3. On the *cathedra*, see Jeremy Haselock, 'Cathedra', *The New SCM Dictionary of Liturgy and Worship*, Paul F. Bradshaw, ed. (London: SCM Press, 2005), 98–9.

4. A summary of the early history of the development of the Liturgy of the Hours can be found in Rubén M. Leikam, 'The Liturgy of the Hours in the First Four Centuries', *Handbook for Liturgical Studies*, Vol. V, *Liturgical Time and Space*, Anscar J. Chupungco, ed. (Collegeville, MN: Liturgical Press, 2000), 3–28.

5. Bernard of Clairvaux dedicates his, *The Life of Saint Malachy* [*Vita Sancti Malachiae episcopi*] to demonstrate this: see especially par. 7, in *The Life and Death of Saint Malachy the Irishman*, ET with commentary by Robert T. Meyer (Kalamazoo, MI: Cistercian Publications, 1978), 22–3.

6. See Aimé George Martimort, 'The Liturgy of the Hours', *The Church at Prayer: An Introduction to the Liturgy*, Vol. IV: *The Liturgy and Time*, A.G. Martimort, et al., eds., rev. ed., ET Matthew J. O'Connell (London: Geoffrey Chapman, 1985), 180–4.

7. Among the better critical studies of the Liturgy of the Hours, as reformed by the Council is Stanislaus Campbell, *From Breviary to Liturgy of the Hours: The Structural Reform of the Roman Office 1964–1971* (Collegeville, MN: Liturgical Press, 1995).

8. A good overview of the history of the development of the RCIA can be found in, Maxwell E. Johnson, *The Rites of Christian Initiation: Their Evolution and Interpretation* (Collegeville, MN: Liturgical Press, 1999).

9. See Kevin Donovan and Veronica Robbins, 'Concentrating the Mind: The Role of Ritual in RCIA', *The Way* 29 (1989), 230–9.

10. Mons Thomas Collins, 'A Bishop's Experience of Lectio Divina', p. 5, found on *Settimana Conclusiva Dell'Anno Centenario del Pontificio*

Instituto Biblico (Rome 2010); www.biblico.it/Centenario/ settimana_conclusiva.html [accessed 23 November 2013].

11. *Ceremonial of Bishops* (Collegeville, MN: Liturgical Press, 1989), no. 44, p. 29.

12. Jeremy Haselock, 'Cathedral', *The New SCM Dictionary of Liturgy and Worship*, 99–101, at 100.

13. See United States Conference of Catholic Bishops, *Sing to the Lord: Music in Divine Worship*, [2007], no. 5. Full text at nccbuscc.org/ liturgy/SingToTheLord.pdf [accessed 25 November, 2013].

14. For an overview see, Adrian Mark Daffen, 'The Liturgical Development of the Cathedrals of the Church of England', unpublished Master's Thesis, University of Durham, 2006.

15. Lecture given by Timothy Radcliffe OP in Westminster Cathedral on 27 April 2008.

16. Henri Daniel-Rops, *Cathedral and Crusade: Studies of the Medieval Church 1050-1350*, ET John Warrington (London: J.M. Dent, 1957), 384-5. Daniel-Rops discusses 'The Cathedral' on 347-92.

17. On this, see Charles M. Murphy, 'The Church and Culture since Vatican II: On the Analogy of Faith and Art', *Theological Studies* 48 (1987), 317–31.

18. Free translation by author from a homily of Paul VI given to artists on Ascension Day, 7 May 1964, in the Sistine Chapel. Original text: 'Noi abbiamo bisogno di voi. Il Nostro ministero ha bisogno della vostra collaborazione. Perchè, come sapete, il Nostro ministero è quello di predicare e di rendere accessibile e comprensibile, anzi commovente, il mondo dello spirito, dell'invisibile, dell'ineffabile, di Dio.' Found on www.vatican.va/holy_father/paul_vi/homilies/ documents/hf_p-vi_hom_19640507_messa-artisti_it.html [accessed 23 November 2013 ...].

19. Reported in *Catholic Herald*, 8 July 1977.

20. On the broader role of the cathedral church within society see, Ian Mac Kenzie, *Cathedrals Now: Their Use and Place in Society* (London: Canterbury Press, 1996), and Stephen Platten and Christopher Lewis, *Flagships of the Spirit: Cathedrals in Society* (London: DLT, 1998).

21. From Address given by Cardinal Basil Hume to the Association of Interchurch Families at its annual Heythrop (London) meeting on 15 February 1997.

22. Archbishops' Council of the Church of England, Research and Statistics; Cathedrals 2012 (London, Church House, August 2013), p. 5. Found at www.churchofengland.org/media/1820547/2012 cathedralstatistics.pdf [accessed 23 November 2013 ...].

MISERERE:
A REFLECTION ON PSALM 51 (50)

ᑐ ᑐ ᑐ

MICHAEL MULLINS

The Psalter or Book of Psalms is a collection of prayers or hymns used in the liturgy of the Second Temple (520 BCE–70 CE). The prayers have been 'processed' and 'canonised' in song through use in the liturgies and festal celebrations, recalling the history of the people, intensifying their sense of identity, reaffirming their response while absorbing personal prayers into the common worship and conversely enhancing personal prayer with the enriching experience of communal celebration. The psalms represent the spiritual heartbeat of God's chosen people. Nourished in the cult, they reflect the many streams of tradition, theology, spiritual awareness and historical experiences that appear throughout the books of the Bible. 'Some were composed expressly for the service of the Temple, to be sung by the Levites and the assembled people during the sacrifices on the occasion of the great festivals; but ... many were [probably] of a purely private character, expressing the sentiments of an individual Israelite, but taken over by the community as a fitting expression of the religious sentiments of the people' when they found themselves in circumstances similar to those experienced by the individual.[1] In his commentary on the psalms John Eaton highlights their essential character when he states that each psalm is a poem and the language 'is not a stilted or artificial form of expression, but a natural outpouring of heart and soul – in need, in gratitude, in sorrow and in joy'.[2]

Saint Athanasius wrote in his letter to Marcellinus:

> The Book of Psalms is like a garden containing all of these kinds [of fruit of all the other books of Scripture, both Old and New Testaments] ... And it seems to me that these words become like a mirror to the person singing them, so that [one] might perceive [oneself] and the emotions of [one's] soul, and thus affected, might recite them.[3]

Saint Athanasius also says that the book of psalms teaches those whose primary concern is the worship of God how they should praise him, and in what words they can glorify him worthily.[4] Saint Augustine puts it beautifully: 'God has praised himself in order to give human beings a pattern by which they can praise him in a seemly fashion. Because God has kindly praised himself, people know how to praise him'.[5] Schooled by God in the language of prayer, therefore, the psalmists have left us a unique treasury of spiritual language, imagery and inspiration with which to address the Almighty.

Saint Basil, commenting on the Psalms, states that they are 'the voice of the Church' and he emphasises their reconciling role in the community:

> A psalm forms friendships, unites those separated, conciliates those at enmity. Who, indeed, can still consider as an enemy [a person] with whom [one] has uttered the same prayer to God.[6]

Psalm 51 (50)

Psalm 51, commonly called the *Miserere* from the first word in the Latin version, shows a deep faith in the nature of God as merciful and compassionate. It is also an excellent example of a psalm 'so that [one] might perceive [oneself] and the emotions of [one's] soul'. Significantly it stands at the beginning of the collection of Davidic psalms (Psalms 51–72) and establishes God's relationship with the repentant anointed/chosen one who will figure in these psalms.[7]

Superscription: vv. 1-2

The psalm is introduced for the presider/choir master as a 'psalm of David' and the occasion is presented as 'on the coming to him (David) of the prophet Nathan when he (David) went in to Bathsheba' (see 2 Samuel 11–12).

The superscription at first glance points to a very definite association with David and his personal sin. Taken at face value these circumstances would explain very well the cause of the overwhelming sense of sin and repentance on the part of the individual. However, the content of the psalm following the superscription is general and does not refer again to David's sin with Bathsheba. It is possible, therefore, that the psalm was composed independently of the circumstances described and recited by David on that occasion and /or subsequently ascribed to him as the psalms of David were collected and edited.

Part One. Forgiveness: Liberation from Sin (vv. 3-11)

Appeal for mercy: vv. 3-4

> 3. *Be gracious to me, O God, in your faithful loving kindness; in your abundant compassion blot out my offence*

The appeal begins with a triple cry to God to be gracious, to have mercy and to wash away the sin. The opening word of the appeal *honneni* is a plea for God's grace (*hen*), the unmerited gift of God's forgiveness in the face of one's sin and guilt. It is the gracious forgiveness of an offended 'superior' who is in a position to inflict punishment on an 'inferior' but instead responds with forgiveness and understanding.

The appeal for 'grace' is followed by the appeal to God's *hesed*. *Hesed* signifies 'faithful loving kindness', unswerving loyalty, selfless and self-sacrificing devotion, the unbreakable bond of love, fidelity, and dependability between family members and lovers which endures even in the face of betrayal. The Book of Hosea, for example, is often regarded as a book of *hesed*, where God as the covenant partner, the husband, pursues Israel the beloved and wins her back from her lovers, the false gods (see Hosea 2), and, as father remembers his love for Israel his son, whom he called out of Egypt, in spite of his having been provoked to anger by Israel's hankering after pagan peoples and their false Gods (see Hosea 11).

Rehamim is used of compassion and mercy. Plural in form it represents 'the bowels of compassion', the inner, gut feeling that springs not simply from an intellectual awareness and sense of loyalty and obligation, but rather from fellow feeling, empathy and sympathy. It shares the same root as the word 'womb' (*rhm*) and calls to mind the bond of the mother and child: 'Can a woman forget her nursing child, or show no compassion for the child of her womb?' (Isaiah 49:15 [NRSV]). In using *hen* (in verbal form), *hesed* and *rehamim* there is a wide array of characteristics of loyalty, love, bonding and intense emotion in God's dealings with the penitent, and they reflect the covenant characteristics of *YHWH*, 'a God merciful and gracious, slow to anger and abounding in steadfast love and faithfulness' (Exodus 34:6 [NRSV]).

> 4. *Wash me thoroughly from my transgression (psh⁽⁾) and cleanse me from my iniquity (me'woni)*

God must do the washing and cleansing for, left alone, the penitent feels powerless. Justification comes from the graciousness of God who alone can cancel the heavenly record of sins and wash the penitent clean of impurities as in washing a defiled vessel or garment, cleansing it from disease or some other ritual defilement (see Exodus 19:10).

Confession of guilt: vv. 5-7

> 5. *My transgressions (psh⁽⁾) truly I know them and my sin (chat'ati) is before me always.*

> 6. *Against you alone have I sinned (chat'ti) and that which is evil (hara') in your sight I have done; so you may be justified in your word [in what you say] and blameless in your judgment.*

7. Behold, I was born in iniquity (be'won) and [I am] in sin (bechet') since my mother conceived me

The references to God's merciful qualities and actions are followed by references to the penitent's sinful condition and actions as a rich combination of words paints a broad picture of sin. 'Transgression' *(pesha')* signifies the breaking of God's law and disruption of the moral order. 'Sin' *(chet')* is used in nominal and verbal forms and signifies offense against God in breaking God's law. Iniquity *('awon)* signifies iniquity as in the destruction and harm one causes to others and self. 'Evil' *(ra')* is a general term for all of these, a general term for 'malice'.[8]

Every sin against another is a sin against God. If the psalm was actually composed by David when he had seriously sinned against Bathsheba and Uriah her husband, by adultery and murder, the enormity of the double crime cries out to God. The penitent openly admits the enormity of the crime, not overlooking the harm caused to human beings but expressing the overwhelming sense, the terrible insight that 'in the last analysis every sin is directed against God, for it reflects the basic tendency of the human will which accomplishes 'what is evil in God's sight' and thereby destroys the living contact with God'.[9] Sin is ultimately a religious concept rather than just an ethical one. 'The recognition of his sin becomes for the psalmist the means whereby he is able to know God – the absolute seriousness of [God's] judgment and the abundance of [God's] grace'.[10] So in true repentance 'the supplicant "gives glory to God" (Joshua 7:19) by confessing guilt and declaring that God would be just and justified to condemn him'.[11] Repentance is therefore an act of worship in acknowledging the merciful character of God.

The psalmist displays awareness of 'his own radical waywardness, a sense of being profoundly unworthy of God'.[12] As in a court scene there is an appeal to the judge in terms of mitigating circumstances. The psalmist makes the case of having been born into a sinful world and propelled into its clutches from conception. 'The psalmist not only confesses the faults which were the cause of his chastisement, but admits the sinfulness of his nature since his very conception, [an admission] that [a person] in comparison with God is essentially corrupt'[13] (see Psalm 143:2; Job 4:17ff; 5:7; 14:4; 15:14ff; 25:4).

Inner dispositions and divine guidance: v. 8

8. Behold you love truth in the inward being [in the heart] (bthchot). Then in the secret of my inner self (bsthm) teach me wisdom

A profound sense of unworthiness leads to an appeal to God to act creatively in the life of the penitent, working for restoration at the core of one's being. Left to oneself the penitent feels helpless when faced with the task of renewal and therefore yearns to be purified by God and created anew.

Acknowledging the importance of inner dispositions the psalmist emphasises his awareness that God reads the innermost self ('the heart') and appeals to God to be teacher of wisdom in the inner self (recesses of the heart), the locus of the motivating factors of one's life and conduct.

Kissane points to difficulties with the translation of *bthchot*. It is usually translated as 'inner self'/'heart'. He looks to the use of *bthchot* in Job 38:36 where it has connotations of obscurity (*incerta/absconditum*). It points to a situation where one may err unknowingly due to confusion and incertitude.[14] If that is so the psalmist is here praying to God for the wisdom to walk without fault in times of confusion and unclear situations. The sentiment is close to that in Psalm 19:12: 'But who can detect his errors? Clear me from hidden faults' (NRSV). The psalmist prays to be shown the way in times of confusion and unclear situations.

Appeal for purification: v. 9

9. Purify me with hyssop and I shall be clean. Wash me and I shall be whiter than snow

The psalmist now moves from the language of morality to that of worship, reflecting the ritual cleansing of the sinner. Sprinkling with hyssop recalls the traditional ritual of sprinkling the lustral water on the leper or other persons who had incurred ritual uncleanness (see Leviticus 14:4ff; Ezekiel 36:25; Numbers 19:16ff; Hebrews 9:19). The word 'wash' has ritual connotations as in washing clothes or vessels that have been touched by ritual uncleanness or contact with disease (see Psalm 26:26; Exodus 30:19f). The sacred language of ritual enhances the scene and further emphasises God's role in making the sinner 'whiter than snow' (Isaiah 1:18).

> 10. *Let me hear rejoicing and gladness. The bones you have crushed shall rejoice*

The ritual language continues with the expression 'Let me hear' which recalls the ritual of purification when at the conclusion of the ceremony the priest announced that the person was again admitted to the worship in the sanctuary and to the friendship of God.[15]

The ritual language now moves the process of reconciliation from the heavily laden tones of a penitential pleading to those of a joyful festival when the people, 'like broken bones', will again sing and dance for joy at the renewal of their covenant relationship with God. There is an echo of the revival of the dry bones in Ezekiel 37, revivified by the power of the prophetic word accompanied by the life-giving spirit.

Reference to 'the bones you have crushed' echoes also the sentiment of one suffering alienation from God, neighbour and self, and its debilitating effects on one's life as spelled out graphically in the penitential psalms and the Book of Lamentations (see Psalm 32:3; 42;11; Lamentations 3:4). The illness of sin as a person is ensnared in guilt, cries out for God's healing action.

> 11. *Hide your face from my sins and blot out all my iniquities*

The psalmist again appeals to God to disregard his sin and makes another request like that in the opening appeal for the 'blotting out' of his iniquity (as from the Book of Judgement).

The conclusion of the first part of the Psalm (vv. 9-11) mirrors the opening with the repetition of the themes of blotting out, washing and cleansing, forming an inclusion or frame around the first part with its focus on sin and forgiveness.[16]

Part Two. Renewal: Heart and Spirit (vv. 12-19)

12. *A pure heart create in me, O God, and renew a steadfast sprit within me*

Renewal is not just a cleansing of past sin symbolised by the sprinkling with cleansing/lustral water. It is an entry into a whole new way of life which is impossible without living continually in a life-giving communion with God.[17] Part two of the psalm emphasises God's role in this renewal of the penitent.

Part two opens and closes with a focus on *heart* and *spirit* as the psalmist begs God, to *create* and *renew* at the core of his being. *Heart* and *spirit* are the two basic elements empowering one's life. The heart is the locus in which the inner dialogue of love and hate, good and evil, listening and understanding is played out. It is the seat of reason and decision. The listening heart hears the divine command and the human cry. The spirit empowers one to remain steadfast in following the dictates of the heart.

The psalmist is praying for a renewal of the covenant relationship with God, not in externals but with a new heart and a new firmness of spirit, following a ritual cleansing. The prayer is reminiscent of the promise of a new covenant envisioned in Jeremiah with the law written deep within the heart (see Jeremiah 11–13), and with the gift of a new heart and spirit following the sprinkling with cleansing water in Ezekiel (see Ezekiel 36), and the revival of the dead bones (see Ezekiel 37).

> I will sprinkle clean water upon you, and you shall be clean from all your uncleanness … A new heart I will give

you, and a new spirit I will put within you; and I will remove from your body the heart of stone and give you a heart of flesh. I will put my spirit within you, and make you follow my statutes and be careful to observe my ordinances (Ezekiel 36:25-27 [NRSV]).

13. *Do not cast me from your presence nor take your holy spirit[18] from me.*

14. *Let the joy of your salvation return to me and a willing spirit sustain me*

The Psalmist prays not to be cast from the presence of God (literally 'from before the face of God'). It is the lot of the pure of heart, the upright and the just, to see God, that is, to experience the presence of God, to be under the all-seeing eye of God. The psalmists express it clearly in Psalm 4:6: 'let the light of your face shine on us, O Lord' (NRSV) and in Psalm 80:7: 'Restore us, God of Hosts; let your face shine, that we may be saved' (NRSV).

The sentiment is reflected in the beatitude: 'Blessed (*makarioi*) are the pure in heart for they will see God' (Matthew 5:8). The blessedness is a gift bestowed by God resulting in 'seeing God' in the sense of living with the awareness and assurance of God's presence, providence and protection.

Weiser points out that the joy in the helpful nearness of God is the motivating power of the new way of life which the psalmist envisages.[19] He puts it very well:

Where the soul is not nourished by the power of God, there man cannot rise above a servile obedience nourished by fear. It is the joy in God as the motivating force of man's actions which alone is able to transform ethical obedience into an obedience based on faith. The poet is conscious of this fact when he prays to his God for joy and for help with the new life which he wants to lead.[20]

In the Christian context the Letter to the Colossians reflects very well this empowering role of the Spirit.

> ... we have not ceased praying for you and asking that you may be filled with the knowledge of God's will in all spiritual wisdom and understanding, so that you may live lives worthy of the Lord, fully pleasing to him, as you bear fruit in every good work and as you grow in the knowledge of God. May you be made strong with all the strength that comes from his glorious power, and may you be prepared to endure everything with patience ... (Colossians 1:9-11 [NRSV]).

Witness: v. 15

> 15. *I will teach transgressors your ways and sinners will return to you*

Witnessing to the work of God in one's repentance and restoration lifts the individual's experience from the comfort zone of a self-centred piety and warm glow of spiritual satisfaction to a broader view where the reformed sinner is now the messenger urged on by a renewal of life with God to lead others along the same path of repentance and renewal.

Eaton points out that the prayer for a renewal of inner life in the case of a king, the Lord's anointed, who has been reinstated in God's favour, will enable him to fulfil his royal duties. 'Re-establishing before God, with all the strength given by the Spirit, he will be able and glad to fulfil his duty of teaching, witnessing and admonishing (see Psalm 2:10f; 4:3f; 62:9f; 75:5f)'.[21]

> 16. *Deliver me from blood [bloodguilt / bloodshed], O God, the God of my salvation and my tongue will proclaim your righteousness [justice]*

This appeal has been variously interpreted. If interpreted in the light of David's personal guilt in having Uriah murdered (see 2

Samuel 12:9), it can be seen as an appeal for the wiping out of his blood guilt (see Isaiah 1:18). Since there is no specific reference to that incident in the body of the psalm it has been suggested by Kissane that 'blood' is used in reference to premature death as in Psalm 30:10. According to the popular view premature death was the fate of the sinner (see Job 5:8ff; 8:5ff; 36:8ff) and it is possible that we have here the prayer for deliverance from premature death which is a feature of this class of psalms (see Psalm 6:5ff; 13:4; 22:21; 30:10; 39:12).[22]

If he were to die because of his sins, he would forever be deprived of the opportunity of performing any acts of faith and praising God's righteousness (see Psalm 6:5). Weiser believes that 'the verse becomes understandable ... if it is a question of a peril which threatens [the psalmist's] life'.[23] He points out how this is a very important consideration for the penitent just 'at the very moment when his whole being is deeply affected by the awareness of the new life granted him by God, and of his new task'.[24] It is reminiscent of the psalmist's appeal when a peril threatened his life, 'What profit is in my blood when I go down to the pit' (Psalm 6:5).

Praise: v. 17

> 17. *Lord open my lips and my mouth shall declare your praise*

The psalmist wishes to share his experience of God's mercy and compassion with other sinners. Not only witnessing privately to the nature of God's merciful judgment, the psalmist now feels the urge to proclaim the praise of God in the assembly (probably implying former alienation from the worshipping community due to sin and guilt). 'Lord open my lips' again shows the psalmist's dependence on God even for the grace, ability and language to praise him. This is very much in tune with the comments of Athanasius and Augustine about how God teaches us to pray in the psalms. They are God's words about God and addressed to God.

Ritual Sacrifices: vv. 18-19

18. You take no delight in sacrifice; an offering from me you would not accept.

19. My sacrifice (the sacrifice acceptable to God),[25] is a broken spirit, a broken and contrite heart you will not reject

Because of the statement that God takes 'no delight in sacrifice' and that the penitent believes his sacrificial offering would not be accepted, some scholars have mistakenly concluded that these verses deny the value of ritual sacrifices as such. Eaton counters this argument with the suggestion that it is because of the 'deliberate and extensive sins as are confessed in this psalm [that] ritual expiations' were thought inadequate (Numbers 15:22-31; Ezekiel 45:20); 'hope rested only in God's grace, appealed to by one truly penitent, "broken" and "crushed" in heart and spirit – the antithesis of the arrogant heart of the rebellious sinner'.[26] In similar vein Weiser comments:

> This thought is no restriction and curtailment of piety; on the contrary, it means a final widening and deepening of that piety. God desires not only material gifts and outward acts, but claims the whole man. God has delight in a broken spirit and in a contrite heart; that is to say, he has delight in human beings who do not seek by use of material means to exert an influence on him, be it ever so refined, but who take the reverse course in that they give up all claims to him and face him with a broken spirit – entirely depending on his grace, completely giving themselves up to him and whole-heartedly submitting to him. God is gracious to those who are humble in heart.[27]

Zenger states that 'the one saved from mortal danger responds with a sacrifice of thanksgiving that both celebrates and proclaims YHWH as the good God of salvation'.[28] The sentiment is similar to that in Psalm 69: 'I will praise God's name with a song; I will glorify him with thanksgiving; A gift pleasing God more than oxen; more than beasts prepared for sacrifice' (Psalm 69:30-31; Grail). He puts it in a nutshell as he states that true worship is not giving a gift that symbolises the person but a gift of the person renewed in heart and spirit.[29]

Rebuilding the walls of Jerusalem: v. 20

> 20. *Do good to Zion in your favour [grace]; Rebuild the walls of Jerusalem*

The petition to 'rebuild the walls of Jerusalem' is generally regarded as an addition to the text added during the time when the people were in Exile after 587 BCE and longing for a return from Babylon, or on their return when they found the city walls, the Temple, and the altar destroyed before their reconstruction in 444 BCE. Kissane, for example, implies that at that time the offering of sacrifices was impossible, but would become possible if Zion were restored.[30] Weiser similarly states that 'the author of the appendix wants the psalm to be interpreted in the light of the absence of cultic observances during the Exile, when it was not possible to carry on public worship in the proper way'.[31]

But a real question arises in the context of worship. Why speak of rebuilding the city walls rather than the Temple and altar when lawful sacrifice is the issue? Why should the building of the city walls influence the cult?[32] Is there a broader symbolic meaning to rebuilding the walls? Eaton and Zenger both believe so.

Eaton prefers 'to interpret the text as a whole if reasonably possible', particularly if the psalmist 'has a representative capacity' (as with a royal psalm reflecting a prayer of the king for protection of the city or like the voice in Lamentations 3). He sees the psalm as concluding with prayer for rebuilding the walls in the sense of 'strengthening, repairing and prospering through divine care'. He regards the verse as a vow that 'when the atonement which can only be made by repentance and grace is effected, leader and community will offer sacrifices, costly and in abundance in thanksgiving for restoration of right relationship or fellowship (*sedeq*)'. He points out that this understanding reflects the sentiment of the preceding psalm 'with its guarded approach to sacrifice, and its prizing of offerings for the occasion of thanksgiving'.[33]

Zenger sees 'rebuilding the walls of Jerusalem' as a plea for the eschatological restoration of the city of God. He states that the petition for the rebuilding of Jerusalem is usually, and rightly, understood as a secondary liturgical appendix, and he goes on to describe it as 'an eschatologizing and collectivizing continuation of the originally individual prayer of petition in vv. 3-19'.[34] For Zenger these verses close the psalm with a vision of the eschatological renewal of Zion, 'an eschatological hope surpassing all historical experiences or even possibilities'.[35] This reflects post exilic theology, especially in the school of Isaiah, with its dream that God would make of Zion a place of salvation and righteousness for Israel and all nations.[36]

In the eschatological renewal of Zion, God will rebuild the walls of Jerusalem – not just building walls of defense but building Jerusalem as a city of righteousness (see Isaiah 1:26-27), as a 'city of God' in Zion from which salvation and peace will stream forth (see Isaiah 2:1-5; Psalms 46, 48).[37]

> 21. *Then you shall delight in rightful sacrifices; holocausts and whole burnt offerings; they shall offer bulls on your altar*

At first glance this verse seems to be somewhat at odds with the profoundly radical sentiment of the psalm so far in relation to sacrificial sacrifices and offerings. Weiser states that the reference to 'burnt offerings and whole burnt offerings' is an unnecessary addition and it overloads the verse.[38] Kissane points out that many scholars regard it as a gloss.[39] Zenger on the other hand, regards the reference to total burned offerings as a recognition of the majesty of God and adds that since sacrifices are accompanied by a common sacrificial meal, the reference to them looks forward to the renewal in Zion, through forgiveness, of the covenant people of Sinai.

In such a renewed city of God, whose inhabitants know themselves as having been rescued by God from their involvement in sin and created anew (see vv. 12-19), God 'will have joy in the "sacrifices of righteousness" (v. 21) which will no longer be subject to prophetic critique'.[40] Recognition of and thanksgiving for the presence of the 'God of righteousness' in the midst of his people, and this in a twofold sense: they are public recognition of God's rule over the city of God and over its inhabitants.

This is very much in line with the teaching of the prophets that sacrifice without the due disposition of the heart is useless. Micah states it very clearly:

> With what shall I come into the Lord's presence and bow down before God on high? Shall I come with holocausts, with calves one year old? Will he be pleased with rams by the thousand, with libations of oil in torrents ... What is good has been explained to you, man; this is what the Lord asks of you: only this, to act justly, to love tenderly, and to walk humbly with your God. (Micah 6:6-8 [NRSV]).

Praying this psalm privately or in common one is inspired by its profound confidence in God's compassion and saving grace in the face of human sinfulness so candidly admitted and expressed. One of the most well known and popular psalms, it sets the tone for the penitential season of Lent by its inclusion in the liturgy of Ash Wednesday and it appears each Friday in the Morning Prayer of the Divine Office. It reflects the sentiments of repentance in the Jewish celebration of Yom Kippur. It is a very suitable prayer for inter-Christian or Christian–Jewish prayer services as we admit the failures that have caused division and pray for God's healing work in creating a new heart and a new spirit among all God's people. To repeat the words of St Basil quoted above:

A psalm forms friendships, unites those separated, conciliates those at enmity. Who, indeed, can still consider as an enemy [a person] with whom [one] has uttered the same prayer to God.[41]

᚛ ᚛ ᚛

Notes

1. Edward J. Kissane, *The Book of Psalms. Translated from a Critically Revised Hebrew Text, with a Commentary*, 2 vols (Dublin: Browne and Nolan, 1953, 1954), I, ix.
2. John Eaton, *The Psalms: A Historical and Spiritual Commentary with an Introduction and New Translation*, 3rd ed. (London: T&T Clark/Continuum, 2008), 3.
3. St Athanasius: *Letter to Marcellinus on the Interpretation of the Psalms*, 2 and 12. ET, *Athanasius: The Life of Antony and The Letter to Marcellinus*, Robert C. Gregg, trans. and intro. (New York: Paulist Press, 1980), 102, 111.
4. See St Athanasius: *Letter to Marcellinus*, 10; ET, *Athanasius*, 109.
5. St Augustine, *Homilies on the Psalms: on Psalm 144*; ET, *Saint Augustine: Exposition of the Psalms (Enarrationes in Psalmos) 121-150*, Maria Boulding, intro. and notes, *The Works of Saint Augustine: A Translation for the 21st Century*, Part III – Books, Vol. 20 (New York: New City Press, 2004), 379. See also, Augustine, *Confessions* 9: 6.
6. St Basil, *Homily on Psalm 1*; ET, *Saint Basil: Exegetical Homilies*, Agnes Clare Way, trans., The Fathers of the Church 46 (Washington, DC.: Catholic University of America Press, 1963), 152.
7. Unless otherwise stated, all translations of biblical texts are by the author.
8. See Erich Zenger, in *Psalms*, Frank Lothar Hossfeld, and Erich Zenger, eds, 2 vols, *Hermeneia – A Critical and Historical Commentary on the Bible* (Minneapolis: Fortress Press, 2005), II, 19.
9. Artur Weiser, *The Psalms: A Commentary* (London: SCM Press, 1962), 403.
10. Weiser, *The Psalms: A Commentary*, 404.
11. Eaton, *The Psalms, A Historical and Spiritual Commentary*, 206.
12. Ibid.
13. Kissane, *The Book of Psalms,* 227.
14. Ibid., 228.
15. See Kissane, *The Book of Psalms*, 228.
16. See Zenger, *Psalms*, 17, 21.

17. See Weiser, *The Psalms: A Commentary*, 407–8.
18. Literally, *the spirit of your holiness.*
19. See Weiser, *The Psalms: A Commentary*, 407.
20. Ibid., 408.
21. Eaton, *The Psalms, A Historical and Spiritual Commentary*, 207.
22. See Kissane, *The Book of Psalms*, 229.
23. Weiser, *The Psalms: A Commentary*, 407.
24. Ibid., 407–8.
25. There are two readings in the mss.
26. Eaton, *The Psalms, A Historical and Spiritual Commentary*, 207.
27. Weiser, *The Psalms: A Commentary*, 409.
28. Zenger, *Psalms*, 22.
29. See Zenger, *Psalms*, 22.
30. See Kissane, *The Book of Psalms*, 229.
31. Weiser, *The Psalms: A Commentary*, 410.
32. See Zenger, *Psalms*, 18.
33. Eaton, *The Psalms, A Historical and Spiritual Commentary*, 207–208.
34. Zenger, *Psalms*, 16.
35. Ibid., 18, citing W. H. Schmidt, 'Individuelle Eschatologie im Gebet: Psalm 51', *Neue Wege der Psalmenforschung*, Klaus Seybold and Erich Zenger, eds, 2nd ed. HBS 1 (Freiburg: Herder, 1995), 345–60, at 353–4.
36. See Zenger, *Psalms*, 22.
37. Ibid., 22–23.
38. See Weiser, *The Psalms: A Commentary*, 410.
39. Kissane, *The Book of Psalms*, 229.
40. Zenger, *Psalms*, 23.
41. St Basil, *Homily on Psalm 1*. See note 6, above.

THE CONTINUING LITURGICAL FORMATION OF CLERGY AND PEOPLE

༝ ༝ ༝

SEÁN SWAYNE

1. Conciliar and Post-Conciliar Directives: An Overview

I would like to begin with a brief overview of official conciliar and post-conciliar statements relating to the continuing liturgical education of priests and people. I would draw your attention particularly to the following: *Sacrosanctum concilium*, esp. pars 14-19; *Motu Propio* of Paul VI, 25 January 1964;[1] *Inter oecumenici*, 26 September 1964;[2] *Eucharisticum mysterium*, 25 May 1967;[3] *Inaestimabile donum*, 3 April 1980.[4a] A look at these statements, from the first to the latest, shows liturgical formation as an absolute pre-condition for the reform of the liturgy: to hope for liturgical renewal without prior liturgical formation is futile (SC 14); moreover, the difficulties encountered since the Council in putting liturgical reform into practice are seen to stem from the fact that neither priests nor people have received an adequate liturgical formation. Hence the need (*Inaestimabile donum*) for proper liturgical formation in seminaries and religious houses, up-dating courses for priests already engaged in pastoral work, and effective liturgical catechesis of the faithful.[b]

---

[a] Seán Swayne wrote a commentary on *Inaestimabile donum* which appeared in *New Liturgy* 27 (1980): 2-11.

[b] All of Swayne's teaching and writing was directed to liturgical formation, and this ministry became his principal preoccupation. See, among his many writings that can be cited, 'The Priest's Preparation for Daily Mass: Three Useful Books', *New Liturgy* 22 (1979): 16-17. SC 14-19 proposes that the task of 'imbuing the

May I add, as far as the European scene is concerned, that the concern for liturgical formation as expressed in the aforementioned documents has been re-echoed with particular insistence in the various meetings of European National Secretaries that have been held over the past nine years.[c]

2. Implementation of these Directives

To what extent have these directives been implemented? That question can best be answered for our various countries by the different representatives gathered here at this meeting.[d] As far as

---

faithful with the spirit and power of the liturgy' is a top-down exercise: bishops ensure that clergy are appropriately trained and that these in turn bring the faithful into a deeper sense of the liturgy. This educational model remains valid. However Swayne suggests a different approach whereby the liturgy itself, well celebrated, becomes a school of a deep formation in liturgy which is primarily experiential and spiritual, and which forms the basis of a mystagogical approach to liturgical formation. In his Post-Synodal Apostolic Exhortation, *Sacramentum caritatis* (2007), Benedict XVI stated that 'The best catechesis on the Eucharist is the Eucharist itself, celebrated well' (no. 64). The question of what we mean by 'liturgical formation' today is explored in Thomas R. Whelan, 'Liturgical Formation: To What End?' *Anaphora* 2:2 (2008): 1-20.

[c] Beginning in 1973, meetings of the Association of National Liturgy Secretaries of Europe took place, with one exception, every two years, and they gathered in different European cities and allowed a particular theme direct their deliberations. They were attended by Secretaries from 26 countries with Belgium being represented by both Flemish and French language Secretaries, and Switzerland being represented by Secretaries from French, German and Italian sectors. Meetings took place, mostly in the month of May, and lasted for approximately five days. The themes discussed were as follows: 1973 (Geneva): Translation and Adaptation of Liturgical Books; 1975 (Luxemburg): New Code and Penitential Liturgy; 1976 (Innsbruck): Liturgical Formation; 1978 (Salzburg): Interiorisation; 1980 (Syros, Greece): Development of Liturgical Science; Formation of Priests and Laity; 1982 (Rome): Christian Initiation; 1984 (Dublin): Sunday Assembly; 1986 (Lisbon): The Role of Laity; 1988 (Leányfalu, Hungary): Liturgy and Popular Piety; 1990 (Burges): Liturgical Presidency; 1992 (Berlin): Funerals in Europe; 1994 (Malta): Diocesan Commissions; 1996 (Madrid): Liturgical Language and Inculturation; 1998 (Munich): Liturgy of Marriage; and 2000 (Brussels). Among the reasons given for the discontinuity of the Association after its final meeting in Hungry in 2003 were the increased controlling presence of representation from the Roman Dicastery in charge of Worship as well as the increased membership that resulted from what was now former 'Eastern Europe' and the very different liturgical agenda that these countries presented.

[d] Swayne offered a brief 'diary' or overview of the implementation of the liturgy reforms in Ireland in, 'Liturgical Renewal in Ireland 1963-1983', in *New Liturgy*

my own country is concerned I would see the standard of liturgical formation varying quite considerably from one diocese to another, and from one parish to another – depending for the most part on the degree to which bishops have been exercising their responsibility in guiding, directing and stimulating liturgical renewal (see *Liturgiae instaurationes*, 5 September 1970).[5] May I be permitted to add that we are fortunate in having at our service the Irish Institute of Pastoral Liturgy which, since its inception in 1974, has provided a one-year course in pastoral liturgy to over two hundred people, and through its shorter courses, study-days, seminars, etc. has touched directly upwards of thirty thousand people.[3] For the situation in England and Wales I would refer you to Monsignor Boylan's excellent report *Living Liturgy* of 19 March 1981 in which he refers to the 'completely inadequate' number of trained liturgists in England, and describes the scene in those countries generally as 'not very encouraging'.[f]

However, the malaise in liturgical formation, as I see it, lies not at the organisational level (by and large the structures are there – courses, seminary programmes, institutes, training

---

40/41 (Winter 1983/Spring 1984), 12-29. This must be supplemented by the review by Patrick Jones, 'Sacrosanctum Concilium at Fifty: Reports from Five English-Speaking Countries: 4. Ireland', *Worship* 87 (2013): 503-609. See also Eugene Duffy, 'The Reception of the Conciliar Liturgical Reform in Ireland', *Questions Liturgiques* 95 (2014): 110-27. For a brief history of liturgy in Ireland, see Edmond Gerard Cullinan, *The Story of the Liturgy in Ireland* (Dublin: Columba, 2010). Little attention is given to the early Irish translations of the Liturgy Constitution and the 1964 *motu proprio* of Paul VI, *Sacram liturgiam* made by Diarmuid Ó Laoghaire SJ, *An Liotúirge: Bunreacht agus Motu Proprio* [full title: *An Bunreacht um an Liotúirge Naofa agus Motu Proprio Phól VI, Pápa faoin mBunreacht céanna*] (Baile Átha Cliath: Foilseacháin Ábhar Spioradálta, 1966).

[e] See, 'Irish Institute of Pastoral Liturgy', *New Liturgy* 22 (1979): 10-11. On the move of the Institute from Portarlington to Carlow, see *New Liturgy* 19 (1978): 3-5.

[f] *Living Liturgy: A Report to the Bishops of England and Wales*, prepared by Anthony B. Boylan, the then National Adviser for Liturgical Formation (Slough: St Paul's Publications, 1981). Here Swayne cites from no. 51, p. 30 and no. 48, p. 29. Extracts from this important Report were published in *Notitiae* 17 (1981): 625-39.

programmes etc.),[g] but rather at the level of *motivation*. The incentives of the 1960s have by and large evaporated. Liturgical renewal, with the novelty of change in old styles and patterns of worship, no longer has the same curiosity value as of twenty years ago. We need a new motivation. And that, I contend, will come through the actual experience of liturgical celebrations of quality, with the nourishment and strengthening of the faith which they are seen to effect. Let us look therefore at the present shape of liturgical celebration as written into our post-conciliar books, with a view to appraising and in turn enhancing the quality of our celebrations.[h]

3. Appraisal of Liturgical Celebration in General

A reading of the history of the liturgy and of certain behavioural patterns in contemporary society suggests a number of qualities which ought to the celebration of the liturgy:

i) *Awareness of the presence of the Easter Jesus.* Every celebration of the liturgy ought to be a veritable resurrection experience for the participants.[i] I like to think

---

[g] Much work of facilitating the training of various ministries has taken place in Ireland. See, for example, from the Dublin Diocesan Liturgy Commission, *Proclaiming the Word: A Guide for Ministers of the Word*, text by Jane Ferguson and Liam Tracey (Dublin: Levins Press, [ND]). Patrick Jones has published a monthly column on liturgy in *Intercom* over many years which offered, among other things, reflections on some practical issues relating to the celebration of Liturgy. The liturgist and composer, Columba McCann, acknowledges this as one important influence on his publication, *101 Liturgical Suggestions: Practical Ideas for Those Who Prepare the Liturgy* (Dublin: Veritas, 2014). McCann's book stands alongside other parish resources that have been published in Ireland over the last number of decades. In simple language that reflects both historical and theological depth, the book sets out to help parish liturgy groups improve the quality of their liturgical celebrations.

[h] See Swayne, 'The Mass, Twenty Years Later: Gains and Losses', *New Liturgy* 40-41 (1983-84): 2-11. One critical appraisal that invites a reflection on the relationship between worship and culture, as well as examining the theological grounding that celebrating assemblies and their liturgical minsters, not least the Presider, seem to presume, is Eamonn Bredin, *Praxis and Praise: A Sense of Direction in Liturgy* (Dublin: Columba Press, 1994).

[i] This was a favourite theme of Swayne: see for example, *Gather Around the Lord: A Vision for the Renewal of the Sunday Eucharist* (Dublin: Columba Press, 1987), 11-17.

of our Sunday assembly, for example, as our weekly 'Galilee experience' (see Matthew 28:7) when we encounter the risen Lord in as real a manner – even if it is with the eyes of faith – as the first Christians did to whom the Lord appeared.[j] We know the effect that those first Easter encounters with the Lord had on the early Christians. They rejoiced. Their hearts burned within them. The effect of 'resurrection encounter' on us today should be no less profound. But first we need to recover this vivid sense of the presence of the risen Lord in our midst, in the liturgical assembly (see John 20:19, 26).

ii)   *Joy.* Related to the foregoing is the quality of joy.[k] Every Christian is, or ought to be, a person of joy. Joy characterized the life of Mary, of John the Baptist, of Paul, of Jesus himself. Joy ought also to characterise the life of the Christian – the joy of knowing that God is, that God has entered human history in the person of Jesus, that God knows me by my name, that God has called me to an unimaginably wonderful destiny. This joy ought also to characterize our liturgical celebration, finding a reflection in the attitude and behaviour of the participants, and giving festive character to the entire celebration.

iii)   *Reverence.* Here I am thinking of that sense of awe, esteem and wonderment which follows from our appreciation of the fact that the God of the liturgy, although coming to us in the person of Jesus, a servant with flesh and blood, remains nevertheless the God of glory and majesty; our celebrations are celebrations of sacred things, sacred mysteries.[l] A mental attitude of awe

---

[j] Swayne developed ideas around Sunday Assembly in *Gather Around the Lord*, 18-24.

[k] See Swayne, 'Joy in the Mass', *New Liturgy* 44 (1984-95): 2-6; and Swayne, *Gather Around the Lord*, 63-7.

[l] See the rather developed thought of Swayne on this theme in, 'Mass: An Experience of God', *New Liturgy* 45-46 (1985): 24-9; 47 (1985): 2-4; 49 (1986): 6-11; and 50 (1986): 2-7. The theme of reverence is taken up by Swayne again in *Gather Around the Lord*, 25-31.

ought therefore to permeate the entire liturgical celebration,[m] registering in our way of using words and music, in our gestures and movements, as well as in the whole visual setting and ceremonial.

iv) *A sense of belonging.* To what extent have our congregations recovered their sense of *assembly*? In this connection our challenge is to liberate people from the individualism which is a legacy of a decadent period of our Christian history and which prevents them from seeing themselves worshipping as a *People*, a community united in a common belief in, love for, and commitment to the risen Lord, a community making their pilgrim Way through life in a fellowship of love for the Lord and for one another.[n]

v) *Engaging us in our whole person: Inwardly and Bodily.*

a. Inwardly: the participants in the eucharistic celebration ought to go through an experience of (1) *Listening* (aware of the presence of the Lord speaking to us today in the Word; aware of the power of that Word to 'penetrate' [Hebrews], to accomplish its purpose [Isaiah]); (2) *Praising* (aware that our prayer of praise blends with that of the Lord, is 'divinised' and reaches the Father through Christ, with Christ and in Christ); (3) *Commitment* (the experience of covenant/commitment renewal).

b. Bodily: aware that in the Eucharist we lift up our whole being (*totus homo*) to God, body as well as spirit, in

---

[m] At this point in the text, Swayne refers to Ambrose Verheul: *Introduction to the Liturgy: Towards a Theology of Worship* (London: Burns and Oates, 1969), 17-19, 21.

[n] Reflection today cautions about any simplistic statement on how assembly is understood, and the influences that are placed upon it: see, Liam M. Tracey, 'Liturgy and Assembly in Dialogue with Postmodernity', in *City Limits: Mission Issues in Postmodern Times*, Joe Egan and Thomas R. Whelan, eds., Explorations in Faith and Culture 2 (Dublin: Milltown Institute of Theology and Philosophy, 2004), 109-18.

word, song,[o] gesture, and movement with full sensitiveness also to the value of order and beauty in worship.[p]

vi) *Authenticity.* People today, especially young people, are thirsting for authenticity. They are quick to identify and reject the sham and the hollow. To emphasize the need for authenticity of celebration is in no way to question the sincerity of those involved. Rather it is to invite appraisal of each moment of celebration and to verify that there is a correspondence between words, gestures, actions, and the meaning behind them. Celebration which does not come from the heart will not reach the heart. All must ring true, not only the words and gestures of the individual minister, but the corporate participation of the people. The Great Amen must be 'great' Amen, a full throated yes to everything the Mass implies.[q]

vii) *Celestial Quality.* Vladimir's followers, when they experienced the liturgy of Constantinople, commented: 'We cannot be sure whether we were on earth or in

---

[o] The fact that Swayne does not include in this paper any comment on music in liturgy belies the deep commitment he had to it, working towards a day when the singing of even the shortest responses (refrain for the Responsorial Psalm, Gospel Acclamation, Great Amen) at daily Eucharist could be presumed. He was responsible for the appointment in 1974 of Margaret Daly as the first resident musician and an integral part of the team of the Mount St Anne's Liturgy Centre in Portarlington, and then in the Irish Institute of Pastoral Liturgy, Carlow (to where the Centre moved in June 1978). This post remains an integral part of the work of its successor, the current National Centre for Liturgy in Maynooth. Margaret Daly was responsible for editing *Alleluia! Amen!* (Dublin: Veritas, 1978; Supplement published in 1981), prepared by the Centre, and which includes a number of her own compositions. Some years later *Hosanna! A National Liturgical Songbook for Ireland*, Paul Kenny, ed. (Dublin: Columba Press, 1987) was published under the auspices of the Advisory Committee on Church Music. See contribution of Moira Bergin for an account of the work and publications of this body.

[p] Not much attention was given to the idea of 'body' in worship at this time: however, see Swayne, *Gather Around the Lord*, 68-74.

[q] See, Swayne, 'Authenticity in Liturgical Celebration', *New Liturgy* 42-43 (1984): 19-25.

heaven'.[r] We must recover our sense of union with the heavenly liturgy, for in the liturgy 'heaven comes down upon earth'. Participation in the mass is participation in the heavenly liturgy behind a veil. Death is the drawing aside of that veil, allowing us to worship 'face to face' in company with Mary, the heavenly beings, and our own loved ones with God in heaven. Again, this quality must once again register in our celebration of the liturgy.[s]

Other questions could be raised here at the level of our general appraisal. Suffice it to mention them. Have priests in general an adequate understanding of liturgical leadership and presidency (replacing the former 'confecting' notion)?[t] What of our concept, at this stage, of 'full, active and conscious' participation? How do we understand 'creativity', and how do we relate development in worship patterns to tradition?[u] Are we taking cognizance of and profiting from the richness of the Eastern tradition of worship?

[r] Reference here is to a tenth century account of the visit of a delegation send by the Grand Prince of Kiev, Vladimir I, to garner information about the religions of others in neighbouring regions, including Byzantium and that of the Roman-Germanic Empire. The relevant part of the account said: 'Afterwards, we went to the Germans and we saw many offices performed in their churches, but we saw nothing of beauty. We went to the Greeks, who took us to the place where they render worship to God. And we did not know whether we were in heaven or on earth. For there is neither comparable wonder, not such a beauty on earth, and we are unable to express either. But we do know that it is there that God dwells with humankind'. Cited from Marcel Metzger, *History of the Liturgy: The Major Stages* (Collegeville, MN: Liturgical Press, 1977), 86.

[s] Swayne addressed the idea of 'Heavenly Liturgy' in *New Liturgy* 36 (1982-83): 2-5; and in his *Gather Around the Lord*, 75-8.

[t] As noted above [annotation c], Seán Swayne was active in the Association of National Liturgy Secretaries of Europe which produced the booklet, *Leading the Prayer of God's People: Liturgical Presiding for Priests and Laity* (Dublin: Columba, 1991) after its biennial meeting in Burges in 1990. On this topic, see also Thomas R. Whelan, 'Presiding at Eucharist: The *Ars Celebrandi*', in *Priesthood Today: Ministry in a Changing Church*, Eamonn Conway, ed. (Dublin: Veritas, 2013), 325-35.

[u] This question could be responded to in so many ways and begs diverse considerations. One example of allowing contemporary pastoral concerns make demands that emerge from liturgy to related forms of ritual gathering is, Pat O'Donoghue, ed., *Circle of Care: Liturgies for Times of Special Need* (Dublin: Veritas, 2000).

4. Appraisal of the Liturgy in its Component Parts[v]

The Eucharist: Problem Areas

i   *Homily* One sometimes hears it said that the great Christian truths are no longer preached at Sunday Mass, and that some form of catechetical instruction programme should be re-introduced. Hasty solutions to the problem could do violence to the principle that 'Scripture is the soul of theology'.[w] The homily, although it is open to exhortatory and catechetical elements, is essentially the application of the scriptures which have been proclaimed to the lives of the people assembled, moving them to an inner attitude of praise (for what God is doing today in our lives).[x] 'The purpose of the

---

[v] Swayne's two books, *Communion: The New Rite of Mass* (Dublin: Veritas, 1974) and *Gather Around the Table* [see annotation i, above] both address the celebration of Eucharist and remain relevant today. See also, Vincent Ryan, *Welcome to Sunday: The Lord's Day. History, Spirituality, Celebration* (Dublin: Veritas, 1980); and his, *The Shaping of Sunday: Sunday and Eucharist in the Irish Tradition* (Dublin: Veritas, 1997). For a contemporary Irish example of a mystagogical approach to liturgical formation, see Julie Kavanagh, *Signposts on the Road to Emmaus: Exploring the Mass* (Dublin: Veritas, 2012), as well as the earlier work by Donal Harrington, *Exploring Eucharist: Thoughts, Meditations, Ideas* (Dublin: Columba, 2007). Patrick Jones edited two introductory booklets on the celebration of the Mass: National Centre for Liturgy: *Celebrating the Mystery of Faith: A Guide to the Mass* (Dublin: Irish Liturgical Publications, 2005; rev. ed. Dublin: Veritas, 2011); and National Centre for Liturgy, *The New Missal: Explaining the Changes* (Dublin: Veritas, 2011). The Liturgy Commission joined with the Theology Commission and prepared a document for the Irish Catholic Bishops' Conference on Sunday Eucharist: *O Sacred Banquet: Revitalising the Sunday Celebration of the Eucharist* (Dublin: Veritas, 2011). This text is also found in PDF format at http://www.iec2012.ie/media/OSacredBanquetVeritas1.pdf.

[w] The concern for the proper celebration of the Liturgy of the Word (with all of its various moments of readings, psalm, homily) was a topic on which Swayne wrote frequently: see, for example, 'The Liturgy of the Word: Creating an Atmosphere for Celebration', *New Liturgy* 22 (1979): 4-9; and his 'The Scriptures in Sunday Mass: Pastoral Suggestions', *New Liturgy* 50 (1986): 8-12.

[x] Here Swayne makes reference to 'Broccolo in *The Chicago Catholic*, 28 July 1978'. See a guide and study prepared under the auspices of the Irish Commission for Liturgy, edited by Brian Gogan, *We Bring Good News: A Guide to Preaching and the Celebration of the Word* (Dublin: Veritas, 1989). Numerous collections of sample homilies exist which aspire to serve as a model of good preaching. See that edited by Patrick Jones, *At the Breaking of Bread: Homilies on the Eucharist* (Dublin: Veritas, 2005).

homily at Mass is that the spoken word of God and the liturgy of the Eucharist may together become 'a proclamation of God's wonderful works in the history of salvation, the mystery of Christ'. [... the homily] must always lead the community of the faithful to celebrate the Eucharist wholeheartedly.' (*General Introduction to the Lectionary*, 24)

ii. *The Old Testament Readings.* Too many are still unconvinced of the relevance and value of the Old Testament readings in the liturgy. The fact is that God speaks through the Old Testament readings no less than through the New. It is the same eternal God who speaks through both. That is why Jerome said, without distinguishing Old Testament from New Testament, 'ignorance of the scriptures is ignorance of Christ'. Hence the 'lasting value' of the Old Testament readings (*Constitution on Divine Revelation*, par 14); they should throw light upon and explain New Testament message. Knowing the Old Testament is knowing Christ's roots, knowing him from within, knowing his indispensable back ground.[y]

iii. *Responsorial Psalm.* This, in many liturgies of my experience, is simply a non-event as far as prayerful involvement of the people is concerned; one wonders have people even yet grasped its true meaning? When God speaks we cannot remain passive. Within our hearts there wells up a response which seeks expression in word, in song and in prayer. The Responsorial Psalm is the vehicle

---

[y] A number of Irish publications have developed over the years which supply excellent homiletic notes, and these help bring the Old Testament readings into relationship with the gospel readings (for Sundays), or offer a consideration of them in their own right in the semi-continuous readings found on weekdays. See especially, *The Furrow* (Maynooth), *Intercom* (Maynooth), and *Scripture in Church* (Dublin: Dominican Publications). A general introduction to the Lectionary is supplied by Thomas O'Loughlin, *Explaining the Lectionary for Readers* (Dublin: Columba, 2008); and his *Making the Most of the Lectionary: A User's Guide* (London: SPCK, 2012).

of this response, the great 'yes' with which the congregation responds to God. And to give proper beauty and lyricism to that response we must draw upon the aid of song.

iv.   *The Prayer of the Faithful.* Often times the prayer of the faithful becomes introverted, giving the impression of a holy 'interruption' of the Mass to allow people to intervene with petitions of an individualistic nature. Sometimes indeed it occasions a spontaneous barrage of talk of dubious theological value. In reality the prayer of the faithful is the prayer of the assembly, the 'faithful', exercising in the very heart of the mass its priestly function of interceding for the world.[z]

v.   *The Eucharistic Prayer.* A common difficulty here is the matter of securing the congregation's attention to what the president is saying and doing.[aa] Should we be working towards further interventions from the assembly, as is the case in masses with children and some Eastern Rite liturgies? One questions too whether or not the unity of the eucharistic prayer is always evident – especially if militating against that unity is the practice of changing posture (sitting/standing to kneeling) or making announcements (e.g. after the preface).[bb] One

---

[z] Among the resources available are, Donal Harrington, *Eucharist: Enhancing the Prayer. Including the Prayer of the Faithful for the Three Year Cycle* (Dublin: Columba, 2007); and Eltin Griffin, ed., *The Prayer of the Faithful for Weekdays: A Resource Book* (Oxford: Blackfriars Publications; Dublin: Dominican Publications; NY: Costello Publications, 1985).

[aa] See also Swayne, 'Praying the Mass: The Eucharistic Prayer', *New Liturgy* 25 (1980): 2-6. A scholarly study of the text of the four principal Eucharistic Prayers (which remains useful with the 2011 translation of the Roman Missal) is found in Raymond Moloney, *The Eucharistic Prayers in Worship, Preaching and Study* (Dublin: Dominican Publications, 1985).

[bb] Here Swayne refers to how the unity of the Eucharistic Prayer (which begins with the Preface Dialogue, and not after the Sanctus) is undermined and not respected when there is a change in posture at the Sanctus or when a presider announces which Eucharistic Prayer will be prayed.

wonders too if the moment of 'consecration' is still being isolated out of the context of the entire eucharistic prayer?[cc]

vi. *Some particular problems.* Opening greeting: I mention this as an example of 'words without meaning'.[dd] Do presiders adequately appreciate the richness of meaning in words like 'grace', 'fellowship', 'peace', etc.

vii. *Veracity of Signs.* Here we might examine our celebration from the point of view of authenticity of sign and symbol. Do our gestures and processions speak? How effective is the 'one bread – one cup' symbol? How can we highlight the 'breaking of the bread'?

viii. *Architectural and artistic setting.* Jesus himself gives us a precedent in the gospels for 'setting the scene' for worship

---

[cc] The first scholarly study of the Eucharist published in Ireland after Vatican Two was edited by Patrick McGoldrick, bringing together some leading Irish theological voices of the time, along with contributors like Joachim Jeremias, Louis Bouyer, John Coventry, Nicholas Lash, and Irish theologians from Anglican, Methodist and Presbyterian Churches. This publication, the tenth of an annual series of Maynooth Union Summer Schools, is significant in that it included a paper on ecumenical considerations as well as a study of the new Eucharistic Prayers of the Roman Rite, then available only in draft form. The revised Order of the Mass was promulgated a year later on 1969, and the Latin original of the full Roman Missal in March 1970. The editor, Patrick McGoldrick, later Professor of Liturgy at Maynooth, worked closely with Swayne in Portarlington and Carlow, and as a member of the National Commission on Liturgy: *Understanding the Eucharist: Papers of the Maynooth Union Summer School 1968* (Dublin: Gill and MacMillan, 1969). See his reflection on the Eucharistic Prayer in this volume.

[dd] Swayne developed, over a number of years, a collection of short reflections on various words used in liturgy. These were initially published in *Reality*, and reprinted in *New Liturgy*, to be expanded in later years: 'Words of the Mass: Understanding What we Say', *New Liturgy* 15 (1977): 18-20; 16 (1977-78): 19-21; 17 (1978): 14-17; 21 (1979): 6-10; 25 (1980): 2-6; 26 (1980): 10-13; 27 (1980): 12; 28 (1980-81): 13-15; 33 (1982); 6-8; 34-35 (1982): 26-8; 48 (1985-86): 4-8. [Words reflected upon include, in order, Alleluia, Amen, Bread, Catholic, Celebrate, Come, Communion, Confess, Death, Eucharist, Go, Gospel, Hosanna, Jesus, Lamb of God, Mass, Mercy, Mystery, Offer, Peace, Praise, Accept, Almighty, Altar, Angels. Anxiety, Apostles, Ascension, Believe, Bishops, Bless].

(cf. e.g. Luke 22:8; Luke 4:16ff.). Because we are human, creatures of flesh and blood, the atmosphere and environment for worship does have its effect on the quality of worship.[ee] In this connection one might ask: Have we yet been liberated from the poor quality commercial art and soulless architecture which swamped the Catholic Church in the past? Paul the Sixth's famous apology to artists on 7 May 1964 might yet have to be reiterated in our time: 'We ask your pardon ... we ourselves have abandoned you ... we have had recourse to substitutes, to 'oleography', to inexpensive works of art of little merit ... we have taken by-roads along which art and

---

[ee] Swayne is noted for working closely with artists and architects, helping them to become imbued with a deep sense of the liturgy so that they, in turn, will bring this to bear on their artistic and professional work in church design. He wrote on the architectural setting in 'Building and Churches', *New Liturgy* [then the Kildare and Leighlin Bulletin] 3 (1969): 12-17. He returned to this theme later, giving a brief report on the work of the Art and Architecture Commission: 'An Irish Contribution to Sacred Art and Architecture', *New Liturgy* 81 (1994): 14-17. A seminar on 'Redesigning Existing Churches' (12 December 1965) led to the production of the *Pastoral Directory on the Building and Reorganization of Churches* (22 June 1966) from the Advisory Committee on Sacred Art and Architecture of the Episcopal Commission for Liturgy (published in *The Furrow* 17 (1966): 471-77. This document was revised and expanded in August 1972 (see comments on this in *Notitiae* 9 (1973): 102-3). Swayne was instrumental in the preparation of the *Guidelines for Diocesan Commissions on Sacred Art and Architecture* (from the Advisory Committee on Sacred Art and Architecture), published in *The Furrow* 27 (1976): 504-10. Mount St. Anne's Liturgy Centre published, *Maintenance Manual for Church Buildings* in 1976, followed by two statements from the Advisory Committee on *Renewal of Sanctuaries: Adaptation of Existing Altars* (December 1976), and *Designing Confessionals for the New Rite of Penance* (January 1977) – both found in *New Liturgy* 12 (Winter 1976-1977): 12-15 and 16. In 1979 the *Pastoral Directory on Confessionals* was issued by the Advisory Committee along with a *Statement on the Disposal of Liturgical and Devotional Objects*, both of which were published in *New Liturgy* 21 (Spring 1979): 23-4. In January 1983 the Advisory Committee published *Alterations in Newly Built or Reordered Churches*, published in *New Liturgy* 36 (Winter 1982-83): 15. Currently work is taking place on a revision of the publication of the Irish Episcopal Commission for Liturgy, *The Place of Worship: Pastoral Directory on the Building and Reordering of Churches* (Dublin: Veritas; Carlow: Irish Institute of Pastoral Liturgy, 1994). Swayne's commitment to good architecture is witnessed in the chapel that was designed for the Irish Institute of Pastoral Liturgy in Carlow: see, Richard Hurley, 'The Eucharistic Room at Carlow Liturgy Centre', *Worship* 70 (1996): 238-50.

beauty and, what is worse for us, the worship of God have been badly served'.[ff]

The Sacraments: Problem Areas

i. *Initiation.* The tendency, in countries where children are normally baptized at birth, and where adult baptisms are rare, has been to ignore the new *Rite of Christian Initiation of Adults*.[gg] But, to ignore it is to be unaware of rich implications of the *Order* for Catholics baptised in infancy; one thinks of the magnificent vision of Church, priesthood of the faithful, Christian commitment, etc. as well as the highly thorough approach to formation in Christian living written into the RCIA. Places like Chicago, where so many people baptized in infancy are being re-formed in Christian belief and living as a result of the RCIA ought to be a headline for all.[hh]

ii. *Devotion to the Eucharist outside Mass.* The desirability of fostering popular devotions and devotion to the Eucharist outside Mass has been increasingly recognized in recent years (cf. *Marialis cultus*, 1974,[6] *Evangelii nuntiandi*, 1975[7]). There is need for care, at the same time, to safeguard such devotions from any mistaken

---

[ff] Swayne commented on this in an article, 'The "Oleography" Bait', *New Liturgy* 14 (1977): 13-14. Related, even if not mentioned in Swayne's paper, was his concern for the contribution to liturgy that can be made by the proper employment of a good organ: see his, 'Buying an Organ', *New Liturgy* 15 (1977): 13-15.

[gg] The comment of Swayne is generally taken to be a truism. The pastoral reality continues to be baptism of children. An attempt to deal with the baptism in a broad way, permitting the RICA to model how it is celebrated, even with children, is found in Michael Drumm and Tom Gunning, *A Sacramental People*, Volume 1: *Initiation* (Dublin: Columba Press, 1999). For a pastoral guide for initiation of children see, Raymond Topley, *Parish Baptism Team Manual* (Maynooth: TS Publications, 1993), and Julie Kavanagh, *A Welcome for your Child: A Guide to Baptism for Parents* (Dublin: Veritas, 2009). Swayne addressed Confirmation in, 'Theology of Confirmation', *New Liturgy* 26 (New Series) (1980): 2-4.

[hh] Seán Swayne edited an important collection of texts relating to the sacraments (along with sections on Christian Burial, Ministers of Lector and Acolyte, the Function of the Deacon, and Music in the Liturgy): *The Sacraments: A Pastoral Directory of the Irish Episcopal Conference* (Dublin: Veritas, 1976).

emphases and to ground them on a solid liturgical, theological and biblical basis. In this matter guidance will be found above all, in relation to eucharistic devotion, in the beautiful *Eucharisticum mysterium* of 1967 and *Holy Communion and Worship of the Eucharist outside Mass* of 1973.[8ii] Meantime we search, at times in vain, for evidence that the emphasis in these documents is being translated in pastoral terms and having its effect on the *pia exercitia* of the faithful.

iii.   *Reconciliation.* Writing and comment on the new rite has not been lacking. Nor, it would seem, study at local (diocesan, etc.) level. And yet there is an obvious malaise. Pastoral practice has altered but little – apart from a decline in frequency of use of the sacrament.[jj] One asks why?

iv.   *Christian Burial.* The present *Ordo exsequiorum* contains rich possibilities. To what extent are they being availed of? Vatican II looked forward to a new emphasis on the paschal character of Christian death.[kk] Is this emphasis, in practice, being confined to marginal matters such as colour of vestments, type of music selected, etc? And what of the integration of the great Requiem chants with their beautifully distanced quality and highly distinctive Catholic identity being integrated into the celebration of Christian burial today?

[ii] See Swayne, 'Exposition of the Blessed Sacrament', *New Liturgy* 34-35 (1982): 3-5.

[jj] Swayne commented on this rite in, 'The New Rite of Penance', *New Liturgy* 12 (N.S.) (1976-77): 2-5. Among the large number of publications relating to this sacrament is Oliver Crilly, ed., *Penitential Services*, New Enlarged Edition (Dublin: Columba, 1993).

[kk] The paschal character of death was an important theme for Swayne: see *inter alia* his 'Death through the Back Door', *New Liturgy* 13 (N.S.) (1977): 9-14. Among the resources available alongside the *Order of Christian Funerals* (1991), see Eltin Griffin, ed. *The Funeral Book: Pastoral Commentaries, Creative Ideas and Funeral Homilies* (Dublin: Columba, 1998). A serious pastoral and theological consideration of death in a paschal key was the subject matter of a collection of essays dedicated to Dermot Lane: Donal Harrington, ed., *Death and*

Liturgy of the Hours

'The liturgy of the hours got off to a bad start. It may never recover. ... What we have inherited is the cathedral version, but what we need is the parish version.'[ll] One of the hopes behind the restoration of the Liturgy of the Hours was that the people of God generally would rediscover it as their prayer and no longer look at it as the preserve of the clergy.[mm] Academic formation in its understanding seems to achieve little; what is needed is the experience of effective celebration of the Hours.[nn]

New Life: Pastoral and Theological Reflections (Dublin: Dominican Publications, 1993). Included is a contribution by the late Brian Magee CM co-writing with Catherine Gorman, 'Celebrating the Paschal Mystery: Words of Commentary for the Paschal Vigil', 48-54. The National Advisory Committee on Church Music produced *Rite of Christian Funerals: Music for the Reception of the Body at the Church*, Patrick O'Donoghue, ed. (Dublin: Veritas, 1998).

[ll] From an Editorial by Virgil C. Funk, in *Pastoral Music* 7:5 (June/July, 1982), 2.

[mm] A number of publications have creatively looked to producing forms of the Prayer of the Church which would be accessible to groups: see, for example, Margaret Daly, *Nunc Dimittis: Night Prayer of the Church as Celebrated at Gort Muire* (Dublin: Veritas, 1991). Some resources for the principal hours were published by Austin Flannery, ed., *Making the Most of the Breviary*, Supplement to Doctrine and Life, Vol. 13, nos. 56, 57 (Dublin: Dominican Publications, [ND]); and Brian Magee: *Psalm Prayers for Morning and Evening Arranged for the Daily Hours* (Dublin: Veritas, 1990). Among Irish publications which are used by parishes and smaller groups of people are, John McCann, *Weekday Celebrations* (Dublin: Veritas, 2000), esp. chapter 4, pp 41-60; *The Glenstal Book of Prayer* (Dublin: Columba Press, 2001, rev. ed. 2008); a publication that includes a form of Evening Prayer was produced jointly by nine dioceses: *Taking Our Hearts to the Lord: Lenten Resource for Scripture Sharing Prayer Groups* (Strokestown: Pastoral Diocesan Office, 2010).

[nn] Swayne co-authored an article with Patrick J. McGoldrick, 'The New Office', *New Liturgy* 4 (New Series) (1974-75): 8-14. The first part (pp. 8-12), 'The Psalms' was written by Swayne while McGoldrick supplied a brief history of the Hours (pp. 13-14). See also, Swayne, 'Praying the Breviary', *New Liturgy* 38-39 (1983): 5-13. Studies relating to the psalms have been offered by Margaret Daly-Denton, 'Psalmody as "Word of Christ"', *Finding Voice to Give God Praise: Essays in the Many Languages of the Liturgy*, Kathleen Hughes, ed. (Collegeville, MN.: Liturgical Press, 1998), 73-86; and her more recent, *Psalm-Shaped Prayerfulness: A Guide to the Christian Reception of the Psalms* (Dublin: Columba, 2010).

Seasons and Festivals

'The Easter Vigil is the prime target in setting up any programme. From this point in time all the rest of the parish/Church calendar flows. Lent becomes a time of training.[oo] Eastertime a time to relish the development[pp] The other seasons and feasts then fall into place' (Fr Dan Coughlan, Meeting of European National Liturgy Secretaries at Syros).[qq] In practice the Vigil is scarcely seen as the high-point in the Church's year.[rr] Its neglect points to the hiatus between Church teaching (seeing the Vigil as the climax of the Christian's year) and practice. Time was when the celebration of the Vigil was the Christian's identity badge (cf. Tertullian, Augustine). What, one may ask, is lacking today in our manner of celebration of the Vigil which leaves so many Christians uninvolved and uninterested?

[oo] See, Swayne, 'Holy Week and Easter', *New Liturgy* 37 (1983): 2-17. A brief but excellent presentation on Lent is found in Vincent Ryan, *Lent and Holy Week*, 2d edition (Dublin: Veritas/Leominster, Herefordshire: Fowler Wright Books, 1983).

[pp] Vincent Ryan offers a brief but full exploration in his *Eastertime and Feasts of the Lord*, 2d edition (Dublin: Veritas, 1985).

[qq] The theme of the second part of the gathering of the Association of European National Liturgy Secretaries which took place in Syros, Greece in 1980, was 'Formation of Priests and Laity'.

[rr] This statement places the Advent/Christmas cycle in a paschal context, as it does also for the celebration of saints. See, Swayne, 'Advent', *New Liturgy* 42-43 (1984): 2-9; and, Vincent Ryan, *Advent to Epiphany* (Dublin: Veritas, 1993); Eltin Griffin, ed., *Celebrating the Season of Advent* (Dublin: Columba/Collegeville, MN: Liturgical Press, 1986; repr.: Dublin: Columba, 2004); and Austin Flannery, ed., *The Saints in Season: A Companion to the Lectionary* (Dublin: Dominican Publications/Northport, NY: Costello Publishing, 1976).

For pastoral material on the Triduum see, Eugene Duffy, ed. *Celebrating the Triduum* (Dublin: Columba, 1999); and, John McCann and Pat O'Donoghue, eds., *Those Three Days: A Resource for the Celebration of the Easter Triduum* (Dublin: Veritas, 2002).

For a guide to celebrating Eucharist throughout the entire year see, National Centre for Liturgy (Patrick Jones, ed.), *Celebrating the Mass Throughout the Year: Eucharist and the Liturgical Year* (Dublin: Veritas, 2011). Music resources can be found in John O'Keeffe, ed., *Feasts and Seasons: Liturgical Music for Parish Choirs, Congregations and Cantors* (Maynooth: St Patrick's College, 2003).

5. Conclusion

My contention is that even where the structures for liturgical formation exist many remain unconvinced of the priority it should hold in the Church's pastoral plans today. A new motivation is necessary, and this will come most effectively through the faithful's actual experience of liturgies of quality. Liturgy is learned not so much through academic intake as through worthy celebration. Once people are convinced through experience of the value of good celebration they will want to learn the 'how' of celebration. And the means are there.

** This is the text of an unpublished paper read by Monsignor Seán Swayne (1933–1996), then Secretary to the Irish Episcopal Commission on Liturgy, at a meeting of the National Secretaries of the member and associate member Conferences which constitute the International Commission on English in the Liturgy (ICEL) held in Rome on 26–31 October 1982. Two other papers delivered at this meeting, all of which were followed by lengthy discussion, were 'Inculturation of the Liturgy' by Camilo J. Marivoet CICM, Liturgy Secretary in The Philippines, and 'Rite of Christian Initiation of Adults' presented by Joseph V. McCabe MM, Liturgy Secretary to the Bishops' Conference in Tanzania. While couched in the language of the 1980s, the issues raised by Swayne remain a concern for today and constitute a significant part of the ongoing task of liturgical formation. Apart from being the first Episcopal Secretary for Liturgy, Swayne was also the founding Director of the Irish Institute of Pastoral Liturgy (Portarlington). This Institute later moved to Carlow and is now in Maynooth as the National Centre for Liturgy. See contribution of Moira Bergin for more on the liturgical work and influence of Seán Swayne.

The contribution of Seán Swayne to liturgical renewal in Ireland is outlined in three articles published after his death on 9 May 1996. See, Patrick Jones, 'Seán Swayne (1933–1996)', *New Liturgy* 90-91-92 (1996), 4–9; J. D. Crichton, "A Personal Memory"', Ibid., 10–11; and Margaret Daly-Denton, 'Seán Swayne: The Memory and the Challenge', *New Liturgy* 94 (1997), 2–9.

These annotations have been compiled and written by Liam M. Tracey and Thomas R. Whelan.

Notes

1. Paul VI, Motu Proprio, *Sacram liturgiam*, On putting into effect some prescriptions of the Constitution the Sacred Liturgy, 25 January 1964, AAS 56 (1964): 139-44.

2. Sacred Congregation of Rites (*Consilium*), [First] Instruction, *Inter oecumenici*, On the orderly carrying out of the Constitution on the Sacred Liturgy, 26 September, 1964: AAS 56 (1964): 877-900.

3. Sacred Congregation of Rites (*Consilium*), Instruction, *Eucharisticum mysterium*, on the worship of Eucharist, 25 May 1967: AAS 59 (1967): 539-73; *Notitiae* 3 (1967): 225-60.

4. Congregation for Sacraments and Divine Worship, Instruction *Inaestimabile donum*, on certain norms concerning the worship of the Eucharistic mystery, 3 April 1980, AAS 72 (1980): 331-43; *Notitiae* 16 (1980): 287-96.

5. Congregation for Divine Worship, [Third] Instruction *Liturgicae instaurationes*, on the orderly carrying out of the Constitution on the Liturgy, 5 September 1970: AAS 62 (1970): 692-704; *Notitiae* 7 (1971): 10-26.

6. Paul VI, Apostolic Exhortation, *Marialis cultus*, on rightly grounding and increasing Marian devotion, 2 February 1974: AAS 66 (1974): 113-68; *Notitiae* 10 (1974): 153-97.

7. Paul VI, Apostolic Exhortation, *Evangelii nuntiandi*, on evangelization in the modern world, 8 December 1975: AAS 68 (1976): 5-76.

8. SC Divine Worship, *Holy Communion and Worship of the Eucharistic outside Mass*, 21 June 1973.

LITURGICAL RENEWAL
IN IRELAND

THE WORK OF LITURGICAL RENEWAL IN IRELAND – AND PATRICK JONES

༆ ༆ ༆

MOIRA BERGIN RSM

Sacrosanctum concilium, the Constitution on the Sacred Liturgy, was the first document of the Second Vatican Council to be promulgated (on 4 December 1963). Its opening chapter, which outlines the general principles for the restoration and promotion of the sacred liturgy, refers to the setting up of a liturgical commission by the competent territorial ecclesiastical authority. It set out the task of this commission, working under the direction of the ecclesiastical authority, as regulating pastoral liturgical action throughout the territory and promoting 'studies and necessary experiments whenever there is a question of adaptations to be proposed to the Apostolic See'. It also noted, 'So far as possible the commission should be aided by some kind of Institute for Pastoral Liturgy ...' (SC 44).

Following the Council the work of renewal of the liturgy took hold of our dioceses and parishes. The Latin editions (*editiones typicae*) of the new liturgical books were translated by the International Commission on English in the Liturgy (ICEL), which was formed by bishops from Conferences where English was spoken,[1] just some weeks before the promulgation of *Sacrosanctum concilium*.[2] The preparation for their publication in Ireland was put on a formal basis by the appointment of a secretary to the Episcopal Commission for Liturgy in April 1973.[3]

Seán Swayne, a priest of the diocese of Kildare and Leighlin, studied liturgy at the Institut Superieur de Liturgie in Paris, having worked in the parish of Naas for nine years after his ordination on 23 June 1957.[4] From the time of his return to Ireland in 1968, he lectured in liturgy at St Patrick's College, Carlow, until his appointment as parish priest of Graignamanagh, Co. Kilkenny in 1986. During all of this time he also served as National Secretary for Liturgy. Later he wrote, 'From my student days in Paris I had dreamed of having our own liturgy centre in Ireland where we could have courses, resource material, etc.'[5]

Swayne created, in liaison with the pastoral panel of the Episcopal Commission for Liturgy, a small diocesan liturgy centre at Carlow College, providing a service to the diocese and began publishing a quarterly bulletin, *New Liturgy*.[6] For him, liturgy was always new: 'Our liturgy is the *new* liturgy of the Christian dispensation, which keeps the Church ever young and fresh and beautiful as a bride (Revelations 21:2)'.[7]

Founding of an Institute for Pastoral Liturgy

After his appointment as National Secretary, a notice appeared in the summer 1974 issue of *New Liturgy* (by now published as a National Bulletin):

> Ireland is to have an institute for pastoral liturgy. Over the past few years there has been a growing conviction, among people involved in the renewal of the liturgy, that the key to success lies in the formation of a corps of priests, religious and laity having some specialised training in liturgy. With this in mind the Irish hierarchy, at their meeting last March in Maynooth, approved of the setting up of an institute for pastoral liturgy at Mount St Anne's, Portarlington. Mount St Anne's, which also serves as a retreat house, has been put at the disposal of the institute through the generosity of the owners, the Presentation Sisters of Kildare and Leighlin.[8]

The Institute began a residential one year programme in pastoral liturgy on 29 September 1974.[9] Music played an important dimension in the course and Margaret Daly [-Denton], a student of the first year, became its Director of Music in 1975.[10] The Institute attracted students from Ireland and from more than thirty other counties over the next years. Lecturers were drawn from a panel of people teaching liturgy and related subjects throughout the country. Staff and students formed a daily worshipping community with the celebration of the Liturgy of the Hours and Eucharist. Preparation for these celebrations was time-tabled into the daily programme.

In 1978, the Institute had developed to the point that it needed a permanent, independent location. It moved to St Patrick's College, Carlow, on 30 June 1978, where it had its own administration within the college. Under the patronage of the then Bishop of Kildare and Leighlin, Bishop Patrick Lennon, it was renamed the Irish Institute of Pastoral Liturgy. A wing of the college had been made available and was renovated under the direction of the architect, Dr Richard Hurley (1932–2011). 'Above all', wrote Seán Swayne,

> we wanted the new Institute to be welcoming, hospitable, a place of 're-freshment' (Fr A.B. O'Shea's word [a member of the staff at that time]), reflecting simplicity and detachment, and not 'aggressively religious' from a visual point of view.[11]

Its chapel or liturgy room was unique and admired at home and abroad, exercising its own special influence on the places we design for our worship.[12]

The Institute housed the secretariat for the Bishops' Commission for Liturgy and was a place of formation. It continued the one year programme with the Diploma in Liturgy, recognised by the Faculty of Theology of the Pontifical University of St Patrick's College, Maynooth. There were outreaches as an advisory service in matters relating to liturgy and through short courses and seminars in pastoral liturgy and theology at Carlow and throughout the country.

A significant annual event in Carlow were the May Seminars, first conducted in 1972 before the appointment of Seán Swayne as secretary but at his initiative. Each May for twenty-five years, about two hundred people attended the two day seminar in mid-May. The participants were priests, religious, students of the Centre, seminarians and lay men and women. They were presiders, teachers, ministers of the Word and Eucharist, music ministers and people with leadership responsibilities in parishes. They were exposed to a wide range of liturgical issues and scholarship, from the first seminar on aspects of celebration by the French liturgist and composer, Lucien Deiss CSSp to the twentieth-fifth seminar in 1996 by Andrew D Ciferni, Professor of Liturgy at the Washington Theological Union on the theme of 'The Next Thirty Years'. Topics explored over the years included the major themes of liturgical study and celebration and areas like RCIA, liturgical spirituality, and the ministry of presider. The seminars offered Irish audiences the insights of scholars such as Robert Taft, Aidan Kavanagh, Mary Collins, Kathleen Hughes, John Fitzsimmons, David Power, Kevin Seasoltz and John Shea.[13] Though overlapping a little with the Glenstal Liturgical Congresses,[14] which prepared many for Vatican II and its immediate aftermath, the May Seminars, along with other conferences which have been a constant part of the Centre's programme, have made a significant mark on liturgical renewal in Ireland. The rich understandings of worship given at these events have been of great benefit to those who participated and, through them, to many others.

Fr Seán Collins succeeds Mgr Seán Swayne
When Seán Swayne was appointed parish priest of Graignamanagh in 1986, Fr Seán Collins OFM became National Secretary and the second director of the Irish Institute of Pastoral Liturgy. He had come to Carlow two years earlier as assistant director.[15] His love of Irish made him the appropriate secretary of the working group on the revision of the Irish Calendar and on the provision of new prayer texts for its feasts.[16]

Seán continued his predecessor's work in liturgical formation, taking every opportunity to share his understanding and love of the Church's worship. As National Secretary he served on the National Commission for Liturgy, Church Music, and Sacred Art and Architecture, and later as a member of *an Coiste Comhairleach um an Liotúirge i nGaeilge*.[17] Seán Collins completed his term as Secretary and Director in June 1992.

Appointment of Patrick Jones as National Secretary and Director

The honouree of this volume, Patrick Jones, was appointed Director of the National Centre for Liturgy (as it came to be know from August 1996), and National Secretary for liturgy from June 1992 to 31 August 2013. He had served as a part-time staff member and assistant director to Seán Collins in Carlow from 1987 (and before that as an occasional lecturer) after his return from studies at Sant Anselmo in 1978. A native of Greystones, Co. Wicklow he has often acknowledged the importance of that parish and his parents and family for his understanding of faith and its expression in worship.[18] Greystones, with its significant Church mix, also gave him a particular interest in ecumenism but it is an early acquaintance with the Liturgical Movement that is recalled here.

The comment of Bernard Botte, citing an Irish correspondent, on the Liturgical Movement in Ireland, is often quoted: 'The history of the liturgical movement in Ireland is as simple as that of the snake: there have never been any snakes in Ireland'.[19] But the Liturgical Movement reflected the movement for the renewal of worship.[20] The re-establishment of the monastery of Solesmes in 1833 and the work of its founder, Prosper Guéranger may be seen as the beginnings of the Liturgical Movement. The more parish based call for a democratisation of the liturgy by Lambert Beauduin at the Malines Congress in 1909 may be regarded as another beginning point. The call for 'active participation', that echoed at this time had already been included in the *motu proprio, Tra le sollecitudine* of Pope Pius X, issued on 22 November 1903.[21]

Endorsement of the Liturgical Movement came with the encyclical *Mediator Dei* of Pope Pius XII on 11 November 1947.[22] The Movement, now affecting many places, received the seal of approval with this encyclical, even if cautiously.

In Ireland the papal endorsement and reforms had begun to take effect.[23] The reforms of Pius X were well received. Children began to receive communion at the earlier age of around seven years. People received Holy Communion more often. There were many courses in Gregorian Chant and liturgical festivals, though these engaged schools rather than parishes, therefore the fruits of the festivals did not filter into the parishes. The reforms of Holy Week in 1956 were received with enthusiasm and attracted large numbers of the faithful.

Yet the Irish congregation was perceived as passive. In this regard the work of Fr John Fennelly, parish priest of Greystones, Co. Wicklow in the 1950s and early 1960s, is exceptional. He sought to put into practice the ideals of the Movement, encouraging congregational singing, with simple chants and vernacular hymns, and the use of a form of the dialogue Mass but using English, patterned after the *Betsingmesse* of Pius Parsch.[24] He was 'a zealous and courageous pioneer of the Liturgical Movement in Ireland' given much to advocacy 'and indeed to advocacy of a particularly robust and indefatigable kind'.[25]

Maynooth, the Third Home of the Liturgy Centre

Liturgical formation has been the work of the Centre through the years since 1974 with its course on pastoral liturgy and the practical living out and celebrating what was learned. The Centre continuously goes back to the founding vision of 1973 which reached out to priests, parishes, choirs, composers, artists and architects.[26] This vision together with its formation principles have continued at the National Centre for Liturgy, the new name given to the Institute since its transfer to St Patrick's College, Maynooth in 1996. Writing at the time, Patrick Jones said:

> Times change and our circumstances change. At Maynooth
> we will work with the resources already here and explore
> how together we can organise courses in liturgical
> formation and the lived experience of worship. This will be
> our task in the first year here at our new home.[27]

In 1996, following the transfer, Patrick Jones sought to have the
status of the Diploma in Pastoral Liturgy raised to an award by
the Faculty of Theology, St Patrick's College, Maynooth and
conferred by the Pontifical University. He negotiated with the
Faculty of Theology in 2000 to approve the award of the
Higher Diploma in Pastoral Liturgy and establish a Master's
programme in Theology, specialising in liturgy.[28] This
development has also enabled the Centre, working with the
Faculty of Theology, to bring several leading liturgical scholars
to present seminars and courses at Maynooth.[29] The first
graduates of this Master degree were conferred in 2002.
Students have been from home and abroad and, though the
great majority are Roman Catholic, several from other
Churches, Anglican and Orthodox, have studied at the Centre.
    Since 1999 the National Centre for Liturgy has worked with
the Department of Music, Maynooth University, on the Diploma
in Arts (Church Music) programme. The liturgy component for
the Diploma is taught through the Centre. Although the liturgy
Centre cannot any longer provide a residential course at its new
home in Maynooth, unlike at its previous locations, an important
part of the daily programme of the Centre continues to include
common worship. In September 2001 new links were established
with the Chaplaincy at Maynooth University in providing
weekday Mass, which takes place in St Mary's Oratory at midday.
    Patrick Jones had established night courses in liturgy in
Carlow before the transfer to Maynooth and such courses,
organised by the National Centre for Liturgy at Maynooth,
have been conducted in several places throughout the country
from time to time. Many one day seminars have been conducted
there and this, in many ways, continues the so-called 'May
Seminars' which had previously been conducted in Carlow.

Liturgical formation outside of the National Centre for Liturgy strengthened as a result of these programmes. 'But there are limits to this work!'[30] Patrick Jones has continuously emphasised the need to invest in liturgical formation in order to train the trainers.

The National Agencies – Liturgy

On 8 November 1964, during the third session of Vatican II, the Irish bishops announced their decision to introduce the vernacular into certain parts of the Mass. They stated that 'the changes will be introduced in several stages in order to achieve as smooth a transition as possible in the ceremonies of this central act of Catholic worship'.[31] By the First Sunday of Advent, 1 December 1968, the Mass was completely in the vernacular. The translated texts were made available by ICEL and while the vernacular was introduced in stages over a short period of time, a New York produced *Altar Missal*[32] was adapted for use in Ireland and published in March-April 1967. The vernacular was also introduced into other liturgies, including marriage and funerals.

In December 1963 an Episcopal Commission for Liturgy was appointed and initially it was assisted in its work by five panels or committees – in music, sacred art and architecture, pastoral liturgy, catechetics and translations. Much of their work was taken over in 1974 after the establishment of National Secretariat for Liturgy, but from these panels in the following year the Irish Commission for Liturgy, as the primary consultative body, was appointed. The Episcopal Commission for Liturgy and the Irish Commission for Liturgy were later amalgamated in March 2010, and now known as the 'Council for Liturgy'. The panels on sacred art and architecture and music became the Advisory Committees on Sacred Art and Architecture, and on Church Music, respectively.[33]

Ensuring the availability of the new liturgical books in Ireland was the responsibility of the Episcopal Conference, which was facilitated and directed by the Episcopal Commission for Liturgy and the National Secretary for Liturgy.

Similarly the task of liturgical formation rests with them, with the National Centre for Liturgy serving as a unique resource.

In the immediate years following the promulgation of the Constitution on the Sacred Liturgy (4 December 1963), the use of the vernacular was extended using the existing books or interim texts. Scripture readings used available translations and led to the publication of the Lectionary, in RSV and Jerusalem Bible editions, permitted for use from Advent 1969 and mandatory from the following Lent.[34] *An Leicseanáir* was also published in 1970.

The task of translating the revised *Missale Romanum* of 1969 into English was entrusted to ICEL and the task of publishing was given to the Episcopal Conferences. ICEL issued reports, consultation material and segments of the translation to the Conferences and a final complete text was available in 1973. Final editing on behalf of the publisher was given to a small task force,[35] was then approved by the Episcopal Conference before receiving the Roman *confirmatio* on 4 February 1974. Published on 7 January 1975, the *Roman Missal* was used throughout the country from 16 March 1975, the eve of the feast of St Patrick.[36] At the same time, the work of producing an Irish translation was completed and *An Leabhar Aifrinn Rómánach* [lit. 'The Roman Mass Book'][37] was published in late 1973, even before the English edition.[38]

The ritual books were also translated in English and Irish, the first of which was the rites of Marriage,[39] Baptism of Children,[40] Penance,[41] Anointing,[42] and Exposition of the Blessed Sacrament.[43] The funerals rites were produced in both Irish and English[44] but the expanded Ritual was published with a small amount of the Irish language rite.[45] This was the first 'second generation' book of ICEL and contained much material not in the Latin *editio typica*.[46] Earlier, supplementary material, in particular music and the provision of an Office of Evening Prayer for the Dead, was made available in Christian Burial, published by the National Centre for Liturgy.[47] The RCIA was a later publication.[48] *The Divine Office*, as the book for the Liturgy of the Hours, was produced by a committee working from Glenstal Abbey, with Dom Placid Murray as principal editor. This was published in 1974.[49] The *Roman Pontifical*, as used for the ordination rites, was published by ICEL.[50]

ICEL began work on the revision of the *Roman Missal* with consultations of Episcopal Conferences in 1982 and 1985. Reports with the new translations and newly composed texts were issued in the late 1980s and the complete revision was presented to the Bishops between 1993 and 1997. Each of the eight segments was carefully examined by the Conference and the Irish Commission for Liturgy. This work was co-ordinated by Patrick Jones as National Secretary.[51] The revised *Sacramentary*, as it was called, was approved by the Episcopal Conference and by the other ten Conferences for whom ICEL was a joint commission. It was submitted as a common *Missal* by the three neighbouring Conferences for the *recognitio* of the Congregation for Divine Worship in December 1998.[52] The revised *Sacramentary* was not given *recognitio*.

A new, third Latin edition of the *Missale Romanum* was published in March 2002, with an amended reprint in 2008. Its *Institutio Generalis* was translated by ICEL and published after receiving *recognitio* on 26 January 2005.[53] An Instruction on the use of vernacular translations, along with norms for translation and the process to be followed for approval, was published in April 2001. It called for the Latin texts to be 'translated integrally and in the most exact manner, without omissions or additions in terms of their content, and without paraphrases or glosses'.[54] Under the direction of Patrick Jones, a team from the National Centre for Liturgy put together *Celebrating the Mystery of Faith, A Guide to the Mass*,[55] based on the new edition of the *General Instruction of the Roman Missal*. It was published as a study book for priests, on their own or in groups, for liturgy teams, for ministers of the Word, music and communion, for parishes, and for all who want to understand better this *mysterium fidei*.

ICEL, which was newly constituted in 2003,[56] worked on the translation of the *Missale Romanum* according to the 2001 Roman Instruction, issuing its first segment, a draft translation of the *Ordo Missae* in February 2004. After having received comments from various of its member Conferences, ICEL redrafted the Order of Mass, or more accurately, 'parts of the Order of Mass', which was published in mid-2008. Over a six-year period, ICEL issued twelve segments of the translation of the new edition of the *Missale Romanum*, each was reviewed by the Episcopal Conference and its consultors on the Commission for Liturgy. After submitting the final text of the new translation of the Missal to Rome, and the subsequent granting of the *recognitio*, an Episcopal Conference statement of 19 April 2011 stated that the new *Roman Missal* would be introduced from the first Sunday of Advent, 27 November 2011.[57]

A very full programme of catechesis and preparation had already begun at the National Centre for Liturgy. Days for diocesan representatives were held and workshops for priests in several dioceses took place. Further resource material was made available from the Centre, including *The New Missal, Explaining the Mass*, with Patrick Jones as chief author,[58] and *Celebrating the Mass Throughout the Year*,[59] which offers a catechesis on the Mass using several of the new texts.

The Liturgy Centre prepared material for parish bulletins and missalettes, and Jones published articles in *Intercom* to support and facilitate the many dioceses which began to introduce the people's parts of the Mass from 11 September 2011.[60] Full implementation and use of the third edition of *The Roman Missal*[61] took place throughout the country from the first Sunday of Advent following.

At this time preparations were in place for the International Eucharistic Congress, held in Dublin, 10–17 June 2012. The Liturgy Centre, including its staff, its panel of lecturers, and many present and former students contributed to the preparation for and the celebration of the Congress through their membership of committees, as presenters of workshops, and as members of the liturgy and music teams.[62]

The National Agencies: Art and Architecture – Music – Liotúirge i nGaeilge

The establishment of the agency for sacred art and architecture was much aided by the work of the Church Exhibitions Committee, later called the Sacred Arts Committee, founded by the Royal Institute of the Architects of Ireland in 1956. The Committee held exhibitions of French and German church architecture which drew big numbers (for example, the 1962 German churches exhibition in Dublin attracted some twenty-five thousand visitors). The Committee also handled the Irish contribution to the biennial international exhibition of sacred art and architecture. Such exhibitions and seminars were very helpful as church sanctuaries were reordered. The new Advisory Committee set about offering guidelines on such reordering and in June 1966 prepared for the Episcopal Commission for Liturgy a *Pastoral Directory on the Building and Reorganisation of Churches*.[63] This short directory led to an extended edition in 1972.[64] Its chapter on the tabernacle was published in *Notitiae*, the periodical of the Congregation for Divine Worship[65] and Archbishop Annibale Bugnini described it as 'an excellent summary of the legislation and norms regulating the construction and location of the tabernacle'.[66] A further edition published in 1994, *The Place of Worship*,[67] continues to serve as the current guide for the organisation of liturgical environment in Ireland.

Two exhibitions of sacred art for the home were organised by the Advisory Committee. Seven artists were selected to produce a work in a limited edition of a maximum of 100 copies for the exhibition held in 1974. Fifteen artists participated in 'Christian Art 90', an exhibition held 1990–91 in several centres throughout the country. Working with the National Centre for Liturgy, the Advisory Committee has held occasional days for artists and architects.

The Local Government (Planning and Development) Act, in force since 2000, gave rise to much discussion and many meetings in order to produce *Architectural Heritage Protection Guidelines for the Planning Authorities*, and thus 'to respect liturgical requirements', as called for by the Act. The Advisory Committee strongly recommended the establishment of Historic Churches Advisory Committees on a diocesan or inter-diocesan basis. A sub-committee of the Advisory Committee, co-ordinated by Patrick Jones, worked with the Department for the Environment, Heritage and Local Government to produce these guidelines in 2005 and, in particular, its important fifth chapter on Places of Public Worship.[68] This chapter was agreed by the four main Christian Churches on the island of Ireland, with Jones acting as liaison with the Church representatives.

When the Irish Commission for Liturgy was established as a commission of consultors in December 1963, one of its panels was music, which later became the Advisory Committee on Church Music.[69] In late 1966 it published the *New Liturgy Hymn Book* containing forty hymns in Irish and English. Cardinal Conway, in his foreword, hoped 'that this hymn-book will both encourage choirs to fulfil their ministerial office in the revised liturgy, and also contribute towards the ideal of congregation participation which the new Constitution so strongly advocates'.[70] Congregational singing in those early days of liturgical renewal was often seen in terms of hymns.[71] The most important hymnal of the time was, without doubt, *The Veritas Hymnal* (1973), edited by Fr Jerry Threadgold, a long-time member of the Advisory Committee. It contained one hundred and forty-six hymns in Irish and English and enjoyed great popularity for many years.[72]

The Church Music Panel, at the request of Cardinal Conway, founded the Irish Church Music Association (ICMA) on 22 November 1969. The Association held its first summer school in St Patrick's College, Maynooth, 13–17 July 1970.[73] Professor Gerard Gillen, one of the founding members of the Association, said in his address to the twenty-ninth summer school in 1998 that 'over the years this annual week has become firmly established in the musical, ecclesiastical and educational calendar of this country as one of perennial importance in the ongoing work of shaping the musical constituents of the post-Vatican II liturgy'.[74]

Another initiative was the founding of the Schola Cantorum, based in St Finian's College, Mullingar, Co. Westmeath in September 1970 under the directorship of Fr Frank McNamara. Scholarships were provided for boys who studied music, including Church music, together with their other subjects of second level education. While they had the freedom to choose their own career, it was hoped that some would fill posts in cathedrals and diocesan schools, a hope fulfilled in several cases.

While in these early years the emphasis was on hymn singing, Mass settings were also being published, including four commissioned by the Advisory Committee from well-known composers, Seoirse Bodley, T.C. Kelly, Gerard Victory and Fintan O'Carroll.[75] Though not commissioned by the Advisory Committee, noted here is the Mass setting of Seán Ó Ríada, a Gael-Linn production, has been used extensively by parishes.[76]

Now the emphasis, endorsed in the deliberations of the Advisory Committee, was moving towards the singing of acclamations and the psalm. Margaret Daly, a member of the Advisory Committee and then director of music at the Institute, edited the hymnal *Alleluia! Amen!*[77] containing music used at worship at the Institute for Pastoral Liturgy. It was unique in its inclusion of music for the Liturgy of the Hours. Bishop Dermot O'Mahony in his foreword commented:

> It contains not only a selection of hymns, but also music for the parts of the Mass. It is perhaps the presentation of this hymnal, which makes it a significant step forward in the renewal of liturgical music in Ireland. Not only are the priorities for music in the Liturgy clearly indicated, but the notes which accompany each section provide the priest, the organist and the congregation with a kind of 'teach yourself' kit for understanding the role of music and song and its appropriate application to any specific celebration.[78]

The Advisory Committee has produced occasional memoranda and guidelines and here is noted the *Guidelines for Payment of*

Parish Church Musicians. First prepared and presented to the Episcopal Conference in December 2002. The rates have been updated annually and since 2006 the guidelines have been jointly published by the Advisory Committee and the Church Music Committee of the Church of Ireland Dioceses of Dublin and Glendalough.

The Advisory Committee produced *Seinn Alleluia 2000*, a collection of music for the Jubilee Year 2000 which was edited by Patrick O'Donoghue.[79] But the biggest project in recent years was the production of music for the third edition of the *Roman Missal*. The National Centre for Liturgy in association with the Advisory Committee, prepared *Sing the Mass*, an anthology of Mass settings, including new settings as well as older ones which were amended in line with the revised translation.[80] It was launched at the annual summer school of the Irish Church Music Association, five months before the use of the new edition of the *Roman Missal* and at a time when the Catholic Church in Ireland was preparing for the International Eucharistic Congress, held June 2012. Members of the Advisory Committee, staff and lecturers at the Centre took a very active part in the promotion of the music through the dioceses of the country. *Sing the Mass* is published in two editions, choir/people and accompaniment. A CD-ROM is included with the accompaniment edition. It also includes JPG images of congregational parts that may be reprinted for non-commercial use for congregations.[81]

The most recently established advisory committee is *an Coiste Comhairleach um an Liotúirge i nGaeilge*, formed in February 1993. Earlier translation work into Irish has been done on an *ad hoc* basis by individuals and working groups and it was decided to put in place an advisory committee enjoying the same status as the other commissions in liturgy, music and art and architecture.[82] The work of providing texts not translated was undertaken, including the *Collectio Missarum de Beata Maria Virgine*.[83] Several other texts had been translated, approved by the Episcopal Conference, but the *recognitio* of the Congregation for Divine Worship was not received.[84]

The task of providing an Irish language translation of the third edition of the *Missale Romanum* began with that translation of its *Institutio generalis*.[85] When the *Missale Romanum* became available in March 2002, translation of its texts commenced, according to the norms set out in *Liturgiam authenticam*. It was satisfying to note that the fuller translation required by this Instruction had already been honoured in *An Leabhar Aifrinnn* (1973). As segments were translated, they were submitted to the Episcopal Conference and then to the Congregation for Divine Worship and its review committee (*Sapienti*) which was set up in 2010. The translation of *Ordo Missae* was given the Roman *recognitio* and subsequently published.[86]

This brief account may not convey fully the enormous commitment and work of the members of the Irish language advisory committee under the able guidance of Canon John Terry. For instance, when the *Coiste* gathered to translate the *Missale Romanum*, it involved working throughout an entire afternoon, evening and following morning, eight times per year. There was also frustration when Irish language texts, approved by the Episcopal Conference, did not receive Roman *recognitio*.

The Contribution of Patrick Jones
In his service from 1992–2013 as Director of the National Centre for Liturgy and as Executive Secretary to the Council for Liturgy, Patrick Jones has made an enormous contribution to the liturgical life of Ireland through his dedication and commitment to the full and worthy celebration of liturgy, and to liturgical formation. Working with the Episcopal Conference, the Episcopal Commission for Liturgy and with their agencies in Liturgy, Church Music, Sacred Art and Architecture, and *Liotúirge i nGaeilge*, he strove to ensure that liturgy was given its rightful place of priority in the life of the Church, as well as at the table of the Episcopal Conference. At the same time, as Director of the National Centre for Liturgy, he maintained the ethos of welcome, hospitality, reflection, study and mission created by his predecessors – and friends – the late Seán Swayne and Seán Collins.

During his twenty-one years as National Secretary for Liturgy, much of his energy has been given to processing liturgical books for publication, and, in more recent years, the translation of the third edition of the *Roman Missal*. His years as Secretary oversaw many publications. The first books he worked on in 1992 were the *Order of Christian Funerals*, and then the *Rite of Baptism for Children*, this being a common edition for Ireland, England and Wales, and Scotland. He worked closely with his colleagues, who were also friends, in the liturgy offices of the neighbouring Conferences of Scotland, and of England and Wales. With them he facilitated the Roman submission of the revised *Sacramentary* as a common edition for the three Conferences in 1998. Prior to that he coordinated the process of comment and review of the eight segments of the *Sacramentary* as this was issued by ICEL, and guided it through the Episcopal Conference for its eventual approval. He was a member of ICEL's Advisory Board and Consultants' Committee, 1997–2003.

Working with Veritas Publications, he succeeded his close friend, the late Fr Brian Magee, in editing the annual *Liturgical Calendar* (Ordo) since 2004. He has been writing a monthly 'Liturgy Page' for *Intercom* since September 1999. At the request of Veritas, he edited *At the Breaking of Bread* for the Year of the Eucharist.[87]

Other publications linked with the new edition of the *Roman Missal* and to which he contributed, include *Celebrating the Mystery of Faith: A Guide to the Mass* (based on the *General Instruction of the Roman Missal*); *The New Missal: Explaining the Changes*; *Sing the Mass* (an anthology of music for the *Roman Missal*), and *Celebrating the Mass throughout the Year*.

While the earlier Diploma course at Mount St Anne's and Carlow enjoyed the recognition of the Faculty of Theology at Maynooth, Jones worked towards the recognition of the programmes of the Centre at Award level by the Pontifical University when the Centre transferred to Maynooth in 1996. To this also was added the Higher Diploma in Pastoral Liturgy and a Master's programme in Theology, specialising in Liturgy.

He was also instrumental in forging the association of the Liturgy Centre with Diploma in Arts (Church Music) programme offered through the Department of Music, Maynooth University.

Patrick Jones organised many outreach programmes over the years, and liturgical formation outside of the National Centre for Liturgy was strengthened as a result. He continuously emphasised the need to invest in liturgical formation so that dioceses and parishes have structures to ensure good liturgy. Liturgy and liturgical formation were at the centre of his life. He often quotes what Pope Paul VI said on the day that the Constitution on the Sacred Liturgy was promulgated at the end of the second period of Vatican II Council:

> Treated before all others, in a sense [the sacred liturgy] has a priority over all others for its intrinsic dignity and importance to the life of the Church and today we will solemnly promulgate the document on the liturgy. Our spirit, therefore, exults with true joy, for in this way things have gone we note respect for a right scale of values and duties. God must hold first place; prayer to him is our first duty. The liturgy is the first source of the divine communion in which God shares his own life with us. It is also the first school of the spiritual life. The liturgy is the first gift we must make to the Christian people united to us by faith and the fervour of their prayers.[88]

These words, essentially, that the liturgy is the summit and source of all our Christian activity, were the charter that guided Jones as executive secretary to the Council for Liturgy and director of the National Centre for Liturgy. They were part of the legacy he generated in his students coming from over thirty countries. They encapsulate the vision of *Sacrosanctum concilium* to this day which the now Blessed Paul VI was tasked with embedding in the Church post Vatican II.

Patrick Jones steps down from posts in which he selflessly served the Irish Church, having consolidated the work of both his predecessors and secured the place of liturgical formation in the Church in Ireland. He now is parish priest of St Columba's Parish, Iona Road, Dublin where he continues the work of the liturgy in a parish setting which always was the focus and his interest in his work at the Centre.

Notes

1. Ireland was represented by Archbishop Joseph Walsh of Tuam (1940–1969), who had been a consultor with the Council's preparatory commission on liturgy, attended the four Council sessions. He became of the first president of the Episcopal Commission for Liturgy when formed in response to SC.

2. For an overview of the history of ICEL and the role it played in the translation of liturgical text since its inception, see Thomas R. Whelan, 'Liturgy Reform since Vatican II: The Role Played by Bishops in the English-Speaking World', *Questions Liturgiques 95* (2014), 81–109.

3. While most of the *editiones typicae* were translated by ICEL, the Divine Office was translated in these islands and is often known as the Headingly-Glenstal translation. *The Rite of Marriage* was translated by a group of Irish scholars and pastors.
    The Irish translation of *Missale Romanum* and *Ordo Lectionum Missae* were also prepared, with much of the work been done by priests in St Patrick's College, Maynooth. Monsignor Padraig Ó Fiannachta prepared *An Leabhar Aifrinn* and several other ritual books. *An Leiceanáir* was prepared by Dr Cathal Ó Háinle. The translation of various books of the Bible had begun many years previously and would become *An Bíobla Naofa*, published 1981 under the general editorship of Mgr Ó Fiannachta. Both Mgr Ó Fiannachta and Dr Ó Háinle have contributed greatly to the work of *an Coiste Comhairleach um an Liotúirge i nGaeilge* [Advisory Committee on Liturgy in the Irish Language].

4. Seán Swayne was born in Charters Towers, Queensland, Australia, 9 May 1933. His father had emigrated to Australia and later returned to Ireland with his family. Seán grew up in Ballon, Co. Carlow, attending the local national school and Knockbeg College. He was ordained in 1957 after having completed studies in science and theology at St Patrick's College, Maynooth. He had served as a consultor to ICEL, a role he served in also with the Congregation for Divine Worship. He was later honoured with the title of Monsignor. In Graignamanagh, he took a special interest in the restored 13th-century church, Duiske Abbey. He edited *New Liturgy* from its

beginning in 1968 to 1986. Among his books are *Communion* (Dublin: Veritas, 1974), *Gather Around the Lord* (Dublin: Columba Press, 1987), and *The Old Grey Mouse, Graignamanagh Remembered* (Graignamanagh, Abbey Centre, 1991). He was editor of *The Sacraments: A Pastoral Directory* (Dublin: Veritas, 1976), and *Pocket Book of Blessings* (Dublin: Columba Press, 1995). He died after a short illness on 2 May 1996. Idir dhá láimh Chríost go raibh sé [May he be between the two hands of Christ].

For a more comprehensive overview of the thought of Swayne, see an annotated version of a previously unpublished article of his, 'The Continuing Liturgical Education of Clergy and People', found elsewhere in this volume.

5. From notes by Seán Swayne lodged in the archives of the National Centre for Liturgy.
6. *New Liturgy* was published from autumn 1968 as the bulletin of the diocesan liturgy commission before it became a national bulletin in spring 1974.
7. Quoted in Patrick Jones, 'Seán Swayne (1933–1996)', *New Liturgy* 90-91-92 (1996), 5.
8. *New Liturgy*, 2 (1974), 3. Sister Dolores Fitzgerald RSM, Carlow, was appointed as assistant to Mgr Swayne, and she worked at Mount St Anne's in Portarlington, and then later in Carlow.
9. Archbishop Joseph Cunnane, archbishop of Tuam 1969–1987, and Chair of the Episcopal Commission for Liturgy, preached at the opening Mass. He strongly supported the establishment of the Institute, and later its move to Carlow. The programme was devised by Mgr Swayne who was greatly helped by Fr Patrick McGoldrick, Professor of Liturgy at St Patrick's College, Maynooth from 1967 until his retirement in 1998 and a fellow student at the Institut Superieur de Liturgie in Paris, and by Fr Liam Walsh OP, later Professor of Sacramental Theology in Fribourg, Switzerland – both of whom have contributed to this *Festschrift*. Mgr Swayne noted that 'Fr Crichton helped later to finalise the planning' (from his notes, referred to in note 5, above). J.D. Crichton (1907–2001), author, retired pastor of Pershore, Worcestershire, editor of the journal of the Society of St Gregory (1952–72) and respected as the doyen of liturgists in these islands, strongly stressed the importance of the pastoral aspect of the programme, as well as the work and title of the Institute. Patrick McGoldrick, a priest of the diocese of Derry, gave enormous support to the Institute at each of its three homes. He served on ICEL's advisory committee, 1984–91, including on its working group on translation.
10. In 1980, Sr Gerard (Eileen) McLoughlin RSM, who had taught at Mount Lourdes Grammar School, Enniskillen, succeeded Margaret

Daly-Denton. The present author was appointed a staff member in 1993, which includes the responsibility of direction of music.

11. From his notes, referred to in 5, above. The notes describe in detail the renovations of Junior House of the College into the new Institute.

12. See Richard Hurley, 'The Eucharist Room at Carlow Liturgy Center', *Worship* 70 (1996), 238–50.

13. See Moira Bergin, 'May Seminars 1972–1996. A Study of the People and Issues in Liturgical Renewal', unpublished MTh thesis, Pontifical University, St Patrick's College, Maynooth, 2003.

14. See Julie Kavanagh, 'The Glenstal Liturgical Congresses 1954–1975', *Worship* 72 (1998), 421–44. From its foundation at Mount St Anne's, the National Centre for Liturgy (as it is now called) has enjoyed great support and friendship with Glenstal Abbey. Fr Placid Murray OSB and the late Fr Vincent Ryan OSB taught at the Centre for many years from its inaugural programme in 1974. Later, Fr Seán Ó Duinn OSB also taught there and was a member of *an Coiste Comlairleach um an Liotúirge i nGaeilge*. Father Columba McCann OSB served for some years as a part-time member of staff and continues to teach on the programme.

15. Seán Collins was born in Ennis, Co. Clare on 20 October 1945. He entered the Franciscan Order, making his solemn profession in 1966 and was ordained priest in 1972. He studied at University College Galway, the Catholic University of Louvain, and the Antonianum in Rome before taking a doctorate in liturgy at Sant Anselmo, Rome in 1982. He taught at the Antonianum and the Beda College before returning to teach at the Milltown Institute. He fulfilled various services in the Irish Franciscan province, including those of assistant novice master, guardian at Multyfarnham Abbey, definitor and vicar provincial. He was appointed general secretary of the Order, taking up the post in January 2007 but returned to Ireland with serious illness in the following July. He died on 24 December 2007. *Ar dheis Dé go raibh a anam uasal* [May his gentle soul be at the right hand of God].

16. The *Liturgical Calendar for Ireland* was approved by the Congregation for Divine Worship in October 1988. The prayer texts, published in 2009, appear in a slightly amended form in the third edition of the *Roman Missal*, 2011.

17. See Patrick Jones, 'Fr Seán Collins OFM (1945–2007). A Tribute to a Friend and Colleague', *New Liturgy* 136 (2007), 2–3.

18. Patrick Jones, son of John (Jack) Jones and Mary Warde, born 14 August 1943, grew up in Greystones, attended the Holy Faith and Christian Brothers Schools before secondary education at St Brendan's School, Bray. He entered the seminary of Clonliffe College

in October 1961, taking a Degree in Philosophy at UCD and in theology, awarded by the Angelicum University, Rome. He was ordained priest on 26 May 1968, and served as chaplain and, later, curate in Castledermot, Co. Kildare, 1968–1975. Sometime after that he was appointed 'parish chaplain' in the parish of Marino, Dublin, for a few years in the late 1970s and early 1980s. He studied at the Pontifical Liturgical Institute at Sant Anselmo, Rome, 1975–78 and has taught at Clonliffe College, Mater Dei Institute, and the National Centre for Liturgy.

19. Bernard Botte, *From Silence to Participation* (Washington, DC: Pastoral Press, 1988), 57.

20. The Liturgical Movement has been a particular interest of Patrick Jones [see note 23, below]. For a summary of its history, see Virgil Funk, 'The Liturgical Movement (1830–1969)', *The New Dictionary of Sacramental Worship*, Peter E. Fink, ed. (Dublin, Gill and Macmillan, 1990), 695–715. See also Kathleen Hughes, *How Firm a Foundation: Voices of the Early Liturgical Movement* (Chicago: Liturgy Training Publications, 1990), and Robert L. Tuzik, *How Firm a Foundation: Leaders of the Liturgical Movement* (Chicago: Liturgy Training Publications, 1990).

21. See R. Kevin Seasoltz, ed., *The New Liturgy: A Documentation 1903 to 1965* (New York, Herder & Herder, 1966), 3–10. The use of the expression here included engagement and activity whereas in later writings 'participation' was used in a more spiritualised sense.

22. See Seasoltz, *The New Liturgy*, 107–159.

23. The most complete research of the Liturgical Movement in Ireland has been undertaken by Patrick Jones, 'Irish Traditions and Liturgical Renewal from 1903 to 1962', Rome: Pontifical Liturgical Institute at Sant Anselmo, unpublished tessina, 1977. The work was prepared under the direction of the late Anscar J. Chupungco OSB. For an overview of the years since the Council, see Patrick Jones, '*Sacrosanctum Concilium* at Fifty: Reports from Five English-Speaking Countries – Ireland', *Worship* 87 (2013), 503–9. See also the review and assessment by Eugene Duffy, 'The Reception of the Conciliar Liturgical Reforms in Ireland', *Questions Liturgiques* 95 (2014), 110–27.

24. See John Fennelly, *The People's Mass Book* [original title: *The Children's Mass Book*] (Dublin: Gill, 1952).

25. These comments are made, respectively, by J. B. O'Connell in supplementary material to Joseph A. Jungmann, *Liturgical Renewal* (London: Burns, 1965), 45, and by Austin Flannery in a very fine introduction on the Liturgical Movement and architecture in Richard Hurley and Wilfrid Cantwell, *Contemporary Irish Church*

Architecture (Dublin: Gill and Macmillan, 1985), 12. For a fuller account of John Fennelly, see Patrick Jones, 'John Fennelly 1890–1966', *New Liturgy* 55 (1987), 13–16. In this personal reflection, he suggests that a lasting reminder of John Fennelly is the hymn 'Christ be near at either hand' which is set to an Irish traditional tune 'aptly called *Greystones* in our Office Book'.

26. See Patrick Jones, 'Spring follows Winter', *New Liturgy* 89 (1996), 3.
27. Patrick Jones, 'National Centre for Liturgy', *New Liturgy* 90-91-92 (1996), 13. The Episcopal Commission for Liturgy (Bishops Joseph Duffy, John Magee, Fiachra Ó Ceallaigh and Bill Murphy) was involved with this move and gave it their full support in 1995–1996 when it became the most viable option.
28. See Patrick Jones, 'National Centre for Liturgy', *New Liturgy* 106 (2000), 2.
29. Overseas scholars included Professor Paul Bradshaw, Professor John Baldovin, Dr R. Kevin Seasoltz and Dr Jan Michel Joncas.
30. See Patrick Jones, 'Three remarks', *New Liturgy* 112 (2001), 3.
31. Quoted in Jones, '*Sacrosanctum Concilium* at Fifty – Ireland', 505.
32. *Altar Missal*, produced by Benzinger Brothers, New York and adapted for use in Ireland (published by Geoffrey Chapman, London, Dublin, and Melbourne).
33. See a diary of significant events for the twenty years after the promulgation of SC, Seán Swayne, 'Liturgical Renewal in Ireland 1963–1983', *New Liturgy* 40–41 (1983–1984), 12–29.
34. These were co-published and approved for use in the dioceses of England and Wales, Scotland and Ireland. The current second edition was published in 1981. The main work of publication was done in England but it is worth noting that Bishop Michael Harty was one of the two who gave the *imprimatur*. Bishop Harty, while Dean at St Patrick's College, Maynooth, 1947–67, edited the annual *Liturgical Calendar* and acted as Secretary to the Episcopal Commission for Liturgy. Ordained bishop of Killaloe in 1967, he was appointed to that Commission, serving until his death on 8 August 1994. He was also a member of ICEL's Episcopal Board, 1967–1989.

Bishop Harty was the first of four Chairs or Presidents of the Episcopal Commission in which Patrick Jones served as Secretary. Bishop Joseph Duffy, Clogher, who had been a member and Chair (1984–95) of the Advisory Committee on Sacred Art and Architecture and a member of the Episcopal Commission for Liturgy (1981–1986), was appointed Chair after Bishop Harty. In December 1997, Bishop John Magee became Chair, having been a member of the Episcopal Commission since shortly after been ordained bishop of Cloyne in 1987. On his resignation as Bishop of Cloyne, Patrick

Jones wrote of him, 'Bishop Magee rarely missed any meetings of the Commission and the Irish Commission for Liturgy and undertook his duties with great care, which included reporting to the Episcopal Conference on the deliberations of the Commissions and the Advisory Committees' (*New Liturgy* 145–146 [2010], 32–3). The current Chair, Bishop Martin Drennan, Galway, succeeded Bishop Magee.

35. Fr William Yeomans SJ was chief editor, with Liam Miller, designer and typographer, Fr John Whelan, Dublin liturgist, and Eileen Power, editorial assistant.

36. *Roman Missal* (Dublin: Liturgical Books, 1974).

37. *An Leabhar Aifrinn Rómánach* (Maigh Nuad: An Sagart, 1973).

38. This material is taken from the *relatio* prepared by Patrick Jones for the submission of the *Revised Sacramentary* in December 1998 and now lodged in the archive of the National Centre for Liturgy.

39. *The Celebration of Marriage: Gnás an Phósadh* (Dublin: Veritas, 1970). A revised and extended edition was published by Veritas in 1980.

40. *Rite of Baptism for Children: Órd an Bhaiste le haghaidh na Leanaí* (Dublin: Catholic Communications Institute/Veritas, 1971). Later it was published for England and Wales, Scotland and Ireland in a common edition, *Rite of Baptism for Children* (Dublin, Veritas; London, Geoffrey Chapman, 1992).

41. *Rite of Penance: Gnás na hAithrí* (Dublin: Veritas, 1976).

42. *Rite of Anointing and Pastoral Care of the Sick* (Dublin: Liturgical Books, 1974). This interim book was later replaced by *Pastoral Care of the Sick and Dying* (Dublin: Veritas, 1983).

43. *Exposition and Benediction of the Blessed Sacrament: Taispeáint agus Beannacht na Naomh-Shacraiminte* (Carlow: Irish Institute of Pastoral Liturgy, 1982).

44. *Rite of Funerals: Deasghnátha na Marbh* (Dublin: Veritas, 1972).

45. *Order of Christian Funerals* (Dublin: Veritas, 1991).

46. From early on, ICEL itself realised that the task of translating liturgical text required continued reflection and critique, and that this meant that the 'first generation' of English language liturgical Ritual Books, which were often produced in a short space of time as bishops often required English texts quickly after the reformed Rites were published in their Latin *editiones typicae*. The Episcopal Board of ICEL (representing eleven full-member English-speaking Bishops' Conferences throughout the world) soon asked for revised translations that would respond to their specific pastoral needs and incorporate extra prayer texts, as permitted by liturgical law. These revised translations were known as 'second generation' books. Much

of Patrick Jones' time was occupied with this work, both as a Consultant with ICEL, and as National Secretary. See, John R. Page, 'ICEL, 1966–1989: Weaving the Words of Our Common Christian Prayer', *Shaping English Liturgy: Studies in Honour of Archbishop Denis Hurley*, Peter C. Finn and James M. Schellman, eds (Washington, DC: Pastoral Press, 1990), 473–89, esp. 486–9.

47. *Christian Burial* (Mount St Anne's Liturgy Centre, 1976/Irish Institute of Pastoral Liturgy, 1983).

48. *Rite of Christian Initiation of Adults* (London: Geoffrey Chapman/ Dublin: Veritas, 1987).

49. *The Divine Office* in three volumes was a co-publication by Collins, London; E. J. Dwyer, Sydney; and Talbot, Dublin. It is approved for use in Australia, England and Wales, Ireland, New Zealand and Scotland. The design is by the late Liam Millar, who also designed the English edition of the *Roman Missal*.

50. *Roman Pontifical* (Washington, DC: 1978).

51. This involves working closely with Bishop Diarmuid Ó Suilleabháin and, after his death, Bishop Bill Murphy who, as members of ICEL's episcopal board, had responsibility for processing each segment for the approval of the Conference.

52. The Irish Episcopal Conference worked closely with those of England and Wales, and of Scotland. This material is taken from the *relatio* prepared by Patrick Jones for the submission of the revised *Sacramentary* in December 1998 and lodged in the archive of the National Centre for Liturgy.

53. Irish Catholic Bishops' Conference, *General Instruction of the Roman Missal* (Dublin: Irish Liturgical Publications, 2005). Some minor adaptations had been accepted for Ireland, e.g., wood for the altar, wood, stone or metal for sacred furnishings, white as an optional colour at Masses for the Dead.

54. Congregation for Divine Worship and the Discipline of the Sacraments, *Liturgam authenticam*, Fifth Instruction on the Right Implementation of *Sacrosancum concilium* (SC 36), effective 25 April 2001.

55. National Centre for Liturgy, *Celebrating the Mystery of Faith: A Guide to the Mass* (Dublin: Irish Liturgical Publications, 2005; rev. ed. Dublin, Veritas, 2011).

56. ICEL's Constitution, by mandate from Rome, was replaced by new Statutes, approved in 2002, which created new structures of the Commission. Bishop John McAreavey of Dromore was the Irish member of the Episcopal Board of ICEL during this period.

57. For statement and other material, see 'The *Roman Missal*, Update', *New Liturgy* 148-149 (2010–2011), 5–13.

58. National Centre for Liturgy, *The New Missal, Explaining the Changes* (Dublin: Veritas, 2011). Patrick Jones was assisted by Moira Bergin, Julie Kavanagh and Liam Tracey.

59. National Centre for Liturgy, *Celebrating the Mass through the Year* (Dublin: Veritas, 2011).

60. Using his regular 'Liturgy Page', *Intercom* as well as through the pages of *New Liturgy*, Patrick Jones kept readers informed of the work of translation of the Missal since shortly after Rome mandated this new version in 2001.

61. *The Roman Missal* (Dublin: Veritas, 2011).

62. The Centre had also been involved with the International Eucharistic Congress held at Lourdes in 1981 when it was given responsibility for the planning and organisation of liturgies in the English language.

63. *The Furrow*, July 1966, and Austin Flannery OP, ed., *Liturgy, Renewal and Adaptation* (Dublin: Scepter Books, 1966), 70*–75*. The earlier edition of this commentary, *Vatican II, The Liturgy Constitution*, edited by Austin Flannery OP (1925–2008) was published in April 1964, making it one of the first commentaries to appear on SC. His edition of the sixteen constitutions and decrees of Vatican II (*Vatican Council II: Conciliar and Post-Conciliar Documents* [Dublin: Dominican Publications – various editions]) is often simply known as 'Flannery'.

64. Irish Episcopal Commission for Liturgy, *Pastoral Directory on the Building and Reorganistion of Churches* (Dublin: Veritas, 1972). Cardinal Cahal Daly, who served as the chair of the Advisory Committee wrote the Foreword. Later his successor, Bishop Joseph Duffy, contributed the Foreword to 1994 edition.

65. Congregation for Divine Worship, *Notitiae* 8 (1972), 171–7.

66. Annibale Bugnini, *The Reform of the Liturgy 1948–1975* (Collegeville, MN: Liturgical Press, 1990), 856.

67. Irish Episcopal Commission for Liturgy, *The Place of Worship: Pastoral Directory on the Building and Reorganistion of Churches* (Dublin: Veritas; Carlow, Irish Institute of Pastoral Liturgy, 1994).

68. Department for the Environment, Heritage and Local Government, *Architectural Heritage Protection. Guidelines for the Planning Authorities* (Dublin: Government Publications Office, 2005).

69. From notes supplied by Canon John Terry, who had served, from 1976, for some seventeen years as Secretary of the Advisory Committee on Church Music. He was asked to resign this post in order to become *Rúnaí* [Secretary] of *an Coiste Comhairleach um an Liotúirge i nGaeilge* which was created by the Episcopal Commission for Liturgy in February 1993. He has also been a long-serving member of the Irish Commission for Liturgy/Council for Liturgy.

70. *New Liturgy Hymn Book*, prepared and published by the Sacred Commission established by the Irish Hierarchy, 1966, foreword. As president of the Episcopal Conference, Cardinal William Conway oversaw the implementation of Vatican II which he had attended. He died 17 April 1977.

71. The *College Hymnal,* edited by Fr Séamus O'Byrne, St Peter's College, Wexford, published in 1964, was probably the first hymnal to be published after Vatican II. The editor was secretary of the Church Music panel.

72. *The Veritas Hymnal* (Dublin: Veritas, 1973), 'commissioned by the National Commission for Sacred Music and approved by the Irish Church Music Association'. It was reprinted several times, including as recently as 2010.

73. Since the beginning of its foundation the Association has conducted a summer school each year, with a gathering of church musicians, choir directors and choir members from all over Ireland and has a membership of up to two hundred and fifty. The ICMA also publishes some liturgical music. The Association published its own quarterly magazine *Hosanna* from autumn 1975 until 1985.

74. Gerard T. Gillen, 'Looking Back, Looking Forward', *New Liturgy* 98 (1998), 5.

75. The four Masses were published by the Irish Commission for Liturgy Music Panel: Seóirse Bodley, *Mass of Peace* (1976); T.C. Kelly, *Mass for Peace* (1976); Gerard Victory, *Mass of the Resurrection* (1977) and Fintan P. O'Carroll, *Mass of the Immaculate Conception* (1977). For a detailed survey of music settings of Mass in both Irish and English languages, see the contribution of John O'Keeffe to this volume, 'Singing the Mass: Mass Composition in Ireland Since Vatican II'.

76. *Ceol an Aifrinn* (Dublin: Gael Linn, 1971). It includes the well-known *Ár nAthair* and *Ag Críost an Síol* and predates the introduction of acclamations in the Eucharistic Prayer.

77. *Alleluia! Amen! Music for the Liturgy*, Margaret Daly, ed. (Dublin: Veritas, 1978). A supplement to this hymnal was published in 1981.

78. *Alleluia! Amen! Music for the Liturgy*, 6.

79. *Seinn Alleluia 2000, Music for the Jubilee Year*, Patrick O'Donoghue, ed. (Dublin: Columba Press, 1999).

80. The National Centre for Liturgy in association with the Advisory Committee on Church Music, *Sing the Mass: Anthology of Music for the Irish Church* (Dublin: Veritas, 2011). Four new settings were included: Mass of St Paul (Ephrem Feeley), The Glendalough Mass (Liam Lawton), Mass of St Columba (Columba McCann) and Mass of Renewal (Bernard Sexton). Among the amended settings were

Mass of Peace (Seóirse Bodley), Mass of Our Lady of Lourdes (Paul Décha, Jean-Paul Lécot, Lucien Deiss) and Mass of the Immaculate Conception (Fintan O'Carroll).

81. For a review of this anthology, see Thomas R. Whelan, 'Singing the Mass', *The Furrow* 62 (2011), 587–94

82. See Seán Terry and Patrick Jones, 'CCLG, fiche bliain d'aois', *New Liturgy* 155–156 (2012), 27–31. The support of the Episcopal Commission for Liturgy (Bishops Michael Harty, Joseph Duffy, Diarmuid Ó Súilleabháin, and John Magee, with Patrick Jones, secretary) is acknowledged. John Terry, who was appointed secretary of the new Advisory Committee, writes, 'While Bishops Joseph Duffy and Diarmuid Ó Súilleabháin were acknowledged scholars in Gaeilge, all were committed to the establishment of such an advisory committee, including Patrick Jones, who admits that he is a man of "cúpla focal"' (from notes supplied to the author).

83. As well as twenty-eight Masses from the *Collectio*, published as *Díolaim d'Aifrinn na Maighdine Beannaithe Muire* (An Daingean: An Sagart, 2000), other published texts included *Leabhar Póca Beannachtaí* (1993), *Léachtaí do Dheasghnátha na Marbh* (1995), *An Pósadh: treoracha, léachtaí, guí an phobail* (1996), all published by An Sagart.

84. In particular, *Deasghnátha na Marbh*, which contained a translation of much of *The Order of Christian Burial*. Two other texts, *Paidir Eocairisteach d'Aifrinn do Riachtanais agus Ócáidí Éagsúla*, submitted for *recognitio* in 1992 and in a revised form in 2002, and *Féilire Naoimh na hÉireann*, submitted 1998 and in a revised form in 2007, await *recognitio* as part of the new edition of *An Leabhar Aifrinn*.

85. A draft translation was published in *Irisleabhar Mhá Nuad* (An Daingean: An Sagart, 2001).

86. *Ord an Aifrinn* (Baile Átha Cliath: Veritas, 2011). Segments on Advent, Christmas, and some of Ordinary Time also received *recognitio* and were published.

87. Patrick Jones, ed., *At the Breaking of Bread: Homilies on the Eucharist* (Dublin: Veritas, 2005).

88. *Documents on the Liturgy 1963–1979, Conciliar, Papal, and Curial Texts*, International Commission on English in the Liturgy, trans. (Collegeville, MN: Liturgical Press, 1982), 27.

CONTRIBUTORS

ℨ ℨ ℨ

John F. Baldovin is a Jesuit priest and Professor of Historical and Liturgical Theology at Boston College School of Theology and Ministry. He has also taught at Fordham University, the Jesuit School of Theology at Berkeley, as well as at various other places as a visiting professor. Father Baldovin served on the US Catholic Bishops Advisory Committee on the Liturgy as well as on the advisory committee of ICEL from 1994–2003. He has been president of the North American Academy of Liturgy, of the international ecumenical Societas Liturgica, and of the Jungmann Society for Jesuits and Liturgy. He has published a number of essays and reviews in theological journals. Along with Edward Foley, Mary Collins and Joanne Pierce he edited a commentary on the new translation of the order of Mass, published by Liturgical Press in 2012. His latest book is *Reforming the Liturgy: A Response to the Critics* (2008).

Moira Bergin has been a staff member of the National Centre for Liturgy since 1993. A native of Camross, Co. Laois, she is a Sister of Mercy, joining the community in Borris-in-Ossory and now in Maynooth. She studied piano at the Royal Academy of Music (LRAM), theology and music at St Patrick's College, Maynooth (BATh) and education (H Dip Ed) and Church music (Dip Arts – Church Music) at NUIM. Bergin is an accomplished composer of psalmody. In 2003 she received MTh in liturgy from the Pontifical University at Maynooth. She serves as a member of the Council for Liturgy and the Advisory Committee on Church Music, agencies of the Irish Episcopal Conference. She is also a council member of the Irish Church Music Association (ICMA).

Paul F. Bradshaw is Emeritus Professor of Liturgy at the University of Notre Dame, USA, priest-vicar emeritus of Westminster Abbey, and an honorary canon of the Episcopal Diocese of Northern Indiana. He has been a member of Societas Liturgica since 1977, serving on its Council from 1989 to 2005 and as President, 1993–95. He was also editor-in-chief of *Studia Liturgica* from 1987 to 2005. His most recent book is *Rites of Ordination: Their History and Theology* (2013).

Margaret Daly-Denton holds degrees in music, liturgy and Scripture, and is a well-known organist and composer. Her *Alleluia, Amen: Music for the Liturgy* (1978) was a seminal resource and her music for the Liturgy of the Hours is sung in monasteries world-wide. She was Director of Music at the Irish Institute of Pastoral Liturgy from 1975 until 1980, and served extensively on the International Committee on English in the Liturgy (ICEL). Her doctoral thesis from Trinity College Dublin (TCD) on early Christian reception of the psalms was published as *David in the Fourth Gospel: The Johannine Reception of the Psalms* (2000). She has taught Bible and liturgy at various institutions in Ireland including The Church of Ireland Theological College, The Milltown Institute, and the Priory Institute. She is currently the Wallace Adjunct Assistant Professor in the Department of Religions and Theology at TCD. Among her recent publications is *Psalm-Shaped Prayerfulness: A Guide to the Christian Reception of the Psalms* (2009), and she is currently completing a volume for the 'Earth Bible Commentary' series, *'Supposing Him to Be the Gardener': An Earth-Conscious Reading of the Fourth Gospel (forthcoming)*.

Gerard Gillen is Emeritus Professor of Music at Maynooth University and has been Titular Organist of Dublin's Pro-Cathedral since 1976. A graduate of UCD, the University of Oxford and the Royal Conservatoire of Music, Antwerp, he has an international reputation as an organ recitalist. Visiting John Betts Fellow at Oxford in 1992, Gillen has been chair of the National Episcopal Advisory Committee on Church Music for many years, and has written extensively on matters relating to the organ and its place in the liturgy. He was subject editor for Catholic Church for the *Encyclopaedia of Music in Ireland* (2013).

Patrick Hannon is a priest of the diocese of Cloyne and emeritus professor of moral theology at Maynooth College. He holds doctorates in theology (Maynooth) and law (Cambridge) and is a member of the Irish Bar. He has written extensively on issues at the intersection of religion, law and politics, and his publications include *Church, State, Morality and Law* (Dublin and Westminster MD, 1992). *Right or Wrong: Essays in Moral Theology* (Dublin, 2009) is his most recent book. He is currently parish chaplain in Donabate, Co Dublin, and teaches courses at Mater Dei Institute, Dublin City University, and the Loyola Institute, Trinity College, Dublin.

Wilfrid John Harrington, STM, LSS, is a Dominican. He is Emeritus Professor of Scripture at Dominican House of Studies, Tallaght; Senior Lecturer at Milltown Institute; and Visiting Lecturer at Church of Ireland Theological College. He lectured at the Liturgy Centre from its beginning until 2013, and is author of over fifty books – mainly in the area of biblical studies. Among his more recent books are, *What Was Mark At? A Commentary* (2008); *Jesus Our Brother: The Humanity of the Lord* (2010); and *The Loving God* (2012).

Julie Kavanagh has been a member of the panel of lecturers of the National Centre for Liturgy since 1997 and has extensive experience lecturing in the area of liturgy, ministry and sacramental theology in Ireland and abroad, both in academic institutions as well as in parish and diocesan forums. She has been a visiting lecturer at the Margaret Beaufort Institute, Cambridge, and was a member of the Theological Commission for the International Eucharistic Congress 2012. Kavanagh serves on the Council for Liturgy of the Episcopal Conference of Ireland and is currently employed as a resource person for Kildare and Leighlin Faith Development Services. She contributes to journals such as *Worship*, *New Liturgy* and *Anaphora*, and has contributed chapters to publication of the National Centre for Liturgy such as, *Celebrating the Mystery of Faith* (2005) and *Celebrating the Mass Throughout the Year* (2011). Among her books are *Prayer for Parish Groups* (1999), *A Welcome for Your Child* (2008), and *Signposts on the Road to Emmaus: An Exploration of the Mass* (2012).

John Keating is a member of the Irish Province of Carmelites, living in Rome. From 1988 until 2002 he was a lecturer in liturgy and Carmelite spirituality at the Milltown Institute of Philosophy and Theology in Dublin. He was also a guest lecturer at the National Centre for Liturgy in Carlow and St Patrick's College, Maynooth. Until moving to Rome in 2007 he was a member of the Irish Commission for Liturgy for nine years. In 2007 he was elected General Councillor for Europe for his Order, a position he still holds, and from 2007 until 2013 was the Order's Delegate for Formation.

Hugh P. Kennedy studied at Queen's University, Belfast, the Gregorian University, Rome, and at the Institut Supérieur de Liturgie, Paris. He was awarded a Doctorate by the Pontifical University, Maynooth for his thesis on *The Stowe Missal*. Kennedy has contributed to various journals, as well as to the important collection of essays, *Prex Eucharistica: Studia*, vol. 3 (2005). He served on the Irish Episcopal Commission for Liturgy and on the Advisory Committee on Art and Architecture and was a founding member of the Ulster Historic Churches' Trust. He is the Administrator of St Peter's

Cathedral, Belfast and at present is also pursuing studies in Spirituality at Heythrop College, University of London.

Brendan McConvery is a member of the Irish Province of the Redemptorists. He studied Scripture in Rome and Jerusalem and taught for many years at St Patrick's College, Maynooth and at the National Centre for Liturgy. He has published *Redemptorists in Ireland 1851–2011* (2012) and, in association with Ciaran O'Callaghan, *The Three Faces of Christ: Reading the Sunday Gospels with the Liturgical Year* (2013). He is currently working on a history of the interpretation of the Song of Songs.

Patrick McGolderick, a presbyter of the diocese of Derry, is Professor Emeritus of Liturgy at St. Patrick's College, Maynooth, the first person to be appointed to this post in 1967. After his retirement from Maynooth in 1998, he returned to his diocese where he took up pastoral ministry. A student with Seán Swayne at the Institut Supérieur de Liturgie in Paris, he later worked closely with him in Portarlington and Carlow on the creation of the earlier structure and programmes for liturgical renewal in Ireland. He was a member of the National Commission on Liturgy of the Episcopal Conference from its inception until recently, and also served on the Advisory Board of ICEL from 1984 to 1991, including on its working group on translation. Among his edited publications is *Understanding the Eucharist: Papers of the Maynooth Union Summer School 1968* (1969).

Michael Mullins has taught a course on 'Praying the Psalms' in the National Centre for Liturgy for the last thirty seven years. He was formerly Professor of Scripture and President of St John's College Waterford, and lecturer and Associate Professor of Scripture in the Pontifical University of Maynooth. He is author of *Called to be Saints: Christian Living in First Century Rome* (1991), a study of the moral teaching of the first Roman Christians; as well as commentaries on all four gospels and the

Acts of the Apostles. He is a regular contributor to *Scripture in Church* and is currently parish priest of Ballybricken in Waterford city.

Daniel Murphy was appointed Executive Secretary of the Council for Liturgy and Director of the National Centre for Liturgy in September 2013. A native of Macroom, Co. Cork was ordained presbyter for the local church of Cloyne in 1991 and served as curate at St Colman's Cathedral, Cobh and as Cathedral and Diocesan Master of Ceremonies. He studied at St John's University, Collegeville where he completed an MA in Liturgical Studies in 2000. He was the Cloyne Diocesan Director of Liturgy on his return and in 2004 was appointed the Director of the Cloyne Commission for Liturgical Formation. He has served as a member of the Council for Liturgy since 1999.

Neil Xavier O'Donoghue is a presbyter of the Archdiocese of Newark, NJ. He has studied at Seton Hall University and has graduate qualifications in the field of liturgical studies from St. Vladimir's Orthodox Theological Seminary and the University of Notre Dame. He earned a doctorate in theology from St. Patrick's College, Maynooth. He is author of *St. Patrick His Confession and Other Works* (2009), *The Eucharist in Pre-Norman Ireland* (2011), and is a frequent contributor to various theological journals and collections of essays. Currently he serves as Vice Rector at Redemptoris Mater House of Formation in the Archdiocese of Armagh, Ireland, and as a Parochial Vicar at Holy Redeemer Parish in Dundalk.

John O'Keeffe is Director of Sacred Music at the National Seminary of St Patrick's College, Maynooth and Director of Choral Groups at Maynooth University. His doctoral work was a study on *Music and Text in the Mass Settings of Seán and Peadar Ó Riada: Models, Modes and Motifs* (2007). Co-director, with Professor Liam Tracey, of the Pontifical University's 'Master's in Liturgical Music' programme, he also co-ordinates the 'Diploma in Church Music' programme offered by Maynooth University in conjunction with the National Centre for Liturgy. Editor of the Church music collection *Feasts and Seasons: Music for the Church Year* (2003), and composer of a large number of settings for the daily liturgies of the seminary, he is currently completing a congregational *Mass of St Mel*, commissioned for the re-dedication of St Mel's Cathedral, Longford.

Salvador Ryan is Professor of Ecclesiastical History at St Patrick's College, Maynooth. His area of research is late medieval and early modern popular religious culture. He is co-editor (with Rachel Moss and Colmán Ó Clabaigh) of *Art and Devotion in Late Medieval Ireland* (2006); (with Henning Laugerud) of *Devotional Cultures of European Christianity, 1790-1960* (2012), and (with Brendan Leahy) three volumes of *Treasures of Irish Christianity* (2012, 2013 and 2015). He is currently preparing (with Henning Laugerud and Laura Katrine Skinnebach) *The Materiality of Devotion in Late Medieval Northern Europe* for publication by Four Courts Press in 2015.

Seán Swayne was ordained a presbyter of the diocese of Kildare and Leighlin on 23 June 1957 after which he worked for nine years in parish ministry in Naas. Born in Australia in 1933, his parents and family returned to Ireland and lived in Ballon, Co. Carlow. His university studies at St Patrick's College, Maynooth embraced both science and later, theology. After studies in liturgy at the Institut Supérieur de Liturgie in Paris, Swayne returned to Ireland in 1968 where he began lecturing at St Patrick's College in Carlow. Shortly after he was appointed National Secretary for Liturgy. It was because of his vision that the Institute for Pastoral Liturgy was founded, originally in Portarlington, before it moved to Carlow and eventually to its present location in Maynooth. He began *New Liturgy*, a bulletin promoting renewal which he edited from its foundation in 1968 to 1986. He served for many years as a consultor to ICEL, a role he served in also with the Congregation for Divine Worship. He was author of three books, and edited two other publications on liturgy. Monsignor Swayne took up an appointment as parish priest of Graignamanagh, Co. Kilkenny in 1986 where he remained until he died, after a short illness, in 1996.

Liam M. Tracey is a presbyter of the Order of Friar Servants of Mary (OSM) and Professor of Liturgy at St Patrick's College, Maynooth. He undertook undergraduate studies in Dublin and Rome, after which he worked for a number of years in parish ministry. He returned to Rome to pursue graduate studies in liturgy at the Pontifical Liturgical Institute, Sant' Anselmo, culminating in a doctorate. He has taught and lectured in many parts of Ireland and Australia, Ghana, Italy, UK, and the USA. He was Appointed Director of Postgraduate Studies at the Pontifical University at Maynooth in 2009 and again in 2012. He is a long-time member of the Irish Council for Liturgy and several of its work groups. He is also currently Review Editor of the *Irish Theological Quarterly*. His latest publication 'Liturgical Reform and Renewal in the Roman Church and Its Impact on Christian Jewish Relations', in Gilbert S. Rosenthal, editor, *A Jubilee for All Time: The Copernican Revolution in Jewish-Christian Relations* (Eugene, OR: Pickwick Publications, 2014), reflects his long-term interest in the role of liturgy in the Christian Jewish encounter.

Liam G. Walsh is a member of the Irish Dominican Province. He studied theology in Dominican Studia, at Tallaght (Ireland), at *Le Saulchoir* (France) and at the *Angelicum* (Rome). He has spent his life teaching theology, including liturgy, in Ireland, in Rome at the *Angelicum*, and in Switzerland as Professor of Dogmatic Theology at the University of Fribourg. He was Consultor to Irish National Episcopal Commission on Liturgy 1968–1975 and worked with Mgr Seán Swayne when he was setting up the Institute of Pastoral Liturgy in Portarlington. The theology of sacraments has been a central part of his research. Hillenbrands reprints recently published a second edition of his *Sacraments of Initiation: A Theology of Rite, Word and Life* (2011).

Thomas R. Whelan is an Irish Spiritan missionary and holds degrees in music (UCD), theology (Gregorian University, Rome), and liturgical theology (Sant' Anselmo, Rome). He has lectured and has held academic leadership posts at the Kimmage Mission Institute, and then later at the Milltown Institute in Dublin where he currently serves as Rector and Acting President. Associate Professor of Theology at the Milltown Institute, he lectures in liturgical and sacramental theology, and also teaches at the National Centre for Liturgy, as well as on the MA in Liturgical Studies programme at Sarum College (UK). He has guest-lectured in parts of Ireland, UK, as well as in France, Italy and the USA. As Episcopal Secretary for Liturgy in the Bishops' Conference of The Gambia, Liberia and Sierra Leone, he was involved with the work of ICEL since 1982, and later served as a member of the ICEL Advisory/Consultants Committee from 1999–2003. Whelan has edited a number of collections of essays, and has published in Irish and international journals. He has a particular interest in issues relating to liturgical theology; early liturgical sources; Eucharist; ordained ministry; theology and music; and the relationship between worship and justice.